*Giving Account
of Faith and Hope
in Africa*

Giving Account of Faith and Hope in Africa

John Samuel Pobee

WIPF & STOCK · Eugene, Oregon

GIVING ACCOUNT OF FAITH AND HOPE IN AFRICA

Copyright © 2017 John Samuel Pobee. All rights reserved. Except for brief quotations in critical publications or reviews, no part of this book may be reproduced in any manner without prior written permission from the publisher. Write: Permissions, Wipf and Stock Publishers, 199 W. 8th Ave., Suite 3, Eugene, OR 97401.

Wipf & Stock
An Imprint of Wipf and Stock Publishers
199 W. 8th Ave., Suite 3
Eugene, OR 97401

www.wipfandstock.com

PAPERBACK ISBN: 978-1-4982-9545-1
HARDCOVER ISBN: 978-1-4982-9547-5
EBOOK ISBN: 978-1-4982-9546-8

Manufactured in the U.S.A.   JUNE 27, 2017

To
Leah and Desmond Mpilo Tutu
and
Rosemary and Walter Khotso Makhulu

Archbishop Emeritus Desmond Mpilo Tutu and Leah Tutu

Archbishop Emeritus Walter Khotso Makhulu and Rosemary Makhulu

Contents

Preface | ix
Acknowledgments | xiii
Abbreviations | xv

1 Taking the Land | 1
2 Africa | 21
3 Culture | 41
4 And What Is Theology? | 58
5 *Residuum Evangelium* | 82
6 Many Designations, One Gospel | 105
7 Is There an African Theology and What Is It? | 128
8 Multitudes before the Lamb: Pluralism and Theology | 133
9 I Am an African Christian | 158
10 God and the Social Order | 171
11 Sex: Uncovering the Nakedness of the Other | 183
12 Our Mothers and Sisters | 192
13 The Altar and the *Polis* | 215
14 The Altar in the Marketplace | 226
15 Human Dignity—Human Rights | 252
16 African Initiatives in Christianity | 276

Bibliography | 293
Author Index | 315
Subject Index | 323

Preface

IN 1979 THERE APPEARED on the market under my name the book *Toward an African Theology* (Nashville: Abingdon). In 1981 that volume was issued in German as *Grundlinien einer afrikanischen Theologie* in the Vandenhoeck and Ruprecht series Theologie der Ökoumene. The word "Toward" in the title signaled a tentative, exploratory attempt. Time and distance can and do change and mature one's perspective. Thirty years and more have passed. I myself have grown through many experiences and encounters. So a revisit to this topic is overdue and appropriate.

This volume is dedicated with heartfelt appreciation to two couples: Desmond Mpilo Tutu and his wife, Leah, and Walter Khotso Makhulu and his late wife, Rosemary. They not only encouraged me but also represent experiences I went through myself that proved most profound in my life and theological evolution. Like me, both of them were Anglicans of the High Church tradition. As destiny had it, we were involved in the Anglican Communion at about the same time. Tutu and Makhulu were archbishops; I was for years a lay theologian, and later was ordained. We collaborated and the encounter gave me a sense of a bigger Anglican family beyond my local Anglican experience. In that relationship I learned that the temptation to place the academy and the church—scholarship over against faith and mission—at odds with each other is misguided. Thus I have come to the conviction that whatever else theology does for renewal of oneself, it is also an agency for renewal of the church and her mission.

Both of these churchmen were of South African origin. They were called to leadership in the frightful and urgent days of apartheid in South Africa and Southern Africa. I was from Ghana in West Africa, which had been the home of Kwame Nkrumah, the prince of African nationalism. I had learned from Nkrumah's famous dictum that "the independence of Ghana is meaningless unless it is linked to the total liberation of Africa." Our encounters soon forced on me questions of theology's role and what it had to contribute to sociopolitical issues, if, indeed, theology is to be taken seriously as a scientific identification of good news (gospel). Confronting these questions was to be for me almost a conversion experience. I came to see that theology could not be simply a mandarin's art in the academy or even the church; it is also concerned with the public sphere and with life and death issues and challenges. Such a conversion experience demanded a revisit to my earlier study.

Embarking on a Journey

Walter Khotso Makhulu, after a stint as Africa Secretary of Refugee Services of the World Council of Churches, became bishop of the Anglican Diocese of Botswana and archbishop of the Church of the Province of Central Africa (CPCA). From that position he became also a facilitator in the struggle for justice, peace, and human dignity in Southern Africa, especially in South Africa. I was to learn through my contacts with him that theology is also to be lived and not only learned and talked.

My encounter with Desmond Mpilo Tutu in 1973 was to issue in an invitation for me to serve as a commissioner on the Committee of the Theological Education Fund (TEF) of the World Council of Churches (WCC) at Geneva, Switzerland. I was to be invited further to become executive director of its Programme on Theological Education (PTE), the successor for some fifteen years of TEF. (The program went through various metamorphoses in nomenclature, such as Ecumenical Theological Education, abbreviated ETE.) This phase of my life was to be a journey both literally and metaphorically. The position entailed extensive travel across the world, from the base in Geneva to regions of Africa—south of the Sahara as well as Egypt, Eastern, Western, Southern, and Central Africa—the Pacific and Oceania, North and South America, the Caribbean, Asia, and Europe itself. The travels and my assignment were not just ecumenical tourism. The purpose was to challenge churches and theological institutions to seek vital, vibrant, and viable ministerial and theological education and formation marked by integrity, authenticity, and creativity.

These years were a journey in yet another sense, namely, in my own growth as a theological educator. I was to learn that as a dabbler in the discipline of theology, I was at once concerned with theology and with education. One without the other was crippled. I was to learn that the ecumenical imperative is a catalyst for renewal of theology and theological institutions. I was further to learn that theology, in addition to its intellectual vocation, is also an agency at the service of the community of faith for its renewal and transformation—in short, for mission. Such was my baptism into the ecumenical movement, accomplished through its "privileged instrument" of the WCC. Desmond Tutu was the one who initially brought me into the ecumenical movement. The rest is history.

Wider Orbit

In this wider orbit I learned that religion, like theology, is fundamentally concerned with humans and what is human; its foremost concerns reach beyond and go deeper than doctrines, dogma, erudition, and theories. The ecumenical perspective, I learned, is an invitation to make connections and reach out to others outside my group. It offers an invitation to forge connections between the God-Word and social, economic, and political factors that have implications and consequences for human well-being.

As I made this journey, both Desmond Tutu and Walter Makhulu and their families were also in the WCC orbit. In an institution which *was* very much dominated by Caucasians, it became a wise step for people of color to team up. Tutu and Makhulu were natural comrades, making for mutually enriching experiences that lasted beyond the duration of our time together.

As a bonus, being one of three African Anglican colleagues working as friends in a WCC composed of many churches taught me that the tendency to see denominationalism and ecumenism as opposed was unnecessary, if not misguided.

The TEF and WCC as a whole were in those days the high priests of contextual theology. In that context I was exposed to and socialized in theologies from Asia, Latin America, North America, the Pacific, and, of course, Europe and my own Africa. The first monograph I published on African theology came out of that crucible. And now, decades afterward and enriched by further ecumenical and global encounters, it is fitting that I revisit that initial work and that I dedicate it to the two elders who traveled with me, challenged me, encouraged me, and worshipped and prayed with me. I have grown in the consciousness that theology is not first of all regurgitating a body of knowledge, but, more fundamentally and more deeply, a dialogue between *text* and *context*. Every theological construct, I have learned, is necessarily contextual. Mine has been a conversion to a sense of humility and provisionality—not to be confused with reckless relativism—and to the necessity to hold universality and contextuality as two sides of a coin.

Contributions of the Tutus and Makhulus

Leah Tutu and Rosemary Makhulu may not have been formally trained theologians. But their quiet yet strong accompaniment of their spouses helped to wake me up to the important role played by spouses, especially wives. If my curriculum vitae shows that I engaged the topics "Theology by the People" and "Gender Perspectives in Theology," it is the fruit of my encounter with those two women.

The two families exhibited a tremendous sense of humor and socialization. After serious business, sometimes heated, we together trooped to the pubs. Intense business and academic engagement were balanced with humor and sociality. What a lesson!

There was another lesson. In 1973 Tutu secured for me an invitation to South Africa, then in the grip of apartheid. The Organization of African Unity had decreed that the country's racist government should be treated like a leper. For its part, the apartheid government of South Africa was suspicious of independent African states, especially Ghana, which was in the forefront of liberation movements. So the invitation arranged by Desmond Tutu posed a challenge. On the one hand, could I muster the courage to defy the government of Ghana to break the ban? On the other hand, would I by bowing to the OAU and the government of Ghana be prevented from going to South Africa and thus from showing solidarity with the excluded and marginalized? For me it was a moment of sensitization to the qualities of commitment, conviction, and courage that must characterize one who dares walk in theological corridors. Getting a visa for South Africa took until 1980, again at the invitation of the South Africa Council of Churches, of which Desmond Tutu was general secretary. The visit gave me personal experience of how the color divide operated on the ground and of the obtrusive presence of the security agencies.

I came away from the experience with a vivid sense of blacks and whites who were fighting apartheid. The experience impressed on me the necessity not to be part of any scheme that isolated them. I have been enriched with and by many blacks and whites, especially whites who paid the price for standing out to be counted against apartheid.

In dedicating this volume to them, I pay tribute from a grateful heart to Desmond and Leah Tutu and to Walter and Rosemary Makhulu for experience gained and conscientization accomplished in their company. This book is a confession that through them I learned that the theological enterprise is a multifaceted activity: theology is not only thought out and written down but also done and lived. Theology does not consist of scholarly erudition alone; it is also a confession of faith convictions, potentially leading even to martyrdom.

> Leah and Desmond, I salute you and thank you.
>
> Rosemary, I salute and bless your memory as you have journeyed to Elysium.
>
> Walter, I salute you and thank you.

Acknowledgments

ACCORDING TO AKAN TRADITION, "Wisdom is pieced together from divergent perspectives." This maxim asserts that two heads are better than one. So I shared a draft of this volume with long-standing friends, colleagues, associates, and former students. I have benefitted from the trenchant and generous critique of Dr. Jan G. Platvoet, retired senior lecturer, University of Leiden, The Netherlands; Prof. Mercy Amba Oduyoye, director of the Institute of Religion and Gender Studies, Trinity Theological Seminary, Legon, Ghana; Prof. Johnson Kwabena Asamoah-Gyadu, Baëta-Grau Professor of African Christianity and Pentecostal Theology, Trinity Theological Seminary, Legon, Ghana; the late Prof. Gerrie Lubbe, University of South Africa (UNISA), Pretoria, South Africa; Prof. Christo Lombard, University of Western Cape, Belleville, South Africa; Prof. Patrick J. Ryan, SJ, Laurence J. McGinley Professor of Religion and Society, Fordham University, New York; Prof. Deji Ayegboyin, formerly president of Nigerian Baptist Theological Seminary, Ogbomoso, Nigeria, and now professor and head, Department of Religious Studies, University of Ibadan, Nigeria; and Prof. Emeritus John W. de Gruchy, University of Cape Town, South Africa. I am most grateful to all of them but I take full responsibility for whatever blemishes may remain in the manuscript.

I am deeply indebted to the Rt. Rev. Sebastian Bakare, retired bishop of the Anglican Diocese of Mutare, Zimbabwe, and his wife, Ruth, for the insight they brought to improve the manuscript. Their comments were most helpful for, unlike all the other comments, theirs were rooted in the congregation.

I owe a debt of gratitude to two other persons and an institution. Mrs. Martha Ama Akyaa Pobee, the Minister of Interior and Home Affairs in the Pobee Home, not only provided me with a most happy home both in Ghana and in all the countries to which she has been posted as a career diplomat—Russia, Israel, the United States, South Africa, and now as Ghana's ambassador and permanent representative to the United Nations in New York—but also for her sharp challenges and critique. Her formation in philosophy and English at the University of Ghana and her graduate studies at the Institute of Social Studies, The Hague, The Netherlands, enable her to offer helpful, clear, and astute criticism.

My colleague and adopted son, Benjamin Ayitey-Okine, has, over the years, patiently, devotedly, conscientiously, and cheerfully word processed my very poor and trying handwriting into finished text. I am all the more grateful that he also raised serious and fundamental questions that challenged me to sharpen my thoughts. I salute you, Ben. My beloved niece, Dada Pobee, visiting us in Pretoria, South Africa, worked on the corrections. Dada, I thank you. Finally, when I worked through the critique of reviewers, my adopted daughter, Eullan Akosua Asiedu, from whom I have learned much, also processed the final text. Eullan, I salute and thank you. To have received so much help from others may be a sign that the Creator wanted this book to be completed for the sake of God's faithful servants.

Symbols, symbolism and therefore art are the stock-in-trade of religion and theology. With that conviction, I include some select pictures not only of the persons to whom the volume is dedicated but also several that illustrate aspects of what they represent for me. The picture from the sanctuary of the Anglican Church of St. Cyrene represents the congregation's dedication to religion and Christian worship, which is the fulcrum of theology. The altar reminds us of the sacrifice of the Holy Eucharist.

The Rt. Rev. Cleopas Lunga, bishop of Matabeleland, and his assistant Ron Lumbiwa made available to me the picture of the African paintings of Christ the High Priest; of St. Simon of Cyrene, the African who was compelled to carry the cross of Christ on his way to his crucifixion; and of Bernard Mizeki, a nineteenth-century catechist from Southern Rhodesia (Zimbabwe) who died a martyr. I am grateful to them.

I thank also Dwight Baker and his wife, Lois Baker, who gave the manuscript sensitive final copyediting in preparation for sending it to the publisher.

To the publisher who accepted the manuscript to bring it to the light of day I express deepest gratitude. Many manuscripts are not published for various reasons that have nothing to do with quality. The publisher's acceptance of the manuscript, whatever else it may be, is an affirmation of faith in me, which for one in his late seventies is a great encouragement. At the time of putting final touches to the manuscript, I was a sojourner as diplomatic spouse in Pretoria, South Africa. For that reason, I deem it proper to take up issues in this volume—and to offer illustrations—that arise from my home base of Ghana and West Africa as well as from South Africa, the homeland of the two to whom this study is dedicated and which was my land of sojourn.

John S. Pobee
Accra, Ghana
Eastertide 2017

Abbreviations

List of Bible versions cited in the chapters. All citations are of minor length.

	The African Bible
KJV	King James Version
MSG	The Message
NAB	New American Bible
NABRE	New American Bible Revised Edition
NASB	New American Standard Bible
NRSV	New Revised Standard Version

1

Taking the Land

IN SUBSTANCE, THE TITLE of this book, *Giving Account of Faith and Hope in Africa*, is a paraphrase of 1 Peter 3:15: "Always have an answer ready when you are called upon to account for your hope, but give it simply and with respect" (*The African Bible*). It contains part of the experience of a revered Christian disciple of Jesus, a fisherman, not particularly learned, from a backwater of the Roman Empire. Yet he became one of the pillars of the church, going in the end to the capital of the empire, Rome, to preach the gospel and to die a martyr for it. Perhaps here is a reminder that scholars do not hold a monopoly on knowledge, gems, and insights; mere mortals too may, on occasion, utter gems.

The biblical text is part of Peter's admonition and encouragement to the Christians of the Roman province of Asia, who were encountering persecution on account of their faith. He offers encouragement to persevere in the faith, which he takes for granted and does not attempt to expound. Equally important is it for them to give account of their hope rooted in the faith, issuing in their willingness to persevere in it, in spite of persecution. Theology may be written in lives living out the tenets of the faith.

The writer offers a further injunction to give the account in humility and simplicity. In the face of persecution, humility is, perhaps, the last attitude that naturally comes to the victim. But it is consistent with the teaching of Jesus to love even one's enemies (Matt 5:38–48; Luke 6:27–36). In any case, Paul charges his followers to imitate the humility of Christ (see Phil 2:5–8). Equally striking is the note of simplicity, given the rather convoluted theology characteristic of academia. The *logos-ratio* of theology may not be the last word—there is room to employ the primordial symbolism of the people to mediate deep insights of theology.

Some striking lessons can be drawn from the injunction vis-à-vis theology. First, theology is the responsibility and task of each believer and not, as is often made out, the exclusive business of the specialist or an initiated, select few. The corollary of the foregoing is that rational process, on the one hand, and faith and belief, on the other hand, are not alternatives; they complement one another. "Priest like lay, professional theologian like the simple church-goer/believer, rich like the poor, are obliged by the word of God to reflect on and practice the faith."[1] In theology, faith, belief, and the rational feed each other.

Faith takes us to the realm of religion, which is as old as human existence. According to the wisdom of the ages, *homo sapiens = homo religiosus*—that is, the modern species of humans is religious.[2] A Pew Foundation survey has, however, found that 1.1 billion people, that is, one in six human beings, claims to have no religious affiliation. This group includes atheists and agnostics as well as many who are either unidentified with or unaffiliated to a particular faith and who yet hold some religious or spiritual beliefs such as belief in God or some universal spirit.[3]

Of the rest of *homo sapiens*, the Pew survey reports the following:

Religion	Adherents	Percent
Christian	2.2 billion	32
Muslim	1.6 billion	23
Hindu	1.0 billion	15
Buddhist	500 million	7
Folk/Traditional Religions	400 million	6
Jews/Judaism	14 million	0.2

The foregoing statistics testify that religion of one type or another is a significant reality in the world and human life. Further, religious pluralism and diversity characterize the world and society. This reality means that each religion must have its space. It also means that religious pluralism is put on the agenda of theology, especially the question of how pluralism may be negotiated to allow each human created in God's image and likeness to have their space and to live in dignity and peace with justice.

Folk Religion and Universal Religion

Scholars have drawn a distinction between folk religion and universal religion. In folk religion, a society as a vital community is the carrier of religion. Universal religion by definition is supranational. Further distinction is drawn between official religion and popular religion, sometimes termed common religion.[4] The present study does not

---

1. Amirtham and Pobee, *Theology by the People*, 2.

2. Developments in affluent parts of the world, especially Europe, give reason to revisit this age-old wisdom, especially as regards its continued truth for humankind's future.

3. Pew Research Center, "Global Religious Landscape."

4. Platvoet, "The Akan Believer and His Religions," in Vrijhof and Waardenburg, *Official and Popular Religion*, 584–85, argues that the conceptual pair, official/popular religion, consists of biased and one-sided concepts that have little analytical value for twentieth- and twenty-first-century African indigenous religions. In the same volume, see also P. H. Virjhof, "Official and Popular Religion in Twentieth Century Western Christianity," 217–43.

focus on such distinctions but assumes such knowledge. For purposes of this study, Traditional African Religions fall into the category of popular religion, while Christianity, Islam, Hinduism, and Buddhism fit within the category of universal religions.

But, first, the story is much more complex than has just been laid out. What used to be termed African Traditional Religion (ATR) is today preferably styled African Indigenous Religions (AIR). This new language is preferred because Christianity and Islam are also being seen as traditional religions in Africa by virtue of their having been around and dominant in many African societies for quite some time. Before 1900 those traditional religions could be described as indigenous, oral, or preliterate religions. But they were not closed systems, because they were open, receptive, pluralist religions, full of internal diversity. They were adoptive and adaptive religions. Presently in some African societies, Christianity or Islam has become the mainline religion, speaking demographically and in terms of institutional dominance. In these circumstances the old traditional religion may best be termed popular/common or folk religion.

Again, whether to put Hinduism in the same bracket as Christianity, Islam, and Buddhism is arguable. Christianity, Islam, and Buddhism claim salvific unicity and aspire to become the religion of all, irrespective of cultures and histories. Hinduism makes no such claims. Of it, Jan Platvoet states, "Morphologically it is a totally different religion, much more in the vein of a demographically huge, internally diversified, adoptive and adaptive indigenous religion, co-extensive with Hindu societies (and diasporas), than a missionary religion with global aspirations."[5]

Second, theology at its best is reflection on experience; it is thus a second step. Theology is an exercise in attempting to make sense of and understand an experience and assess its consequences. In that sense, theology begins with experience and passion; that is, it starts with what excites one, whether positively or negatively, and thus propels one to wish to understand it in its depth. That note of passion is the key to creative theology.

Third, the experience, so far as theology is concerned, is inextricably tied into faith. A casual reading of Scripture, the charter document of the Christian religion, reveals a variety of senses in which the word "faith" is used, such as intellectual assent to some propositions and a way of life among others. Scholars too have distinguished between experienced faith, affective faith, searching faith, and owned faith.[6]

Experienced faith is marked by trust, love, and acceptance, qualities that mature only over time and through experience. *Affective faith* comes when a person identifies with a faith community and acts according to its norms. It is like being baptized into becoming a member of the community of faith. But such faith is often accompanied by uncritical acceptance of the beliefs and religious practices of the community and, perhaps, does not go deep enough. It corresponds, as in the parable of the sower, to

---

5. Personal correspondance with the author.
6. See Westerhoff, *Will Our Children Have Faith?*

the seed that fell on rocks; the seed sprouted and sprang up quickly in the shallow soil but withered because it had no deep roots and soil (Mark 4:5). Many an African Christian has not penetrated beyond the surface of the gospel as minted in Europe, and therefore their Christianity constitutes only a thin veneer.

There is also *searching faith*. This faith is comparable to Anselm's *fides quaerens intellectum*, that is, faith seeking understanding. Uncritical acceptance of beliefs and religious practices is inadequate. In some cases, people's faith consists in doubting all the time. The significance of such constant doubting and questioning is a search after meaning and should not be despised and castigated as agnosticism or atheism.

Fourth is *owned faith*. In this category—through searching and learning—new meaning is found in and through story, symbol, and ritual. Owned faith gives personal integrity and social action to faith. This faith is what African theology should be seeking to foster. The key to owned faith is the willingness and ability to correct course. It calls for grit and resolve, displaying character under pressure.

Hope

Hope may be identified as a measure and test of relevant theology, especially in Africa. For one thing, because the core of the Christian faith is the incarnation, a test of sound theology is a theology's relevance to the context. For another thing, the African context has become synonymous with poverty, violence, and political instability, not to mention what Charles Winquist has called "epiphanies of darkness."[7] These epiphanies translate as the genocide in Rwanda and Burundi in 1994, the civil wars in Sierra Leone and Liberia, the violent political crisis and enormous carnage in Côte d'Ivoire (2010–11), the genocide in Darfur, the post-election violence in Kenya in January 2008, not forgetting the enormous destruction that accompanied racist ideologies in Southern Africa, Mozambique, and Angola.

In some cases the project of modernity and progress has issued in suffering and death and has uprooted peoples. Thus relevant theology has no alternative but to address the offer of hope in realistic and meaningful ways. But hope must be related to, if not rooted in, people's past. Hope and inspiration may also be found in the African past, in spite of all the negative elements of the past. Hope may be located in the ability of Africans to mobilize political and social movements to overcome situations of injustice, hatred, and exclusion. Religious institutions are part of the social movements reaching even to the grassroots level.

The word "hope" in the title of this volume is deliberately meant to signal that Christian theology is also an agent of hope. The various crises on the continent of Africa represent a culture of despair and a crisis of hope. Insofar as Christianity claims to offer a gospel of hope, theology's vocation includes constructing hope. Since much of

---

7. Winquist, *Epiphanies of Darkness*.

the "hope" on offer functions like drug abuse, putting forward empty pious hopes and "celestial dope"—or to quote from Karl Marx (1818–83), "religion [is] . . . the opium of the people"—Christian theology must endeavor to construct realistic, rational, viable hope.[8] In the depths of theology resides a commitment to rebuilding utopia in new times. As Elsa Tamez puts it, "a reason for living, or the meaning of life, is one of the most profound and universal questions that human beings have asked through the centuries. It entails an effort, often beyond earthly existence. To seek reason for living is not just a philosophical concern; it comes from the desire to live with dignity in the face of cultures, social or political."[9]

The crash of 1929 initiated the Great Depression. In that context James Tuslo Adams wrote *The Epic of America* in which he articulated the idea of hope, identifying a human penchant for hope. For theology such an agenda entails at least two strands. First, the primary resource of the Christian faith, namely the Bible, contains much that arises amidst a culture of despair and crises of hope. To name but a few examples, the crises of the Jews under the Assyrians, Babylonians, and Seleucids formed the backdrop for the books of Isaiah, Daniel, and the Maccabean writings. The construction of hope will entail critical review of the insights of such books. Use of the word "insights" here is critical, for simple repeating of scriptural phrases and careless bandying about of biblical texts is not sufficient. The mere words of Scripture are not immutable, because there is evidence of evolution in Scripture itself, for example, in the evolution of the sacrificial cult, the roles of priests and prophets, and the dietary laws.

Second, the construction of hope cannot be just a reminting of doctrinal statements. Hope may emerge from critical engagement with the text of Scripture in social crises and changes. This means engaging faith and politics, faith and economics, and similar issues. One must endeavor to understand the details of these topics before venturing an opinion and, if I may add, to do so carefully, wisely, and cautiously. In this exercise the equipment of the theologian, above all, is wisdom and to avoid force, curses, manipulation, or bludgeoning into submission (see Eccl 10:20).

Schemes of theology have not always met the historical challenges of the time, constituting situations incongruous with everyday experiences. For example, the messianic promises of the prophet do not appear to be congruent with everyday experiences. Hope is rather an elusive word. Sometimes, hope serves as a substitute for utopia. Hope has horizons, sometimes impossible, that transcend the human condition.[10] As Tamez states, "Utopian horizon represents trusting faith in an all-powerful and unknown God, who at some point in history will do what human beings cannot do, precisely because they are human."[11]

---

8. Marx, *Contribution to the Critique of the Hegelian Philosophy of Right*.

9. Tamez, *When the Horizons Close*, 1.

10. Hinkelammert, *Crítica a la razón utópica*; Hinkelammert, "El cautiverio de la utopía"; Hinkelammert, "La lógica de la expulsión del mercado capitalista mundial."

11. Tamez, *When the Horizons Close*, 18.

The dissonance that is evident between theological affirmation, on the one hand, and Christian practice on the ground, on the other hand, raises the question of the link between the theology of hope and reform. Rhetorically, the church's commitment has been *ecclesia semper reformanda*; that is, the church is always being reformed by the Spirit. To limit such reforming to structures, however, is inadequate, for structures themselves can be defective in ways that undercut renewal and hope. Therefore, whatever the steps of reform, renewal and hope must also reach the interior being—must reach into people's personal and communal core—so that they can "be perfect as the heavenly Father is perfect" (Matt 5:48 *The African Bible*) and so as to foster the values of the kingdom of God.

The Letter to the Hebrews articulates the linking of faith and hope in a striking manner: "The fundamental fact of existence is that this trust in God, this faith, is the firm foundation under everything that makes life worth living. It's our handle on what we can't see. The act of faith is what distinguished our ancestors, set them above the crowd" (Heb 11:1–2 The Message). Faith is not just some intimate conviction. Human decisions are inspired by faith and humans act according to faith. Thus examples abound of people willing to risk everything for faith. Moses undertook the seemingly impossible task of leading a slave people, thus foregoing a promising future in Pharaoh's court. Abraham's emigration from Ur in his old age makes sense only because he had hope and faith. Against all hope, Abraham, at a ripe old age, took God at his word when he was given a promise of a child by the elderly Sarah, past the age of childbearing (Rom 4:18–19). The birth of Isaac by Sarah defied human wisdom and natural laws of procreation (Gen 17, 21). The hope offered by the Christian gospel is founded on God, the Creator, Redeemer, and Sustainer. Hope is entirely God's work and free gift of love and fidelity.

Christian theology in Africa must be concerned to give account of faith and hope when the empirical facts and experiences of poverty, marginalization, exclusion, AIDS, and political oppression seem to go against all hope of life in the image and likeness of God. Faith and knowledge rest on hope in God (see Titus 1:2). Theology is the accounting for and the reason for the hope that we have.

The world press gives the impression that Africa, year in, year out, lives dangerously. If I may borrow a phrase from Dr. Benjamin Carson, the African American director of pediatric neurosurgery at Johns Hopkins Medical Institution, Baltimore, Maryland, USA, Africa too is made up of countries "of yellow bellies": "What we're buying and what everyone is selling us is the promise of security. Yet the only thing we can be sure of is that someday every one of us will die."[12] This is the context for setting hope before the peoples of Africa.

Carson continues with a profound plea, urging people not to focus on the possible circumstances of their death, but on how they should live. This, I suggest, is part

---

12. Carson, *Take the Risk*, 8.

of the ministry of theology. This is an invitation to focus on what quality of life means today.

Hope has proved a very elusive concept in part because too many times it has been pie in the sky, not rooted in reality and realism. Hope, dreams, and change go together and are run through the prism of faith in God, Creator, Redeemer, and Enabler/Sustainer. Hope is an endeavor to reach common understanding and entails a commitment of never abandoning conviction for the sake of expediency. Hope at the end of the day concerns people and, therefore, may never be divorced from human beings, or from their hopes and their fears. Hope is about possibility and humankind's unity in spite of diversity. Hope is a big and loud "yes" to justice and equality for all peoples, opportunity and prosperity for all peoples. As such, hope entails investing in common humanity, repairing the world, healing all nations, guided by a clear sense of what *together* we stand for.

The prophets are often heard declaring a message of doom. But there is another side to their ministry; it is a ministry to deliver the message of hope, restoration, and salvation. The prophet Amos articulates that ministry when he says to the people of Israel, "Seek good and not evil, that you may live. . . . Hate evil and love good" (Amos 5:14–15 NRSV; cf. Hos 8:3; Isa 5:20; Mic 3:2; Prov 14:31).

Theology and Religion

Theology's raw material is religion. The word has two etymologies: in pre-Christian times, it was derived from *religere*, a frequentative of *re-legere*, that is, to read time and again or to consider with great attention and repeatedly. It links "religion" especially to divination, that is, to attentiveness to the omens and prodigies through which the divinities revealed their messages to humans when they were believed to have caused or were expected to cause misfortune.

The other derivation is the Christian one. It is inspired theologically by central tenets of the Christian faith as a religion of obedience and submission. Thus Lactantius, for example, derives *religio* from *re-ligare*, to bind again, that is, to renew one's submission to God by renouncing Adam's "original sin" and thereby find post-temporal salvation.[13]

Wilfred Cantwell Smith has argued that religion is a misnomer, because what is known is a religious person or act and not the phenomenon itself. Religion (with an uppercase R)—that is, as homogenous, monolithic, completely of one piece—is an illusion. Religion is more like Joseph's coat of many colors. A religious tradition is not the same everywhere; time and geography influence it and issue in varieties. Indeed, different groupings of adherents may understand a religious tradition differently. So, Religion is a multiheaded phenomenon. There has always been a human penchant for

---

13. Jan G. Platvoet, "Contexts, Concepts, and Contests: Towards a Pragmatics of Defining Religion," in Platvoet and Molendijk, *Pragmatics*, 463–515.

hope. As James Tuslow Adams writes, the "dream of hope has been present from the start . . . dream of a better, richer and happier life for all our citizens of every rank." It is thinking that tomorrow will be better than today. The past is clear, the present is often confused, and the future is to be plotted. Theology has contributed to making life sustainable and renewing hope.

Accordingly, Cantwell Smith distinguishes between *belief* and *faith*. "Belief" describes the body of creeds, rituals, laws, and specific formulations of a particular religious tradition. He reserves "faith" for the human clinging to the Transcendent.[14]

Not infrequently, religious traditions become idols. Tillich articulates this when he states, "Faith, if it takes its symbols literally, becomes idolatrous! It calls something ultimate which is less than ultimate. Faith, conscious of the symbolic character of its symbols, gives God the honor which is due to him."[15]

The reference to idolatry calls for a brief comment. Eric Fromm, a psychologist, has an apt brief statement: "Idolatry is not the worship of this or that particular idol. . . . [It is] the deification of things, of partial aspects of the world and man's submission to such things. . . . It is not only pictures in stone and wood that are idols. Words can become idols, and machines can become idols; leaders, the state, power. . . . Science and the opinion of one's neighbor can become idols."[16] To Fromm's insight we may add Francis Bacon's submission that "there are four classes of idols which beset men's minds . . . the first class, Idols of the Tribe; the second, Idols of the Cave; the third, Idols of the Market Place; the fourth, Idols of the Theatre."[17] There is a human penchant for creating idols.

Belief may be compared to a lever that has the capacity to move everything else in a person's life. Such belief as a person holds defines his/her vision of the world and dictates his/her behavior, as well as determining the person's emotional responses to others. Thus belief is part of a person's apparatus of mind, shaping his or her desires, fears, aspirations, and behavior.

The Three Cornerstones of Religion

Scholars have identified three cornerstones of religion: experience, belief, and ritual. Belief, like ritual, presupposes or is built on ecstatic/spiritual/religious experience.[18]

Thus, to take a random example from the Christian religion, the experiences of Abraham (Gen 12) and Moses (Exod 3) ushered them into belief in Yahweh. Similarly, the ecstatic experiences of Isaiah (Isa 6) and Amos (Amos 6) were the bases of their

---

14. Smith, *Faith and Belief; Meaning and End of Religion*; and *Faith of Other Men*.
15. Tillich, *Dynamics of Faith*, 52.
16. Fromm, *Sane Society*, 121–22.
17. Bacon, *Novum Organum*, 1.39.
18. Lewis, *Ecstatic Religion*; Zahan, *Réincarnation et vie mystique*; Zaehner, *Mysticism, Sacred and Profane*; Parrinder, "Mysticism in African Religion," in Pobee, *Religion in a Pluralistic Society*, 48–59.

message from the Holy God who demands of God's devotees holiness, righteousness, and justice. Similarly, the ecstatic experience of the resurrected Jesus by Saul of Tarsus turned the one-time persecutor of followers of Jesus into a follower of Jesus and an apostle of Christ (1 Cor 15:8–10).

Lewis has argued that religious/spiritual experience is the most important of the three cornerstones of religion. Any attempt at engaging a religion, at the bottom line, entails an engagement with the claims of people as regards their ecstatic experiences as expressed through belief and ritual. It goes without saying that ritual becomes a critical avenue to learn and understand the religion, especially of the nonliterate. In that light it is questionable to limit the word theology to universal religions and deny that African traditional religions have theology. Their theology is in their ritual.

Ecstatic experience is fundamental, crucial, and of critical importance for the being, understanding, and articulation of religion, which leads one to spend a little longer with it and to do so from a Christian perspective.

A careful study of the prophets reveals that the call of a prophet, as well his message, always took off from what he *saw* (Ezek 1:1, 3, 4, 15; 2:1–3; Amos 8:1–4 *The African Bible*). In the New Testament, 1 John reiterates the same seeing and hearing: "What we have heard, what we have seen with our own eyes, what we looked upon and touched with our hands. . . . We have seen it and testify to it and proclaim to you the eternal life" (1 John 1:1–3 *The African Bible*). So, ecstatic experience is pivotal for religion and its articulation. However, in the case of Christian religion, ecstatic experience may not be reduced to visions and esoteric knowledge; it is made manifest in the real physical presence of Jesus.

Equally instructive is the encounter in John 4 between Jesus and the Samaritan woman at the well of Sychar, a Samaritan town: seeing, hearing, and listening to Jesus became more than just an encounter for the woman. It was an ecstatic experience that led her to reflect and go home to tell the story: "Come and see a man who told me everything I have ever done" (John 4:29 NRSV).

The experience engaged her, so much so that she wondered, "Could he possibly be the Messiah?" (John 4:29). The ecstatic experience was a revelation that had consequences and demanded a response in the real world. It struck a cord of friendship. The response could be anything but indifference. Ecstatic experience reveals and starts a conversation. Theological endeavor is part of that elicited conversation and challenge to proclaim boldly. So ecstatic experience is at once reference point and life defining.

Ecstatic experience, as the Bible portrays it, represents God's search for us and God's will to encounter us, rather than human search for God. Biblical narratives of God's encounter with Abraham (Gen 15–17), Moses (Exod 3), and others demonstrate Divinity reaching out to humans, with weighty consequences that far exceed going through the motions of cultus. This encounter demands cultivating Divinity (Jesus) as Friend and cultivating fellowship and community and communion.

The Sacred and the Secular

Two other words come into focus in any study of the phenomenon of religion: sacred and secular.[19] Religion is concerned with the sacred, that is, with integrity and order beyond humanity's control, which challenges humanity to the pursuit of development and perfection. The other concern of religion is the secular, that is, with integrity and order within the comprehensive control of human beings. Contrary to the usual assumption that the two are in opposition, the sacred and the secular are complementary ways of looking at reality.

The idea of the sacred often is expressed as the Holy. On this word the world of scholarship is indebted to the writings of Rudolf Otto, professor of systematic theology at the Universities of Breslau and Marburg, and especially to his 1923 book *The Idea of the Holy: An Inquiry into the Non-Rational Factor in the Idea of the Divine and Its Relation to the Rational*. He argues that the idea of the Holy is essential to every theistic conception of God, designating and characterizing deity "by the attributes spirit, reason, purpose, good will, supreme power, unity, and selfhood. The nature of God is thus thought of by analogy with our human nature of reason and personality."[20]

Holiness is a category of interpretation and valuation peculiar to the realm of religion. It signals the Numinous, the *mysterium tremendum et fascinans*, that is, a mystery at once overawing, daunting, and repelling, and yet fascinating, attracting, and alluring. Its alluring character is spoken of in such terms as goodness, mercy, love, and grace. As such, "the Holy" signals the "Wholly Other" and what is beyond human grasp, which nevertheless reaches out to mortals.

Belief and talk of God that does not transform people's lives in the world and interpersonal relationships is worth nothing. The foregoing observation brings us straight to African epistemology and ontology. The African scholar John Mbiti has argued that "for Africans it [religion] is an ontological phenomenon; it pertains to the question of existence and being."[21]

This statement does not mean, however, that Africans are sacralists in the sense of being so preoccupied with the sacred as to prejudice their material well-being, even though the borders of the supernatural sphere may be much broader for Africans than for Europeans, for example. Human beings have an innate capacity to grasp the transcendent. The sacred is conveyed and necessarily understood through symbols and myths. Indeed, as Louis Dupré has argued, without the mediating action of language, symbols cannot bear religious meaning. Similarly, myths are essential for conveying meaning, and there is a vital relationship between religious symbol and myth: "The myth is the exegesis of the symbol and the symbol is the exegesis of the myth."[22] Cul-

---

19. Eliade, *Sacred and the Profane*.
20. Waardenburg, *Classical Approaches*, vol. 1, 432–33.
21. Mbiti, *African Religions and Philosophy*, 181.
22. Dupré, *Symbols of the Sacred*.

ture is the solvent of religion and culture is its bearer, helping to shape one's thinking, expression—in short, one's theology.[23]

Language

Language is a means of communication, and theology is a function of communication. Language itself is symbolic. Religions are linguistically based, precisely because language has the capacity for both metaphorical and literal meaning. Language is not only the written word; it reflects the oral and aural traditions of a people. Africans, for example, are proverbial for their love for storytelling. Words have power and connect with the mind's eye. Through the use of language, imagery, symbols, lyricism, and poetical feat, people are woven into the web of identity and culture—in our case, African identities. Vivid imagery engenders a conflation between the human voice of love, sensuality, loss, hope, and survival as well as wider politics and the poetics of national reconstruction and reconciliation.

Language, therefore, is key to identity and culture and is concerned with literary accuracy and cultural sensitivity. Cultural codes are embedded as language; a person's speech is his/her self-definition and self-expression. For this reason it may be claimed that theology is biography.[24] It is what connects people and it has the capacity to work on people. Whoever controls the language has power.

In the light of the foregoing, African theology ideally must be developed in African languages. The present situation of writing African theology in the colonial languages of English, French, and Portuguese can only be second best. African theology cannot be isolated, pushed off into a corner of the global village. So if African theologians may draw on foreign theological artifacts, their translations must be culturally sensitive.

For this reason, it is necessary to hear, loudly and clearly, the critique that emerged from a consultation, "Problems and Promises for the Mission of the Church in Africa," held in Mombasa, Kenya, in 1992, under the auspices of the All-Africa Conference of Churches. It stated that theological education in Africa is experienced as being inadequate, because it is still beholden to Western theology and is not sufficiently sensitive and attentive to the African context.

Language: Theology's Key

Language is key to theology, because theology is essentially an exercise in translating and interpreting a revelation and a vision. Such language implies some philosophy and/or worldview. For example, the central Christian rite of the Eucharist is said to be

---

23. Tillich, *Theology of Culture*. The metaphor of culture as solvent is not a fully happy one. A solvent dissolves materials to which it is applied. But can specific cultures be said to "dissolve" religion?

24. Pobee, "Theology as Biography," in Trompf and Hamel, *World of Religions*, 308–28.

a rite by which Christ becomes present in the form of bread and wine. The technical word in the Roman Catholic tradition is transubstantiation. This is language taken from Aristotelian philosophy, which employs the categories of "substance" and "accidents." While the accidents of bread and wine retain their appearance as bread and wine, it is believed that their substance is changed into the body and blood of Christ. This language was adopted by the Council of Trent in October 1551.[25] Needless to say, Aristotelian philosophical language is not an African's language. Therefore, it becomes the agenda of an African theologian to translate across the lines. In any case, modern secular man's philosophical and scientific beliefs are not present in the earliest forms of the kerygma. Theology is obliged to *translate* formulations of yesteryears and to *interpret* those insights into another idiom relevant to the new times and settings.

Music as a Language of Theology

Language is often heard as words and sentences. Let me signal without further comment that silence can be a strong form of speech and statement. Silence between two persons or peoples has a powerful presence, message, and utterance. Language is not only verbosity. The prophet Elijah, fleeing from the threats of Jezebel, queen of Israel—after he had dared to challenge her for her cultural colonization of Israel—took refuge in a cave on Mount Horeb. After experiencing a frightening wind, earthquake, and fire, he encountered God in "a tiny whispering sound" (1 Kgs 19:12), which symbolizes intimacy of relationship and conversation between God and those who dare to articulate their experience of the Divinity.

Similarly, music is both a form of language and its own proper language. Even without words, music communicates emotions; those who hear the music love the melodies, the sound, and even the voices. Thus, music has the capacity to reach and affect the emotions, which are essential for any transformation, a goal of theology as servant of mission.

The West African nation state of Mali offers us an example of the crucial importance of music as a medium of communication. The hereditary castes of griots, traditional praise singers, are charged with handing down oral history and resolving disputes. For example, when a husband and wife are contemplating divorce, a griot is called in to intervene with a song to urge them to be mindful of the implications for their children and thus to calm the situation. The aid of beautiful voices enables people to hear messages and the voice of reason much better than does straight talking.

Thus in African societies music has been demonstrated to have moral authority, socially, culturally, and politically. There is no reason why similar authority may not be demonstrated in religion and theology.[26] Music is one of the most potent forms of

---

25. Schillebeeckx, *Eucharist*, 58; Aristotle, *Metaphysics*, 167.

26. For instance, consider Fatoumata Diawara, cited by Tracy McNicoll, "A Voice Raised in Joy," 47; Nketia, "African Music," in Skinner, *Peoples and Cultures of Africa*, 580–99; Nketia, *Folk Songs of*

communication. It serves, especially in Africa, an important role in expressing and forming identities. Music and song are media for commenting on society through their lyrics, rhythm, and performance, regularly mirroring the political and social situation of the country. Examples of this role of music are soul music and folk stories such as Akan Spider stories, *Anansesem*.[27]

In the 1970s the soul music of Marvin Gaye and Curtis Mayfield depicted the issues of race and the Vietnam War, which constituted the political and social turmoil of the United States, especially in African American society. For example, Gaye's *What's Going On?* (1971) portrayed through music the gloom and doom facing the world, particularly African Americans.

He sings:

> Mother, mother
> There's too many of you crying
> Brother, brother, brother
> There's far too many of you dying
> You know you've got to find a way
> To bring some lovin' here today—Ya

Blacks were victims of the American society, which caused them much pain, and they pled for love. The curious irony is that Gaye was shot by his own father. In Black South Africa during the excruciatingly painful apartheid era (as well as with the resistance in the Unites States to a racism oiled by Jim Crow statutes), writing and music captured the spirit of the civil rights movement, especially the movement's dream for South Africa and the United States that had yet to be fully realized.

Gloria Blakely's comments related to Martin Luther King, in her *Voices: Reflections on an American Icon through Word and Song*, contain gems that are worthy of being quoted. The chorals start, she writes,

> with the music that once powered bruised bones to rise, sore feet to march forward and weary souls to keep struggling for freedom. . . . Freedom songs, so rousing and integral to the movement, such as *Lift Every Voice and Sing, Guide My Feet*, and a King favorite, *Precious Lord, Take My Hand*, merited a place beside narratives about the movement. The spirit that changed America soars as Voices, music and book parallel the Discord accompanying the non-violent protests . . . leading to the famous March on Washington for Jobs and Freedom, the Harmony desired from comprehensive legislation for equal rights.[28]

Ghana; Nketia, *Music in African Cultures*; Williamson, "The Lyric in the Fante Methodist Church," 126–34.

27. See Rattray, *Akan-Ashanti Folktales*.
28. Blakely, "Giving a Voice to a Dream," 27.

The thrust of this long quotation is that music is a vehicle of remembrances, capturing a dream close to the heart. The music of the liberation movement captured the dream that skin color, ethnicity, and religion would not matter and that all people would be recognized as equal and live in peace. The civil rights movement was a striving after this hope, the engine of which is peace, justice, and freedom.

The goal is an eschatological hope, in the sense that it is not realized as yet, but hope is the motor powering the fulfillment of the vision. Indeed, the last section of Miri Ben-Ari's "Symphony of Brotherhood" is, so to speak, the uplifting of strength and confidence. These considerations serve as a reminder that theology needs allies and agencies to fill peoples with a dream that challenges them to act and live a certain quality of life. Crudely put, what *prima facie* may look like a political word or activity may well be a religious-spiritual-theological quest.

It is often overlooked that hymns and canticles are a vital part of the Christian church's tradition and memory. They are treasure troves of theological, religious, and spiritual insight. So, theological constructs need not be expressed *only* in propositions or prose.

On the African continent a striking institution is the African Initiatives in Christianity (AICs). The popularity and dynamism of these churches is very much due to their ability to communicate the message of the gospel through song and music. Well did Martin Luther state that "music is an endowment and a gift of God. It also drives away the devil and makes people cheerful; one forgets all anger, unchasteness, pride and other vices. I place music next to theology and give it the highest praise."[29]

The subplot of this whole study is that theology must have an ecumenical perspective and hermeneutic. In that endeavor music may play a solid and important role in forging ecumenism. Music does not immediately present any theological problems—listeners and performers alike are able to enjoy and approach the beauty and wonder of the creation of God—while at the same time fostering evangelism. Even nonbelievers can respond favorably to beautiful sacred music. As Colin Mawby asks, "How can one listen to sacred music without questioning its ultimate source? In a spiritually troubled world, it forms a deeply rooted and spiritual anchor to which most people can cling."[30]

Art as a Language of Theology

In all societies art has been used to express religious ideas.[31] Thus Christian art is replete with examples of funerary art, for example, crypts reminding us of death lurking

---

29. Cited from Robin A. Leaver, "Luther on Music," in Wengert, *Pastoral Luther*, 271n1.

30. Mawby, "How Can You Hear Sacred Music without Thinking of God?," 11.

31. Lennart Ryden, "The Role of the Icon in Byzantine Piety," in *Humanitas Religiosa*, 41–52; Pagha, *Glittering Images*; Walter De Maria, *The Lightning Field* (a work of land art situated in a remote area of the high desert of western New Mexico; see http://www.diaart.org/visit/visit/

around the corner as well as of the offer of hope beyond the grave, notably the resurrection of the dead. The tomb of Cardinal Antonio Barberini, brother of Pope Urban VIII (1568–1644), bears the inscription "Here lies dust and ashes—nothing more," conveying the message that all are equal in death.

Similarly, a seventeenth-century Capuchin church in Rome carries on the ceiling a painting of a skeleton with a set of scales dangling on its arm. The scales depict the weighing of the good and the bad on the Day of Judgment, with the promise of hell for sinners and heaven for pure souls. The Sistine Chapel ceiling houses Michelangelo's two-part panel of the Temptation and the Expulsion from the Garden of Eden. Much great art of the West has religious themes, and the Bible forms the basis of much great art. Art is almost the quintessential spiritual quest, capturing transcendental meaning. I sympathize with the view that a society that forgets art risks losing its soul.

Throughout history and across the length and breadth of the world, Africa included, graphic art and design have been modes of capturing reality and matters of faith and belief. Such art includes symbolism of nature, time, persons, action, and language, culminating in the sacraments of Baptism and Eucharist.[32] Especially in Africa, which is home to large numbers of nonliterates, symbolism and art have been most welcome and effective tools for communicating truth and matters of faith, belief, and hope. In Ghana, Adinkra symbols have been celebrated modes of intimating religious messages; for example, the Adinkra symbol of Gye Nyame (Except God) asserts God's omnipotence.

A celebrated painting of the Last Supper from Cameroon portrays an African perspective on the Supper, as does another in the Democratic Republic of Congo (pictures of both can be found on the Internet). To illustrate how art has been employed in an African context to articulate aspects of religious-theological-spiritual convictions and positions, however, let us consider the reredos on the east wall behind the altar in the sanctuary of the Anglican Church of Cyrene, Bulawayo, Zimbabwe.

---

walter-de-maria-the-lightning-field); Rattray, *Religion and Art in Ashanti*.

32. Dillistone, *Christianity and Symbolism*.

Fig. 1.1. Paintings in Sanctuary of the Anglican Church of Cyrene, Bulawayo, Zimbabwe
(Reproduced with the permission of Bishop Cleopas Lunga, Matabeleland, Zimbabwe.)

At the center, high and lifted up, is an African portrayal of Jesus clothed in Eucharistic vestments and with the ciborum in his hand, thus articulating belief in Christ as the great High Priest who offered and offers the great sacrifice for salvation. The Eucharist, whatever else it is, is a sacrifice for salvation. Strikingly, the feet which just about touch the altar still have the nails of his crucifixion, thus asserting that the crucifixion and death of Jesus is the sacrifice which avails for the salvation of the world. It is not without significance that these ideas are present in that church and diocese, because they reflect the Pusian High Church tradition of the Tractarian Oxford Movement in which that diocese stands.

To the right of Jesus the priest—crucified, risen, and ascended high up—is a painting of Simon of Cyrene, who according to Mark 15:21–22 was compelled to help Jesus carry his cross. Simon is barefoot and in shorts, signaling the humble—neither sophisticated nor wealthy nor famous—who nevertheless show commitment and courage in the face of adversity to follow Christ. Simon thus represents simple local members of the African community of faith. When we recall that Southern Rhodesia, now Zimbabwe, for years smarted under racist ideology and, indeed, for years was subjected to struggle for liberation, then Simon also represents the afflicted Africans, especially Christians. As such the entire presentation is biblical, capturing Paul's statement that "not many" of the converts and followers of Christ "were wise by human standards, not many were powerful, not many were of noble birth. But God chose what is foolish in the world to shame the wise; God chose what is weak in the world to shame the strong. God chose what is low and despised in the world, things that are not, to reduce to nothing things that are, so that no one might boast in the presence of God" (1 Cor 1:26–29 NRSV). Thus humility (Phil 2:5–8) is a major principle of exhortation made manifest through the lives of the faithful in Zimbabwe. At the same time, all are admonished to rely on Christ for the ability to live as followers of God and of Christ (1 Cor 1:30–31), who is not a foreigner but an African God.

To Jesus' right is Bernard Mizeki, a Shona evangelist of the late 1890s who was martyred, a fact commemorated by the sword Mizeki is carrying, a reminder of how he was murdered. Mizeki's sartorial apparel of cassock and surplice intimates the call to worship even if through martyrdom. Africans venerate ancestors in the spirit world.

The painting in the Church of Cyrene proclaims the centrality of Christ and his sacrifice for the life of Christians. All, irrespective of status and calling, are called to imitate Christ even if it means martyrdom. The central rite of the sacrament of Eucharist is an exercise in living that vocation. Art then is a most helpful mode of inculcating faith and hope in a manner that the most humble would-be followers of Christ can absorb. Even if all are called to discipleship even unto death, Christ is the unique, unparalleled exemplar and model. The propositional style thus may not be the only mode of articulating theology in Africa; its expression can also be achieved effectively in art and craft.

Art is a potentially powerful language of theology. This capacity of art is most apposite in largely nonliterate societies such as are found in many African rural contexts.

Theology as Story

It may sound odd to use the word "story" of theology. Parents read and tell stories to put their children to bed. Preachers use stories to illustrate points of a sermon. Today, however, academics also make use of oral history to make serious points; consider, for example, the seventeenth-century mathematician and philosopher Blaise Pascal, the English novelist D. H. Lawrence, the German and then US physicist Albert Einstein, the US Protestant theologian H. Richard Niebuhr, and the Nigerian critic and writer Chinua Achebe.

Narrative is a fundamental category of human experience and thinking, because stories create meanings. Stories are used to explain everyday life. Barbara Hardy writes, "We dream in narrative, daydream in narrative, remember, anticipate, hope, despair, believe, doubt, plan, revise, criticize, construct, gossip, learn, hate, and love by narrative."[33] Facts, propositions, dogmas, and doctrines all have meaning when put in the context and form of a story. Jesus was a teacher *par excellence* because of his skillful use of parables to inculcate profound insights. He used stories from everyday life, so as to make sense of life and to open up possibilities in life.

---

33. Hardy, *Tellers and Listeners*, 4; Paul Ricoeur, "Life in Quest of Narrative," in Wood, *On Paul Ricoeur*, 188–99; Brown, "My Story and 'The Story,'" 166–73; Balcond, "Narrative," 11–21.

Authenticity, Integrity and Creativity: Marks of Contextual Theology

The World Council of Churches' Theological Education Fund—on through its subsequent incarnations as the Program on Theological Education and, later, Ecumenical Theological Education—identified authenticity, integrity, and creativity as marks of contextual theology. These were styled the threefold Asian Critical Principle.[34]

Under the banner "Viability of Theological Education," led by the Program on Theological Education, the threefold principle was tweaked to its canonical formula of authenticity, integrity, and creativity by which theological construction was to be "biblically based, missiologically oriented, educationally shaped, pastorally advocated and spiritually empowered."[35] The Africa Region preparatory conference elaborated the formula further by putting creativity first in the threefold principle. John de Gruchy comments as follows:

> A quality theological education requires that we must resist the temptation to give priority to one aspect of theological education at the expense of others, and seek rather to develop approaches which are holistic, coherent and integrated. Quality theological education does not mean scientific training at the expense of spiritual formation or being equipped for pastoral ministry . . . , social witness or vice versa. All these are indispensable. A quality theological education is likewise not one which is fragmented into disparate and competing parts, whether this is understood in terms of academic disciplines, visions of ministry, or models of education. A quality theological education requires technical ability then, but for the sake of producing the authentic and creative pastor and prophet, indeed, the authentic Christian community. A quality theological education, in other words, is grounded in a particular understanding of theologian. If there is uncertainty, shallowness or misunderstanding at this point, it will affect the whole enterprise, no matter how technically competent its products.[36]

An African theology that is viable and faithful to the gospel must be doxological, scientific, contextual, and missiological. These tests have ongoing validity, but, be that as it may, story is an epistemological category. The propositional style may not be the only mode of theologizing.

Several and Diverse Religions

Religion has been evident for as long as humans have been in existence. And so comes the equation *homo sapiens = homo religiosus*, that is, to be human is to be religious. Some have argued that religion is characteristic of primitive cultures. In an age of

---

34. Theological Education Fund, *Learning in Context*.
35. Thu, "Revisiting Mission and Vision in ATESEA," 14–15.
36. De Gruchy, "Quality, Authenticity, Creativity, and Ecumenical Theological Education," 46–48.

science and rationality, religion has taken a pummeling, often being shunted into a corner as old wives' tales. In spite of that a stubborn sense perdures of the reality of a sacred dimension to human existence, with which reality it seems the highest purpose of human life to come to terms. Indeed, *homo africanus = homo religiosus radicaliter*.[37] Mainstream religion appears, prima facie, to address human emotional and spiritual needs.

Religions, many and diverse, are a universal phenomenon. Scholars distinguish between preliterate religions and major religions of the world. The traditional ethnic religions of Africa, Asia, the Pacific, and Central and Southern America fit within the category of preliterate religions. Buddhism, Christianity, and Islam are described as world religions. Often they are treated as systems of belief. This line of theology often reduces particular religions to an ideology. What is human, however, is what should be uppermost and be thought determinative of religious experience and practice. In the words of the German scholar Dietrich Bonhoeffer, "To be religious is not to make a saint or a penitent of yourself but to be human."[38]

If from the beginning of time and space religion has been evident, then it has been run through various ideological prisms. We shall return to this point. Suffice it to affirm here that each religion has its own theology, and particular cultures have been colored by the atmosphere of particular religions. For that reason, attempts to disenfranchise any one religion are unrealistic, especially in an age that intones freedom of conscience and lifts up religion as a human right. This fact means that the theological constructions of any one religion must not be insensitive to other religions. In the globalized village of today, pluralism forms the context for theological construction undertaken by every religion.

In Africa the major religions are African Traditional Religions, Christianity, and Islam, and in some cases Hinduism. Although Platvoet has identified some thirteen kinds of religions in Africa,[39] they often do not live in watertight compartments. In an extended family, two or more religions live side by side without any hostility. In any case, the same person may exhibit traits drawn from both African Traditional Religions and Christianity. This blending fingers the issues of identity and religion, religious pluralism and peaceful coexistence, as well as the nature of conversion in a context of religious-cultural pluralism.

---

37. On this point Platvoet has argued for a dissenting position. See Platvoet and van Rinsum, "Is Africa Incurably Religious?," 123–53; Platvoet and van Rinsum, "Is Africa Incurably Religious?, III: A Reply to a Rhetorical Response," 156–73; Richard E. Elphick, "Introduction: Christianity in South African History," in Elphick and Davenport, *Christianity in South Africa*, 1–15; Shorter, "Secularism in Africa."

38. Bonhoeffer, *Letters and Papers from Prison*, 118.

39. Jan Platvoet, "The Religions of Africa in their Historical Order," in Platvoet et al., *Study of Religions in Africa*, 46–102.

Earlier the argument was put forward that theology is tied into faith; this is no reason, however, for despising persons of no faith. Daniel Polish, spiritual leader of Congregation Shir Chadash, Hudson Valley, New York, writes,

> This may be the greatest gift we receive from those of no faith, the gift of spiritual humility. They stand as reminders to us all that we know less about God, than we would aspire to; perhaps than we pretend to. They remind us that much as we are on a journey toward God we have not arrived at the destination and we need to be more modest in the claims we make for ourselves and more forgiving of those who have achieved different insight. From the vantage point of that modesty we can greet one another in peace, respect and love.[40]

Theology, like religion—its raw material, so to speak—serves as a vision of hope. Hope is not just a sentiment; it is a vision to be worked at. Just as Scripture speaks of *doing* the truth and not just thinking it, a vision of hope must be discerned in the midst of challenges that threaten our well-being and militate against the vision of hope. Hope may not be dismissed as illusions that, so to speak, lull children to sleep. The hope that theology and religion serve must show the capacity to carry out the required reforms that will shore up the peace, security, humanity, and human dignity of all people as persons bearing the image and likeness of God.

---

40. Polish, "The Atheistic Imagination: A Jewish Response," in Ryan, *Atheistic Imagination*, 29.

2

Africa

THE EPITHET "AFRICAN" IN the theme of this study has to do principally with the continent of Africa. In today's world Africa is often spoken of in negative terms: a basket case, primitive, violent, inhuman, or even failed states. Whatever else may be said of it, Africa is the second largest continent, stretching between longitudes 20°W and 50°E and latitudes 76°N and 30°S, an area of 11,677,000 square miles (30,243,000 sq km). It is a continent, not a country, bounded by the Mediterranean Sea, Atlantic Ocean, and Indian Ocean. Indeed, it is a continent of fifty-four nation-states, encompassing tremendous differences and variations. Africa is crossed by the Greenwich or Prime Meridian, the Equator, and the Tropics of Cancer and Capricorn. As such, it is a continent of peoples, "all sorts and conditions" of humanity, and situations, geographic and climatological. It cannot be overlooked nor should it be spoken of without a sense of the variations and diversities and various particularities and peculiarities on the continent. One cut may not fit for all.

As a continent of peoples and languages, Africa has been the home of aboriginal peoples such as the Hottentots of South Africa, Bushmen of the Kalahari, and Pygmies of the Congo forest; Afro-Asians, Saharan nomads, Berbers, and Arabs; Negroids; and Caucasoids, each group with its own identity. All too often people assume the Negroids *are* the Africans. But the picture is more variegated and nuanced than the popular image takes into account. The Caucasoids in Africa, originally Indo-Europeans, migrated from Holland and England to Southern Africa after 1652 and the 1820s respectively. They know and have no other home than Southern Africa.

If in the past particular races and peoples have been associated with particular areas, today there is much moving across borders. With colonialism as a catalyst, Africa, as a continent and as a collective of nation-states, is polyethnic, polysemous, and polycultural. A single country may be polyethnic and polylingual. Thus Kenya in East Africa (EA) is a loose collection of forty-two peoples, principally Kikuyu, Luo, Massai, and Kalenjin. Sudan is also a collection of many peoples, predominantly Arab, Dinka, Nuer, and Nubian.

Nigeria in West Africa has about one hundred peoples and languages, with 50 percent of Nigerians as native speakers of Hausa, Igbo, or Yoruba. Ghana, also in West Africa, is polyethnic, with people from such language groups as Guan (4.4 percent), Mole-Dagbani (16.5 percent), Akan (49.1 percent), Ewe (12.7 percent), Ga-Adangbe (8 percent), Gurma (3.9 percent), Grusi (2.8 percent), Mande-Bwanga (1.1 percent) and others (1.5 percent).[1]

So Ghana, like the other African states, has multiple facets, which warns us to beware of talk about *the* African; it is more true to speak in terms of *an* African. This reality provided the rationale behind the title of my earlier publication *Toward an African Theology*. Pluralism forms the context of Africa and of theologizing. The consciousness of pluralism in Africa is different from the Christendom ideology that shaped theologies inherited from colonial times.

Today consciousness of a search for African unity is growing, as institutions such as the African Union (AU), Economic Community of West Africa States (ECOWAS), and Southern African Development Community (SADC) signify. But these developments do not erase the multiple ethnic identities that are to be found on the continent of Africa and within its countries and nation-states.

A further complicating factor is that Africa is at once ancient and modern. Through time and across space, travel has resulted in contacts with other peoples, cultures, religions, and influences. These contacts have meant ongoing struggles to come to terms with new times and influences. In any one country, the advanced modern and the simple old can be found, standing side by side. That is why it is presumptuous to suggest that one cut fits all.

Since Africa and homo africanus have not been static, a single construct may not be adequate to communicate to homo africanus in his/her various shades and shapes. The long and short is to make us conscious that pluralism is the context for theologizing in Africa and it must be the hermeneutic for making constructs. Further, pluralism signals that various cultures are to be engaged.

In light of Africa's long history and its contacts with others, all talk that presumes a pristine African is suspect. For now, let us indicate some of the factors that have left almost indelible marks on Africa and Africans.

Slavery

Traditional African societies did practice slavery, especially during the wars between the emerging traditional states. But such slaves became members of host households in due time and were not denied their humanity and humanness.[2]

---

1. Ghana Statistical Service, Population and Housing Census, 2012.

2. Perbi, *History of Indigenous Slavery in Ghana*; Blyden, *Christianity, Islam, and the Negro Race*; Patterson, *Sociology of Slavery*.

Contact with the Arabs in Eastern Africa and Europeans in Western Africa, however, introduced a new face to slavery by which the slave became a *res*, that is, a thing, not a human and with no rights. By some estimates, from 1770 onwards some 100,000 slaves a year were sold and shipped to the Western Hemisphere, especially to the West Indies. In the eighteenth-century slave trade, commerce, warfare, welfare, and the national security of Great Britain were inextricably mixed.

It is not as if only the "evil" engaged in slavery. Church people were involved. John Newton, before his dramatic conversion, was a notorious slave dealer. And even when he was converted, he owed his curacy at Olney to the Earl of Dartmouth, an influential slavery supporter. Thomas Thompson, the first missionary sent by the Society for the Propagation of the Gospel (SPG) to the Gold Coast (Ghana), published a pamphlet in 1772 with the eloquent title *The African Trade for Negro Slaves; Shewn to Be Consistent with the Principles of Humanity, and with the Laws of Revealed Religion*. At General Synod of the Church of England on February 8, 2006, Rowan Williams, the 104th Archbishop of Canterbury (2003–12), had this to say in his presidential address:

> The Body of Christ is not just a body that exists at any one time; it exists across history and we, therefore, share the shame and the sinfulness of our predecessors, and part of what we can do, with them and for them, the Body of Christ, is prayerful acknowledgement of the failure that is part of us, not just of some distant "them." To speak here of repentance and apology is not words alone; it is part of our witness to the gospel, to a world that needs to hear that the past must be faced and healed and cannot be ignored.[3]

Further, it is sobering to recall that though much credit is given to William Wilberforce (1759–1833), the English politician, abolitionist, and philanthropist, and to the Clapham Sect for pursuing the abolition of the slave trade, bishops in the House of Lords armed with biblical authority voted against the abolition of slavery.[4] Alongside the foregoing, we must note papal reaction against Portuguese slaving in the seventeenth century.[5]

Two consequences may be derived from the story of slavery. First, since the Christian churches' story in Africa has, in some cases, been tarnished by the slave trade, any attempt to commend Christianity and Christian theology must show penitence and humility. The credibility of what the theologian says has been compromised by the facts of history. So it cannot be a case of a superior, upright agent talking down at benighted African infidels.

Second, the long, inhuman experience cannot but have affected, if not damaged, the psyche of homo africanus. As F. K. Buah, a late Ghanaian historian, has written,

---

3. Rowan Williams, Presidential Address, General Synod of the Church of England, cited in *New African* 440 (March 2006) 36.
4. Howse, *Saints in Politics*; Lean, *God's Politician*; Jakobsson, *Am I Not a Man and a Brother?*
5. Gray, *Black Christians and White Missionaries*, chronicles the papal reaction.

"The African came to regard their white trading partners and white races as superior to their own, and to accept the white cultures and values in preference to their own heritage. This unfortunate attitude became more and more pronounced right through the colonial days, to such an extent that the complex has not entirely disappeared from the African society to this day."[6] This damage to the African psyche is often made evident by the temptation in Africa to copy even the bad legacies of the northern nations.

Against that background, the agenda of constructing African theology must seek to do two things—on the one hand, to take on board and engage the slave mentality that lingers on in the psyche of homo africanus and, on the other hand, to seek to affirm both Africans' humanity and their African identity. In any case, Christianity beyond the level of doctrine is fundamentally about what is human. At the time of writing, the press carried reports of modern-day slavery. It is not as if slavery and what it represents is passé and has faded into history. Indeed, Pope Francis drew attention to modern day slavery in his 2015 New Year's Peace Exhortation.

In 1985 as an executive director of the World Council of Churches' Program on Ecumenical Theological Education, I organized an All-Africa Consultation in Ghana with the title *Theological Education in Africa: Quo Vadimus?*[7] At the end of the consultation, I organized for some seventeen members of the Board of PTE an excursion to Elmina Castle, which was a point of exit for slaves from the Gold Coast in the seventeenth and eighteenth centuries. After my colleagues had gone through the rather inhuman facilities slaves had to contend with, they were overcome by a sudden hush. As the silence grew deafening, Maria Assaad, moderator of Unit III in which PTE stood in the structure of the WCC, piped out, "It is a miracle that Christianity has grown in West Africa." The inhumanity of the slave trade, which the Portuguese, Dutch, and British missionaries seemed to condone, made the embracing of Christian faith by Africans an incredible miracle. But in spite of human folly, in the final analysis, the Word of the Lord found its own way to take root and flourish. When we have finished our mission and theologizing, there remains the mystery of God who, according to the hymnodist and English poet William Cowper (1731–1800), "moves in a mysterious way, His wonders to perform."

Racism

Next door to slavery is racism. Racism is an ideology and a social outlook that peddles the idea that Negroes/Blacks are by nature inferior to whites, especially in intellect. On that premise, Blacks were systematically discriminated against and were consequently at the bottom of the social heap, with tragic consequences for Black peoples. The late Daniel Patrick Moynihan, who later in his life became a senator from New York, in a

---

6. Buah, *History of Ghana*, 74; Fage, *History of Africa*; Gray, *Black Christians and White Missionaries*.
7. Pobee and Kudadjie, *Theological Education in Africa*.

1965 report wrote of the Black family as a "tangle of pathology."[8] The Black American elite, of course, have not taken kindly to his study, though it seems to be realistic.

The intertwining of racism and slavery in combination led to absent fathers, high rates of illegitimacy in Black societies in the United States and Southern Africa, and female-headed households. Other consequences have been poverty, backwardness, stunted economic and educational facilities and opportunities, high unemployment, racist mortgage practices, weakened child-care support, stunted training programs, and a resounding need for secure family life if people were to be able to pull themselves out of poverty. Within white racist and slave culture, survival itself was an urgent task for Blacks; also urgent was the need for the individual to have a voice. Insidiously, racism as an ideology nurtured and conditioned a slave inferiority complex. Such conditioning could be most destructive of any attempt to rise up and walk tall. It struck at the heart of the biblical conviction of humanity as bearing the image and likeness of God (Gen 1:27).

On the African continent, the ideologies of apartheid and assimilation issued forth in violent repression and in violation of the fundamental rights of the peoples of Mozambique and Angola. The tragic fact is that the Roman Catholic Church and its missions there became accomplices in massive destruction and in violations of human dignity and rights.[9] In this regard, attention may be drawn to some complaints of missionary roots for racist practice. In the bull *Dum diversas* (1452), Pope Nicholas V authorized the King of Portugal to make war against the heathen and reduce them to serfdom. His bull *Romanus Pontifex* (1455) reinforced the order to subject heathen Africa to Christian and civilizing Portuguese influence. The implication was that non–Roman Catholics had no rights, because they lived without the light of Christ.

South Africa became the pinnacle of racism. The ideology of apartheid undergirded a theology minted in the Afrikaner Dutch Reformed Church. So it is not as if the Christian church has been clean, untouched by racist ideology. Desmond Tutu wrote, "Christianity and the Church must start off with a massive *mea culpa* when it comes to speaking about their records relating to democracy and human rights. . . . We must be duly mollified and suitably humble and modest in our claims as we look at the track record of the Church and Christianity over the past several centuries of their existence."[10] Namibia from the late 1940s to the 1980s stood as the paragon of white racism in which churches were accomplices. And so, in Southern Africa even theology was very strongly colored by racism. This fact accounts in part for the difference in emphasis between West African theologians and Southern African theologians.

Life experienced in the context of racism has informed the African's perception and understanding of the Christian religion; therefore, the legacy of racism must be reckoned

---

8. Glazer and Moynihan, *Beyond the Melting Pot*.

9. Moreira, *Portugal's Stand in Africa*, 89–90; Hastings, *Wiriyamu*; Césaire, *Discours sur le colonialisme*.

10. Tutu, "Postscript: To Be Human Is to Be Free," 311. Smith, "Apartheid in South Africa," 143–52; UNESCO, Statement on Race and Racial Prejudice.

with when we dare to do Christian theology in Africa, especially Southern Africa. Racism has been registered, if not imprinted, on the psyche of homo africanus—who yet seek, as mentioned, to affirm their common humanity as well as their African identity.

The story of racism in apartheid South Africa was such a momentous experience and challenge to the Christian faith that I must dwell on it a little longer. In the middle of the nineteenth century, the Dutch Reformed Church was faced with radical social and political changes as a result of the Great Trek and the emancipation of slaves. These changes raised in an acute form the question of how "people of colour may be incorporated into the Church. The solution of the Cape Synod in 1857 was separate carriage on the basis of colour. It is a matter of convenience which gave birth to the secular gospel of apartheid."[11]

But what started as a matter of temporary missionary policy to facilitate evangelism developed its own momentum and went on to become a rigid theological principle with ideological overtones, the Boers becoming Super-Afrikaners.[12] In 1959 the Commission of the Nederduitse Gereformeerde Kerk stated the matter as follows:

> God divided humanity into races, languages and nations. Differences are not only called by God but are perpetuated by Him, also between the Natives, Coloureds and Europeans. This includes the appreciation of the fact that God, in His providence, made people into different races and nations. . . . Far from the Word of God encouraging equality, it is an established scriptural principle that in every community there is ordination, that is, fixed relations between authorities. Those who are culturally and spiritually advanced have a mission to leadership and protection of the less advanced. . . . The Natives must be led or formed towards independence, so that eventually they will be equal to Europeans, but each on his own territory and each serving in his own fatherland.

As William Vatcher observes, "Racial differences are nevertheless underlined and are reinterpreted as superiority and inferiority. Apartheid became a religio-political concept which issued in a *Laager mentality*, i.e., a siege mentality."[13]

Apartheid, the South Africa version of racism, became an ideology of death and was life-denying for blacks in spite of claiming to have Christian religious roots. It was against that background that South African Black Theology evolved as a quest for hope.

Colonialism

The experience of colonialism was one of the most formative factors of the African story. Kwame Nkrumah, the prince of African nationalism who on March 6, 1957,

---

11. David Botha, "Church and Kingdom in South Africa: Dutch Reformed Perspective," in Nash, *Your Kingdom Come*, 69.

12. Wilkins and Strydom, *Super-Afrikaners*, 29; David J. Bosch, "The Roots and Fruits of Afrikaner Civil Religion," in Hofmeyer and Vorster, *New Faces of Africa*, 15.

13. Vatcher, *White Laager*.

led the Gold Coast to independent sovereign statehood as the new nation of Ghana and thus opened the gates for one African state after another to come into being, said, "The stage opens with the appearance of missionaries and anthropologists, traders and concessionaires and administrators. While the 'missionaries' with 'Christianity' implore the colonial subject to lay up his 'treasures in Heaven where neither moth nor rust doth corrupt,' the traders and concessionaires and administrators acquire his mineral and land resources, destroy his arts, crafts, home industries."[14]

We may wish to dispute some caricature of the story, but Nkrumah laid out the mix of adventure, exploration, mercantilism, Christian missions, and colonialism that made an indelible impact on the continent of Africa. That story has been, by and large, the story of the encounter between Europe and Africa; it has been the fulcrum for the development of Africa, African states, African peoples, and African theology. Of course, we may not forget that Nkrumah himself also trod on the rights and dignity of Ghanaians; for example, the death of J. B. Danquah, "doyen of Gold Coast politics," in jail.

The British historian Arnold Toynbee argued that the Portuguese navigator and explorer Bartholomew Dias provided the key to the "modern age" when he rounded the Cape of Good Hope, South Africa, in 1488. His adventure in exploration opened the way for another Portuguese explorer and colonial administrator, Vasco da Gama, in 1498, to set eyes on Calicut (modern Calcutta), India. That was *the* meeting of the East and the West that inaugurated the encounter between European and Asian civilizations.

The encounter developed its own momentum, as various European nations developed an interest in a share in the lucrative mercantile activity and possibilities. In due time Chancellor Wilhelm Von Bismarck called the Berlin International Conference of 1884–85 at which Africa was balkanized. Balkanization signifies the breaking up of the continent into small, mutually hostile political units at the behest of European nations. The earlier mercantilism gave way to colonialism properly understood, by which Africa was carved up as colonies of European nations: England, Portugal, Germany, France, and Spain. Colonialism maintained "effective occupation of the area by sending administrators to govern the territory."[15] The divisions were made at the behest of and according to the logic and interest of the European nations. The Africans themselves had no say, even though ethnic groups were often divided across colonial boundaries, thus setting the stage for some of the African continent's continuing instability both between and within countries.

Trade was key to and characteristic of the European encounter with Africa. In 1897 the British prime minister, the Third Marquis of Salisbury, stated it clearly:

> The objects [of the colonial mission in Africa] we have in our view are strictly business objects. We wish to extend the commerce, the trade, the industry and the civilization of mankind. We wish to open as many markets as possible, to

14. Nkrumah, *Speech at Conference of Independent African States*, 13; Pobee, "Church and State in the Gold Coast," 217–37.

15. Buah, *History of Ghana*, 199–200.

> bring as many consumers and producers into contact as possible: to throw open the great national highways, the great waterways of this great continent. We wish that trade should pursue its unchecked and unhindered course upon the Niger, the Nile and the Zambezi.[16]

Europe needed spices, silk, and other precious items from Asia. Asia for her part needed gold, iron, ivory, and other items. These latter items were obtainable from Africa, especially Zimbabwe. And so gold, iron, and ivory from Zimbabwe served as the mainstay of the Portuguese trade with India and Asia.

The idea was that colonialism was not some philanthropy; it was a mandate to make money as well as to develop the colonies for the benefit of the indigenous people themselves. Lord Lugard wrote, "Let it be admitted at the outset that European brains, capital, energy have not been, and never will be, expended in developing the resources of Africa from motives of pure philanthropy; that Europe is in Africa for the benefit of her own industrial classes, and of the native races in their progress to a Higher plane."[17]

Lugard, described as the theorist of imperialism, coined in Nigeria the phrase "dual mandate," a euphemism for indirect rule, that is, the policy of maintaining the traditional indigenous authorities but as subservient to and as collaborators with the foreign rulers.[18] Another strand of the colonial ideology was the doctrine of *indirect rule*. As long as European trade was unimpeded, local rulers were left to enjoy their traditional powers. In Ghana, Nana Otumfuo Asantehene, Nene Mate Korle of Krobo-Land, Nana Ofori-Atta of Akim, and Sir Tsibu Darku of Assin were among such powerful chiefs. Indirect rule was by no means a theory; it was a practical necessity if the native peoples were to be kept happy. Curiously, Lugard also suggested that in indirect rule, rulers would be under the guidance of "higher civilization," thus exemplifying the colonialists' patronizing attitude toward Africans and African cultures.[19]

The doctrine of indirect rule implied a concept of empire in which the role of gentleman played a cardinal role: "Behind indirect rule was the notion that the natural rulers of society, if they could be educated as gentlemen, formed the best type of ruling class."[20]

Colonialism was not all of one type: it consisted in various degrees of domination of Africans by Whites. For the African it entailed the experience of exploitation, paternalism, repression, and tyranny, all of which generated in the Africans a need for hope. As an ideology, colonialism contained a strain of the German philosopher Friedrich Nietzsche's idea of the "Superman," a being "beyond good and evil."

---

16. Vandeleur, *Campaigning*, 263; Kwarteng, *Ghosts of Empire*, 274.

17. Lugard, *Dual Mandate*, 617.

18. Perham, *Lugard*; A. E. Afigbo, "The Establishment of Colonial Rule, 1900–1918," in Ajayi and Crowder, *History of West Africa*, 424–83, esp. 453–65.

19. Lugard, *Dependencies of the British Empire*, 8–10.

20. Kwarteng, *Ghosts of Empire*, 293.

The Superman took the form of the colonial administrator, often a soldier, an administrator who could write manly accounts of his achievements for his desk-bound political masters at home.[21] Hence such personalities as George Taubman, later Goldie of Nigeria fame, and Lord Lugard. In the nineteenth century, Africa was the great unknown continent described as the "white man's grave." Cannibalism, paganism, and so forth—much of which was fantasy—flourished as stereotypes in that story. Bellicosity was another element of colonial rule; it issued, for example, in the West Africa Frontier Force that undertook military campaigns which reduced the independent states of Northern Nigeria to subordinate status.

As attractive as the practice of indirect rule may sound at first, in the sense of preserving traditional authority structures, its preservation was done, ironically, at the expense of citizens in the rural areas. African nationalists saw indirect rule as corrupt because it represented divide-and-rule tactics. Especially when the chiefs were paid by the colonial government, the reward or remuneration of the chiefs was unrelated to performance, whether or not they promoted the prosperity of all. Hence the common slogan of nationalists such as Kwame Nkrumah of Ghana and the Convention Peoples Party that "the chiefs will remove their native sandals [a mark of their authority and dignity] and run before the African nationalist." African nationalists saw chieftaincy, when accommodated to the colonial structure, to be a corrupt system and not in the best interest of the native peoples. The struggle between traditional rulers and African nationalist governments forms the backdrop of the search for peace with dignity in African societies. In any case, the nationalists analyzed colonialism as an ideology for assimilating Africa and Africans to the image of the White Person.

Africans who dared to challenge colonialism were denounced and condemned as troublemakers, saboteurs, terrorists, and so on—for example, Jomo Kenyatta and the Mau Mau uprising in Kenya; Nelson Mandela and the African National Congress (ANC) in South Africa; Robert Mugabe and the Zimbabwe African National Union Popular Front (ZANU-PF); and Kwame Nkrumah and the other five of the "Big Six" of the Ghana Independence struggle.

Be that as it may, the experience of colonialism is deeply imprinted on the psyche and rhetoric of African politicians, historians, writers of African literature, theologians, and church people. For this reason colonialism features prominently in African literature such as in the works of Ngũgĩ wa Thiong'o (Kenya), Sembène Ousmane (Senegal), Camara Laye (Guinea), Ferdinand Oyono (Cameroon); Yambo Ouologuem (Mali), Wole Soyinka (Nigeria), and Ayi Kwei Armah (Ghana).[22] It would be surprising indeed if theology were not also impacted by colonialism.

21. Nkrumah, *Neo-colonialism*; Nkrumah, *Ghana: The Autobiography of Kwame Nkrumah*; Hetherington, *British Paternalism and Africa*; Chabal, *History of Postcolonial Lusophone Africa*; Kwarteng, *Ghosts of Empire*, 274; Robinson and Gallagher, *Africa and the Victorians*, 395.

22. Armah, *The Beautiful Ones Are Not Yet Born*; Beti, *The Poor Christ of Bomba*; four by Ngũgĩ: *The Black Hermit*; *Weep Not, Child*; *The River Between*; and *A Grain of Wheat*; Ouologuem, *Bound to Violence*; Oyono, *Houseboy*; two by Sembène: *God's Bits of Wood* and *The Money-Order with White Genesis*.

The Nigerian Chinua Achebe's celebrated novel *Things Fall Apart* is a classic case. It gives a response of sorts to a former colonial officer's publication *Mister Johnson*, which had suggested that colonialism was the best thing that had happened to Africans.[23] Achebe's response was that whether or not colonialism and contact with the West had been good for Africa and had done good to Africa, it had induced the breakdown of traditional society through the denial of fundamental rights such as the right to create space for each legitimate identity in a plural world. *Things Fall Apart* portrays an African society caught between its traditional Igbo roots and the demands of a rapidly changing world. His two other books *No Longer at Ease* and *Arrow of God* also examine personal and moral struggles in the context of turbulent social conflicts and colonialism.

To pick up a point made earlier regarding the influence of colonialism on African writers, the outlook expressed by Martinique-born playwright and politician Aimé Fernand Césaire had wide currency. "Europe is accountable," he wrote, "to the rest of the human community for the highest pile of corpses in history."[24] This characterization of the colonial story was very influential.

Publications by Franz Fanon influenced anticolonial writers in Africa, including Kenya's Ngũgĩ wa Thiong'o, Zimbabwe's Tsiti Dangaremgba, and Senegal's Sembène Ousmane.[25] If colonialism as an ideology has so influenced the African psyche, it hardly needs arguing that it must have had some impact within the religious sphere. That impact will be addressed under the next section, "Christian Missions." For now, let us register that the other side of colonialism was African nationalism, the high priests of which were Edward Wilmot Blyden, Kwame Nkrumah (Ghana), Nnamdi Azikiwe (Nigeria), Julius Nyerere (Tanzania), Patrice Lumumba (Congo), and Kenneth Kaunda (Zambia), among others. The thing not to miss is that these leaders were nurtured in the womb of the Christian church, so much so that their political rhetoric was soaked in and peppered with Christian language and imagery. The Christian church and Christian faith have been described as "the guardian angel of African nationalism."[26]

Fanon was a self-styled Marxist and, therefore, could not be expected to be sympathetic to religion, especially Christianity. But his critique of religion, Christianity, and church cannot simply be dismissed. His critique was that for postcolonial Africa to continue to mimic the colonial bourgeois with all the trappings of capitalism was a recipe for ruin. Fanon wrote, "The national bourgeoisie will be greatly helped on its way towards decadence by the Western bourgeoisies, who come to it as tourists avid for the exotic, for big-game hunting and for casinos. The national bourgeoisie organizes centres of rest

---

23. Cary, *Mister Johnson*.

24. Césaire, *Discours sur le colonialisme*, 25.

25. Fanon, *Wretched of the Earth*; *Black Skin, White Masks*; *Dying Colonialism*; and *Toward the African Revolution*; Bulhan, *Frantz Fanon and the Psychology of Oppression*; and Gibson, *Fanon: The Postcolonial Imagination*.

26. Sithole, *African Nationalism*, 55; Pobee, *Kwame Nkrumah and the Church in Ghana*; Kimble, *Political History of Ghana*, 161.

and relaxation and pleasure resorts to meet the wishes of the Western bourgeoisie. Such activity is given the name of tourism, and for the occasion will be built up as a national industry."[27] The tourist industry of Kenya, the Gambia, and South Africa make Fanon's critique relevant, even for the church and theology's search for the well-being of peoples.

The experience of slavery was marked by violence and the degradation of Blacks. Colonialism with its tinge of racism and paternalism rubbed it in, so to speak, that Blacks were not equals of Whites. One consequence of this experience is that Blacks around the world developed a sense of solidarity in suffering, marginalization, and exclusion.

That awareness was the fulcrum for Pan-Africanism by which Blacks in mainland Africa and Blacks of the diaspora forged solidarity to fight imperialism and colonialism. The high priests of that development include W. E. B. Du Bois, US historian, educator, and civil rights leader; Marcus Garvey, Jamaican political leader; George Padmore, journalist born in Trinidad; Kwame Nkrumah, Ghanaian statesman; and Nnamdi Azikiwe, Nigerian head of state. Though Christian missions sometimes took a drubbing from Pan-Africanists, they themselves, in varying degrees, had the marks of Christian faith on them. We must not forget the number of African American theologians and church persons who pioneered theology and the practice of liberation as an instrument for affirming the identity, integrity, and dignity of Black Persons. Slavery and colonialism represent the constellation of issues composed of structural inequality, poverty, and drugs. But the story of colonialism was also a story of interaction. It was not a one-way street; Africa received but also gave, just as Europe received and gave. For example, the Shona language, especially the Chi-Manyika dialect, owes much to the Portuguese language. Conversely, the Portuguese language borrowed from Shona (see table).

Shona	*Portuguese*	*Meaning*
Mupeto	empata	tax, tribute
Murandu	milando	lawsuit, fault
Kuruva	curva	pay tax or tribute
Kupembera	pemberar	dance for joy
Tsapalo	sapalo	boot, shoe
Sumburero	sombreiro	umbrella
Puranga	prancha	plank
Fofo	fosforo	match
Rata	lata	tinplate
Bakayao	bacalhau	salt fish
Vhakacha	vaccacao	rest, leisure
Purazi	prazo	farm

With Portuguese colonialism, Portuguese culture and Portuguese Roman Catholic religion also came to Africa. But the Portuguese also carried Africans from Angola

27. Fanon, *Toward the African Revolution*.

to Brazil. Those Africans went with their culture and music; samba and lundu music have their roots in Angolan history. The music was really those Africans' religious and cultural affirmation of identity and their expression of joy and love of life.

By mentioning several examples of two-way influence, I wish to suggest that mutual influence was extensive and not accidental. That truth should give Africans the conviction that they need not always be at the receiving end and, therefore, they may have confidence also to give. A globalized world must be characterized by give and take.

Church Missions

Christian missions was one of the faces worn by the European adventure of exploration into Africa.[28] Consequently, Christian missions and churches have been lampooned as not only another face but also a conscious agent of imperialism and colonialism. In actual fact Christianity came to Africa long before colonialism. The story of the Scillitan Martyrs (AD 180) in Roman North Africa is evidence that a vibrant church was present in North Africa very early. North Africa produced such giant churchmen and theologians as Tertullian (ca. 160–225), Augustine of Hippo Regius (354–430), and Cyprian of Carthage (d. 258), each of whom exerted profound and enduring influence on the theology and character of the Latin church of the West. Early North African Christianity, of course, was embedded in a Latin-speaking Roman colonial culture. Egyptian Coptic Christianity was more indigenous.

Though the Christian lands in North Africa were overrun by Islam in the seventh and eighth centuries, from them Christianity reached Africa south of the Sahara. Christianity in Nubia-Ethiopia was legendary, motivating Christian missionaries from Europe to dare to travel to Africa to see the mythical medieval Christian prince, Prester John.[29]

Missionaries from Europe, however, when they later came to Africa, came with their European cultural constructs and artifacts firmly in place. Consequently, the denominational divisions of Europe were introduced into Africa, further complicating already existing divisions related to ethnicity and racism. This situation posed questions to church and theology; as articulated by Kwame Nkrumah, "How can there be good will if Churches think more of their differences than of their wholehearted devotion to the God of all? Above all, how can the Christian message be spread effectively to the hopeful inquiring mass of Africa, if it does not come to them rooted in charity, which is the bond of perfection?"[30] This signals that an ecumenical perspective in theological construction is essential for credible Christian faith in Africa.

---

28. Pobee, "Church and State in the Gold Coast," 217–37. Latourette, *History of Christianity*; Latourette, *History of the Expansion of Christianity*; Groves, *Planting of Christianity in Africa*; Ajayi, *Christian Missions in Nigeria*; Ayandele, *Missionary Impact on Modern Nigeria*.

29. Adams, *Nubia*.

30. Orchard, *Ghana Assembly of the International Missionary Council*, 149.

Because missionary constructs were cloned in Africa, Christian theology in Africa at first was also a clone of European models. Let us here delineate four examples of this. First, the social services of education and health care were, and continue to be, handmaids of mission. These services have contributed immensely to African consciousness and development. Through them Christianity became the guardian angel of African nationalism, giving churches so much clout in national life that during the post-independence period in most African societies the church and the nationalist political party have become the "heavyweights." We may add that having quality theological education beyond the primary and secondary levels is a logical development of the work of the earliest missions.

Second, a most important contribution made by the missions was their pioneer work in reducing African languages to writing. Thus in the Gold Coast (Ghana), the Basel missionary Johannes Gottlieb Christaller reduced the Twi language to writing. Similarly, Johannes Zimmerman reduced the Ga language to writing. Curiously, rarely did the earliest missionaries take the logical step of writing theological treatises in African languages. While language work was consistent with the core Christian message of the incarnation, the missionaries were trapped in the ideology then current that European languages, especially English, were the languages of civilization.

Third, the Christian faith carried by the early missionaries was permeated with an intrinsic racism. This taken-for-granted racism owed much to the anthropological racists of the time, for example, James Hunt's denial of anything like a common humanity shared between Europeans and Negroes. He wrote:

1. "That there is as good reason for classifying the Negro as a distinct species from the European, as there is for making the ass a distinct species from the zebra; and if, in classification, we take the intelligence into consideration, there is a far greater difference between the Negro and European than between the gorilla and chimpanzee.

2. That the analogies are far more numerous between the Negro and the ape, than between the European and the ape.

3. That the Negro is inferior intellectually to the European.

4. That the Negro becomes more humanised when in his natural subordination to the European than under any other circumstances.

5. That the Negro race can only be humanised and civilised by Europeans.

6. That European civilization is not suited to the Negro's requirements or character."[31]

Even if the missionaries may have denied being racist, they were, at the least, accomplices in the ideology of racism. Certainly in the 1940s and 1980s some of the churches and missions and apartheid governments were hand in glove with each other

---

31. Hunt, "On the Negro's Place in Nature," 51–52; see also 26–27.

in Namibia and South Africa, Portuguese Angola, and Portuguese Mozambique. This fact accounts in part for differences of emphasis to be found between West African and Southern African theologies and theologians.

Fourth, importation to Africa of the ideology of Christendom came as a legacy of North Atlantic missionary contact. The idea of Christendom itself may be said to have originated in the declaration of Theodosius I, Roman general and emperor (379–95), making the Christian faith the official religion of the empire.[32] An ideology of power, Christendom tended to be intolerant of non-Christian religions. It developed its own momentum, being caught up in the politics and power games of the world. Two particular rulers mark significant developments, Charlemagne (742–814) and Charles V (1500–1558).

Charles I, known as Charlemagne or Charles the Great, king of the Franks and emperor of the Holy Roman Empire (800–14), was a champion of Christ against infidels, establishing the kingdom of Christ in Europe. The other ruler, Charles V (also known as Charles I of Spain), became the thirteenth successor of Charlemagne to hold the title of Holy Roman Emperor (1516–56). After the battle of Pavia, February 1525, he consolidated Christian dominance in Europe. This development represented the joining together of a universal empire and a universal religion. The union of spiritual power and temporal power presented by Christendom was considered the ideal.

Charles V's oath of coronation as emperor of the Holy Roman Empire is instructive and worthy of quotation: "In the name of Christ, I, Charles of Spain, the Emperor, promise, undertake, and protest in the presence of God that I will be protector and defender of the Holy Roman Church in all ways that I can be of help, so far as I shall be supported by Divine aid, according to my knowledge and ability."[33] For our purposes, the operative phrase is "protector and defender of the Holy Roman Church." The *una sancta* was sundered before long, but the idea of the Christian ruler standing up for the Christian faith has lingered on in diverse ways, even in the colonies of Europe.

The claim of universal empire joined with universal religion became a source of irritation in relations with Islam, also a temporally and territorially powerful religion, especially under Sulayman the Magnificent (1520–66).[34] Earlier the Crusades, the military expeditions undertaken between the end of the eleventh and the end of the thirteenth centuries at the instigation of the church to recover the Holy Land from Muslim hands, had been sources of contention as well.

Those Crusades set the stage for difficult, bitter, and acrimonious relations between Christians and Muslims. So though Judaism, Christianity, and Islam were from the same root and stock and were considered siblings, usually no love was lost between them. Further, the relationship of Christianity to all other religions has had

---

32. King, *Emperor Theodosius*; Meyendorff, *Imperial Unity and Christian Divisions*; Herrin, *Formation of Christendom*.
33. See Reston, *Defenders of the Faith*, chap. 5.
34. Reston, *Defenders of the Faith*.

a tinge of the Crusader spirit. In Africa that spirit led to the exclusion of traditional African religions and to de facto discounting of the pluralism that marked Africa. After independence the situation was reversed, and Departments of Divinity/Theology became Departments for the Study of Religions or Departments of Religious Studies, recognizing the pluralism present in the African context. The principles of other religions such as Islam, Buddhism, Hinduism, and African Traditional Religion were given recognition alongside fundamental Judaic-Christian principles. It was in that light that the first Festschrift from Black Africa had pluralism as its focus.[35]

Europe and Africa: A Story of Contradictions

Slavery, mercantilism, colonialism, and missions are aspects of the interface between Europe and Africa that has impacted Africa and the African psyche. The interface, however, has also introduced Africa to science and technology. The story of twentieth-century Africa reveals the way that tremendous changes have come to the continent culturally, theologically, scientifically, and ethically. The net result is that today Africa is a continent of contradictions.

Three sets of facts serve to substantiate this story of contradictions. First is the picture of the potential wealth juxtaposed to the abject poverty that characterizes even the well-endowed countries. On the one hand, Africa is endowed with rich natural resources such as extensive and expansive waterways. Among its rivers are the Congo (2,718 miles), Nile (4,160 miles), Zambezi (1,599 miles), Niger (2,590 miles), and Volta (1,000 miles). It has considerable arable land and timber. It is well endowed with mineral resources such as gold (Ghana, Tanzania, Congo), diamonds (Democratic Republic of Congo, Liberia, Ghana, Angola), uranium (Democratic Republic of Congo), and oil and gas (Nigeria, Sudan, Angola, Central African Republic, Uganda, Ghana), not to mention manganese and bauxite. Africa is blessed by God with natural resources.

On the other hand, Africa has tragically also become synonymous with abject poverty, famine, disease, and particularly AIDS. Relatively rich and stable African countries have slums such as Kibari and Athare in Kenya. These slums are explosive reservoirs of frustration ready to erupt into violence.

Second, Africa has become a byword for political instability and eruptions of genocide. Liberia underwent a ruthless and painful civil war from the mid-1980s until 2003. Angola and Ivory Coast also went through years of bloody civil war. So, too, Mozambique and Sierra Leone. Rwanda is forever identified with genocide, and in 2008, genocide's grim shadow fell across Kenya also. Violence, pain, and suffering—and masses of in-between people—are the backdrop for all theological endeavors in Africa. At the heart of these endeavors lie the issues of what it means to be human, and those of justice, peace, value systems, and morality. Economics also becomes, as it were, a religious-spiritual issue.

35. Pobee, *Religion in a Pluralistic Society*.

In all of Africa's crises, the evidence shows that whatever the role and fault of African nations may be, there is also massive interference from nations outside Africa.[36] As such, issues on the continent may be not African only but intercontinental and transnational as well.

Third, Africa has become a byword for corruption. Thirty-six of the fifty-four African states have been reported as being afflicted by rampant greed and corruption so extensive that it is stunting Africa's growth and hurting people. Governments have not been held responsible and accountable for graft and misrule, generating disgruntlement. Elected leaders—sometimes with accomplices from Europe and America—are cited for racketeering, money laundering, fraud, and bribery. While we deplore violence and armaments in Africa, France has been implicated in arms deals in South Africa that, further, are tainted by corruption. Meanwhile, the people suffer, and religious bodies, time and again, have had to care for the victims of corruption and of the irresponsibility of politicians.

Fourth, amid all the negatives, economic and political resurgence in Africa offers signs of hope. Almost all African nations have gone through democratic elections. Liberia, after emerging from its tunnel experience, in 2007 posted economic growth of 13.3 percent. Some measures, unfortunately, appear to be little more than palliatives, rather than going to the root for the sake of enduring results. But no step on the positive side should be dismissed out of hand.

This long tale of negatives with its few bright lights of hope comes with issues and challenges, but religion and theology risk irrelevance if they ignore them. Through all the changing scenes of life in Africa—from science and technology, industrialization and urbanization, living standards, peace, and scale of growth, to the "epiphanies of darkness"[37]—religion seems, in fact, to be of continuing relevance. Even as heralds of doom have prophesied religion's final demise and in spite of shifts from conservative stances to moderation and tolerance, religion remains a significant factor and a major player in African society. Africa seems to be experiencing now a high tide for religion, for Africa has become the heartland of World Christianity, and other religions are also finding a place on the continent.

Since the core of the Christian faith is the incarnation, theology in Africa necessarily can be constructed only against the backdrop of the African reality and context. But that context must be approached in diachronic terms; it must include a sense of past traditions and the experiences that have gone into molding the African psyche as well as a critical sense of the present and a mobilizing vision for the future.

Africa is not monochrome: there are Africas and Africans many and diverse. They are at once ancient and modern, at once primal and developed. They consist of peoples with their own identities, worldviews, hopes, and fears. There may, as well, not be a sole "African Theology." In the situation we find today, African theologies,

36. See, e.g., Hahn, "US Covert Operations in Liberia: Washington Removes Three Governments."
37. Winquist, *Epiphanies of Darkness*.

plural, are the only option. Equally important is that African theologies are a dialogue between the Word of God and the African reality. Just as the Word of God comes to Africa and homo africanus with questions, so, too, do Africa and homo africanus come to the Word of God with questions and challenges. Only in that way can the tabernacling of the Word of God become authentic in Africa.

Faith as preached by missionaries sometimes confused true faith with European culture and other European artifacts. The Cameroonian novelist Mongo Beti's *Poor Christ of Bomba* articulates this confusion. In that novel, the missionary Fr. Drumont expresses disgust at the drumming and dancing of the villagers of Evindi on Friday. Seeking to destroy their xylophones and drums, he goes further, "I simply want to make you understand that you can't dance like this on the first Friday of the month, because Jesus—"[38]

Strikingly the chief of Evindi responds: "Go and stuff yourself with your first Friday and all the other Fridays! Jesus Christ . . . another damned White! Another that I would like to crush with my left foot. What? Jesus Christ? Do I know this fellow? Do I come and tell you about my ancestors, huh? Jesus Christ? I scorn him, your Jesus Christ. Just let me pull your ears a moment to make them a bit less red. . . . Jesus Christ!"[39] Later the chief adds, "Father, it seems to me that if Jesus Christ had really thought of us he would have come himself, to discuss the matter with us."[40]

In that same novel a dialogue takes place between the French colonial servant, Vidal, and Fr. Drumont. It throws additional light on the practice of mission and theology.

> Vidal: Might it not be that we merely adapted Christianity to suit our own stomach, Father? . . . In Christ's conception, it was to be a universal religion, wasn't it? And Christ was no fool. . . . Why not present a Christianity that is suited to the blacks?
>
> Fr. Drumont: If we really have to adapt Christianity for Africa, then I'll be more useful back home than I will be here.[41]

As Christian faith has gone about its mission, it has been associated with and has been refracted through the prism of other ideologies—ideologies that had non-Christian elements. This reality reminds us of the need to distinguish between the essential gospel and the accidents of language and ideology, between the *residuum evangelium* and the temporal expression of it. As church and theology have negotiated the contours of culture and ideology, mistakes have been made of which Christians need to repent. But the core message remains on offer: to secure the well-being of Africa as of other continents. The conversations between Fr. Drumont, on the one hand, and the chief of Evindi and Vidal, on the other hand, finger the critical issues of universality and contextuality, catholicity and incarnation.

38. Beti, *Poor Christ of Bomba*, 55.
39. Ibid.
40. Ibid., 56.
41. Ibid., 156–57, 159.

Theology in an Age of Science and Technology

Whatever may be said of the overall development of Africa, the continent in varying degrees has come under the influence of science and technology. So religious faith and theology have to face the challenges posed by the world of science and technology, because of the latter's commitment to rational analysis and processes. Today, even with rational analysis and processes, evidence is abundant of continuing resort—in feeling for the unknown—to persons variously called intuitionists, mentalists, psychic consultants, or those who use their sixth sense and crystal-ball-gazing. This phenomenon of discernment is as old as the book of Genesis, where in chapter 41 Joseph uncannily interprets Pharaoh's dream. Today psychic advisers have been crossing over into the world of legitimate business. With no desire to be judgmental, we notice that when the prospects of business are bleak and in times of great change and stress, such as war and recession, politicians, corporate titans, and other celebrities have been consulting psychics.

In 2008, the Harvard Business School Network of Women Alumnae scheduled sessions led by a psychic, Laura Day, to train them to use their sixth sense.[42] A more glorified language, that is, more masculine sounding, for the phenomenon is the appeal to gut feeling made by many leaders such as President George W. Bush and Michael Cherloff, onetime chief of homeland security in the United States. The amazing thing is that big business concerns and even attorneys resort to Laura Day, a stylish New Yorker, a forty-nine-year-old mother with no tech experience.

Communications Revolution

A particular dimension of the scientific-technological revolution of our time is the communication revolution—as well as the improved transportation possibilities by air, rail, and road—which has contributed to the shrinking of the world into a globalized village. Telephones, faxes, the Internet, e-mail, the websites YouTube and Facebook, and bloggers have forced all to come together, so that none can be an isolated island to himself or herself. The new communications technologies have unleashed a vast flow of information, often defined in terms of warp speed. The media now offer twenty-four-hour-a-day coverage of news, seven days a week, bombarding people with information. These developments have repercussions for theology and mission.

First, the new communications technologies make it possible to reveal more than is necessary or desirable. In the process, the sense of mystery is often shortchanged. At a very crude level, we may recall the words of Yuri Alekseyevich Gagarin, the first Russian cosmonaut, when he returned in 1961 from space: "I have been to space and I did not see God." The statement had ideological undertones of challenge to people's

---

42. Dokopil, "The $10,000-a-Month Psychic," 44–45; Shermer, *Why People Believe Weird Things*; Day, *Practical Intuition*.

religiosity and faith. In any case, the statement challenged some to rethink the meaning of the prayer "Our Father in heaven."

Second, today's scientific/technological culture embodies a secular spirit. In the words of Charles Winquist, "Intelligibility is bounded by a sense of contingency, relativity, transience and autonomy. There is no warrant for an absolute, fixed, eternal, theonomous world-view that is acceptable for secular understanding."[43]

Third, scientific and technological achievement offers ethical and moral challenges to the theological enterprise. What goes under the label of development has sometimes become a boomerang and a plague to humanity, human dignity, and security. With the acquisition of armaments, Nigeria went through a most painful and destructive civil war from 1967 to 1970. Liberia, Sierra Leone, and Côte d'Ivoire also underwent agonizing civil wars with enormous destruction of life and resources. In 1998, US embassies in East Africa (Kenya and Tanzania) were bombed with tremendous destruction. In 2000, the USS *Cole* was attacked in Yemen. These happenings are of a piece with occurrences in other parts of the world. On September 11, 2001, the World Trade Center in New York was attacked. About 2,750 persons perished, not to mention the wounded and displaced.

Three conclusions may be drawn from these examples. First, in today's globalized village, what happens in one part has consequences for other parts, even regions far distant. That fact argues for the need of having an ecumenical vision on all things. Second, several of these examples blight hope and induce hopelessness. Third, we live today in an age of omnipresent "mediacracy" in which anyone may have access to an idea anytime. This plethora of ideation has been described as a science-fiction society. Outlandish ideas can be easily disseminated. Almost unlimited possibilities exist to get a message out. Whether such output communicates new vision to society is another matter. The output can, however, fuel divisions in society, feasting on emotions of anxiety, anger, and resentment. The communications revolution is pandering to populism.

These observations are not intended to suggest that the fact of mediacracy's existence must necessarily lead to its uncritical use. Communications can consist of more than scoops, as it has tended to be; it can be a dialogue between the gatekeepers of community and pockets of opinion within the community. That note of dialogue signals the necessity for an ecumenical perspective on theologizing.

Theology must, therefore, be pursued with an acute awareness of the communications revolution with all its evident pluses and minuses. As such, theology has its work cut out for it: how it is to appropriate communication technology's possibilities while avoiding its negatives—and, indeed, to offer a critique of it. In practical terms, it means that theology will avoid communications that principally offer mere shock value and entertainment. Instead of being divisive, theological communications should seek to help people to see beyond their particular circumstances and to make connections with what is shared in common. It should seek to build bridges within

---

43. Winquist, *Epiphanies of Darkness*, 106.

diverse circumstances, assisting in-between people to belong to the same community as part of the human community and to celebrate life together.

Information and communications technology (ICT) has enabled a dramatic evolution in how business is done today, and it structures the storage, retrieval, manipulation, transmission, and receipt of digital data. No doubt, the new capabilities ICT offers have been of tremendous benefit to institutions and business. But they have facilitated concerns and threats that face us as well. The art of sending e-mails falsely claiming to represent an established legitimate enterprise tricks users into providing pieces of information that turn out to be used for identity theft. Hackers are another headache; they gain unauthorized access to other persons' computer systems to get at confidential information. And if all that were not enough, malignant individuals disperse computer viruses that destroy files.

Thus as excellent as the technology of communications has become, the communications revolution has spawned ethical issues as to how the technology can be put to good and effective use. William Deresiwicz asks,

> What does the contemporary self want? The camera has created a culture of celebrity; the computer is creating a culture of connectivity. As the two cultures converge—broadband tipping the Web from text to image; social networking sites spreading the mesh of interconnection even wider—the two cultures betray a common impulse. Celebrity and connectivity are both ways of becoming well known. That is what the contemporary self wants. It wants to be recognized, wants to be connected: It wants to be visible. If not to millions, on Survivor or Oprah, then to the hundreds on Twitter or Facebook. This is the quality that validates us, this is how we become real to ourselves—by being seen by others. The great contemporary terror is anonymity. In postmodernism, if the property that grounded the self in Romanticism was sincerity and in modernism was authenticity, then . . . it is visibility now.[44]

The culture of visibility raises questions about the key tenets of a manufactured vision that pretends to generate unrelenting optimism and happiness.

Africa is a continent, indeed, the second largest, but it is inextricably part of a worldwide whole that is shaped to the core by a world economy. Even the United States, the world's so-called richest nation, has undergone economic tremors issuing in the experience of insecurity and uncertainty. Politically, too, Africa—like Europe, the Middle East, and the United States—stands in fear of violent ideologies. Some of them don the guise of religion, which fuels fear and insecurity. Family life appears to be collapsing, leaving people vulnerable. This tumult is the real context in which Christian theology must communicate a gospel of faith and hope. And Christian theology does so in the face of other offers. That is why we have signaled that the ecumenical imperative of the gospel is a necessary perspective for doing theology today—and even more so in Africa.

---

44. Deresiewicz, "The End of Solitude," B6, 21.

3

Culture

DURING THE AGE OF nationalism in Africa, African politicians such as Kwame Nkrumah of Ghana and Leopold Senghor of Senegal proclaimed the ideologies of the African personality and Négritude from the rooftops.[1] Those ideologies were at once protests against colonialism, imperialism, white racism as in apartheid South Africa, and the appalling racism in the Portuguese African countries of Angola and Mozambique, on the one hand, and a desire, on the other hand, for *owning* African identity. The inspiration for such ideologies owes much to Aimé Césaire. Long before the politicians of the 1950s and 1960s arrived on the scene, movements had been current in Africa urging ownership of and respect for—and thereby rehabilitation of—African identities. That was the significance of the nineteenth-century movements of Ethiopianism and the Aborigines Rights Protection Society (ARPS) of the Gold Coast, both of which were not unrelated to Christian churches and mission.[2]

Today, that the gospel should be contextualized is hardly a matter of dispute. But when viewed against the background formed by the ideology of colonialism and the missionary practice of *tabula rasa*, the efforts made by the ARPS to reappropriate African cultures as a medium for communicating the gospel are seen to have been revolutionary. Colonialism, however enlightened and benevolent the form it may have taken, was based on the premise that the colonialist was master and knew what was best for the colonized peoples—and, in so many words, claimed to be purveyor of civilization and culture.

Christian missions manifested a similar superiority complex. The familiar language of missionaries as purveyors of "Christian civilization" was coupled with a condescending attitude toward African cultures. The classic articulation of that condescending and negative outlook comes from Richard Sibbes (1577–1635), Master

---

1. Nkrumah, *Axioms of Kwame Nkrumah*, 3–4; Senghor, *On African Socialism*; Jean-Paul Sartre, "Orphée noir," introduction to Senghor, *Anthologie de la nouvelle poésie nègre et malgache de langue française*, ix–xliv; "Orphée noir" published separately as Sartre, *Black Orpheus*.

2. Ahuma, *Gold Coast Nation*; Hayford, *Ethiopia Unbound*; David Brown Vincent, *Africa and the Gospel* ([Lagos: King], 1889), cited in Ayandele, *Missionary Impact*, 200; Pobee, *Skenosis of Christian Faith in an African Context*.

of St. Catherine's College, Cambridge, and a founding father of modern Protestant missionary thinking. In his sermon entitled "Lydia's Conversion," Sibbes states:

> Now, God in preparation for the most part civiliseth people, and then Christianiseth them, as I may say; for the Spirit of God will not be effectual in a rude, wild and barbarous soul, in men that are not men. Therefore, they must be brought to civility, and not only to civility, but there must be a work of the law to cast them down, and then they are brought to Christianity. Therefore they take a good course that labour to break them from their natural rudeness and fierceness.... There is no forcing of grace on a soul so far indisposed, that is, not brought to civility. Rude and barbarous souls, therefore, God's manner is to bring them into the compass of civility, and then seeing what their estate is in the corruption of nature, to deject them and then to bring them to Christianity.[3]

This lengthy quotation is so clear as not to need commentary, except to underline, first, that Christianity and Western civilization and culture are deemed to be coterminous and, second, that Christian theology and faith may be built only on Western civilization and culture. Thus the rich kente cloth Nkrumah wore to Britain in the nationalist period was described by a British writer as a bedspread. Such a response represents an imperialist attitude toward the cultures of others.

Humility is needed if a person wants to understand and to be initiated into another person's culture or its meaning and significance. The plea for humility is often sidestepped—if it does not trigger confusion—for the cognate word "cultured" signals a person who shows good taste or manners. This lack of clarity on the distinction between cultures in the anthropological sense and being cultured too easily leads to imperialistic attitudes, because it often goes with judging other persons' cultures by one's own culture and standards. For example, having a stream of Africans visiting an African in a flat often causes the English to feel uneasy. Their uneasiness stems from their individualism and sense of privacy, which have marked their culture, in contrast to the communitarian and welcoming epistemology and ontology of homo africanus.

The Character of Culture

"Culture" derives from the third conjugation of the Latin verb *colo, coleri, colui, cultus*. The configuration yields such English words as colony, agriculture, cultivation, and culture, all deriving from the same root. As such, culture is a social reality, a human achievement, rather than a natural phenomenon; it is something good for human beings, is concerned with temporal and material realization of values, and is pluralistic.[4]

---

3. Richard Sibbes as quoted in Rooy, *Theology of Missions in the Puritan Tradition*, 30.
4. Niebuhr, *Christ and Culture*, 32–39.

E. B. Tylor formulated the classic definition of culture as "that complex whole which includes knowledge, belief, art, morals, law, custom, and any other capabilities and habits acquired by man as a member of society."[5] This definition makes culture total and all-inclusive. Hence culture is not just a matter of dance or kente cloth or the fly-whisk: it includes all facets of a particular people's life and existence, especially their psyche and value systems. It includes the realm of meanings. Even ephemeral life patterns and values can be part of culture, for they are acquired as a member of a society, that is, after birth, during one's lifetime, by learning and other processes of communication.

First, Tylor opposes "culture," as something inherently human, to something acquired genetically, such as instinctive behavior. In this definition, a baby's sucking of its mother's breast is not culture, but walking is, for it has to be learned. A language and the speaking of a language, by the same token, are culture.

Second, culture is collective tradition: it is done and exhibited by a group of people, especially when they work together on an enterprise and share its benefits. In other words, it is not enough for one person to be doing it; there must be evidence that others, a community, respond in much the same way.

Third, two other elements are important in the definition of culture. Culture has the capacity to exert a dynamic directive or conversely constraining influence over its group. If you belong to a particular culture, certain things are just not done, because the group frowns on them; or you are obliged to do them, as they are the norm or what the society expects of its members. Thus, for example, one does not wait for an invitation to attend a funeral or call on the bereaved; it is a duty, an obligation. Conversely, no invitation is needed for joyful occasions; one just shows up.

Culture, fourth, is not static. It grows and develops through and with time as well as in response to challenges posed by particular times. As new challenges emerge, the society needs to find new solutions and ways of responding to the challenges. If sensitive responses to new situations and challenges are not forthcoming, then the responses on offer and the persons clinging to them are described as antiquated, out of date. The exposure of African peoples to the colonial experience, Western culture, the missionary experience, and the communications revolution has meant that African cultures have not remained static but are *in statu nascendi*, a state of growth and development. For now, let the point be registered that culture needs to be seen as both ancient and modern.

Culture, like social life, is an interpretation, or to use the theologian's term, an exegesis and an understanding, reflecting memories of the past which are necessarily multifaceted and multi-determined. Contrary to popular belief, the past is dynamic in the sense that it has the capability to influence the present and future. The use of proverbs in African cultures as marks of wisdom represents the use of the past and of memory as exegesis and understanding. At this point an important detail is easily

---

5. Tylor, *Origins of Culture*, 1:1; Malinowski, *Scientific Theory of Culture*; Malinowski and Kaberry, *Dynamics of Culture Change*.

overlooked: grappling with the past and people's memories involves reinterpretation of their lives and their times. This step of reinterpretation has sometimes been called the "double hermeneutic."

That culture is not static is indicated by the fact that the son of one ethnic group, known to be very exclusivist, may marry a woman from another exclusivistic society. Similarly, chiefs and kings have been known to marry into nations with which they have been at war for generations.

Culture represents the identity of a people, that is, the persona or personality and individuality of the group. Culture is what distinguishes "Africanness" from "Caucasianness," even though both are human. To change images, culture is the code of a people. In this age of unprecedented systems of communications, we speak of country codes and ZIP codes without which addressees cannot be reached by mail and of country codes and area codes without which we cannot reach people by telephone. Culture is a necessary code without which a particular people cannot be reached or engaged. Communication, which theology is, necessarily demands identifying with a people, their stories, their expressions, and their hopes and fears. More important even than hearing their stories is to allow my story to be challenged, critiqued, or even shattered by the story of the other person—and to be reconstructed.[6] Reconstruction brought about by the challenge of stories and cultures is what Alasdair MacIntyre has spoken of as epistemological crisis.[7]

If we identify culture as the code of a people (their perception and understanding of reality), in the global and ecumenical village into which the world has shrunk, the task becomes not simply one of replacing received statements about God derived from Europe with African cultural artifacts; it demands that we search for shared schemata which underlie and underline intelligible action on the part of all parties in the dialogue. As MacIntyre succinctly puts it, "My ability to understand what you are doing and my ability to act intelligibly (both to myself and others) are one and the same ability."[8] Culture's role is to help in laying out the schemata of intelligibility, given the diversity of cultures, codes, and identities.

Epistemological Crisis

When we observe the impressive activities of the African Initiatives in Christianity (AIC) churches, the contours of the epistemological crisis in Africa become clearly evident. S. R. B. Attoh Ahuma, of ARPS fame, spoke in terms of "the denationalization of the African."[9] The attempt to denationalize Africans represented the imposition

---

6. Brown, "My Story and 'The Story.'"

7. Alasdair MacIntyre, "Epistemological Crises, Dramatic Narrative, and the Philosophy of Science," in Hauerwas and Jones, *Why Narrative?*, 139.

8. MacIntyre, "Epistemological Crises," 159.

9. "Editorial," *Gold Coast Leader*, April 20, 1907.

of cultural hegemony in the creation and maintenance of a new country's national consciousness. To the degree that the attempt succeeded, the result is well illustrated by Frantz Fanon's cogent and expressive phrase "black skin, white masks."[10] So making culture integral to theologizing is a way of resolving epistemological crises in Africa. That entails the construction of a new narrative that enables Africans as agents to render intelligible both how they could have held their original beliefs *and* how they could have been so drastically misled by them.

The narrative in terms of which Africans at first understood and ordered experience is itself made into the subject of an enlarged narrative. They thus come to understand as agents how the criteria of truth and understanding may be formulated. "He has had to become epistemologically self-conscious and at a certain point he may have come to acknowledge two conclusions: the first is that his new forms of understanding may themselves in turn come to be put in question at any time; the second is that, because in such crisis the criteria of truth, intelligibility, and rationality may always themselves be put in question. . . . We are never in a position to claim that we possess the truth or now we are fully rational."[11]

Epistemological crisis may seem to cause anxiety about faith. But a careful reading of Scripture reveals that cocksureness is not part of faith. Indeed, doubts and questioning of God and faith are part of faith. For example, Elijah's doubts are revealed in his fear of the threatening King Ahab and Queen Jezebel (1 Kgs 19:1–8). The prophet Jeremiah had doubts when, after twenty years of prophesying, his prophecies seemed unfulfilled (Jer 20:7–9). The temptations of Jesus himself may be read as questioning of the baptismal experience: "Has God really said that I am Son of God?" So, taking culture seriously as a catalyst in nurturing epistemological crisis can be a healthy sign of a process of renewal and transformation.

I do not intend to critique the dominant ideology of mission here. But I wish to pursue the logical consequence of taking seriously the essential core of the Christian message of the incarnation, namely, that God became human in a particular culture (Gal 4:4) and would be ensouled and incarnated in each and every culture. Displays of local customs and art are expressions of the creativity of particular societies. Normally, such expressions and artifacts have particular significance and meanings, ones that are easily missed by people who do not belong to those particular societies.

"Etic" and "Emic" Readings of Culture

In anthropological analysis, "emic" refers to the attempt of an observer, especially one from a different culture, to be descriptively as objective as it is possible for a foreigner to be, that is, to approach as closely as possible—in the language of the foreigner and for a foreign audience—to the meanings a certain cultural item has for those who practice the

---

10. See Fanon, *Black Skin, White Masks* and *Wretched of the Earth*.
11. MacIntyre, "Epistemological Crises," 143.

culture. "Etic," for its part, is a further reworking and reinterpretation—at the contextualization, comparative, and classificatory and theoretical levels—of the emic meanings. That is, etic analysis is scholarly interpretation at a meta-level. All three, but particularly the level of contextualization, may introduce elements of interpretation into etic analysis that are foreign to the emic meanings as the members of a culture would formulate them. Such interpretations may at times be experienced as alien, denigrating, or profaning if members of the culture become aware of them. Etic analysis, however, is not simply and only the imposition of alien, hostile, or dismissive meanings.

The seeming success of Christian missions and Western culture in Africa has led students of Africa to suggest that African culture can be and has been replaced by Christian and Western cultures. Margaret Field, however, is correct in her conclusion that "though it is not difficult by warfare, foreign administration, modern industry and other means, to smash up an ancient religious organization, the ideas which sustained it are not easily destroyed. They are only disbanded, vagrant and unattached. But given sufficient sense of need, they will mobilize again."[12] Indeed, the appeal and success of AIC churches today have been attributed to their appeal to primal expectations, finding a fertile ground in the all-pervasive primal religious traditions, especially in their cosmology and in their concept of salvation.[13]

African cultural reality must be engaged seriously, especially when constructing theology in Africa. Africa must be approached in diachronic terms: one must possess a sense of the past of the traditions and experiences that have gone into forming the African psyche, a sense of the present in real terms, and a mobilizing vision of the future. Correspondingly, Christian theology becomes a kind of relay: From whence have we come theologically? What do we find today, and what are the challenges, hopes, and fears of society? Where do we wish to go under God?

Cultures Many: Culture of Pluralism

Given the different races and contexts to be found in Africa, it is not surprising to find many cultures also present on the continent. So it is more realistic to speak of African cultures rather than *the* African culture. Besides, other types of culture exist in addition to cultures in the sense of differing worldviews. In a continent both literally and metaphorically almost synonymous with poverty, there exists a culture of poverty, which is as important as a worldview. Whether in a multiethnic society or a multireligious one, the pervasive presence of the culture of pluralism affects how we live—whether at peace or otherwise. Through contact with Western civilization, African nations have received the legacy of Enlightenment culture with its hallmarks of rationality and individualism, as well as versions of the culture of patriarchy. Other "cultures" could be mentioned.

12. Field, "Some New Shrines of the Gold Coast," 138; Field, *Search for Security*.
13. Larbi, *Pentecostalism*, 3.

Clearly, many cultures are present simultaneously on the continent of Africa—and even within a single nation—that willy-nilly encounter one another. What is demanded is to give attentive identification to the various cultures on offer and to bring them into dialogue one with another and with the gospel.

Contours of Traditional African Cultures

Since homo africanus is a multiheaded hydra and one cannot pretend to claim familiarity with all the racial groups of Africa, this study will be confined to the race that, for lack of a better word, is described as Negroid. Of that group we may delineate the following characteristic emphases.

Religious and Spiritual Epistemology and Ontology

Though they are not sacralists, so far Negroid Africans seem, both at the individual and at the group levels, unable to explain life without a religious and spiritual frame of reference. The African's life is punctuated by crisis points: birth, puberty, marriage, death. These points are marked by rites that are religious as well as social. Illness, for example, is traced to spirits, instead of to bacteriological or physiological causes; impecunious circumstances are attributed to witches, or similar entities, who have made a hole in the palm that causes any money one earns to fall through. Alcoholism is assigned to the evil machinations of relatives who are said to be witches. Such beliefs may sound ridiculous and laughable. But simply dismissing them has not been known to facilitate communication and renewal.

The success of the African Indigenous/Instituted Churches (AICs) is, in part, due to this cultural mentality. A catechist of the Musama Disco Christo Church (Ghana), founded in 1929 by Prophet Jemisemiham Jehu-Appiah (1893–1948), alias Joseph William Egyankaba Appiah, said at an evening prayer meeting: "We are all in this Church because we have found healing here. But for this Church the great majority of us here assembled would not be alive today. This is the reason why we are here: is that not so?" The researcher, Christian G. Baeta, records: "To that question came from the congregation as answer, a unanimous and most decided 'Yes.'"[14] This eloquent statement needs no comment. But even medicine has a religious and theological reference in African traditional societies.

Political organization, too, is linked with religion and spirituality. For example, traditional rulers were at the same time political and religious/spiritual leaders. Thus the office of the king (*ohene*) of Ashanti was a composite institution: judge, priest, commander-in-chief, legislator, and executive and administrative head of the

---

14. Baëta, *Prophetism in Ghana*, 54.

community.[15] Here we may add a clarification. The ritual duties of Akan *ahemfo* (rulers) normally respect only their royal *nsamanfo* (forebears), and their own *kra* (soul) and *sunsum/ntoro* (personality soul),[16] and hardly ever relate to Nyame, Asase Yaa, or the *abosom*. The designation "priest," therefore, seems dubious. But it is difficult to suggest an alternative etic or classificatory term that fits the emic situation better.

Related to this religious/spiritual epistemology and ontology is a certain characteristic African cultural sense of finitude. That is the significance of the pervasive African preoccupation with spirits, especially with witchcraft, and the fear of death. For Akan indigenous religion and social life, preoccupation with funerals is tied into the central position of the *nsamanfo* (the ancestors as "the living dead").

In light of Negroid Africans' religious/spiritual epistemology and ontology, the seeming agnosticism, if not atheism, inherent in the epistemology of the Enlightenment (as signaled by such "hallowed" words as fact, objectivity, and theory) is viewed with suspicion.[17] And so, Ela writes:

> Our church must express a Passover of Language, or the meaning of the Christian message will not be understood. One of the primary tasks of Christian reflection in Black Africa is to totally reformulate our basic faith through the mediation of African culture. In place of the cultural presuppositions of Western Christianity, namely *logos* and *ratio*, we must now substitute African symbolism. Beginning with the ecclesiastical furrow where the language of faith germinates, we must restore the Gospel's power to speak to Africans through the primordial symbol of their existence.[18]

Since homo africanus's reality is rooted in a religious paradigm, reality is constructed on the basis of a sacred universe. Reality is perceived in terms essentially spiritual and transcendental.[19] So homo africanus is homo religiosus radicaliter.

From a West African perspective, the traditional spiritual ontology and epistemology fall into four categories: the Supreme Being, the divinities/gods, the ancestors,

---

15. Busia, *Africa in Search of Democracy*, 26; Busia, *Position of the Chief*.

16. Akan beliefs pertaining to the soul are complex. Each human is believed to be endowed with three souls: *mogya*, the "blood-soul," thought to derive from one's mother; *sunsum*, the "personality-soul," regarded as an individuation of one's father's *ntoro*, a patrilineal descent group worshipping a particular water god; and *kra*, the "destiny-soul," believed to be obtained at birth on taking leave from the sky god Nyame with a particular *hyebea/nkrabea* or commission in life. See Bartle, "The Universe Has Three Souls," 85–114.

17. Nearly all the major eighteenth-century propagators of the Enlightenment were deists rather than agnostics or atheists; that is, they were believers in a retired and remote God, a transcendent being that is in retreat. Exclusively materialistic and naturalist views, such as the mechanistic and explicitly atheistic views of Julien Offray de la Mettrie (1709–51)—see his *L'Histoire naturelle de l'âme* (The natural history of the soul), published anonymously in 1745, and his *L'Homme machine* (Man a machine), published in 1747—were rare, were banned, and were not acceptable to such pillars of the Enlightenment as Diderot.

18. Ela, *My Faith as an African*, 44.

19. Mbiti, *African Religions and Philosophy*.

and the charms/amulets.[20] In the epistemology of Africans, the spiritual and the physical do not constitute a dualistic frame. Though distinguishable, they are inseparable and they interpenetrate. And so, ailment may also be attributed to spirit beings.

Characteristic of Holism

Chapter 1 addressed the complementarity of the language of sacred and secular. The preceding paragraphs have also denied that dualism is inherent in the sacred-secular distinction. Both claims are ways of affirming that metaphysical holism is characteristic of African cultures and societies. Thus ailments are interpreted not only in bacteriological or psychological or physiological terms but also in spiritual categories. Inability to have biological children of one's own is explained in terms of the machinations of a witch. If after much difficulty a child is born, it is named *Nyamekye* (gift from God), implying the defeat of the evil spirit by the Supreme Being. Conversely, the loss of a child at birth, especially if such loss occurs more than once, is interpreted as the doing of some spiritual being. On a second or third occasion, if the child lives to the stage of naming, it is given a crude name. A child may also be called *Ababio* (he/she has come again) to signal that the child is the return of a revered ancestor to the family. In this holistic epistemology and ontology, the borders of the spiritual are broader than is usual in the West.

The name Ababio signals that the holistic epistemology and ontology is also diachronic. That an African is named after an ancestor in the family gives evidence of the belief both that the child is the return of a deceased forbear and also that the child will replicate the character and characteristics of that forbear.

Institutionalized Religion and . . .

A phrase that has been suggested is that homo africanus is homo religiosus radicaliter. But today even some Africans claim to be atheists and agnostics or to belong to the group now styled Nones, that is, persons who have no religious affiliation.[21] That organized religion has been party to injustices, intolerance, violence, and arrogance has caused people to become disaffected and led them to turn away from institutional religion.

Institutional congregational life is symbolic of organized religion. In a congregation, people engage each other in spiritual conversation and prayer, deliver food to the sick, and work together in serving the poor. The community of faith is the instrument of building communion, fellowship, and solidarity. Abuses of religion do not do away with the true purpose of religion; the hunger for spiritual conversion and community continues.

---

20. Parrinder, *West African Religion*, 16–17.
21. Bass, *Christianity after Religion*.

Communitarian Epistemology and Ontology

Africans characteristically define themselves by community, the prototype of which is the family, and that community is seen in diachronic terms. It consists of the living (that is, contemporary society), the living dead (ancestors), and those yet to be born. The rites of passage mentioned earlier concern incorporation into or departure from the community. The individualistic epistemology and ontology of the Enlightenment culture have proven unsatisfactory to Africans. In any case, an epistemology that is individualistic can only produce individualism, which is not the option of Scripture.

In South Africa people claim to live by the precepts of *ubuntu*, which places deep interconnectedness at the center of human beings and their consciousness. By implication ubuntu acknowledges the human dignity of fellow human beings. The revered Nelson Mandela articulates this option for interconnectedness in a lecture presented at the Oxford Centre for Islamic Studies on July 11, 1997: "As with other aspects of its heritage, African traditional religion is increasingly recognized for its contribution to the world. No longer seen as despised superstition which had to be superseded by superior forms of belief, today its enrichment of humanity's spiritual heritage is acknowledged. The spirit of *Ubuntu*—that profound African sense that we are human only through the humanity of other human beings—is not a parochial phenomenon, but has added globally to our common search for a better world."[22] Ubuntu is an option for recognizing the other as human and for mutual recognition of each other as human beings who are not to be toyed with but to be accorded love, respect, dignity, and welcome. Ubuntu is an option for the mutual faithful service and support that alone make for progress.

The Bantu say, "*Aungumtu mpela*" (he is a real person). A similar idea is found among the Akan, who say, "*Oyè nyimpa dè*" (which also means "he is a real person"), and the Gã say, "*Gbomo dze lè*" (that is, "he or she is a real person"). The humaneness of a person shines through everything he or she does. But to those who do not show the cherished humaneness, the Bantu say, "*Ungumtu onjane na?*" (which means "what kind of person are you?"). To these may be added the Bantu expression "*Batho bat la reng na?*" (meaning "what will decent people say about your behavior?"). In other words, anyone worth the epithet *human* must exhibit behavior which that person's community identifies as appropriate for his or her age and standing.

This outlook, typical of agrarian societies, that humanity and all of creation are interconnected is strikingly expressed by the celebrated Native American Chief Seattle (ca. 1786–1866): "Humankind has not woven the web of life. We are but one thread within it. Whatever we do to the web, we do to ourselves. All things are bound together. All things connect."[23]

Even secular life and society display increasing awareness that our salvation as nations on the continent of Africa lies, in part at any rate, in our solidarity. From

---

22. Mandela, "Renewal and Renaissance."
23. See http://www.californiaindianeducation.org/famous_indian_chiefs/chief_seattle/.

this realization rises the significance of the New Partnership for African Development (NEPAD), African Union (AU), Economic Community of West African States (ECOWAS), Southern African Development Cooperation (SADC), and many other partnerships. This trend of development is consistent with Africa's traditional communitarian epistemology and ontology and, therefore, can be a model for theologizing in Africa. All combine to inculcate the lesson that "united we stand, divided we fall." The force of this outlook is further strengthened when we take into account the earliest Christian community's self-understanding as consisting of *koinonia*—communion/community/fellowship/solidarity/sharing (Acts 2:42–47). In the twentieth century, the ecumenical movement rediscovered this basic ecclesiology.[24] Presumably it has implications for the style in which theologizing should be done.

Thus from the African's cultural background, it can be argued that theology should foster community/communion and healthy communication. In part, this effort may entail endeavoring to develop an ideology of communication that corresponds to Africa. But it will also mean questioning and critiquing some aspects of African epistemology and ontology themselves, for overly narrow definitions of community, especially in kinship terms, have been known to contribute to ethnocentrism, violence, and other negative results. Therefore, critique of African epistemology cannot be avoided.

Africa's communitarian epistemology and ontology have tended to induce or foster a culture of silence and acquiescence that is expressed in five ways: (1) conformity and eschewing of individual speculation, (2) unquestioning acquiescence, (3) lack of self-reliance because of the extended family's pervasive influence, (4) blind worship of authority and charismatic leaders, and (5) hatred of criticism. The traditional epistemology and ontology are not sacrosanct; they need constant critique.

Community Epistemology and Ontology?

Even if African societies have had a communitarian epistemology and ontology, in our globalized world we will do well to recognize also a development present in the Northern Hemisphere, especially in the United States. A growing number of persons now *live alone* (that is, as soloists).[25] Is living alone the same thing as being alone or feeling lonely? Is being alone the same as being disconnected? Is this phenomenon indicative of the ultimate atomization of modern society? Does splintering of society and community result in diminished quality of life?[26] What consequences does greater social isolation have for health and happiness?

Twenty-eight percent of all households in the United States now consist of persons who live alone. The trend is found in other parts of the world as well, with Sweden (47 percent of households consist of a single person) taking the lead; others

24. Best and Gassmann, *On the Way to Fuller Koinonia*; Birmelé, *La communion ecclésiale*.
25. Klinenberg, *Going Solo*; Putnam, *Bowling Alone*.
26. Olds and Schwartz, *Lonely Americans*.

include Britain (34 percent), Japan (31 percent), Italy (29 percent), Canada (27 percent), Russia (25 percent), South Africa (24 percent), and Kenya (15 percent).[27] It is only a matter of time before being and living alone becomes an issue in West Africa, also, with consequences for the traditional epistemology of homo africanus.

Massive research has been conducted on this matter; it suggests that a distinction needs to be made between quantity of social interactions and quality of social interactions.[28] Living alone is not the same as feeling lonely. In fact, living with the wrong person can be hell. Further, persons who live alone may find ways to compensate, so as to be socially active. Digital media and expanding online social networks provide both opportunities for connection and the option of time and space for restorative solitude. Persons who live alone have time and space to pursue the sacred values of modernity such as individual freedom, personal control, and self-realization.

Ritual, Excessive Ceremonialism, and Symbolism

Ceremonialism and symbolism have been characteristic of African societies.[29] The British anthropologist Robert Marett (1866–1943) used to say that "primitive man dances out his religion." Marett significantly does not use the word "savage." It is primitive religion, not the theology, that is danced out. Today, we are wiser and know that love for ceremonies, ritual, and symbolism is not a sign of a level of development, but a human penchant for communication in all cultures and in all ages. Symbols and ceremonies are attempts to interpret and reenact the activities of human societies in terms of the supernatural. According to social scientists, humanity lives by symbols and finds stability and satisfaction through adequate symbols. Symbols also bind people into community.[30]

Symbols, signs, and sacraments go together, and ceremonies employ these categories. F. W. Dillistone comments helpfully on the distinction between signs and symbols: "The sign indicates, the symbol represents; the sign transmits directly, the symbol indirectly or obliquely; the sign announces, the symbol reminds or refers; the sign operates in the immediate context of space and time; the symbol extends the frame of reference indefinitely."[31] Here it is sufficient to draw attention to the fact that African societies spend more time on ceremonials, symbolism, and ritual than do European societies. Max Gluckman has explained this fact in terms of the structural

---

27. See "Living Alone Statistics," Statistic Brain, http://www.statisticbrain.com/living-alone-statistics/.

28. Cacioppo and Patrick, *Loneliness*.

29. Busia, *Challenge of Africa*, 37.

30. Marett, *Anthropology*; Marett, *The Threshold of Religion*; Waardenburg, *Classical Approaches to the Study of Religion*, 257.

31. Dillistone, *Christianity and Symbolism*, 24; Langer, *Philosophy in a New Key*; Swantz, *Ritual and Symbol in Transitional Zaramo Society*; Dillistone, *Myth and Symbol*.

relationships within ethnic or preliterate societies in which each social relation of its subsistence economy tends to serve multifold purposes.[32]

Such ceremonialism fosters the "we-feeling" of the group. Busia comments, "The community comes together, to join in song and dance or in ritual, to give expression to the sense of the group's solidarity or the sense of dependence on the ancestors or one or other spirit powers."[33] Ritual, symbolism, and ceremonialism are useful avenues for establishing and undergirding koinonia. Besides, in a context in which many of the adherents are nonliterate, ritual, ceremonies, and symbols are highly effective ways of communicating and creating a sense of belonging and participation. Thus the African cultural characteristic of ceremonialism and related phenomena may be treated as *preparatio evangelica* for the deeper insights of Christianity.

As I wrote in an earlier publication, "Western Christianity is highly intellectualized. But African Christianity is expressed in ceremonies, in colourful robes, in rites, in gestures and art, beautifully oral rather than written. It is celebrative faith and not so much cerebrative. We may not just transplant the forms of ceremonies and art minted in the North to Africa; rather we seek ceremonies in African symbolism, transmitting the same [today I would add the word 'essential'] faith through different signs. This is particularly important in an Africa which is largely non-literate."[34]

Theology is at once scientific elucidation of the Word of God *and* education/formation. As a scientific quest, theology is mindful of and indebted to the project of progress as measured in terms of science and technology. But that environment influences education/formation has long been understood. Further, there are two types of environment: outward and inward.[35] The former falls in the category of science and technology, for example, functional modern buildings, the ever-present E-word of our time (e-mail), and IT (information technology). The interior environment—such as a people's value-system, their concept of beauty, and similar constructs—has a more enduring influence on communication and transformation.

During the presidency of Kwame Nkrumah in Ghana, the government put up modern buildings at OLA-Bentsir for the fisher-folk who lived around the Cape Coast Castle. But the fisher-folk refused to move. They understood well enough the words of the regional commissioner instructing them to relocate. But they declared that the very idea was incomprehensible. At stake was the fact that they could not see themselves leaving their ancestral land and home, and, more so, the gods of that particular place which had protected them down the ages. Here we have an example of the influence of traditional culture on Africans. African theology cannot but be in dialogue with African cultures.

---

32. Gluckman, *Custom and Conflict in Africa*; Gluckman, "Social Aspects of First Fruit Ceremonies among the South-Eastern Bantu," 25–41.
33. Busia, *Challenge of Africa*, 7–8, 37.
34. Pobee, *Skenosis*, 69–70.
35. Niblett, "Neutrality or Profession of Faith," in *Science and Freedom*, 234.

Because, as Paul Tillich states, culture is the environment of religion, the missionary travels of the gospel have led various cultures to become the environment(s) of the gospel.[36] As a continent of diverse peoples and cultures, Africa offers various and varied models of the incarnation as particular expressions of the gospel-culture dynamic. The biblical model(s), however, cannot just be repeated in new times with their new language and new challenges. It is reasonable, therefore, to take lessons from the history of the church as well.

One model found in church history has been that of "Christ against culture," by which Christ's authority is uncompromisingly asserted against any claims of culture. Proponents for drawing such a hard line have leaned for support on the contrast Christ draws between the old law and the new law (Matt 5:17–20, 21–48; 23:1–3) and the book of Revelation's apparent rejection of the world. In the Christ against culture model, loyalty to Christ has meant rejection of the cultural influences of society. Culture and society have been linked with lies, hatred, and murder (see 1 John 5:19). As C. H. Dodd put it, the surrounding culture is inevitably deformed by "pagan society, with its sensuality and superficiality, its materialism and its egoism."[37]

The Christ against culture approach is found in such early church documents as *Didache: The Teaching of the Twelve Apostles*; *The Shepherd of Hermas*; *The Epistle of Barnabas*; and *First Epistle of Clement*.[38] Christians described themselves as *tertium gens*, that is, a third race, alongside Jews and Gentiles (see 1 Clem 14:1; Ep. Barnabas 13–14). Perhaps the most uncompromising exponent of the genre was Tertullian (ca. 155–ca. 240), for whom culture was the place where sin resides.[39] For that reason, social relations tainted by pagan religion with its polytheism and idolatry, its beliefs and rites, its sensuality and commercialization had to be shunned.[40]

Even Tertullian, however, could not consistently sustain the Christ against culture stance. H. Richard Niebuhr concludes, "The great North African theologian seems, then, to present the epitome of the 'Christ-against-culture' position. Yet he sounds both more radical and more consistent than he really was. . . . He could not in fact emancipate himself and the church from reliance on and participation in culture, paganist though it was. Nevertheless he remains one of the foremost of the anticultural movement to be found in the history of the church."[41]

The Russian author, philosopher, and social theoretician Leo Tolstoy (1828–1910) is another important exemplar of the Christ against culture movement. Tolstoy underwent a deep experience of the meaninglessness of existence and a sense that

---

36. Tillich, *Theology of Culture*.

37. Dodd, *Johannine Epistles*, 42.

38. Lietzmann, *Beginnings of the Christian Church*, 173–261.

39. Tertullian, *Prescriptions against the Heretics*, chap. 20; *Apology*, 23.20; *De spectaculis*; *De corona*; *De paenitentia* (On repentance).

40. Tertullian, *On Idolatry*; *Apology*, 10–15.

41. Niebuhr, *Christ and Culture*, 55.

contemporary social values were cheap, showy, and sleazy. The experience presented him with a crisis. Against that background, he writes,

> I have understood Christ's teaching. I see their [the commandments'] fulfillment offers blessedness to me and all men . . . the Source of all from which my life has also come . . . the only possibility of salvation. . . . Jesus is not only the Messiah . . . but . . . is really the Saviour of the world. I know that there is no other exit either for me or for all those who together with me are tormented in this life. I know that for all, and for me together with them, there is no escape except by fulfilling those commandments of Christ which offer to all humanity the highest welfare of which I can conceive.[42]

A second approach has been to embrace the "Christ of culture" by which Christ is accommodated to culture. Gnosticism and the thought of Peter Abelard (1079–1142), French theologian and philosopher, are classic examples of this approach.[43] The Christ of culture approach stresses the universal meaning of the gospel and that Christ is savior of the entire world. Already in the early church some found linkages of Christ not just with the Hebrew peoples, but also with the Greek moral philosophers and the Roman Stoics. Lactantius (ca. 240–320), a Christian apologist, attempted to amalgamate the Christian faith and Romanism.[44]

The statement found in the funeral oration that St. Gregory Nazianzen (d. 389; bishop of Sasima, 372, and of Constantinople, 379–81) wrote on the occasion of his father's death is highly significant. "Even before he entered our [Christian] fold he was one of us. Just as many of our own are not with us because their lives alienate them from the common body of the faithful, in like manner many of those outside are with us, in so far as by their way of life they anticipate the faith and only lack in the name what they possess in attitude. My father was one of these, an alien branch, but inclined toward us by his way of living."[45]

Culture is a kind of collective memory of a people and a key index of one's identity. Bongani Finca, a South African minister, tells how a friend said to him: "Young man, you talk a lot about people in the book. You talk about the Abrahams, the Davids, the Samsons, the Pauls and the Peters. Talk also a bit about your father, your uncles, your grandparents, your great-grandparents, the people who made you who you are. In life, my son, you will not amount to anything until you learn to bless your origins." He concludes, "Our capacity to be effective in our ministry depends, to a large extent, on our ability to feel confident about our identity and to tell the story of the experience that defines us as unique human beings."[46]

---

42. Leo Tolstoy, "What I Believe," in *The Christian Teaching*, vol. 11 of *The Works of Leo Tolstoy*, 447–48; see Troeltsch, *Social Teaching of the Christian Churches*, 328–30, 691–93.

43. McCallum, *Abelard's Christian Theology*, 90; Abelard, *Abelard's Ethics*.

44. Cochrane, *Christianity and Classical Culture*, part 2, chap. 5.

45. *Funeral Orations by St. Gregory Nazianzen and St. Ambrose*, 123.

46. Bongani Finca, "Learning to Bless Our Memories," in Denis, *Orality*, 13.

If we are to communicate the Word of God effectively to homo africanus, we will necessarily need to take culture seriously. The Sepede of South Africa say, "*Rita bona ditaola, o se yɛ natso badimong*" (teach insights into the secrets of life to your children; you are not to take them with you when you depart to the land of the ancestors). Every group of people has a culture of its own that mediates the wisdom and insights of the ages of that particular people. Their culture is a measure of their consciousness.

In devoting time to culture I am making a claim that in pursuing theology we are also rooted in our past, our story, our memory, and our history. History recalls experiences that constitute a society's memory and identity. George Santayana, the Spanish-born American educator, philosopher, and poet, wrote a wise word that "those who cannot remember the past are condemned to repeat it."[47] Without memory, we repeat the errors of the past. In rehearsing African culture I seek to place the story of Africans on the table as the "universe constructing, foundation laying, certainty guaranteeing, and goal clarifying means of understanding reality."[48]

Though we must take culture seriously as a world-taken-for-granted, we dare not forget that the popularization of culture too frequently leads to total degradation. As the philosopher Hannah Arendt articulates,

> The result of this is not disintegration but decay, and those who promote it are not the Tin Pan Alley composers but a special kind of intellectual, often well read and well informed, whose sole function is to organize, disseminate, and change cultural objects in order to persuade the masses that *Hamlet* can be as entertaining as *My Fair Lady*, and perhaps as educational as well. There are many great authors of the past who have survived centuries of oblivion and neglect, but it is still an open question whether they will be able to survive an entertaining version of what they have to say.[49]

When culture is popularized, it often becomes degraded and in the process it is either denied or passively given up, and there is failure to separate illusion from reality. Ghana's story provides an interesting illustration of this process.

During Ghana's independence celebration, the nationalist government of Kwame Nkrumah decided to pour libation to welcome the Duchess of Kent, the representative of the Queen of England. The Christian Council read this move as a resurgence of pagan practices, and therefore it threatened not to attend the ceremony. Nkrumah ignored them. This story illustrates the confusion about custom. On the one hand, Ghana was and is a pluralistic society, and not a Christian country; therefore, the Christian Council had no grounds for its tirades against polytheism. On the other hand, libation is not poured to project African personality, as Nkrumah was arguing; it is to invoke the good wishes and blessings of Ghanaian ancestors. In the traditional religion, libation is

---

47. Santayana, *Life of Reason*.
48. Graham Hayes, "Interviewing the Past: Wulf Sachs for Instance," in Denis, *Orality*, 53.
49. Hannah Arendt, "The Crisis in Culture," in Arendt, *Between Past and Future*, 207.

poured only to one's own ancestors and not to the ancestors of another group. In fact, to do so would be regarded as a declaration of war on the ancestors of the other group, as if to say to them: "You could not protect one of your own; our ancestral spirits have protected her (the Duchess of Kent)." How easily is culture trivialized![50]

Thus, spending time on African culture is not just a matter of idly digging around in the past. It helps us to enter into and engage the treasure trove of Africa's past and to recover the ideals that contributed to the greatness and failure of Africans. Theology then is engagement with and traveling on memory lane vis-à-vis the Word of God, bringing together the memory of the Word of God and the memory of a particular people, so that we might be invigorated in serving our future.

Though language is a, or even *the*, key index of a culture, the language of theology in Africa is problematic. The emergence of African nation-states has meant that individual countries have several and diverse vernacular languages. A situation of multilingualism exists within these newly formed, interconnected, and yet competitive societies. The consequent establishment of second languages, along with use of the colonial language as the official language and sole medium of communication, carried a disadvantage for Africans. As missionaries put it, the vernacular language is the soul of a people. Especially since the incarnation constitutes the core message of Christian theology, African theology at its best must be carried out in the vernacular.

Swayed by the growing tendency toward monolingualism (in spite of their countries' multicultural base), Africans are not encouraging their children to cultivate their mother tongue. This decline is especially evident among those children who attend an international school. If in spite of this challenge one promotes doing theology in various vernaculars, the financial implications may make the undertaking not viable economically. Practical difficulties and financial implications stand in the way of the pursuit of theology and mission in the vernacular. But if Africans are to be *at home* in the gospel, that agenda cannot be avoided.

The place of the Enlightenment in theological construction is addressed in another chapter. The Enlightenment's stress on rationality suggests a philosophical thrust. But the careful reader may notice the use of the epithet "culture" of the Enlightenment. That is a deliberate attempt not to place philosophy and culture at odds with each other as is often done. Indeed, German thinkers of the nineteenth century questioned the foundations of Enlightenment rationality. They asked, to put it crudely, whether it is in fact the case that human beings are first of all calculating, rational beings bent on serving their individual material interests. Those German scholars' emerging thinking identified a relationship between consciousness and culture and developmental and political action. Thus culture was brought into public discourse.[51]

---

50. Pobee, *Kwame Nkrumah and the Church in Ghana, 1949–1966*, 120–24.
51. Hughes, *Consciousness and Society*, 66.

4

And What Is Theology?

THAT A BOOK ON African theology should ask, "And what is theology?" may sound strange. The question serves, however, as a reminder that the familiar is sometimes denuded of specific meaning and that theology may too easily be treated as no more than a vast but nebulous catchall. Therefore this chapter seeks to delineate the contours of theology and the challenges it faces in an ever-changing landscape. It serves also as a reminder that every theological construct is a contextual statement.

The word "theology" combines two Greek words, *theos* (God) and *logos* (reasoned and reasonable word). Therefore, to say "theology" is shorthand for the science of identifying and articulating the God-word, along with related education and formation. Theology has to do with the realm of religion and spirituality; it is a human attempt to use human language to capture, understand, and articulate that part of human life and experience which is described as religion. From the beginning of time and in every place, anthropologists have argued, *homo sapiens* is *homo religiosus*. As a universal human experience, religion takes—and has taken—various forms and shapes and depths. The distinction scholars make between primal religions and universal religions signals plurality and differences of and in religion. Whatever labels we may use, however, each religion has beliefs, practices, rituals, and symbols that articulate or intone the meaning, hopes, and fears of the practitioner of the religion. This statement, in so many words, is an assertion that every religion has a "theology"—some more simple than others—expressed in word, music/song/chant, ritual, art, and craft. To deny that any religion has a theology, it would seem, is incorrect. Theology as it relates to the spectrum of religions is like the range of musical scales on an organ or piano.

But comparing theology to the range of musical notes signals that we do well not to endorse the position just stated in a doctrinaire manner. For example, it can be argued that theology is a quite special and quite late development in the long-term history of human religions, spanning from the Paleolithic Age to now. While all religions have beliefs and a cosmology, the beliefs and cosmology may not be articulated into a formal theology. For one thing, the adherents of oral religions usually do not undertake to articulate their beliefs; they simply have them and live them and use them when they need them, not unlike how we have, live, and use all kinds of notions about social relations without articulating them, leaving such articulation to sociologists. Religions that explicitly articulated beliefs into doctrines—that is, beliefs fit to be discussed, taught, spread, and fought over—emerged only in the course of the first millennium BC, when philosophy also emerged, for example, in India, Greece, and China. Theology, properly so called, was an even later development, rising in early medieval times, when Greek and especially Aristotelian philosophy was merged with and used to further articulate Christian doctrines and cosmology. That theology represented a huge intellectual development. It was part of—indeed, at the heart of—the early European universities and remained so up until the present, when its position and that of philosophy have become more and more insecure in modern universities, especially in Europe. The efflorescence of theology proper is described as an early medieval development even though the Christological controversies of the early church resulted in statements that are arguably incipient theological formulations, drawing as they did on non-Aristotelian Greek philosophy to formalize beliefs into doctrine.

Though all religions potentially have a theology (because all religions have beliefs that can be articulated into a largely consistent set of doctrines by means of theological reflection), we may suggest that only Christianity—and even only particular parts of Christianity limited to certain times and places (especially Latin/Western Christianity) and to certain social categories (elite versus folk Christianity)—has a theological tradition, that is, a tradition of competitive doctrinal reflection that has been organized institutionally. In all other major religions, such as Hinduism, Buddhism, Judaism, and Islam, similar institutionalized reflection has been either absent or minimal and marginal or been the recent by-product of globalization. When the central place theology held in powerful colonial Christianity became apparent, it proved to be an attractive example for adherents of other religions to attempt to develop theologies of their own.

A main reason for the differential development of theology in (Latin/Western) Christianity and in other religions is that the latter placed emphasis more on prescription, on how to behave, than on belief, on how things are. For example, Judaism and Islam stressed *lex* and *regula* rather than *secta* and doctrine; their prescriptive side was strongly developed. One could look, for example, at the place of *Sharia* and the discipline of *fiqh* in Islam. The Quran consists of Allah's commands that require "Islam" (literally "surrender"), whereas the rational side is kept to a minimum and is mostly implicit rather than being the object of explicit articulation. In Islam, the splits and fights are, therefore, mostly not about doctrinal differences, but about differences in law schools and about prescriptive observances.

Finally, if we extend the concept of theology to cover all religions, we immensely widen, and weaken, that notion and that historical phenomenon. We can apply "theology" to preliterate or oral religions only by articulating and systematizing their beliefs. Unintentionally, the act of articulating those beliefs may misrepresent them, because the absence of articulate, systematic belief itself is a crucial element in them. Thus we may delineate theology historically and spatially—and not make it coexistent and coextensive with all religions, all societies, and all cultures.

Theology, deriving from the two Greek words *theos* (God) and *logos* (Word), literally means the God-Word. As the God-Word, it is to be distinguished from the Word of God, the oracles of God that are part of the memory of the community or communities of faith. Initially, the Word of God was couched in the form of narratives, stories, myths, wise sayings, music, song, art, and dance. Other styles of communication, and not only narratives, played a role in the attempt to capture the insights of faith and of experience, especially mystic experiences, in human language.

The God-Word, however, taking off as it does from the Greek word *logos*, is a reasoned word, a rational process. Thus theology is a *rational* attempt to understand and capture a faith. It is not intellectual exercise engaged in merely for the sake of rational delight; it is geared toward making sense of the reality of a particular community of faith. Each attempt at communicating that reality necessarily has a starting point and a guiding principle for reading and constructing the narrative of the Word. Thus black theology in South Africa was a signal achievement of the Black Consciousness movement that, among other things, challenged the intellectual foundation of modernity inherited from Europe. The Black Consciousness movement sought to restore the humanity of downtrodden Africans and to do so in a spirit of nonethnic solidarity that honors the four H's—that is, humanity, honesty, humility, and sense of humor.

Reading

A conundrum presents itself. The familiar expression "reading theology" is connected with literacy. But the preceding paragraphs have suggested that not all theology is read; it can be lived and danced out. Too often, however, this statement is coupled with or implies a not-so-salutary judgment on "nonliterary theology" on the part of philosophical expressions of theology. Such quibbling misses the point. Religion and theology that are worth taking seriously are those that make a difference to people and in their lives. Intellectual excellence, we may therefore suggest, is not the only test of whether a "theology" is worthy of the designation. Rather, theology that merits being taken seriously is one that measures up to the three V's: Vitality, Vibrancy, and Viability, and especially the third. More important than being an intellectual feast, theology is a delineation and articulation of the tenets of a religion as it transforms, makes alive, and renews peoples and communities. For that reason it is a tragic denial of the raison d'etre of a religion when theology becomes an accomplice in unjust, cruel, and inhuman institutions such as slavery and apartheid.

A clarification regarding theology and dance may be in order. R. R. Marett wrote that "primitive" religion is danced out (which is why it is primitive, and not savage), not that theology is danced out. Marett certainly did not suggest that the civilized, established Anglicanism of his time be danced out—though, ironically, in 1906 the Azusa Street Revival, filled with Pentecostal fire and led by the Afro-American preacher William J. Seymour, had already broken out. But many more decades were to pass before that revival would fire "civilized" Anglicans into dancing out their faith.

Again, "reading" implies interpretation, which is always linked with an ideology. Human beings describe and interpret their experience through spectacles or lenses supplied by particular cultures, philosophies, ideologies, idioms, and dogmas. For example, when theology is read with a Christendom ideology, the reality of the plurality of religion—and therefore of theologies—is shortchanged. Indeed, under the canopy of Christendom only Christian theology was granted recognition, and it was often denied that other faiths had a theology. In the African context, African Traditional Religions and Islam compete with Christianity for allegiance. There pluralism and an ecumenical perspective form the outlook from which theology must be read.

Reading entails translation and interpretation, and both functions are necessary for communities as well as for individuals. Therefore, Christian theology can be seen to have gone through the perspectives distinctive of the early apologists, the monks and scholastics, and the Enlightenment. This reality warns us not to talk glibly about normative theology or classical theology.

To put it another way, three intertwined questions shape the coherence, vitality, vibrancy, and viability of a theological construct—namely, theology by whom, for whom, and for what? Christian theology reads and interprets the Word of God in the framework of Christian belief and worship. We shall return below to the Enlightenment ideology and culture that have shaped much of contemporary theology in Europe and, by that route, in Africa.

One example may make concrete the way ideology and culture color interpretation and therefore reading. The Pauline statement of justification by grace through faith (Rom 3:24) zeros in on Christ Jesus, "whom God set forth as *hilastèrion* ... by his blood" (Rom 3:25). In earlier times, *hilastèrion* was translated as propitiation, which suggested an angry Deity out to take revenge. Those, however, who take seriously the character of God as Love and Grace would rather translate *hilastèrion* as expiation. Indeed, this translation interprets the death of Jesus as a sacrifice signaling a divine act of forgiveness of sin, preceding any human response (see Heb 2:17; 8:12; 1 John 2:2; 4:10; Luke 18:14). Thus the question is raised of how a theological construct is faithful to and consistent with the essence and core of the gospel.

Theology Is a Science and More

Theology is science in the sense that it seeks by investigation and questioning to reach ordered knowledge about God's self-disclosure in a plural society and world. The German monk and Protestant religious reformer Martin Luther, however, reminds us that "a theologian is born by living, nay dying and being damned, not by thinking, reading and speculation."[1] Rational processes are an important characteristic of theology. But equally important, if not more so, is that theology is written in the lives of people. Martyrdom can be a witness and a theological statement.

At Once a Scientific Exploration and Education

How are theology and education related? Time and again, we find students passing judgment on their professors by stating, "Professor X knows his subject but is neither a communicator nor a teacher." The use in German circles of *Ausbildung* (training, formation) in speaking of theological education gently reminds us that the concern of theology is as much about formation, the building up of character and vision, as it is about acquisition of book knowledge. Associated with formation in this way, theology is seen to be a tool for developing character and a quality of life. Theology is wisdom, from God, by which to live.

The centrality to education of building up character and vision was articulated by the Greek historian Dionysius of Halicarnassus in the first century before Christ when he wrote, "Contact with manners then is education; and this Thucydides appears to assert when he says history is philosophy learned from examples."[2] Similarly in Africa, traditional Akan society distinguished between *mmoa* (book knowledge) and *yansa* (wisdom). From the United States, William Deresiewicz reminds us that "the true purpose of education is to make minds, not careers," nor is it education's true purpose to develop only one form of intelligence, namely, the analytic. Deresiewicz continues, "While this [focus on analytic intelligence] is broadly true of all universities, elite schools, precisely because their students (and faculty, and administrators) possess this one form of intelligence to such a high degree, are more apt to ignore the value of others. One naturally prizes what one possesses and what most makes for one's advantages. But social intelligence and emotional intelligence and creative ability, to name just three other forms, are not distributed preferentially among the educational elite."[3]

Theological education as formation is also about mentoring and not pulling up the ladder behind one. It means that the relationship between the teacher and tutees must be easy and open, rather than stiff. This openness is not the same as failing to encourage pupils especially to know the boundaries. Freedom of thought and action that are creative are not a license for demolition of all necessary boundaries. Mentoring is about bonding and is characterized by honestly going to the roots of any and every issue.

We are also concerned with education in the sense of study, as Herbert Zorn notes. He writes, "Theological education is theological in the sense that it involves people in a commitment to mission and ministry, a commitment to the 'study of God'

---

1. Luther, *Table Talk*, 352.

2. Dionysius of Halicarnassus, *Ars Rhetorica*, 11.2, in *Bartlett's Familiar Quotations*, 17th ed. (New York: Little, Brown, 2002) 104.

3. Deresiewicz, "Disadvantages of an Elite Education."

in the sense of His revelation in the life, death and resurrection of Jesus Christ and His continuous working through the Holy Spirit."[4] Education is the unveiling of truth about human life and society. It is a community's way of passing on its accumulated knowledge, wisdom, values, and insights to its members so as to enable them to ensure the *continuity* and *continuance* of the society. Thus education is purposeful, and the contours of its purpose include such ponderous words as survival, continuance, socialization, and knowledge.[5]

Theology is not only scientifically validated but is also a process of education. It thereby becomes part of a larger intellectual journey as the life and mind of a pilgrim. Education is concerned both with the transfer of information and with formation. Zorn, who for a time was contracted to do research related to theological education's viability, reminds us that

> theological education is education; commitment is no substitute for competence. Academic excellence, technical proficiency and breadth of experience are necessary components of theological education. The specific problem of . . . Third World theological education concerns the standards by which these components are measured as well as the minimum requirement by which they can be achieved. Precisely at this point, the questions of "hybridizing the transplant" and of "search[ing] for native plants" arise. Standards of evaluating new patterns and methods ultimately have to be found within the context, whether reference is made to western standards or not.[6]

Education is one of the primary pillars for success whether of an individual, an organization, or even a country. To be on target and effective, education must address both a subject matter's theory and its practice, in this case, that of religion. It must introduce students to what is to be done and how it is to be done if it is to secure maximum effect. Education must not merely impart knowledge about individual components; it must also inquire into the processes and technologies that integrate them. It must engage the latest trends and issues. Thus a theologian who affirms the goodness of everything that God created must necessarily address the Revised Kyoto Convention. Also, a theologian who joins Amos in affirming that God is righteous and just is obliged to address circumstances that contradict that affirmation and to identify ways to overcome them.

---

4. Zorn, *Viability in Context*, x.

5. Busia, *Purposeful Education in Africa*; Brown and Tomori, *Handbook of Adult Education in West Africa*.

6. Zorn, *Viability in Context*, x; see also John S. Pobee, "Stretch Forth Thy Wings and Fly: Theological Education in the African Context," in Werner et al., *Handbook of Theological Education in World Christianity*, 337–45.

Exorcising Myths

At death, so the jibe goes, the deceased are faced with a fork in the road marked "Left to theology and hell. Right to faith and heaven." The point is that those who dabble in theology are destined for hell and destruction. Conversely, those who keep themselves from becoming entangled in theology have heaven and salvation as their reward. Despite the grain of truth to which it points, this jibe is a caricature. As the church father Evagrius Ponticus (346–99; a noted preacher of Constantinople, monk of the Nitrian Desert, and disciple of St. Macarius of Egypt) put it, "A theologian is one who truly prays. And one who truly prays is a theologian." The discipline of theology, properly understood, is a commitment to the nurture of deep spirituality.

Historically, the jibe has contained more than a grain of truth. Dissenters have often revolted against theology because it had become part of the establishment. Once freed from an official theology, they found that they could manage very well, or even better, without theology and ministers trained in theology. In particular, nineteenth-century millennialists and holiness movements, such as the Apostolics, Jehovah's Witnesses, and Mormons / Church of Jesus Christ of Latter-day Saints, that claimed to have and to have institutionalized direct revelatory contact with "God" managed very well without theology. They were able to bring about their religious revolutions precisely because they, in the margins of society, were not fettered by theology. But they became interested in theological education for their ministers again as soon as they left the margins and again became part of established society. This process of reintegration usually takes several decades as shown by the example of Dutch Pentecostalism. It launched a Bible school in 1967 and now supports Azusa Theological College as an institute within the Faculty of Theology of the Free University at Amsterdam.

Theology, the preserve of an exclusive group of initiates? Time and again, theology as a discipline has been treated as if it were the business of an exclusive group. But as 1 Peter 3:15 insists, all of Christ's followers—irrespective of gender, age, or social standing—are expected to "give an account of the faith." So it is meaningful to compare the practice of theology to the scales of music on a piano. When each chord is struck, a whole range of sounds issues forth, some soft, some loud, some high notes, some low notes. Changing the figure, at the shallow end of the pool is theology by the people; at the deep end is the academic's theological construct.[7]

Does only Christianity have a theology? Every religion—namely, ecstatic experience, belief, and ritual—has a theology, whether expressed orally (in sermons and homilies) or in drama (liturgy) or propositionally. In consequence, theological discourse and engagement has to be a dialogue or trialogue between the religious and spiritual practices and thought of the three major religions present in Africa, namely, African Traditional Religions, Christianity, and Islam (and a few others).

---

7. Amirtham and Pobee, *Theology by the People*.

The story is even more complicated, however, since culture is the environment within which religion "exists." Therefore, care must be taken to distinguish the religious beliefs from the cultural additives. For example, how may the Semitic three-decker universe of earth, heavens, and Sheol present in the Bible be negotiated in the post–space exploration age?

Zorn, in the earlier of the quotations from him above, focuses on the life, death, and resurrection of Jesus. But his definition must be broadened to include other faith traditions as well. An African, for example, comes to the Christian faith within an African culture that is deeply soaked in African Traditional Religion.

Society as a Factor in Theology

Theology is communicated in and to society. The significance of culture, already mentioned, suggests that the artifacts of society may be used to communicate the substance of theology. Further, since theology is not erudition for erudition's sake but an instrument for the change, transformation, and renewal of society, society becomes a key factor in the construction of theology. The nineteenth-century writer William Hazlitt wrote that "men do not become what by nature they are meant to be, but what society makes them."[8] The simple reality is that by the time people arrive at seminary or university to read theology, they are not empty shells available to be filled with knowledge; they already have been filled with some religious information, good or bad, false or true.

Education in Dialogue with Environment

Communication and hence education can be hindered by its environment, whether external or internal. The external environment consists of physical surroundings, material gadgets, inventions, and so on. The nonquantifiable aspects of human life and existence constitute our internal environment; that is, the values of affection, loyalty, enterprise, shallowness, and lack of purpose or zeal, as well as standards and concepts of beauty, turn out to be the cement of society as well as of the individual. W. R. Niblett writes,

> Much indeed of the education of men is made possible or impossible simply by the environment around them. The most direct way of influencing their education will often be to modify the environment itself. A change of physical surroundings will have its effects but a change of mental and spiritual climate will have many more. It is for this reason that the atmosphere and personality of the school or church can matter so much; families and institutions are important educationally to the extent to which they reach deep down into affections. It is difficult to be energetic and hardworking in a society which freely

---

8. Hazlitt, *Memoirs of Thomas Holcroft*, 2:155.

practices and approves laziness. It is difficult to be enterprising in a society which most of all has faith in the *status quo*.⁹

Theological education as a process of giving orientation and vision to life—of providing it with values—is a crucial instrument for molding both the internal environment and the external environment. The situation is not a one-way street, however, but a two-way street with the environment influencing education and vice versa.

Since theological education gives orientation and vision to life, the German concept of *theologisches Ausbildung*, that is, theological formation, has appeal. Theological and religious education, whatever else they do, must foster values, form a "disposition of the heart," promote personality development, and advance "social conscientization," to use Paolo Freire's phrase. That is the sort of theological education as formation to which Edward Farley has applied the label "theology."¹⁰

Historically, in the West, formation of character was accomplished by immersing students in the classics of Western civilization. Students were enabled to take the classics as partners and to drink deeply of them. Keeping in mind the legacy of the Western hemisphere in Africa, what are some of the elements upon which the West drew in looking to the classics? The list includes, among many others, the Greek epic poet Homer (ca. 850 BC), the Greek philosopher Plato (427?–347 BC), the Greek philosopher Aristotle (384–322 BC), the Roman poet Virgil (70–19 BC), the church father and philosopher Augustine of Hippo Regius, North Africa (AD 354–430), the Italian theologian and philosopher Thomas Aquinas (1225?–1274), the Italian poet Dante Alighieri (1265–1321), the English poet John Milton (1608–74), the English playwright and poet William Shakespeare (1564–1616), and the Spanish author Miguel de Cervantes Saavedra (1547–1616).

By exposure to and immersion in the insights of the classic writings of the West, students' lives "become a practice of the ecumenism of time—and their journey through life is enriched by having [the classic Western thinkers and writers] as partners along the way."¹¹ Scripture is, in addition, *the* classic of biblical religion and culture.

Education in the Age of Communications Revolution

Educational styles and philosophies have not been static. For many years, memory and memorizing were key planks of education. In this exercise the human brain was treated somewhat like a hard drive. But evidence is mounting that the communications revolution of our time is changing cognitive habits. We are, so to speak, outsourcing our memory to search engines and smart phones, and we now expect information to be continually and instantaneously available.

---

9. W. R. Niblett, "Neutrality or Profession of Faith," in *Science and Freedom*, 234.
10. Farley, *Theologia*.
11. Weigel, *Evangelical Catholicism*, 214.

Educationally, the situation unfolding today is new, and it raises questions regarding how information may be processed appropriately in the age of the Internet. This development may have consequences for accreditation procedures. First, rather than focusing on acquisition of the knowledge itself, people instinctively resort to the nearest Web connection. Second, because the new situation encourages us to think that we can recheck information later, we find a corresponding temptation not to feel the need to encode information internally. We are left to look it up, when necessary.

Third, we risk becoming symbiotic with our computer tools. We think first not of the facts but of where to locate the information we want. Betsy Sparrow writes: "We are learning what the computer 'knows' and when we should attend to where we have stored information in our computer-based memories."[12] This may be a variant of what psychologists have called "transactive memory," that is, a system, often implicit, in which information is "doled out" and stored by individuals to be shared with the group when needed.

This development has implications for how we think about learning procedures and accreditation. "Skills like critical thinking and analysis must develop in the context of facts: we need something to think and reason about. . . . And these facts can't be Googled as we go; they need to be stored in the original hard drive, our long-term memory."[13] Factual knowledge precedes skills, especially for children. Even adults resort to stored knowledge to evaluate new information and situations. In any case, context cannot be Googled.

The communications revolution has added another item to theology's agenda: the porn culture, which some would argue falls within people's freedom of choice. But pornography entails warped desires. It entails painful and degrading attitudes toward sex that constitute an affront to the Christian value of the dignity of all as beings made in God's image. Translation and interpretation, to which theology is so closely tied, are instruments of communication. Therefore, theology cannot avoid the modern communications revolution. No longer can theology restrict itself to considering Scripture and dogma; it must also engage the challenging implications of the communications revolution.

Diversities of Models

Theology has a long history; it would be naïve to expect all theologizing to follow a single model or ideology. For one thing, as there are multiple religions, so too there will be diverse theological constructs according to the particular religions, whether Christian, Muslim, Buddhist, or so on. Our specific concern is with the theology of the Christian faith and religion. Throughout its long history and as different cultures have become its environment, Christian theology has taken various forms. African

---

12. Sparrow et al., "Google Effects on Memory," 778.
13. Paul, "Your Head Is in the Cloud," 65.

theology, thanks to contact with the Latin West through colonialism and Western Christian missions, owes much to Enlightenment culture.

The Legacy of the Enlightenment

The Italian-born English prelate and philosopher Archbishop Anselm of Canterbury, England (1033–1109), stands as part of the tradition of the Church of the West. His seminal study defined theology as *fides quaerens intellectum* (faith seeking understanding). If rationality is common to the disciplines of theology and philosophy, the former characteristically starts from faith. If we may use a Pauline phrase out of context, the theology of Anselm is rational activity directed "from faith to faith" and, as such, it becomes peripheral. The thrust of such theologizing has issued in the privatization of religion with far reaching consequences for the practice of faith.

First, a caution needs to be struck regarding the place of reason in theology. The theologian Luther reminded people that "reason is the greatest enemy that faith has: it never comes to the aid of spiritual things, but—more frequently than not—struggles against the divine Word, treating with contempt all that emanates from God."[14] Luther's strong statement is a warning to see rational processes in perspective. In any case, change is not possible without emotion, which is energy in motion and a sign that we are alive.

Second, Enlightenment culture emphasized *ratio*, that is, reason and rationalism, and the three crucial underpinnings of the Enlightenment edifice were fact, theory, and objectivity. The word "fact," which derives from the Latin word *facere* (to do, to make), conjures up the idea of humans crafting order out of chaos on the basis of reason. In view is the idea of crafting and creating with the aid of reason. The "epiphanies of darkness" entailed by science and technology constitute a warning that the total elimination of faith and ideology from the scientific quest has its own dangers.[15] Evidence of the epiphanies of darkness is present all over the world. In Bosnia some prelates of the Serbian Orthodox Church proved helpless and unable to challenge the political and military leaders who were perpetrating genocide. Rwanda and Burundi, which are said to have large Christian populations, witnessed horrendous genocide. World history is replete with evidence of a cavalier approach by governments to empirical facts, leading to political manipulation of science with dire consequences for humanity and what is human. Theology cannot ignore this fact.

The word "theory," which derives from the Greek word *theoros* (a spectator), conjures up ideas of detached analysis and commentary. It connects logic to facts. In theoretical analysis the analyst or scholar may not appear to be an integral part of the drama and vision. Theory implies that the scholar stands outside the "action," observing reality from a distance, and that the scholar may not be an integral part of the action.

14. Luther, *Table Talk*, 353.
15. Winquist, *Epiphanies of Darkness*.

The third underpinning of Enlightenment culture is "objectivity." The word derives from a Latin root that signals "putting against" or "opposing." By cultivating a critical, dispassionate, and neutral attitude, the scholar aims to achieve impartiality or at least as high a degree of objectivity as is methodically possible. But the quest for impartiality itself sometimes becomes an adversary, for theologians cannot be impartial. They are committed. And so, for them the call for neutrality becomes a huge methodological problem. But whatever be the case, critical distancing is a necessity. In social studies, someone writing a thesis begins with a statement of a problem, and this method has been adopted by writers in the arts and humanities. But such an approach tends to raise more problems than answers. The catalyst of creative, renewing study is passion; what excites one positively or negatively stimulates a person to want to find out more. We shall return to this point shortly, but for now let me stay with the Enlightenment style.

Enlightenment Style

The Enlightenment was a particular cultural development with heavy emphasis on rationalism. It developed under the banner of liberation from the tyranny of the church. The protagonists of the Enlightenment were heavily anticlerical, that is, opposed to the powerful position—political, social, and intellectual—held at the time by the Roman Catholic Church. They were determined to destroy the church's hold and thereby became the founders of "modernity." Within modernity religion no longer had primacy of place in creating society.

The later phrase "world-come-of-age," associated with the German Lutheran theologian Dietrich Bonhoeffer, captures well the Enlightenment context for constructing theology.[16] Theology was dethroned from its position as queen of the sciences to become a science like any other science. Theology may well have some unique character and purpose, but only in the way that every discipline should contribute by virtue of offering a vista on reality.

The phrase of the seventeenth-century philosopher and mathematician René Descartes (1596–1650), *cogito ergo sum* (I think, therefore I am) was seminal for Enlightenment culture and the Cartesian mind-set and will repay time spent on it. To that end I offer two observations. First, Descartes's statement, often quoted in this short form, is part of a longer statement: *dubito ergo cogito, cogito ergo sum* (I doubt, therefore I think [and] I think, therefore I am). Knowledge is part of being a human being, and doubting and thinking are catalysts for human consciousness. Yet the Enlightenment emphasis on rationality needs to be leavened by the ubuntu of homo africanus mentioned above.

Second, Descartes's *cogito* was an option for individualism: *I* think. This emphasis, needless to say, was in reaction to the tyranny of the medieval church. Under the

---

16. Bonhoeffer, *Letters and Papers from Prison*; Bosch, *Transforming Mission*, 172–302.

canopy of the Enlightenment, the individual became the emancipated autonomous person. Now it is the individual who decides what to believe, and the church's presupposition of involvement or engagement with faith becomes a matter for critical reflection. At the very least, these underpinnings of the Enlightenment de facto separate epistemology from ethics and ontology. This separation introduces a dichotomy between subject and object that thwarts building bridges between theory and praxis.[17] Hence we find obvious contradictions between supposedly "Christian" nations and individuals within them, on the one hand, and on the other hand, their apparent ability to support dictatorships, to practice inhumanity, and in apartheid South Africa to walk over broken bones—not to mention the slave trade in England.

The ideology of the Enlightenment is a commitment to *rationality*. The *logos* component in the word "theology" corresponds with and answers to the challenging call to exercise our power of reasoning. Certainly, the commitment to rationality has at times been overemphasized and in the process has shortchanged, if not squeezed out, feeling and faith, which are the starting point of theological activity and creativity. Without feeling and passion, theology as an instrument of change, transformation, and renewal can only come to nothing. As the German philosopher Hegel (1770–1831) insightfully observed, "We may affirm absolutely that nothing great in the world has been accomplished without passion."[18] Therefore Enlightenment culture and ideology need to be seen in perspective and complemented with compassion and passion.

The presence of Enlightenment culture as the ideology of modernity is inescapable. But the critique made above suggests that, as unavoidable as it may be, it cannot be endorsed uncritically and in toto. Some measure is needed to ensure that the raison d'etre of theology is not shortchanged. Still, in the light of Anselm's definition, the theological quest entails articulation, clarification, and questioning. It is theology's proper vocation "to provide symbolic resonance and coherence between the history of faith and its contemporary restatement."[19]

Bonaventure (1217–1274), Italian theologian and philosopher, rightly warns against undue emphasis on rational processes, writing, "Let no one believe that he can be content with reading without inspiration, investigation without devotion, research without wonder, circumspection without exaltation, hard work without piety, knowledge without charity, intelligence without humility, zeal apart from divine grace, vision apart from divinely-inspired wisdom."[20] Viable theological education results from rational processes complemented with passion and feeling, emotion and experience.

This insight leads us back to the Old Testament understanding of the Hebrew word *yada'*: "The knowledge is more by the heart than by the mind and conveys

---

17. Cheryl Bridges-Johns, "From Babel to Pentecost: The Renewal of Theological Education," in Pobee, *Towards Viable Theological Education*, 132–34.

18. Hegel, *Lectures in the Philosophy of World History*.

19. Bridges-Johns, "From Babel to Pentecost," 138.

20. Bonaventure, quoted in Mayes, *Spirituality in Ministerial Formation*, 26.

engagement in lived experience, and its dynamics are more of love and response than of subject and object. Knowledge of God, therefore, is not measured by the information one possesses but how one lives in response to God."[21] Such a model represents the inversion of the fund of knowledge and the inversion of the subject/object dichotomy.

A Working Definition of Theology

John Macquarrie has defined theology as "the study which, through participation in and reflection upon a religious faith, seeks to express the content of the faith in the clearest and most coherent language available."[22] But theology—beyond its scientific vocation in the sense of a commitment to intellectual discipline and coherent exposition of its content—also entails participation. As stated above, objectivity as a canon inherited from the Enlightenment needs to be seen in perspective, for theology's raw material consists of the faith experience and practice of a people. Faith is not simply a matter of randomly floating ideas; it is a commitment and it encompasses the lifestyle of a people. The credibility and "salability" of a faith tradition are fostered not only by intellectual criteria, but also and perhaps more crucially by whether the faith tradition has transformed people into becoming movers and shakers of society. The bottom-line question is the capacity and capability of a faith to make a difference in people's lives.

Theology as Biography

The other side of the preceding discussion is the suggestion that theology is biography in the sense that a theological construct cannot be fully understood in isolation from a theological writer's life and formative experiences.[23] For a particular piece of writing to be dynamic and carry conviction, it has to convey the twists and turns in its author's development as a person. Further, it must be rooted in the intellectual and social milieu of the writer's country and context, past and present, including in early church history. The debate between Augustine of Hippo and Pelagius on grace and free will, and the different conclusions they reached, hinged in part on the different lives that had formed them. Earlier the one (Augustine) had lived a reckless, profligate life, while the life of the other (Pelagius, a cloistered Irish monk sheltered in a monastery) had been less tempestuous. Pelagius, visiting Rome in 400, was shocked at what he considered to be the low moral standard prevalent in the city. He also rejected the doctrine of original sin. People sin, he held, not because of inheriting a sinful tendency from Adam, but because of following their own free choice.[24]

21. Bridges-Johns, "From Babel to Pentecost," 138.
22. Macquarrie, *Principles of Christian Theology*, 1.
23. John S. Pobee, "Theology as Biography," in Tromp and Hamel, *World of Religions*, 309–28.
24. Augustine, *On the Spirit and the Letter*; Augustine, *On Nature and Grace*; Barr, "The Pelagian Controversy," 253–64; Greenslade, "Augustine," in *Chambers's Encyclopedia*, 1:774.

Biography is a kind of seismograph, tracing subtle changes in the spiritual and cultural life of one's community, homeland, and world—whether social or religious. Theological constructs, therefore, must be seen as intricate webs of influence and response. For this reason no apology should be made for embracing "An African Theology." Once again we are reminded that all theology is contextual. To describe any theology as classical is to lose sight of the contextual nature of the construct and perhaps even to be imperialistic.

Two things may be said of the contextuality of theology. First, the dynamism of a theological construct flows from continuous innovation, experimentation, adaptation, and change, all of which raise productivity over time. Second, a contextual theology yields probabilities and not absolutes. A theological construct is a confession of faith.

Formative Components of Theology

Macquarie goes on to identify five formative components of theology: reason, faith, culture, experience, and tradition. After the comments given above on the Enlightenment, little needs to be said further on the importance of reason as a formative factor for theology. The same is true of the fundamental importance of faith. The only word to add is to ask, in the globalized village the world has become, how religious pluralism can be prevented from fueling friction, violence, and tragedy. People, whatever differences they have, are made in God's image and likeness and share a common humanity.

The crucial nature of culture in communication, also, hardly needs additional comment except to underline that culture—as the index, code, and wavelength of a people—is key for translation and interpretation.

Language is a critical index of culture. So the observation, common among early missionaries to Africa, that "language is the soul of a people" was quite an insight. The Ghanaian Basel Mission agents David Asante (1830–93), Theophilus Opoku (1842–1913), and Carl Reindorf (1830–1917) did publish some theological pieces in Twi and Ga, two Ghanaian vernaculars. For example, Opoku published *Christoni Akwantu*, a translation of John Bunyan's *Pilgrim's Progress* (1678) and *Onipa Kuma*, a translation of *Man's Heart* (1616), by Daniel Dyke. David Asante also wrote hymns and articles in Twi in the *Christian Messenger*. Whether they undertook the logical consequence of theologizing in the local vernacular is another matter.[25]

If vernacular language is critical for theology, what specific issues must African theologians struggle with? First of all, colonial languages, for good or for ill, have become part of our African makeup today. Language, beyond syntax and morphology, is picturesque and embodies the story of a people. For example, the expression "Good

---

25. In Ghana, Basel Mission agents such as Carl Reindorf, Theophilus Opoku, and David Asante were exceptional in writing pieces in the vernacular. Those, however, were not theological treatises. See Pobee, "Identity, Religion, Nation," 20–29; Sanneh, *Translating the Message*.

Samaritan" in English presupposes the parable of the Good Samaritan in the Gospel of Luke (10:25–37). Knowledge of the biblical parable illuminates the language.

Similarly, the expression "Black Pimpernel" presupposes *The Scarlet Pimpernel*, an English novel written by Baroness Emmuska Orczy Orczy and published in 1905. The novel was set in the time of the French Revolution and told the story of the Scarlet Pimpernel, a clever Englishman who saved innocent persons from deranged bloodthirsty revolutionaries. Risking his life to save people from the guillotine, he cleverly embarrassed and humiliated his pursuers. Language, then, is part of a people's history, and their history (real and imagined) is also part of their language.

The importance of people's mother tongue for communication, however, is more complex than is often realized. For one thing, many Africans today appear to have lost facility in the use of their mother tongue, because English, for instance, has become their society's official language. For another thing, because of the multiplicity of African languages, the colonial languages have been useful instruments of unification, both in individual countries and for the continent as a whole. Were it not for English, it would be difficult, if not impossible, for a Ghanaian to communicate in Kenya or Zambia. This fact should alert us to be on guard against doctrinaire positions vis-à-vis language, even while as a matter of principle we must insist on the necessity of being thoroughly socialized in African cultures and languages so that language can be of service to the development of African theologies. The critical role of language in theologizing indirectly reminds us that theology in Africa cannot achieve the status of a finished product. Theology is reflection on praxis—praxis that is in process and progress. That fact argues for an ecumenical hermeneutic for doing theology in Africa.

Theology Starts from Gospel, Not Dogma

Macquarie's working definition of theology, with its reference to religious faith and its content, easily slides into a focus on doctrine or dogma. Christian theology, however, starts not so much from dogma as from "gospel," the good news of the story of the Christ event. The gospel is, first of all, a narrative. Indeed, making dogma the starting point for the God-Word has led to divisiveness in Christian theology. Thus, in Germany, Tübingen has a Protestant Faculty of Theology and a Catholic Faculty of Theology. As a legacy of colonialism, such divisions have made their way into Africa: Protestant faculties are found in Yaoundé and Kinshasa with Roman Catholic counterparts in the same countries. Such developments further complicate an already divided situation and aggravate divisive tendencies within African societies—not to mention their financial implications which necessitate looking outside Africa for resources.

Starting from gospel, theological statements unfold as portraiture of a common event, the outreach of divinity to humanity in diverse situations. This observation should not be surprising, because the four gospels present four portraits or theological snapshots of the one Christ event.

Pluralization of Theology

As part of its legacy for theology, the Enlightenment has fostered a pluralization of theology as an aggregate of disciplines, and "theology" has tended to mean "systematic theology."[26] Consequently, important dimensions of the discipline, such as pastoral theology and the study of missions, have often been treated like stepchildren of the academy. Even biblical theology, which is the heart of the gospel, is often not given equal rank with systematic theology.

The evidence from Scripture is clear. The Fourth Gospel states that the revealing signs written down in the gospels had the goal of bringing people to faith in Jesus Christ, the Son of God, and thereby set salvation before the reader (John 20:30–31). Theology cannot be allowed to be simply an intellectual pursuit for the sake of satisfying intellectual curiosity or academic criteria or even denominational interests. Theology is, more importantly, an aid to renewal and seeks to offer salvation and hope; it cannot be confined to dogmatic matters. Theology must be an encounter between the God-Word and the social, economic, and political realities and challenges facing society at large as well as the individual.

Modern communication media, as indicated above, are ubiquitous and are always "on." The media have been transformed by multiple global satellites, twenty-four-hour television networks, unending television news coverage, and live coverage of terrorist attacks and strange operations. To this onslaught must be added the saturation of the global Internet with its bloggers, hackers, chat rooms, digital cameras, and camcorders. The net result is that classified, or restricted, information can no longer be kept secret. The slogan popularized by Stewart Brand, that "information wants to be free," buttresses the free flow of information on the Internet. The media have an implied ideology that shapes society and offers a challenge to what religion affirms. Theology cannot escape the challenges posed by the communications revolution; it must be in dialogue with and be involved in the media for the sake of better communication.

The ubiquitous nature of modern communication media is forever unveiling closely held secrets. Consequently, the concepts of revelation and mystery, key ideas in theology, are proving more and more elusive. How theology is to sustain an understanding of the idea of mystery—without which the idea of the Numinous becomes difficult—is becoming a challenge.

Three Publics/Constituencies of Theology

Looking backward, theology contributes dynamic engagement with the legacy or legacies of the Enlightenment, denominational treasures, and cultural riches. Looking beyond itself theology has three publics or constituencies, namely, the academy, the

---

26. Farley, *Theologia*, 43.

church, and the world or society.[27] Hence theology is necessarily a public discourse. Theology that is worthy of the name must meet and satisfy academic criteria and principles; that is, it must follow scientific procedure. It must be an investigation, analysis, and ordered and coherent presentation of data. Making this statement does not entail that Enlightenment culture is the only model. As African theologians, we must drink from our own wells and use language that has meaning for those we address.

Theology in Africa must address African issues in a relevant scientific way. Only in this way will theological constructs intended for Africa be owned in Africa. Developing African theology is more than a matter of transmitting and transferring constructs made in Athens and Rome or England to Africa. The propositional style of theologizing inherited from Europe is not the only option available; it is also possible to articulate theology through drama, music, song, dance, and art. A society that forgets its art risks losing its soul, for art is about spiritual quest.

Since all are called to give an account of the faith, we can rightly expect gradations of theological constructs for different stations in life and society. Further, narrative theology validly stands alongside propositional theology. Differences among types or styles of theologizing provide no reason or justification for lampooning the theological style of another person or school.

As has been suggested, Christian theology, when overly influenced by the divisions in the church, has been divisive. The plurality of peoples and religions makes it necessary that the ecumenical imperative of Scripture (Ps 24:1; Rev 21:1–2) must be part of the essential core of religion as well as of what it is to be human. Dialogue, therefore, is necessary in theology.

Theology and Mission and Worship

Teaching is a cornerstone of mission, and the Christian community defines itself by mission (Matt 28:19–20). In the Jewish community, synagogues and the temple were venues for articulating the message, and the Jewish benedictions and prayer—for example, the Passover Haggadah and the three evangelical canticles: the Benedictus, the Magnificat, and Nunc Dimittis—entered into the theological treasure store of the Christian community.[28] All these are theological nuggets that glow with the fervor of mission and worship. C. F. D. Moule suggests the possibility that "worship early provided a matrix for the formation of Christian exhortation and ethical direction in the shape of the homily or sermon."[29] Theology, we may say, is crafted and shaped with a sense of worship, mission, and ministry.

Moule continues, "Worship is the be-all and end-all of Christian work; . . . if worship and work are distinguished, that is only because of the frailty of human nature

27. Tracy, *Analogical Imagination*.
28. Moule, *Birth of the New Testament*, 30; Moule, *Worship in the New Testament*.
29. Moule, *Birth of the New Testament*, 32.

which cannot do more than one thing at a time. The necessary alternation between lifting up holy hands in prayer and swinging an axe in strong, dedicated hands for the glory of God is the human make-shift for that single, simultaneous, divine life in which work is worship and worship is the highest possible activity."[30] Because worship and mission constitute the matrix of theological work, Evagrius Ponticus's aphorism quoted earlier comes into its own: "A theologian is one who truly prays. And one who truly prays is a theologian."

Theology as a Hermeneutical Process

Too often theological work in Africa has simply regurgitated artifacts from the North Atlantic. If theology, however, has a missiological and liturgical orientation and if it has the three constituencies of academy, community of faith, and the world, then the task of theology in Africa cannot be either to regurgitate the constructs of others or even to administer the institutions of the community of faith. It must, in the words of Jean-Marc Ela, also "create and advance the future. Everything is yet to be done, and nothing is to be decided in advance."[31] Seeking to move beyond the three-dimensional universe composed of a doctrine of sin, sacraments, and grace, theological work in Africa must engage people to "free themselves from oppression, from slavery, poverty and hunger."[32] Such work seeks to do biblical and doctrinal exposition from the African perspective. Theology so conceived pursues a hermeneutical process.[33]

Hermeneutics of Incarnation and Kenosis

For Christian theology, incarnation and *kenosis* are critical hermeneutical principles. The incarnation—in the words of the Fourth Gospel, "the Word became flesh" (John 1:14; see Gal 4:3–5)—is at the heart of the Christian story. When the gospel was mediated in a Semitic context, it assumed Semitic form and artifacts. Similarly, in the Greco-Roman context it assumed Greco-Roman form. Everywhere the gospel has gone, it has taken the shape and form of the locale. And so we have had the Semitic, Greek, Latin, Celtic, Ethiopian, Coptic, and Slav gospels—along with innumerable other contextualized gospels. African theology is the culturing of the gospel in the African context.[34] Such a culturing of the gospel is not, first and foremost, reactionary; it is pursued because that is the character of the incarnation.

---

30. Ibid.
31. Ela, *My Faith as an African*, 63.
32. Ibid., 99.
33. See the observations of De Gruchy, *Doing Christian Theology in the Context of South Africa*, 11.
34. Pobee, *Skenosis*; Pobee, *West Africa: Christ Would Be an African Too*.

Historically, the ideology of Christendom made for a church marked by power and grandeur. But also at the core of the Christian gospel is the message of *kenosis* (self-emptying; Phil 2:5–11). "What we need is a Church that lives *kenosis*, self-emptying, a church and theology that are like Abraham's tent where God encounters a pilgrimage people of God making their pilgrimage of faith throughout history, time and space."[35] Renewal of this vision of the church has strong implications for theology, including kingdom-oriented curricula and identifying with processes that seek justice and freedom.

Theology as Scales of Music

Theology has been mediated through university departments and faculties, theological and religious studies departments, seminaries, Bible schools, and theological education by extension programs. To these we may add the community of faith, that is, the church. These all have different and diverse clientele. So even if all are concerned with the God-Word, the range encompassed by each may be likened to different scales on a piano. A whole range of sounds is made when each chord is struck; one end is high, another end is low. Convoluted theology finds a home at the university end of the scale, more popular theology at the pew level.

Africans are characteristically singing communities. They sing while fishing; they sing while farming; they sing at every community work project. This African characteristic alerts us to the place of music and dance in worship and theologizing. It awakens us to the realization that gems of theology are expressed in Christian hymns. For example, a line in the Christian hymn "All Things Bright and Beautiful" speaks of "the rich man in his castle, the poor man at his gate." Certainly, the hymn recalls the parable of Lazarus and the rich man (Luke 16:19–31). But it also rehearses the contemporary idea that everybody has his place in the order of things. Whether we like the idea or not is beside the point. Our interest here is to say that a music piece in tones can initiate a message.

All groups of people have their own idiom in music, which speaks to them. For example, an earlier chapter referred to the music of African Americans as well as to the role of the lyric in the Ghana Methodist Church. African musical idiom fits well with the idea of participatory, spontaneous, and expressive worship. Since numerous African worshippers are nonliterate, their hymns are easily memorized and enable participation of the people. Writes Pablo Sosa, "Repetition, sometimes frequent, creates a degree of flow in which worshippers momentarily cease to focus on their own identity in order to become one with the larger body of the community."[36] Singing in the vernacular brings the message nearer home to the singers.

---

35. John S. Pobee, "En Voie: Theological Education in Africa," in Pobee and Kudadjie, *Theological Education in Africa*, 183–228.

36. Pablo Sosa, "Hymns," in Lossky, *Dictionary of the Ecumenical Movement*, 557; Williamson, "The Lyric in the Fante Methodist Church," 128; Nketia, "Contribution of African Culture to Christian

Music is a form of art. The culture of the written word is an attempt to capture an experience and a vision. But art is another way of capturing experience. Art is about spiritual quest. A society that forgets its art risks losing its soul. The Akan of Ghana are celebrated for their Adinkra symbols. Gestures also are a form of art. When hands or a drink is raised to the skies, it is in invocation and prayer to the Supreme Being. Dance movements articulate ideas and meaning. Art then, in its own way, may be a mode of theological communication.

Theology for Whom and for What?

The comparison of theology with musical scales is related to the question of theology for whom and for what. The title of this book, taken from 1 Peter 3, enters the claim that theology must be the task of every believer. Theology is for the whole people of God—the community of faith—who are all obliged to give account of the faith. By definition there is room for the whole range of theological work, including "theology by the people." As stated on the cover of *Theology by the People*, a book I coedited,

> Christians who have never had access to formal theology are learning afresh to relate faith to life, worship to work, prayer to action, proclamation to protest, in new creative ways. They discover in the process that they are doing theology and that they need and read theology in their search for new forms of Christian obedience. As we recognize this new phenomenon, we gain new insights and more particularly that theology needs people. Theology needs the reflection of people, committed to certain practices to preserve its vitality and wholeness. The phrase "theology by the people" catches this insight and embodies this vision.[37]

A second broad category of addressees encompasses the equippers of the people of God, popularly known as ministers. Within this broad category we discern differences of role:

- Education-related occupational roles (for example, teachers of religious knowledge in elementary and secondary schools)
- Church-related occupational roles (for example, clergy, catechists, and deacons)
- Academically-oriented occupational roles (for example, professors in seminaries and universities)
- More diffuse groups of occupational roles (for example, those who work in the media and mass communication, welfare work, and adult education)

Worship," 265–78 (also available in Desai, *Christianity in Africa as Seen by Africans*, 112–25); Amu, *Twenty-Five African Songs in the Twi Language*; Laryea, *Ephraim Amu: Nationalist, Poet, and Theologian (1899 1995).*

37. Amirtham and Pobee, *Theology by the People.*

The content of the courses of study pursued by those who work in each of these roles must be related to what they are setting out to do.

In respect to church-related occupational roles, the picture is even more complex. Two groups must be distinguished. One group of ministers labors full time in the ministry of the community of faith. The second group of ministers is to some degree bivocational; their ministry is referred to variously as tentmaking ministry, non-stipendiary ministry, or supplementary ministry.[38] The program of formation appropriate to each will differ.

Since much confusion exists regarding appropriate church-related occupational roles, three brief comments may be helpful. First, a long-recognized category of professional, whole-time ministry is supported by ecclesiastical revenue, trained and set apart for its special function, and debarred from secular employment. Second, in light of a growing church, a growing population, and new social and economic conditions, new opportunities have emerged that require voluntary ministerial assistance. Third, persons of recognized Christian standing and leadership in the local church and in society and public life, who earn their living in secular occupations, may be admitted to Holy Orders and be authorized to assist the whole-time ministry or to minister to small flocks with no shepherd, as is practicable. They do not receive a stipend but may be given something to defray their out-of-pocket expenses. All must go through some formation.

The distinction made between gospel and dogma is important and significant. In a circuitous way, the distinction between conservative and liberal theology and theologians involves the distinction between gospel and dogma. The conservative bent is to seek to go back to dogma, reverting to the way things were in the good old days, if ever such a time existed. Indeed, dogma, as history suggests, emerged from controversy and contention between opposing views. The party that achieved victory often had political power on its side. For example, Nicene orthodoxy was in a real sense imposed with the help of the Roman emperors, for most Christians in the East were adherents of Arian theology.[39] The establishment of what became standard theology, the "Truth," was a more complex process than simply clarifying a straightforward difference between truth and falsehood. The role played by the emperors in the process was not for theological reasons; it was in their interest to restore peace in their empire, troubled as it was by the cleavage between Arians and Athanasians.

A further issue is how far back do we wish to go? The story of theology has been with the church from its inception. Distinctively Christian theology began with the Judeo-Christian effort and moved on to the teaching and treatises of apologists such as Tatian, Tertullian, and Origen of Egypt. The achievements of Augustine of Hippo Regius represent another landmark of theological development. More recently Enlightenment theology rose to dominance. But that step came only in the fifteenth

---

38. Francis and Francis, *Tentmaking*.
39. Williams, *Arius: Heresy and Tradition*.

century with its hallmarks of *ratio* and the canons of fact, theory, and objectivity.[40] So-called liberals take their stand with the Enlightenment model, making pointed the question of how far back we wish to go. Truth be told, the church, in spite of its ancient roots and classical antiquity, has been changing all the time.

As one who belongs to the Anglican tradition, I cannot but recall the seminal book by John Henry Newman, *An Essay on the Development of Christian Doctrine*. Following Hegel, Newman argued that nothing stays the same; everything is in a state of flux and development. The story of theology may be likened, therefore, to a vast plain studded with promontories or theological nuggets. To isolate one model and exalt it as *the only* model for theology is difficult. The case with theological insights is more like juggling balls. Preference for one over the other is influenced by one's psyche and one's situation. Rising above such considerations, though, Scripture is basic and fundamental to all theology, for Scripture gives us the earliest traditions: the traditions standing nearest to the founder of the Christian faith, the earliest witnesses, and the earliest responses to those witnesses. The Scriptures show how the earliest witnesses interpreted and negotiated the *residuum evangelium*, which should be a resource for all who engage in theology. Indeed, the struggles of the Reformation are, crudely put, a quest for a return to Scripture, which had been overlaid by years and years of interpretation (one thinks, for example, of John Wycliffe in the fourteenth century and the Lollards).

Claims to be going back to the good old days are perhaps a deception, pure and simple. The old days were not all good; there were unedifying episodes, often informed by power complexes. Any attempts to return to the good old days, desirable as they might seem, to define what has gone into our present consciousness and identity, must be done in a spirit of penitence, humility, and sensitivity. The call for these heart attitudes may be seen as code for acknowledging our humanity.

The need for sensitivity in theology is illustrated by the furor aroused in the Muslim world by Pope Benedict XVI's citation, in a lecture at Regensburg University in September 2006, of a medieval writer's claim that "essential violence" lies at the heart of Islam. The fact that he spent time apologizing for that statement soon after Regensburg when he made a state visit to Istanbul underlines theology's need for sensitivity and political awareness.

Pope Benedict's first encyclical, *Deus caritas est* (God is love) provides another striking example. In many ways it justified Martin Luther, the father of the Reformation, who held that salvation is a gift of God received by faith in God alone (*sola fide*) and not by the mere performance of religious acts. The course of theology may be

---

40. A case can be made that the seeds of the Enlightenment were sown in the mid-fifteenth century when the siege and fall of Constantinople in 1453 caused quite a number of Greek and Byzantine scholars to flee to North Italy. A renewal of the study of Greek and Greek philosophy, especially of Plotinus, followed. Yet the Enlightenment as a distinct period is normally situated in the eighteenth century, and more narrowly in the mid-eighteenth century, at the time of David Hume and his *Natural History of Religion* (1757), Voltaire, Diderot, d'Alembert, and the "enlightened" king of Prussia, Frederick the Great (who ruled 1740–86).

likened to a *decumanus fluctus* (the tenth wave that towers over the preceding nine); important as the past is, new situations and challenges arise for which the past may not offer us a blueprint or answers. The challenges of crafting a new world order and shaping world peace with justice in a globalized village require more than regurgitating a *depositum fidei* (deposit of faith).[41] Creativity is necessary equipment for theology.

Theology today is obliged to be dynamic, if it is to be up to the task of engaging peoples for God in new times. Therefore, the depositum fidei itself must be seen in dynamic terms, and the language of liberal versus conservative is best avoided. Theological practice must engage, with the help of reason, in sensitive negotiation and structuring of Scripture and tradition. For this sensitive negotiating and structuring, the overarching hermeneutic for Christian theology is commitment to the core Christian message of the incarnation, with its option for contextualization in a specific locale with its particular challenges and resources.

In our pluralistic world of many peoples and religions, the theologian's task is to make real the biblical affirmation that the whole earth is the Lord's and to foster a vision of a new heaven and a new earth. The theologian, so to speak, stands at the gate between the cosmological and the eschatological, enabling peoples to go in and out of that gate to engage the totality of life.

---

41. Von Campenhausen, *Tradition and Life in the Church*, 9; Meyendorff, *Living Tradition*, 307–86.

5

Residuum Evangelium

THE TITLE OF THIS chapter is in Latin. From early times, and still today, Latin has been one of the major languages used for the communication of the Christian faith. But using Latin in a study written in English and intended primarily for an African context may sound an odd note or signal a Roman Catholic background—or even be the sign of a desire to exude erudition and scholarship. Such is not the case nor my aim. Quite simply, the English phrase "residual gospel" does not exactly conjure up a salutary impression.

In resorting to the phrase "*residuum evangelium*," I am making a conscious statement: first, that the gospel (*evangelium*) is a basic, fundamental resource for delineating the essential Christian good news and therefore for any theological construction; and second, that the *evangelium* is good news. Time and again theological approaches have been labeled liberal versus conservative, progressive versus traditionalist, and ecumenical versus evangelical. It is not helpful to define oneself by reacting to another's attempts. Such an approach locks us into camps. It obstructs our ability to hear other persons so as to be able to hold dialogue with them—and in that way to be enriched by the wisdom of others. Worse still, it shifts the focus away from the important and absolutely crucial residuum evangelium, which signals that at bottom, theology should be understood and experienced as good news. Third, the phrase residuum evangelium contains an admission that in approaching the fundamental gospel in the twenty-first century, we come at it with our accumulation of tradition and language. The task demands that the theologian endeavor to cut through accumulated traditions and accretions in seeking the heart of the matter and gospel.

A possible alternate language, that of the *depositum fidei*, belongs to the tradition of finding in memory the key to delineating one's identity. The idea is not without merit; the wise idea that the way forward is the way back is one inculcated by T. S. Elliot's *Four Quartets*. A possible way to teach the Christian tradition's promise of salvation and the renewal of all things through Jesus Christ—crucified, risen, and ascended—is to call to mind the earliest reaches of the church's memory. Such a review is not the same thing as a path of conservatism or liberalism. Still, in the end the language of the "deposit of faith," valuable as it is, conjures up the image of a hardened and not exactly dynamic tradition.

Gospel Is a Story

The Christian faith has been in existence for two millennia. Though it began in a little town in a small country in the Near East, it has spread to all continents of the world. It has a story. Throughout this story, the Christian faith has considered itself to be fundamentally a bearer of the gospel, that is, of good news. This good news is rooted in the story of Jesus himself. When he appeared on the scene, the synoptic writer announced "the beginning of the good news [gospel] of Jesus Christ." He laid out the content of the gospel further: "The time is fulfilled, and the kingdom of God has come near; repent, and believe in the good news" (Mark 1:1, 15 NRSV).

Gospel Is Good News

Whatever else Christian theology does, it must first of all be concerned with and focus on the good news, the kingdom of God, and the call to repentance. Theology is obliged to identify and to articulate the kingdom of God, and it must be focused on leading people to repentance. It is a story with a moral imperative. Therefore, theology necessarily entails more than simply rehearsing the story; it must also sound the challenge to follow Jesus and to be guided by the imperatives of his lifestyle, a point to which we shall return shortly. But whatever else theology may consider itself to be, it must be expressed and understood as good news.

Embracing the fundamental importance of Scripture for theologizing in Africa is not the same thing as to resort to biblicism and fundamentalism. Judaism, Christianity, and Islam, guest religions in Africa that have become native there, respectively put much store by the Torah, the New Testament, and the Quran. Further, states Amir Hussain, "The stories in the Qur'an are intimately linked to those in the New Testament and the Hebrew Bible. The audience that first heard the revelation in Mecca must have been familiar with Jewish and Christian stories, for without them, the Qur'an is hopelessly enigmatic."[1] For example, when the Quran in sura 21:104 (*Al-Anbiya*, The Prophet) speaks of the rolling up of the heavens as a scroll, we recognize an echo of Isaiah 34:4 and Revelation 6:14. So Thomas Aquinas, the Angelic Doctor, is on target when he suggests that Jews and Christians are two phases of the same covenant. Hussain suggests the addition of Islam as the third phase of that covenant.

The texts of Scripture themselves contain evidence of evolution vis-à-vis sacrificial cult; roles of priests and prophets; dietary laws; the structure, content, and

---

1. Hussain, "McGinley Lecture Response: Fall 2010," in response to Ryan, "Prophetic Faith and the Critique of Tradition: Jewish, Christian, and Muslim Perspectives." See also Ryan, "The Descending Scroll," 24–39.

meaning of various festivals; and the names of the Deity. Biblicism, which represents an ahistorical vision of the past, does not and cannot do justice to this process of evolution. Against such a view, John Henry Newman writes, "In a higher world, it is otherwise, but here below to live is to change, and to be perfect is to change often."[2]

Gospel of the Incarnation: Principle of Contextuality and Particularity

The second point to be noted about Christian faith is that the message of the incarnation lies at its core. The exordium, or introduction, of the Fourth Gospel descends from esoteric and ecstatic philosophical language about the Logos to assert, "The Word was made flesh, and dwelt among us, . . . full of grace and truth" (John 1:14 KJV). In like manner, whatever else theology may do, it must identify what is human. It must articulate a call to be human both in general terms and also in concrete, specific contexts. In writing to the church in Galatia, Paul points to the utter necessity of context: "When the fullness of time had come, God sent his Son, born of a woman, born under the law, in order to redeem those who were under the law" (Gal 4:4–5 NRSV). Jesus, the founder of Christian faith, was human, born like every other human being at a particular time and in a particular locality.[3]

The particular people who became his people were a nation that had been shaped by the faith tradition established through Moses. These comments signal that context and particularity are cardinal principles in the articulation and transmission of the Christian gospel.

Jesus Movement Defined Itself by Mission

There is a third factor. When Jesus was leaving his followers physically, he charged them: "God authorized and commanded me to commission you: Go out and train everyone you meet, far and near, in this way of life, marking them by baptism. . . . Then instruct them in the practice of all I have commanded you" (Matt 28:18–20 MSG). The earliest disciples took up Jesus' commission, and the Apostle Paul carried the gospel from its Palestine and Semitic cradle to the Hellenistic and Roman worlds and contexts. Mission is a composite of the proclamation of the good news of Jesus, the making of disciples (that is, evangelism), and a pursuit of the socioethical imperatives and implications of the gospel. Christian theology, like any other theology, serves to clarify the identity and mission of the community of faith. Three aspects of mission—evangelism, the centrality of Christ, and intergenerational thrust—may be drawn out here.

---

2. Newman, *Essay on the Development of Christian Doctrine*, 40.
3. Dodd, *Apostolic Preaching and Its Developments*; Dodd, *According to the Scriptures*.

First is our understanding of evangelism. Albert Luthuli, South African Christian (Congregationalist), chief, activist, and Nobel Laureate for Peace, articulated well the idea of evangelism:

> Evangelism means the unreserved surrender of the individual to God through faith and the regeneration of society through souls. Our aim in evangelism should definitely be to confront the individual with Christ and to challenge him/her to decide for Christ. And we should not be satisfied until the individual unreservedly surrenders himself/herself. Our efforts in evangelism mean little if we do not secure through Christ changed lives; consecrated lives; new men and women living a new way of life, as shown by our Lord and Master Jesus Christ when he said: "I am the Way, the Truth and the Life, no man cometh unto the Father but by Me."[4]

Second, Christian belief is intensely Christocentric. Christian faith also stresses the corporate importance of Christ-centered spirituality. The contours of this spirituality include regeneration of society and service received from others as well as given to others, issuing in interracial, interethnic, intergender, and intergenerational exchange for the sake of winning Africa for Christ. Intergender exchange is important because of the strategic position women have and the role they play in society (see chapter 12, Our Mothers and Sisters: Fellow Citizens in the Human Community and Church).

Third, mission's intergenerational thrust is important not only because the youth constitute a substantial constituency within the academy and because to them belongs the future of church and society, but also because even today they constitute the energy of the church and society. Agencies and institutions which proffer values contrary to the kingdom of God have time and again attempted successfully to recruit youth and to enlist their passion, their potential, and their energy. For their part, theologians must give particular diligence to engage the youth.

Mission, like Theology, Is Translation and Interpretation

In the Hellenistic and Roman contexts, the core phrase "kingdom of God," which is Semitic language, was not in frequent use. Indeed, the Fourth Gospel in addressing a Greek context speaks of "eternal life" (John 12:24–25) where "kingdom of God" would have been used in the Synoptic Gospels. And Paul takes the concept of the "inner man" (or "inner being," Eph 3:16 NRSV), which is not exactly Semitic language, from Greek philosophy.

Here we see initiated a fundamental principle of Christian missions: the telling of the story of the good news of Jesus is not just narrative; it is also translation—from the language and the artifacts of one context to those of another—as well as interpretation. Theology entails translation and interpretation. For example, Paul applies

---

4. Luthuli, "Evangelism for Educated Bantu Youth"; Couper, *Albert Luthuli: Bound by Faith*.

the analogy of the body to the church. This is language that was already present in Roman and Hellenistic society. The Roman historian Livy (59 BC–AD 17) attributes the metaphor of the body to Menenius Agrippa (ca. 494 BC). During the mutiny of the plebeians, Menenius suggested to them that they and the patricians belonged to the same body and therefore they should reconsider committing mutiny. Seneca (ca. 4 BC–AD 65), the Roman philosopher, dramatist, and statesman—and a contemporary of Paul—also wrote, "All this that you see, in which the divine and things human are included, is one [*unum est*], we are members of a great body [*membra corporis magni*]."[5] The idea and language of one body, we see, was already available in Roman society and on hand for Paul to adapt and use.

Thus, from time immemorial, translation and interpretation of biblical insights have borrowed from contemporary idiom and the worldview of the receptors' context to articulate the gospel message. As Christian missions have pursued obedience to Christ's command, missionaries have borrowed the idiom of each new locale and transformed it to suit the new situation and message. The combination of the revelation of God through Christ in the Scriptures, the mission mandate, and the Christian commitment to the incarnation and, therefore, to the vernacular paradigm—along with the twin principles of translation and interpretation across cultures—has meant that the gospel has taken the color and hue of each place. Translation, interpretation, and communication that will be meaningful and gripping to people deals in images and imagery drawn from their context.

In its exordium the Fourth Gospel uses the word "Logos" of Jesus. In the Hellenistic world the word "Logos" had affinity with neo-Platonic thought and religious philosophy, especially that of the Stoics. For example, Augustine comments,

> Thou didst procure for me through a certain person . . . some books of the Platonists translated from Greek into Latin. They indeed—not in so many words, but in substance—supported by many arguments of various kinds that in the beginning was the Word, and the Word was with God, and the Word was God. The same was in the beginning with God. By him were all things made, and without him was not anything made. That which was made in him was life and the life was the light of men. And the light shineth in darkness and the darkness comprehended it not. And that the soul of man, though it bear witness of the light, is not itself the light; but the Word of God, being God, is the true light that lighteth every man that cometh into the world. And that he was in the world and the world was made by him, and the world knew him not. But that he came unto his own and his own received him not, but as many as received him to them gave he power to become sons of God, even to them that believe on his name, I did not read there. Again, I read then that God the Word was born not of the flesh nor of blood, nor of the will of man, nor of

---

5. See Sevenster, *Paul and Seneca*, 170, 170–73.

the will of the flesh, but of God. But that the Word was made flesh and dwelt among us, I did not read there.[6]

Here we see Platonism and Stoicism fused together and used as an organon (or instrument for acquiring knowledge) to justify religion philosophically. The language of the Logos was not invented by the author of the Fourth Gospel, but as Augustine's comments suggest, it was not taken over wholly, lock, stock, and barrel. As Augustine points out, the incarnation was not present in Stoic teaching about the Logos. Also absent from the earlier teaching was the truth that God gives power to become God's children to all who welcome the Logos.

This discussion provides an example of the way forward for African theology. It will borrow from the language and traditions of the locale, but will put a definite Christian imprint on them. This pattern is the same as we recognize in the emergence of Semitic Christianity, Hellenistic Christianity, Latin Christianity, Celtic Christianity, Gothic Christianity, Slavic Christianity, English Christianity, Ethiopic/Coptic Christianity, and endlessly more local forms of Christianity. Several consequences arise.

First, when they go, missionaries and theologians take with them what they know and have, which is the gospel as translated and interpreted in their context. Therefore, theological statements transported to Africa have consisted of the translations and interpretations of the gospel as it was received by the missionaries. The task of African theology then is to seek to build a theology that is in consonance with the identity and story of its addressees. In undertaking this task, it must stand in the African context and engage the text of Scripture from within the African sociocultural milieu, even as it retains full consciousness of the history of translations and interpretations.

Second, through accident of history the *una sancta*—the one, holy, catholic, and apostolic church—has been sundered. Its divisions reflect not only theological differences that express the culturing of the text of Scripture in different contexts but also conscious divisions, reflecting war, often with political admixture. Thus the Great Schism of 1054 between the Church of the East and the Church of the West was the result of political, ecclesiastical, and theological differences as well as of the long embittered relationship between Pope Leo IX and Michael Cerularius, to whom the former would not concede the title "Oecumenical Patriarch."[7] In consequence, theology in Africa today reflects the two strands of Latin (Roman Catholic) Christianity of the West and Greek (Orthodox) Christianity of the East. As if that were not enough, between the fourteenth and seventeenth centuries Latin Christianity experienced further schisms. These ranged from the Lollards, a sect of the fourteenth- and fifteenth-century reformers who were followers of the English religious reformer John Wycliffe (1320–1384); the Hussites, Bohemian reformers who adhered to the cause

---

6. Augustine, *Confessions* 7.9.

7. Meyendorff, *Imperial Unity and Christian Divisions*; Runciman, *The Eastern Schism*; Ullmann, *Origins of the Great Schism*.

of the Czech reformer John Huss (1374–1415); and on to the followers of the German Martin Luther (1483–1546), the French-Swiss John Calvin (1509–1564), and the Swiss religious reformer Ulrich Zwingli (1484–1531).

All the foregoing divisions have been reflected in theological construction to the extent that, as noted earlier, in Tübingen, Germany, one finds both a Catholic Faculty of Theology and a Protestant Faculty of Theology. Whether these schisms and their reflections in theological education are really necessary and relevant to the hopes and fears of Africans and Africa is a matter that must be evaluated in the African setting. They cannot be ignored but must be addressed because of their bearing on the viability of theological education and ministerial formation in the African context. Because of the shape that the Reformation took in Germany, with its *Landeskirche* and the country's division between a Protestant north and Roman Catholic south, the phenomenon of having both Roman Catholic and Protestant faculties of theology in the same university may be to a degree intelligible. But such disunity can only further compound other divisions present in African societies and does not help matters much.

A third, and related, matter is that these divisions have issued in theology's coming out principally as dogma rather than first and foremost as gospel. Dogmatic statements have reduced the historical gospel to creeds: Apostles' Creed, Nicene Creed, Athanasian Creed (or Quicunque Vult), and even African Creed. What should be heard as gospel (that is, good news) has often become a creed, a party line which defines who is in and who is out. F. R. Barry, late bishop of the Church of England, comments, "We are not asked to 'believe in' the creeds. These [i.e. the creeds] are, as it were, diagrams and schedules which need readjustments and redrawing in every generation, as it passes. They are not Christianity itself. Christians are not primarily people who believe in Creeds and formularies of Christendom. They are primarily people who believe in God and Man through Jesus Christ."[8] The language of the creeds, especially those with a Latin or Greek philosophical frame of reference, does not make sense to contemporary Africans, because it stands at a remove from the language of homo africanus.

A fourth matter also needs to be put on the agenda. Theology as minted in the academy (which is one of the constituencies or publics of theology) has been crafted using tools supplied by the ideology of the Enlightenment, especially reason (rationality), individualism, and propositional form. But it is evident not only that the Enlightenment style does not communicate well to homo africanus, but also that other approaches are available that are more appealing and meaningful to homo africanus. Support for this statement comes from the fact that the most vibrant growth of the church in Africa today is found among the African Initiatives in Christianity (AIC) churches, which are not beholden to the style of the Enlightenment.

---

8. Barry, *What Has Christianity to Say?*, 63.

Threefold Cord of Theology

How does African theology measure up when evaluated by the threefold cord of Anglicanism, namely, Scripture, tradition, and reason? First, we can state that rational processes are indispensable. The "-logy" part of the word "theology" commits us to scientific, rational study of the Word of God. Second, mindful that as we stand today we are heritors of millennia of traditions that have in varying degrees entered into our being and understanding, we are obliged to take seriously the various pieces of tradition and to engage with them. But tradition must be seen in dynamic terms and not just as a solidified body of information and practices that must be regurgitated without any sense of contemporary moods, events, and challenges. Scripture, the third part of the cord, is primary because—as the earliest witness to the faith—it is fundamental to the *depositum fidei* (the deposit of the faith).

In light of what has just been stated, to speak of a pure tradition of faith is not possible, for each age and faith takes the message and re-presents it in a way that speaks to its own context. Still the title given to this chapter, *"Residuum Evangelium,"* is significant, for all theological statements down through the ages contain a nonnegotiable kernel that may not be surrendered without losing their Christian identity. The catch phrase residuum evangelium signals the necessity for theological statements to be mindful on many fronts—of the context, of the supernatural nature of religions and faith traditions, and of the pluralism that characterizes the theological formulations that have come to Africa through the missionary movement.

The Bible, a Coat of Many Colors

Even if we affirm Scripture as the primary source for African theological statements, Scripture—like Joseph's coat in Genesis—is most aptly seen as a coat of many colors. For one thing, taking a clue from Wilfred Cantwell Smith's description of religion as a misnomer, one sees in Scripture no religion that is "homogeneous, monolithic, or completely of one piece."[9] Rather, like Joseph's coat, statements of the one and same faith are various, varied, and variegated.

Scripture as theology's primary source shows evidence of evolution. For example, the story of Israel's sacrificial cult undergoes change and development. So too do the roles of priests, prophets, and dietary laws as well as the structure, content, and meaning of festivals. Inclusion of the book of Job in the canon of Scripture is evidence of an attempt to correct a rampantly mechanistic application of the teaching regarding rewards and punishments found in the Deuteronomic tradition of Scripture. Indeed, the development of a text-focused biblical religion is a stream that runs through Scripture.[10]

---

9. See Polish, "McGinley Lecture Response: Fall 2010," 1.
10. Ibid.

The Law and the Prophets present the terms of the special covenant relationship between God and the Hebrews. To be in special or covenant relation with God entails both a call (from God) and a commitment (on the part of people) to certain values stipulated by the Lord Creator God as essential to that relationship. Discipleship without pursuit of a godly way of life, the terms of the special relationship, is a contradiction in terms.

Further, though the character of the covenant relationship is often stated in terms of the Law, the provisions of the Law are intended as helps to a fundamental goal: love of God and love of neighbor as oneself (Rom 13:8–10; see also 12:9–10; Gal 5:13–15). That summary changes the mood of the Law. The issue is not a matter of legalism, but of a bonding relationship informed by love. This law of God is inextricably locked into and embedded in public life and interpersonal relationships.

The Essential Gospel

And what is the essential gospel? First is the affirmation that God is Creator of heaven and earth, of all things visible and invisible (Gen 1–2; Ps 8). The British philosopher and mathematician Bertrand Russell argued in 1903 that the world and humankind are but "accidental collocations of atoms."[11] On the contrary, the evident order and purpose to be seen throughout the universe seem to weigh in favor of the biblical belief in a purposeful Creator God. Biblical faith in the Creator God both entailed repudiation of idols and images and undergirded ethical development. The comments of Daniel Polish, a rabbi, on this latter point are illuminating:

> Biblical religion represents a reconfiguration of the very concept of religion itself. In a way that its neighbors did not, Israel elevated ethical concerns to the central place in religious life. In a world defined by social hierarchy, Israel's major tendency was to advocate social equality. In a cultural context that deferred to the powerful and prominent, the Bible betrays a preferential prejudice for the poor. The very notion of positing the foundational experience to be, not royal derivation, but the escape from slavery is representative of this tendency."[12]

Affirmation of God as Creator is an assertion that all that exists is contingent and depends on God, the Supreme Being, and that such a belief has ethical implications for social equality. "Law cannot go too far beyond the parameters of public morality. It is only love—for that which transcends the individual, God and one's community—that can motivate any variety of food prohibition, any type of abstinence. . . . Love

---

11. Bertrand Russell, "A Free Man's Worship," in Russell, *Why I Am Not a Christian*, 105–6.
12. Daniel F. Polish, "Faith and Culture: A Response," in Ryan, *Faith and Cultures: Jewish, Christian, and Muslim Perspectives*, 28.

of that which ultimately transcends you, usually understood as God, and love of the community of your fellow abstainers, is the key to such freely embraced law."[13]

Minimum Content of Gospel

The minimum content of the particular Christian slant on the gospel is summarized by an English Anglican bishop, F. R. Barry. It is, he writes,

> the story of a Young Man, dedicated to a new age of Love and Truth, Righteousness and Freedom, murdered by a totalitarian State in uttermost agony of mind and body, broken by the hard facts of life, His claim discredited and His cause lost, who held on through disaster and defeat serene in His confidence in God, and in the hour of failure was victorious. He who would reveal God to man must show Him to us not only in the sunshine of the oleanders of the Lake of Galilee, where all conspires to make belief easy, but in the midst of clouds and thick darkness, in the heart of sin, suffering and tragedy, He was offered a religion of Escape, and in the forty days in the wilderness, He decisively rejected it. He refused to live in an inner world of dreams, unrelated to the facts of life and the concrete actualities of the world. He would manifest God's truth here on this earth our habitation.[14]

I have quoted a summary of the gospel written by an Englishman by design. Seeking to write an African theology is no excuse for an ideological rejection of foreign constructs. Barry's statement is simple, yet it contains all the elements a biblical theologian of whatever description might desire. What is left is to expound the various strands of the residuum.

Christian faith is about the teachings of Jesus of Nazareth, a historical personality. In his lifetime, some called him a prophet. He challenged those who wished to follow him to "be perfect . . . as your heavenly Father is perfect" (Matt 5:48 NRSV). The call to Christian faith is an invitation to *imitatio Christi* (imitation of Christ) and *imitatio Dei* (imitation of God). Since in Christian theology, Jesus is at once human and divine, the call to imitate Christ can be troubling, demanding, and challenging. Are we called to become divine?

In Genesis 1:27, however, we find that humanity, male and female, stands at the summit of creation and is made in God's image and likeness. This quality is a matter of ethical vocation and more:

> Human beings too receive God's blessing that empowers them to transmit the life they have received from God. In this way they participate in his work of creation. But to transmit life is to be seen as involving a serious responsibility.

---

13. Ryan, "Law and Love: Jewish, Christian, and Muslim Attitudes," in Ryan, *Law and Love: Jewish, Christian, and Muslim Attitudes*, 14.

14. Barry, *What Has Christianity to Say?*, 45–46.

Parents have to consider their responsibility before they transmit life. Their concerns, for example, must include the education and upbringing of children and provide for their needs. This is also a sense in which they are to subdue the earth. It does not mean exploitation. It means that as God's stewards (Ps. 8:6–8), they have to take good care of what God has created and entrusted to them by using and maintaining the environment in such a way that the earth, the plant life, animal life and human beings can co-exist in harmonious relationship that promotes God's gift of life.[15]

The imitatio Christi and imitatio Dei are the theologian's way of expressing the wonderful scientific and technological developments and achievements of the ages, the procreative activity of humankind, and similar human qualities. What is sometimes left unexpressed is the sense of responsibility that must accompany the privilege of being in God's image and likeness.

Other things are also involved in the imitatio Christi. Imitation of Christ, whatever glory belongs to it, can be challenging and humiliating, and be touched with experience of failure. In the presence of falsehood, truth may seem to be weak. But Christianity is a religion of realism. We shall return to this when we take up the values of the kingdom of God.

Gospel of the Kingdom of God

As a summary of Jesus' mission and message, Mark writes, "Jesus came to Galilee, proclaiming the . . . kingdom of God is at hand. Repent, and believe in the gospel" (Mark 1:14–15 *The African Bible*). Similarly, the family prayer Jesus taught says, "Hallowed be thy name. Thy kingdom come. Thy will be done in earth, as it is in heaven" (Matt 6:9–10 KJV). In Jesus we encounter the kingdom of God. That phrase is a code for the Christian angle of vision, which may be summarized in several key words: truth and truthfulness (John 14:6, 8:32), justice and righteousness (Amos), freedom (John 8:32, 36), love, mercy, compassion, loving-kindness (Hos, Rom 13:8–10), peace (John 14:27), and reconciliation (2 Cor 5:11–21).

Truth and Truthfulness

According to the exordium of the Fourth Gospel, "the Word was made flesh, and dwelt among us . . . full of grace and truth" (John 1:14 KJV). Additionally, Jesus says, "I am the way, the truth, and the life" (John 14:6 KJV). By contrast, those who dislike Jesus have taken their stand with the devil, the father of lies in whom there is no truth (John 8:44). To be a follower of Jesus is to join in Jesus' mission and ministry, which

---

15. *The African Bible*, 26.

is at war with lies and untruth. In 1 Esdras 4:41 (KJV), Ecclesiastes also exalts truth: "Great is Truth, and mighty above all things."

Truth is also exalted outside the Judeo-Christian tradition. For example, Aristotle states that "while both [Plato and truth] are dear, piety requires us to honour truth above our friends" (*Nichomachean Ethics* 1.1). Truth, however, is easier to talk about than to pursue. Michel Eyquem de Montaigne (1533–92) signals the complications that the search for truth can raise when he writes, "Truth itself does not have the privilege to be employed at any time and in every way; its use, noble as it is, has its circumscriptions and limits" (*Essays* 3.13). The persecutions faced by Christ's followers in the early church put the truth of the message to the test. The issue was: what was the good in telling the truth and getting killed? Might it not be more useful to avoid death so as to live to praise God? It is our society's suggestion that truth is never so sacred that it cannot be negotiated. Pilate gave voice to the same issue when he asked Jesus, "And what is truth?" (John 18:38 NAB). The culture of lies and lying that characterizes much of life, however, is discomforting to one who imitates Christ. The follower of Christ is committed to a life of truth and truthfulness. Thus it should be our concern to commit to truth in political rhetoric and ideology as also in economics and in religious and theological statements and belief. Theodore Parker well wrote, "Truth never yet fell dead in the streets; it has such affinity with the soul of man, the seed however broadcast will catch somewhere and produce its hundredfold."[16]

Truth is not just an abstract theological word; it is a challenge in very practical ways. The political climate determines what "truth" can be told and what truth must remain unspoken. Sometimes the truth one knows cannot be expressed, either due to lack of "hard" evidence or to political and personal risks to the sources of the information. Pursuing the truth must be done with wisdom and, sometimes, political sense.

Many times the complex nature of truth is shortchanged if we set up a simplistic opposition between truth and lies or falsehood. That is the significance of Pilate's question. To capture the complexity of truth, three images may help. First, truth is a horizon of intelligibility. The horizon as seen from the shore seems to recede and to broaden as one attempts to sail to it from the shore. Second, truth is a "coat of many colors" (Gen 37:3 LXX). It is multihued, and simple statements may not be adequate for expressing it. For example, all religions claim to present some truth or to be vistas of truth. We need to be humble when we come to address another person's truth. By what criteria may we rule out of court another's sense of truth? Third, in this age of computers, we dare to speak of truth as an operating system that has some or a number of applications. The one truth may find expression in diverse applications.

Truth is more easily invoked as a commitment of Christian life than defined. In part that is because there are different orders of truth, for example, forensic, social, and personal truth. Forensic truth is factual, verifiable, and documentable. Social truth emerges from shared experiences and is established through interaction, debate,

---

16. Parker, *Discourse of Matters Pertaining to Religion*.

and discussion. Personal truth has been described by the South African Justice Ismail Mahomed as "truth of wounded memories" and therefore relates to healing truth. The intense labor of the Truth and Reconciliation Commission following the tragic apartheid experience was a quest for such healing truth. In seeking healing truth we must go beyond understanding and articulating truth as something objective; we must give sensitive *hearing* to the stories and feelings of the victims. The combination of truth and reconciliation obliges us to refuse to sweep things under the carpet; standing for truth entails facing up to the experiences of people even when we understand truth here not as something static but as discernment of a fluid and shifting set of insights. Holding out for truth may entail allowance for diversity in truth, which goes with difference, especially when socially constructed.[17]

Justice and Righteousness

In the Sermon on the Mount, Jesus enjoins the disciples, "Seek ye first the kingdom of God, and his righteousness" (Matt 6:33 KJV). Righteousness, we find, is a keynote word in the letters of Paul as well. Our words "justice" and "righteousness" (or right relationships) translate the Greek word *dikaiosune* and its Hebrew equivalent *tsadaqah*. There can be no justice without right relationships and vice versa. Denials of truth become manifest as corruption, injustice, embezzlement, oppression of the poor, flight of capital, unjust wages, and stolen money, all of which are negations of justice and righteousness. Above all, justification or righteousness is ultimately a gift from God given to those who try to follow the commandments of God and to walk in his holy ways. Justice or righteousness is a quality that needs to be worked out in social, economic, and political life so as to redeem all things to God who is both the creator and the final judge to whom we all are accountable.

No one, however, can establish a claim on God, and therefore the quest for justice and righteousness has no room for legalism or self-sufficiency. What is required in humanity is a new heart that eschews sin. The Christian's service to the world is to show leadership in works of justice and charity.

Freedom

Another quality of the kingdom of God is freedom. In his teaching Jesus insists that "the truth shall make you free" (John 8:32 KJV). A life of falsehood does not make for true and authentic freedom; in the Christian understanding, truth and freedom are yoked together. But this religious value needs to be worked out in social, economic, and political life. Slavery and sectarianism, land seizure, and sectionalism (whether of gender, race, creed, age, or other factors) are denials of freedom. Again Theodore Parker has

17. Bernstein, *Pedagogy, Symbolic Control, and Identity*, 5; Tutu, *No Future without Forgiveness*, 33.

perceptively written of democracy as "a government of all the people, by all the people, for all the people; of course, a government of the principles of eternal justice, the unchanging law of God; for shortness' sake I will call it the idea of Freedom."[18] The religious commitment to freedom as a value of the kingdom of God has everything to do with social, economic, and political life. Impoverishment and disenfranchisement of people are an affront to the Christian principle of freedom, for all are created in God's image and likeness. Freedom concerns the right and ability to make choices in life. In political terms it comes close to a system of participatory democracy.

Love

Love is another characteristic of the kingdom of God. In today's usage, love is often something frivolous and trite. Jesus taught a higher standard: "Thou shalt love the Lord thy God with all thy heart, and with all thy soul, and with all thy mind. This is the first and great commandment. And the second is like unto it, Thou shalt love thy neighbor as thyself. On these two commandments hang all the law and the prophets" (Matt 22:37–40 KJV; see Lev 19:18; Deut 6:5; Rom 13:8, 10). In biblical faith, love (Hebrew *hessed*) is covenantal love and is linked to God's covenant with Abraham. It is the bond of loyalty that exists between God and God's chosen people and is the model for the loyalty that should exist between members of the chosen people.

At the root of love is God's observation that "it is not good for man to be alone" (Gen 2:18 NAB). Love (*hessed*) is redemption from loneliness. Love, in Jonathan Sachs's words, is "the bridge across the ontological abyss between I and Thou."[19] Love is of a piece with compassion, loving-kindness, and mercy. Love issues in hospitality. The writer to the Hebrews (13:2 t) exhorts the faithful: "Do not neglect to show hospitality to strangers, for by doing that some have entertained angels without knowing it." This exhortation refers to the experience of Abraham the patriarch and Sarah the matriarch when they welcomed three strangers at their tent near the Oak of Mamre (Gen 18:1–15; see Quran 51:27–28). Love offers hospitality even to strangers and people who are different. Writes Stephen Carter, "*Hessed* is civility, doing acts of kindness because one is convinced that each person is made in the image of God."[20] Love is a constant theme in theology throughout the ages. At the opening of the second century, Ignatius of Antioch summed it up thus: "Let none of you take a merely natural attitude toward his neighbor, but love one another continually in Jesus Christ."[21]

---

18. Parker, *American Idea*.
19. Sachs, *To Heal a Fractured World*, 47.
20. Carter, *Civility: Manners, Morals, and the Etiquette of Democracy*, 71.
21. Adels, *Wisdom of the Saints*, 123.

Peace

Next door to *hessed* is peace (Hebrew *shalom*, Greek *eirènè*). Not only is Jesus, the model for Christians, styled "the prince of peace" (Isa 9:6–7; see Matt 5:9; Eph 2:14; Heb 12:14; Jas 3:17–18), but also his ministry is characterized as a work of peace (2 Cor 5:17–20).

Peace in the biblical faith is more than the absence of war; it does away with whatever infringes the dignity and well-being of others. Peace, though a gift of God, is to be worked at; therefore, Proverbs 3:17 speaks of *darkhei shalom*, that is, the paths of peace. According to Sachs, peace is basically *hessed* universalized and applied to those who are not members of our faith.[22] Sachs also writes, "The attempt to bring prophetic peace by human action creates not peace but war." The rabbis, he continues, understood that "in this not-yet-fully-redeemed world, peace means *living with difference*—with those who have another faith and other texts."[23] In a world of competing religious absolutisms, Sachs prefers what the rabbis call "the lights of peace (the Sabbath candles) . . . over the lights of victory (the Hanukkah candles)."[24] In simple language, to love is to be civil, one to another.

A further note, added by Martin Luther, is that "peace is more important than all justice; and peace was not made for the sake of justice, but justice for the sake of peace."[25] All too often, however, a problem arises if justice takes a harsh form. As Luther reminds us, "What can only be taught by the rod and with blows will not lead to much good; they will not remain pious any longer than the rod is behind them."[26]

Both Desmond Tutu and Walter Khotso Makhulu have received Scandinavian awards for their work for peace in Southern Africa. Their personal testimonies, therefore, carry weight because they reflect experiences and convictions arrived at from active involvement. Tutu, for example, describes peace as "a priceless goal" demanding of all to "find ways where all are winners rather than to fight; where negotiators make it a point that no one else loses face, that no one emerges empty-handed, with nothing to place before his or her constituency. How one wishes that negotiators would avoid having bottom lines and too many preconditions. In negotiations we are, as in the process of forgiveness, seeking to give all the chance to begin again."[27] This is an option for making "flexible compromises" so that in the end all will be victors. Tutu concludes, "This tired, disillusioned, cynical world hurting so frequently and so grievously has

---

22. Sachs, *To Heal a Fractured World*, 98.
23. Ibid., 101.
24. Ibid., 103.
25. Luther, *On Marriage* (1530).
26. Luther, *The Great Catechism, Second Command* (1529).
27. Tutu, *No Future Without Forgiveness*, 228.

been intrigued by a process that holds out considerable hope in the midst of so much that negates hope."[28]

Tutu argues that beyond theological affirmation stands the need for symbolic acts, however small, "that have a potency and significance beyond what is apparent."[29] Theology must not only be thought out but more importantly be *done*. Such symbolic acts may include the use of temperate language to describe those with whom we strongly disagree, for example, avoiding applying the language of "terrorists" and similar labels. The history of the liberation struggles in Africa reminds us that those who were called terrorists and "Communists" during the anticolonialism struggle often went on to become cabinet ministers. Kwame Nkrumah and Nelson Mandela are two who became heads of state. Tutu further offers a sobering reminder that "negotiations, peace talks, forgiveness, and reconciliation happen most frequently not between friends, not between those who like one another. They happen precisely because people are at loggerheads and detest one another as only enemies can. But enemies are potential allies, friends, colleagues, and collaborators."[30] The propagation of enemy images needs to be discouraged and avoided.

History and destiny located Desmond Tutu at the eye of the storm of the violent ideology of apartheid and its inhuman practice in South Africa. But in the same region was another son of South Africa, Walter Khotso Makhulu, also a churchman and archbishop of the Church of the Province of Central Africa, who resided in Botswana. He may be taken as an illustration of Milton's words that "they also serve who only stand and wait" (*On His Blindness*). For his quiet but highly critical and effective work in the resistance to apartheid, several awards were conferred on him: Officier dans L'Ordre des Palmes Academique (France, 1981); Doctor of Divinity, Honoris Causa (University of Kent, 1988); Doctor of Divinity, Honoris Causa (General Theological Seminary, New York, 1990); Companion of the Most Distinguished Order of St. Michael and George (Archbishop of Canterbury's Award, 2000); Order of St. Mellitus (2008); Presidential Order of Honour (Botswana, 2001). In addition, John Magne Lund and Paul Weinberg published *The Church's Secret Agent: Archbishop Walter Makhulu and the Fight against Apartheid*, a volume dedicated to Makhulu. The book's title and subtitle witness to the story of his principled contribution to the fight against apartheid in collaboration with the church and government of Norway.

The cover of the volume states that Makhulu "became the conduit for millions of Norwegian kroner into anti-apartheid organisations in South Africa. So tight was the security of the operation that, until the publication of this book, few people knew anything about it. Makhulu was convinced he had no alternative. He had to do it if he was to be true to his faith. In the process, he deceived the all-powerful apartheid security network." The message is clear: Makhulu was fundamentally a man of Christian faith

---

28. Ibid., 229.
29. Ibid., 227.
30. Ibid.

with conviction and commitment who lived his theology and spirituality. He was an example of the earlier catechism of Martin Luther that the authentic theologian lives the faith, even if unto death.

Reconciliation and Peace—Related but Not Identical

Peace and reconciliation are two closely related kingdom of God values, but they are not identical. The need for reconciliation presupposes that good relationships have been disturbed or disrupted, especially with one person or party offending and hurting the other. In the Old Testament the Israelites hurt God by turning their backs on God, who not only had created them but also had liberated them from slavery in Egypt. Such behavior, to say the least, was not conducive to maintaining good and harmonious relationships (Amos 5:15; Hos 3:3, 11:11). Similarly, after demanding and taking his share of his father's estate, the younger son in the parable in Luke 15 chose a profligate life outside the home. Those relationships were—at best—not good, if not wholly sour. Only if the offended party could *forgive* (that is, could decide not to allow the wrong or injury done to him to obsess him) could the original good relationship be restored.

Forgiveness is possible if the offender meets certain conditions. He or she must take steps suggesting a change of mind and an awareness that his or her words, behavior, and actions left much to be desired and, indeed, had offended and hurt the offended party. Further, the offender must admit his or her wrongdoing. Those steps taken together constitute what religious language terms repentance. Repentance consists of consciously turning away from wrong and evil so as to face the right way and rebuild relationship. Doing that requires deep contrition and humility.

The change of heart must be acknowledged and not be left to be taken for granted. This is the significance of the statement that the prodigal son "came to himself" (Luke 15:17); that is, he became conscious that he had wronged the father. The next step was that he also appeared before his father to admit his sin: "Father, I have sinned . . . " (15:21). He became conscious that his behavior had disrupted the relationship to the point that hirelings and servants back at home were doing better than he, a son. Consciousness entailed a sense of the degrading consequences of his actions. Acknowledgment of sin must go deeper than just saying the words "I am sorry."

In the story of the tax collector Zacchaeus (Luke 19), beyond an awakened conscience, Zacchaeus promised restitution to the offended parties, giving half his goods to the poor and paying back fourfold to any he may have defrauded. Reconciliation is not a case of seeking a quiet conscience; it is more important to take concrete steps of restitution as a precondition for restoring harmonious relationships. Finally, such steps are a means of returning to participation in God's rule.

In Africa some foreign colonialists ruthlessly robbed natives of their freedom and birthright. The ideology of apartheid practiced in South Africa destroyed lives, killed people, and denied multitudes access to their homes and dignity. In the name of law and order, security agencies did heartless things to Africans. Frank Chikane, general secretary of the South Africa Council of Churches, for example, was nearly killed by poisoning.[31] It took the Truth and Reconciliation Commission to bring resolution to that sordid story.

Reconciliation

Next to peace stands reconciliation. To reconcile the alienated and hostile (Col 1:21–22; 2 Cor 5:11–21) is the very work of Christ. Reconciliation forms a cross—vertical reconciliation with God coupled with horizontal reconciliation between humans and of humans with the rest of creation. Reconciliation is as much religious and spiritual as it is social, economic, or political. For example, the real significance of poverty is marginalization and exclusion. Therefore, biblical commitment to reconciliation is not complete until it is made manifest in social life, in economic life, and in political life. Peace coupled with justice and reconciliation is a matter to which we will return in addressing the issue of human rights.

The language of reconciliation presupposes the existence of its opposite, such as alienation, disharmony, conflict, hatred, and enmity. Reconciliation is an option for a common or open process of unity, harmony, togetherness, friendship, community, family, and a reliable network of interdependence.

In Black Africa, dictatorial regimes have pommelled their own nationals. During the rule in Ghana by the military regime of Flight Lieutenant Jerry Rawlings, three judges—Justice Sarkodie, Justice Adjepong, and Justice Mrs. Koranteng-Addo—and Lieutenant Acquah, a retired soldier, were abducted from their homes and killed at a military security zone facility. To this day no one has admitted being responsible. The story brings enormous complexities. We may well ask whether the children of these four murdered persons can or will be able to forgive, to restore relationships, and to have reconciliation, let alone to have closure on their loss. The challenge of reconciliation posed by the injunction to "seek . . . first the kingdom of God, and his righteousness" (Matt 6:33 KJV) is a very existential issue.

Not only individuals need to hear the challenge of the kingdom of God; governments must also. In Southern Rhodesia, now Zimbabwe, the racist settler government passed the Land Tenure Act of 1969 that enabled them to acquire any land they found fit, thus brazenly dispossessing the natives of their inheritance.[32] But the problem had deeper roots. The mentality can be traced back to 1893 when Cecil Rhodes, English financier and colonizer, and his Pioneer Forces

---

31. Chikane, *Things That Could Not Be Said*, 182–87.
32. Southern Rhodesia, Land Tenure Act of 1969, chap. 48, sec. 69.

took all suitable land in the colony and gave it away free of charge to the settlers. As soon as the settlers were established on expropriated land, they resorted to the normal property acquisition methods of contract, using state powers. The demand for repossession by the dispossessed indigenous was then, of course, criminalized. In other words, the thieves were now owners, and their victims were the criminals to be guarded against. The land grabbers, turned legal owners, proceeded to coerce the dispossessed to work for them.[33]

The kingdom value of reconciliation is not some exclusively or narrowly religious idea; it reaches into the social, economic, and political arenas and, therefore, must be negotiated and made incarnate in other areas besides religion and spirituality. Reconciliation also requires engaging repressive ideologies that undermine the dignity and honor of peoples. A courageous example from within South Africa of such engagement was the denunciation by Christians and theologians of the ideology of apartheid as heresy.[34] More will be said below on the issue of land.

Whatever else African theology may do, it must translate and interpret the values of the kingdom of God, the core of the good news of Jesus of Nazareth, into the African context. As F. R. Barry puts it: "If the religion of Jesus Christ is true, the forces of hope, renewal and goodwill are stronger than those of reaction and decay. For then at the heart of the world there is a will of beauty and truth; through an ambiguous history, there stands the eternal purpose of the Father to draw mankind into one family united in the spirit of Christ Jesus."[35]

According to the biblical faith, in the beginning there is God and at the end there is God. God, the Supreme Being, so to speak, overarches all life, and therefore all are accountable to God. This conviction is an affirmation of the ultimate victory of truth, love, peace, righteousness, and reconciliation. It is an affirmation that, in the final analysis—empirically, sociologically, religiously, and spiritually—Satan and the forces of evil do not have the last word. In Africa, however, the values just articulated are constantly being challenged by events on the ground. Africa's proverbial poverty and the political chaos and human rights violations found there demand that African theology continue to carry on dialogue between those realities and the Word of God. Only then can the Word of God be said to be for well-being and salvation and to be worth taking seriously. The role of theology is not only to reflect and speak; it is also to live out and act upon one's affirmations and convictions.

To claim that Scripture is theology's basic and primary source is not the same thing as being uncritical in one's use of Scripture. The *residuum evangelium* is reached

---

33. O. B. Gutto, "The Political Economy and History of Laws on Land Acquisition in Zimbabwe," unpublished paper, University of Zimbabwe, September 2–3, 1983, 416, cited in Bakare, *My Right to Land, in the Bible and in Zimbabwe*, 59.

34. De Gruchy and Villa-Vicencio, *Apartheid Is a Heresy*; Johannes N. J. Kritzinger, "Liberating Whiteness: Engaging with the Anti-Racist Dialectics of Steve Biko," in du Toit, *The Legacy of Stephen Bantu Biko*, 89–113.

35. Barry, *What Has Christianity to Say?*, 62.

by scientific identification of the Word of God, distilled, translated, and interpreted across time and space to new times and places, this time in the continent of Africa with a sense of the continent's various and varied particularities and contexts. By the same token, such residuum as is distilled may not be paraded as *the* Christian faith. It is *one* attempt. Conversely, there may be a nonnegotiable residuum.

Residuum Evangelium as Story

The point was made earlier that the style of theology inherited from the Enlightenment was propositional in style. Given the theological product's differences in clientele and the diversity of its consumers as well as the spectrum of the varieties of ministries, "story" may be one appropriate mode for couching the residuum evangelium. While I may use a propositional style in the university, the medium of story as a sense-making tool may be a more appropriate mode of couching the same residuum evangelium in the context of the African Initiatives in Christianity (AIC) churches or in a downtown or village congregation. Thus the residuum evangelium may also take the form of a story or narrative of God's grace of salvation, especially through Jesus Christ, that does not engage in legalism and self-sufficiency and that addresses homo africanus's preoccupation with and fear of cosmic powers. The liturgy too is a mode of theologizing.

Residuum Evangelium Crafted in a Context of and with a Sense of Pluralism

The theology inherited from Europe was marked not only by Enlightenment culture but also by the ideology of Christendom. The ideology of Christendom was an ideology of power that tended to be intolerant of and to ignore other religions as well as the nonreligious. Especially it ignored both African Traditional Religion, which has African culture as the medium within which it exists, and the Islamic faith tradition.

The Akan wisdom of Ghana is apropos: "The one who has not ventured into another person's farm may be tempted to think his is the best farm and that he is the best, if not the only farmer." The crafting of the residuum evangelium can be enriched by dialogue with other religions in the same arena and by cooperation. Dialogue is not the same as debate. Theology with a dialogical style is not the same as adopting a combative and confrontational style. We need to remember that one of the emphases of the kingdom of God is peace. In this regard, let us insist that the angle of vision of the residuum evangelium is faith in a purposeful and righteous God. Theology must not be reduced to propaganda.

Christ's Message the Fulfillment of the Old Covenant

Christians claim to be followers of Jesus, the Christ and the Lord, and therefore they follow or try to live according to Jesus' teachings as laid out in the literature of the New Covenant, the New Testament. The Scriptures of the New Covenant, however, are not adequate in themselves. Jesus himself stated, "Do not think that I have come to abolish the law or the prophets. I have come not to abolish but to fulfill. . . . Until heaven and earth pass away, not the smallest letter or the smallest part of a letter will pass from the law, until all things have taken place" (Matt 5:17–18 *The African Bible*). The words "the Law" and "the Prophets" refer to the Old Covenant and to the dispensation of the Hebrew-Jewish story.

In identifying the elements of the residuum evangelium, we have been articulating the values of the kingdom of God, the core of the residuum evangelium. Values define us as a society and define the boundaries of appropriate behavior and attitude. Shared values give order to interpersonal relationships and govern public life. In a 2011 lecture, the South African Ismail Serageldin commented on values as follows: "Values create communities out of individuals. Values enable transactions to take place and bridge intergenerational divides. Values are what make human society worthy of the designation 'human.' We have come to rely on our educational system to reinforce what parents have to do at home in nurturing the correct values in their growing children. In the educational system, values are forged by teachers' example and student practice."[36] To be on target, theology as well as theological education and formation must not only endeavor to identify and articulate the values of the kingdom (the education side), but also, and perhaps more importantly, on the formation side to shape students so they will be equipped for engaging the third constituency of theology, namely, the world and society. This approach is an option for a values-based approach to governance. That is why the residuum evangelium is critical for theological formation. It gives people Christian and religious values and identity.

Land

In articulating the values of the kingdom of God as residuum evangelium, we have so far been silent about a matter that in Africa has many times been critical—indeed, been the very eye of the storm, leading to violence, injustice, and the breakdown of peace—and an obstacle to reconciliation. The issue is that of land.

Everywhere in Africa land has been a major issue; it has been the cause of friction and violence for ages. In the Gold Coast, the Aborigines Rights Protection Society was established to protect Gold Coast land from European encroachment and appropriation. In Kenya, the Rhodesias (now the sovereign states of Zambia and Zimbabwe), and South Africa, the appropriation of native lands by white settlers and

---

36. See Pandor et al., "The Challenge of Science in Building Democracy."

governments issued in liberation wars, such as the first and second *chimurenga* (uprising) of 1880–96 and 1966–80, which entailed enormous carnage, destruction, and numbers of refugees. Questions of land, therefore, are very much an issue in Africa, the consequences of which cannot but offer spiritual and theological challenges to the church and theologians. Even without the intrusion and interference of foreigners, in Africa land has been the cause of intertribal wars and family disputes. Therefore, theology in Africa cannot but have land on its agenda, for it is an existential issue.

Since the theologian has the Bible as a principal resource, we do well to glean insights from it. Walter Brueggemann has argued that in Scripture, land takes center stage.[37] The Hebrews left Egypt, the land of slavery, for the promised land. Since the promise was made by God, the land became a religious and theological issue. The land was God's gift to them, rooted in God's covenant. Being based on love and justice, the covenant implies equitable distribution of land to the tribes of Israel. Besides being a religious and theological issue, land is a title to identity. The law told the story of God's promises and the people's special relation to God.

The biblical narrative indicates that the people of Israel had to fight to defend the land against the Philistines. They were required to raise armies for their defense. As if that were not enough, the prophecy of Samuel (1 Sam 8:11–16) signaled how "the very land that promised to create space for human joy and freedom [would become] the very source of dehumanizing exploitation and oppression. Land was indeed a problem in Israel. Time after time, Israel saw the land of promise become the land of problem. The very land that contained the sources of life drove kings to become agents of death."[38] The biblical insights converge with the story of African experiences with land today.

The story of Naboth (1 Kgs 21) draws out the idea that land is an ancestral inheritance and must be respected as such. It must not be wantonly discarded through sale and purchase (cf. 1 Sam 8:14). Rights to land are also a point at which the kingdom value of justice must be made meaningful.

In African societies, land is a determinant of a people's identity, history, and livelihood. It is sacred in the sense that it ties together the living, the living dead (the ancestors), and those not yet born. The Native American Chief Seattle (ca. 1786–1866) has a word that speaks as well for how Africans see land. He asks, "How can you buy or sell the sky, the warmth of the land? . . . Every shining pine needle, every sand shore, every mist in the dark woods, every clearing and humming insect is holy in the memory and experience of my people. The sap which courses through the tree carries the memories of the red man. . . . Our dead never forget this beautiful earth, for it is the mother of the red man. We are part of the earth and it is part of us."[39]

In the light of the foregoing perspectives on people's understanding of their land, banishing them from their ancestral lands through the use of force amounts to

---

37. Brueggemann, *The Land*; Davies, *The Gospel and the Land*.
38. Brueggemann, *The Land*, 11.
39. Rich, *Chief Seattle's Unanswered Challenge*, 344.

undermining, if not the outright denial, of their identity, their human dignity, and their rights as human beings. Such actions are an affront to Christian theology, which affirms that humanity is made in God's image and likeness. Banishment constitutes disregard for and an attack on their memory of how they have gotten where they are, their identification, their sense of belonging, and their restoration. It is a denial of equal opportunity and of civil rights, which belong to human rights. A version of killing a people, banishment is a type of genocide.

The particular unfolding of the land issue as it transpired in Zimbabwe throws light on another dimension of the land and what it means to be human. Charles D. Rudd, of Kimberley, and two others entered into an agreement with Lobengula, king of the Matabele, that has survived as the Rudd Concession, article 13, October 1888. In the Rudd Concession, the chief granted exclusive rights to mine all minerals and metals within the territories over which he had authority to the company, controlled by Cecil Rhodes, of which Rudd was a partner. He did this in return for armaments and one hundred pounds sterling each month. Later it turned out the text was not exactly what he thought he had signed. Could an uneducated nonliterate African king be fairly signing a contract with a sophisticated British colonizer? In other words, some trickery and dishonesty was involved that took advantage of the illiteracy of the native ruler. At root it was also a human rights issue, for as a person the African leader was not treated as being on a par with Rudd. African governments have undergone similar experiences in their relationships with economic powers regarding minerals and oil.

Land issues have been crux human rights issues in Africa. Sadly, African political leaders are playing the same game with their own people. A century ago a Rhodesian pioneer articulated the idea that the human rights of Africans are of lower value when he said, "Removal [of Africans from their traditional lands] does not entail the same degree of hardship that we contemplate in the dispossession of land in civilized communities."[40] Exploiting others to gain control of land is a basic human rights issue. Jean Marc Ela rightly urges, "We must get involved in this experience and use it as our starting point for a radical critique of all that is happening before our eyes."[41] The issue of land represents the point of confluence of the values of the kingdom of God, the residuum evangelium.

---

40. William Harvey Brown, *The Adventures and Observations of an American in Mashonaland and Matabeleland* (New York: Charles Scribner's Sons, 1899), 397, quoted in Cairns, *Prelude to Imperialism*, 226.

41. Ela, *My Faith as an African*, 91.

6

Many Designations, One Gospel

THE CONCEPT OF A model, in theology, denotes an interpretation of the God-Word that has as its purpose to hold the adherents together, using images and symbols in a reflective manner to deepen a community's theoretical understanding of reality.[1] Given the size, pluralism, and challenges of Africa, numerous models of theology can be found there. They have been variously called African (Christian) Theology, Contextual Theology, Savannah Theology, Theology of Indigenization, Theology of Inculturation, Theology of Adaptation, Theology of Reconstruction, (African) Liberation Theology, and *Aggiornamento*. Each of these models has a particular emphasis, but all are varieties within the same genre. These thrusts in culturing theology in the African context have run parallel to such African political rhetoric as Négritude (Léopold Sédar Senghor), African Personality (Kwame Nkrumah), Authenticité (Mobutu Sese Seko), Black Theology (especially in Southern Africa), and Black Consciousness (Steve Biko).

Designations, especially in the African context, are not just identification labels; they also signal the vocation and character of the particular construct. For example, the name Immanuel in the Bible summarizes the story of God's blessing of miraculous liberation and God's divine presence among the Israelites. Similarly, the name "Samuel" (literally "God has heard"; 1 Sam 1:20) encapsulates the story of God's answer to Hannah's earnest prayers for a child. In a similar way significant names are manifest in African cultures. Winston Ndugane, a former archbishop of the Church of Southern Africa (Anglican), for example, was named by his grandfather "Njongokulu," a compound of "*njongo*" (aim), and "*nkulu*" (big). The name was a prayer for good hopes and big things for the child. Review of the various designations chosen for the theological constructs in Africa yields similar rewards.

---

1. Boulding, *The Image*; Ramsey, *Models of Mystery*; Robert N. Bellah, "Transcendence in Contemporary Piety," in Bellah, *Beyond Belief*, 196–208; Dulles, *Models of the Church*; Minear, *Images of the Church in the New Testament*.

Aggiornamento

In the late 1950s and 1960s *aggiornamento* was the preferred language used within Roman Catholic churches in Africa. An Italian word introduced by Pope John XXIII (1958–63), aggiornamento designated the necessity for bringing the church, her message, and her methods up to date.[2] Pope John's insight grew out of his sense of a triple revolution—political, industrial, and scientific—in which his age and the world stood. With hindsight his very election as pope can be seen as having initiated a quiet revolution in the Roman Catholic Church.

To understand the springs of what Pope John was to become, do, and achieve, it is helpful to outline his story. Angelo Cardinal Roncalli, an Italian, was ordained in April 1904. Beginning as a parish priest, he became a seminary professor and made a career in the church. He was appointed apostolic visitor to Bulgaria in 1924 and then apostolic delegate to Bulgaria until 1934. An apostolic delegate is, as Pope Pius XI (1922–39) explained to a contingent of Catholics from Bulgaria, "an emissary to represent my person among you. He will have my ears that I should hear you, my lips that I should talk to you, and my heart that you should feel how much I love you."[3] In practice the apostolic delegate not only was to report on the Catholics scattered all over Bulgaria but equally importantly was to explore means to improve their relationship to the majority Eastern Orthodox Church. At the same time he was to seek for a more amicable relationship with the rather suspicious hierarchy of the Eastern Orthodox Church.

As if the foregoing were not a full agenda for the apostolic delegate, Bulgaria was living with the consequences of having joined with Germany during World War I. The country lost much of its Macedonian territory to Greece and Serbia, giving rise to an influx of refugees and wholesale executions. In this situation, Roncalli's ministry consisted of free outreach to all affected by the emergency. Rather than focusing on dogma, he followed the instincts of the heart. He endeavored to demonstrate that members of the Eastern Orthodox Church are true brothers and sisters. Further, ideologically Bulgaria was taking shape as a Communist state. Since Communism at the time was most hostile to religion, so as to secure the survival of the Christian faith in Bulgaria, his call demanded that he consciously seek not to be unnecessarily confrontational.

After that experience, Roncalli was appointed apostolic delegate to Turkey, in 1935, and also to Greece. Those two appointments further sharpened his sensitivity to others outside his group. Turkey with its capital Istanbul, the old Constantinople of the early church and the new Rome on the shores of the Bosporus, has been the scene of Orthodox Christian developments reaching back at least to the Emperor Constantine. The city is the seat of the Ecumenical Patriarch of the Orthodox Churches to

---

2. Trevor, *Pope John*; Hebblethwaite, *John XXIII: Pope of the Council.*
3. Elliott, *I Will Be Called John*, 93.

whom autocephalous Orthodox churches and independent self-governing nationalized churches relate. Those autocephalous churches maintain communion with the Ecumenical Patriarch of Phanar, who exercises some ecclesiastical authority over the main groups of the Orthodox churches.

Turkey had been the heart of the Ottoman Empire, and in the mid-1930s it had a predominantly Muslim population of some seventeen million. Prior to Roncalli's appointment, Mustafa Kemal Ataturk—holding that religion was incompatible with a modern nation—had opted in 1924 for a secular state. Lawrence Elliott writes, "He was no less hostile to the Christian minority whose presence had historically given the European powers a convenient pretext to intrude in Turkey's affairs. Catholic and Orthodox, once free to pursue their faiths without hindrance, suddenly found themselves regarded with official suspicion, warned against proselytizing, restricted in those sacraments, such as marriage, which conflicted with state law, and so circumscribed by the new bureaucracy as to find it all but impossible to run their own schools."[4] As apostolic delegate, Archbishop Roncalli began his mission in an explosive atmosphere. The model of church minted by the ideology of Christendom was not viable as part of the Turkish pluralistic scene.

Roncalli's response to an edict of June 13, 1924, banning the wearing of religious dress in public, is of interest. At the behest of the Catholic religious order, the French ambassador protested. But Archbishop Roncalli retorted, "If in Rome Christ is a Roman, let him be a Turk in Turkey."[5] This could be taken as the agenda for theology and a model of church, especially when no inviolable principle is involved.

Bulgaria, Turkey, and Greece were learning experiences for Roncalli. So was Roncalli's next appointment, in December 1944, as papal nuncio to Paris. France carried the honorific title of "eldest daughter of the Church," but in the eighteenth century the country underwent the French Revolution. Just before Roncalli's arrival there, the country had been liberated from Nazi Germany. Further, France was dominated by leftists, and their influence was felt even in the church. At the beginning of the twentieth century, Modernism had posed such a challenge to the Roman Catholic Church that Pope Pius X had declared it a heresy. The France that Roncalli encountered was very much dominated by Modernism.

As his story indicates, Angelo Roncalli's ministry spans a period when the Roman Catholic Church was regularly described as *semper idem* (always the same), yet Roncalli as a leader of that church lived in situations that challenged its vaunted sameness. His life experiences could not but have forced on Roncalli a mission of updating the institution. It was with that background that Cardinal Roncalli came to the *Sancta Sedes* (Holy See) and *Petri Cathedra* (papal chair) as Pope John XXIII. On June 29, 1959, the Feast of St. Peter and St. Paul, he issued his first encyclical, *Ad Petri cathedram*. In that encyclical he invited the faithful to discuss issues "which concern the

---

4. Ibid., 124.
5. Ibid., 127.

spread of the Catholic faith, the revival of Christian standards of morality and to bring ecclesiastical discipline into closer accord with the needs and conditions of our time." This brief paragraph from the encyclical sets out the contours of the agenda of aggiornamento. First, aggiornamento is in the interest of the church's mission. Second, it is concerned with the revival of Christian standards of morality. Third, it is about the necessity of facing up to contemporary challenges.

In his *Discourse at the Opening of the Second Vatican Ecumenical Council*, delivered on October 11, 1962, Pope John gave further exposition of the vision of aggiornamento. He stated,

> Our duty is not only to guard this precious treasure, as if we were concerned only with the past, but to dedicate ourselves with an earnest will and without fear to that work which the era demands of us, pursuing the path which the church has followed for twenty centuries. . . . [Our duty requires] a step forward towards a doctrinal penetration and formation of consciences in faithful and perfect conformity to authentic doctrine which, however, should be studied and expounded through the methods of research and the literary forms of modern thought. The substance of the ancient doctrines of the Deposit of Faith is one thing, but the way it is presented is another.

This is aggiornamento delivered in the words of its architect.

The idea is so clear as to make comments on it almost superfluous, but I would note three things. First, the concept of aggiornamento is not revolutionary, because it is rooted in a sense of history. Since it arises out of a sense of history, the "equipment" it demands are books, years of study, and knowledge of historical method. Recognition of the need for aggiornamento is an admission that church doctrines emerge in historical contexts, answering questions of their time. Second, if aggiornamento demands a sense of history, it also demands sensitivity to new times and new questions. Therefore, aggiornamento demands the endeavor to help find relevant answers. Third, important as doctrinal renewal is, aggiornamento must also have a pastoral orientation.

The quest for aggiornamento proceeds logically from Pope Pius XII's encyclical *Divino afflante Spiritu* (1943), which encouraged what we might call sensitive "liberal" study of Scripture. Liberal study of Scripture encompasses the necessity that we delineate the substance of the message of Scripture from the cosmology, anthropology, legends, myths, and literary conventions of the books of the Bible. Further, political, social, and even doctrinal changes and challenges in new times have always demanded revitalization of the gospel message and the church. Disagreements with society could not be allowed to entrap the church in hostile confrontation. Thus aggiornamento was at once adaptation and updating.

As attractive as aggiornamento is, it was born out of due time. It was a misnomer because the world itself was falling apart when it came. The post–World War II period was struggling to articulate a new vision. In the 1960s, shouts of "God is dead" were in the air and student riots filled the news. An antiestablishmentarian spirit was pervasive, typified by the rebellion against Pope Paul VI's encyclical *Humanae vitae*, July 25, 1968. There was general skepticism about truth and authority, especially that of the church.

The early and untimely death of Pope John XXIII meant that though aggiornamento continued to be on the lips of people, it underwent changes. For example, Pope John XXIII's successor, Pope Paul VI, at a public session on November 18, 1965, stated, "Henceforth *aggiornamento* will mean to us 'the enlightened penetration into the spirit of the Council' and 'the faithful application of the directives so happily and firmly laid out by the Council.'"[6] The starting point for discussion became Vatican II itself, hence deriving aggiornamento not so much from gospel as from dogma.

The Dutch Roman Catholic theologian Edward Schillebeeckx summarizes the significance of this development for the meaning of aggiornamento:

> Before and in the early stages of the Council *aggiornamento* meant throwing open the doors and setting out on a journey of discovery. But in the meantime the Council had taken definite decisions so that from now on *aggiornamento* is channeled. Herein also lurks the danger of a Post-Tridentine Roman Catholicism, at least if only the second part of the Pope's sentence ("faithful application of the council's directives") is pounced upon, while the first part ("penetration into the spirit of the council") is ignored. Because this means that the criterion of every *aggiornamento* is the apostolic spirit of holy scriptures, of which every Council, Vatican II included, can only draw an historically situated profit.[7]

Accommodation

How is the truth of Scripture to be related to the needs, language, and issues of a particular time and place today? In liberal German theological writing of the eighteenth century, *Herablassung* was much in vogue as a model for biblical exposition of Divine communication. In this model, scriptural tenets were held to be divine revelations and therefore timeless and changeless. Consequently, the only option open was to apply or accommodate those tenets to new times, for by definition the idiom of an age is dated and transitory. Unfortunately, as a name or label for this process, the literal English meaning of Herablassung, "condescension," is not a happy choice. But the term "accommodation" lay ready to hand, for well before the liberal German theologians of the eighteenth century arrived on the scene, it had been used to describe the missionary strategy practiced by the Jesuits in sixteenth-century China.

---

6. Schillebeeckx, *Real Achievement of Vatican II*, 13.

7. Ibid., 83–84.

For the sake of communicating the Christian message in a way that would be intelligible to the Chinese, the Italian Jesuit Matteo Ricci (1552–1610) pursued a path of interfaith dialogue. As vehicles he adopted indigenous Chinese forms of worship, customs, and culture. Karl Rahner and Herbert Vorgrimler define accommodation as

> paying due regard to the intellectual world of one's hearers, when preaching the Christian message, and therefore, also in the formal statement of revealed doctrine. It is not simply provisional adaptation to non-Christian civilization, but rather is designed to achieve fixed permanent results. The unity of revelation in the course of its history does not appear in a lifeless uniformity and repetition of ideas, but in the ever creative presence of the Word of God and his salvation for every human age, becoming history in one continuity of the one human race. Continuity requires living contact with sources; historicity requires that the Word of God confront concrete human life in all its forms.[8]

With circumspection and respect for Chinese tradition, Ricci studied the ancient Chinese customs. Following the Chinese characterization of heaven as *sang-Ti* and *Tien*, he designated the Lord of Heaven as *Tien-chu*, a construction with theistic import. Because he understood them to be civil rites, he countenanced the Chinese rites honoring Confucius. Obviously, Ricci adopted a positive attitude toward Chinese culture.

Another missionary, Roberto de Nobili (1577–1656), followed a similar approach in India. He first did a careful and thorough study of Indian life, especially of the Brahmin caste. He mastered Tamil, Telegu, and Sanskrit. De Nobili also wore the attire of a *sanyassi guru*, wearing the red ochre robes of Indian holy men. To avoid suspicion, he avoided associating with the local Christian church. His missionary activity took the form of public discussion of religious themes such as the creation and the unity of God, using Indian terms drawn from his study of the Indian classics. The caste system was not a problem for him because he judged it to be just a social distinction. His missionary efforts began with the higher castes, then moving to lower castes. He finally embarked on a mass movement.

The theology of accommodation takes the revelation of God as nonnegotiable, even though the historic context of that revelation must be engaged in interpreting it. To that extent, the theology of accommodation takes the incarnation seriously and attempts to hold universality and contextuality together in a creative tension. It is an incarnational paradigm. Unfortunately, Ricci's approach was swept up in church politics; the Jesuits were for it, the Dominicans were opposed to it. The disagreement between the two orders led to the Chinese Rites controversy.[9] Consequently, Pope Clement XI banned the practice in 1715, a ban that was reimposed by Pope Benedict XIV in 1742.

---

8. Rahner and Vorgrimler, *Theological Dictionary*, 12; Kollbrunner, "Die Akkommodation im Geist der Katholizität (1919–1959)," 161–84, 264–74; Cross, *Oxford Dictionary of the Christian Church*, 10.

9. "Chinois Rites," *Catholicisme*, 2.1060–63.

At the heart of that ban was *species superstitionis*, that is, a fear of superstition and syncretism, presumably in the minds of converts. Throughout their long history superstition and syncretism have been bad words. But the history of Christianity down the ages is replete with evidence that "Christianity is a syncretism *par excellence*."[10]

Adaptation

"Adaptation" is another word that has been used in mission circles for attempts to restate church theology and practice for use in new conditions. In most cases, however, the adaptation took the form of adapting European artifacts to an African or Asian context.[11] The process often assumed or implied, however, the correctness of European artifacts as the paradigm of civility and civilization. They, instead of Scripture, became the standard against which theological developments in other contexts were expected to be measured.

Adaptation found a strong proponent in Charles Martial Allemand Lavigerie (1825–92) and in the Roman Catholic missionary society he founded in 1868. The Society of Our Lady of Africa, also known as the White Fathers, engaged in the method of adaptation in Gold Coast (Ghana), Algeria, Central Africa, Uganda, Tanganyika/Tanzania, and Upper Congo.[12]

The Rule of the White Fathers articulates the method of adaptation as follows: "The spirit that must prevail in everything is that we must draw as near as is prudently possible to the African way of life: that is to say, in everything compatible with Christian and priestly life."[13] In this method, we can state first that the gospel of God is not negotiable. Second, the pursuit of adaptation is an option for dialogue with African ways of life. Third, prudence is needed.

The approach Lavigerie advocated was consciously opposed to that of the 1889 Berlin Conference with its espousal of the de-Africanization of Africans. What the Berlin Conference envisioned entailed the transformation of Africans by imposing European arts, crafts, and material outlook on them. It was shot through with philanthropic paternalism. In opposition to the Berlin Conference's approach Cardinal Lavigerie writes,

> The divine method of assimilation between ourselves and the African . . . is quite different. It is St. Paul who defines it when he says: "I have become all things to all men, that I might by all means save all." The apostle is primarily concerned with the soul; it is the soul which he seeks to change, knowing that all the rest will be added. And in order to win the soul, it is the apostle

---

10. Boff, *Church, Charism, and Power*, 99, see 92–99; see also Schreiter, *The New Catholicity*, 65, and Walter J. Hollenweger, foreword to Pobee and Oshitelu, *African Initiatives in Christianity*, xi.

11. Kollbrunner, "Die Akkommodation in Geist der Katholizität (1919–1959)."

12. Kittler, *White Fathers*; Burridge, *Destiny Africa*.

13. Burridge, *Destiny Africa*, 104.

who constrains himself, if need be, to give up all his accustomed externals of life. He would become Greek with the Greeks or a primitive with the primitives. . . . The apostles sought to change men's hearts and once this was done, the world was renewed. That is what we must do, following their example.[14]

Much as the White Fathers pursued adaptation to the outward environment, they also paid attention to the inward environment through careful empirical study of the history and customs of Africans, their traditions, and the criteria of their social and moral values. By means of such studies they sought a handle for communicating the Christian message in a manner that would be appropriate and effective in the African context as well as a way to educate their contemporaries back in Europe.

The White Fathers saw the crucial importance of the language of the people in communicating the gospel. Indeed, Lavigerie was unequivocal that "without a knowledge of the language, it is impossible to do any apostolate in Africa."[15] For him the language was an instrument. He required his missionaries to at least compile a vernacular dictionary because the language provided an index to the minds and lives of the people and offered a vehicle for assuming the weight of the culture.

In practice, adaptation tended toward extrinsic contact between a North Atlantic molding of the faith and the culture of the South. What was required, however, was intrinsic symbolism by which the non-Northern—that is, Southern—ethos, cultures, hopes, and fears could be taken seriously as essential to the basic nature of the gospel. As practiced, adaptation was covertly imperialistic. Thus, instead of being liberating, the construct held non-Westerners in a North Atlantic captivity. Wainwright, a former Methodist missionary to Cameroon, comments,

> *Adaptation* may suggest the need for a kind of philosopher-King who from a superior vantage point would bring into satisfactory, theoretical, and then practical relation two originally separate entities. On the one hand, there is the existing norm, whether such a norm be found in the apostolic church imaginatively reconstructed on the basis of New Testament texts or in an ideal quintessential church distilled by theology from the total history of the Church, or in the tradition of the particular missionary denomination; on the other hand, there is the cultural situation in which the norm has to be deliberately given an "adapted" form.[16]

Indigenization

The Aborigines Rights Protection Society, founded in the Gold Coast in 1897, time and again critiqued the work of missionaries, though many in the society were committed

---

14. Lavigerie, quoted ibid., 127.
15. Lavigerie, quoted ibid., 110.
16. Wainwright, "The Localization of Worship," 22.

Christians. Two examples will suffice. Joseph Ephraim Casely Hayford (1866–1930), called "the Great Moses of West Africa," critiqued the work of Christian missions, writing, "The methods of the pioneers of civilization among us were peculiar. They were dangerous. They tended to destroy African nationality."[17] Similarly, Samuel Richard Brew Attoh Ahuma (1866–1930), a Gold Coast Methodist minister, argued that the average product of a mission school was "a black Whiteman who is a creature, a freak and a monstrosity."[18]

These critiques, from before the time of Franz Fanon's *Black Skin, White Masks*, signal the dissatisfaction felt in African circles in regard to the manner of presentation used by missionaries in communicating the content of the Christian message. The Christian gospel itself does not appear to be the problem. The problem is that the presentation appears to undermine African identity.

Two comments may, however, be made on the subject of indigenization. The first concerns the word's etymology. In French colonial times and circles, the word "*indigène*" had about it the ring of "uncivilized" or "uncultured." The word has unhappy associations of judgmentalism and paternalism; it is backward looking in its implications.[19]

Second, because culture is not static but always evolving, the content of what is indigenous can be elusive; the term carries the risk of addressing a creation that no longer represents the heartbeat of a people.

An interesting instance is provided by the use of Swahili. Outsiders unacquainted with Africa, time and again, talk as if Swahili were the language of Africa. True, Swahili is a language that is spoken widely in East Central Africa, and it has become the official language of Tanzania. But in origin, it was the language of the WaSwahili, a coastal Bantu people, who over the years were Arabicized in genes, culture, economy, and language.[20] A real question can be raised of how indigenous Swahili is to East and Central Africa. Similarly, while the overall idea of culturing the gospel in the locale where it is taking root is right and laudable, the ideological implications of the word indigenization can be misleading.

Inculturation

At least as far back as the middle of the twentieth century, French mission scholars have been discussing "*un Catholicisme inculturé*," that is, an inculturated Catholicism.[21]

17. Hayford, *Ethiopia Unbound*, 10.
18. Ahumah, *Gold Coast Nation and National Consciousness*, 40.
19. Wainwright, "Localization of Worship," 26.
20. Alexandre, *Introduction to Languages and Language in Africa*, 39; J. Spencer Trimingham, "The Phases of Islamic Expansion and Islamic Culture Zones in Africa," in Lewis, *Islam in Tropical Africa*, 127–43.
21. Masson, "L'Église ouverte sur le monde," 1032–43.

Yves Congar argues for Japanese origins of the phrase, describing it as a way of modifying acculturation.[22] Whatever its origins, "inculturation" has become the preferred term within Jesuit circles, pointing as it does to the dynamic relationship that should exist between the church and the cultures of the world in all their variety.[23] As exemplified in the writings of John Mary Waliggo, Engelbert Mveng, John Mutiso-Mbinda, and Justin S. Ukpong, especially in Africa inculturation has become an established word for the contextualization of church and theology.[24] As a concept inculturation is indebted to cultural anthropology, where inculturation describes "the process of acquiring the cultural traditions of a society."[25]

In a 2008 review of the content and perspectives of African theologians, especially those from East Africa, Paul Gifford stressed that the fact of African theology's existence is something that cannot be doubted.[26] He examines African theologians' positions on issues of culture, modernity, and the public sphere. On the whole he discerns a certain romanticization of the African past and a rather unconvincing dismissal of some positive contributions of modernity to African civilization.

Reconstruction

One type of theologizing found in South and East Africa is styled "Theology of Reconstruction."[27] Its imagery derives from construction and the building industry. To place the movement in sharper focus, it will be helpful to put it alongside the words revolution, reformation, restoration, and renewal, all of which reflect moments in the life of the church.

At root, revolution refers to the movement of an orbiting celestial body. But the word gained notoriety by its association with or description of some historic events—the American Revolution of 1775, the French Revolution of 1789, the Chinese Revolution

---

22. Congar, "Christianisme comme foi et comme culture," 1:83–103.

23. Thirty-Second General Congregation of the Society of Jesus, December 2, 1974, to March 7, 1975, "Decree 4: Service of Faith and the Promotion of Justice," para. 36, 53–56; "Decree 5: On Promoting the Work of Inculturation of Faith and of Christian Life"; "Decree 6: On Formation," para. 29; Crollius, "What Is So New about Inculturation? A Concept and Its Implications," 721–38; Crollius, "Inculturation and Incarnation: On Speaking of the Christian Faith and Cultures of Humanity," 138–40; Ukpong, *New Testament Essays*; Ary A. Roest Crollius, "Inculturation: Newness and Ongoing Process," in Waliggo, *Inculturation: Its Meaning and Urgency*, 31–45; Schineller, *Handbook on Inculturation*; Sarpong, "Inculturation," 7.

24. Waliggo, *Inculturation: Its Meaning and Urgency*; Mutiso-Mbinda, "Inkulturation," 164–71; Mveng, "Afrikanisches Profil von Theologie und Kirche," 154–63; Shorter, *Toward a Theology of Inculturation*.

25. Theodorson and Theodorson, *Modern Dictionary of Sociology*, 13; Herskovits, *Man and His Works*, 39.

26. Gifford, "Africa's Inculturation Theology," 18–34.

27. Villa-Vicencio, *Theology of Reconstruction*; Mugambi, *Christian Theology and Social Reconstruction*; Mugambi, *From Liberation to Reconstruction*.

of 1911, and the Russian Revolution of 1917. Those revolutions represented the forceful overthrow of one government and its replacement by another government. Therefore, the word revolution is often understood as meaning radical change, often characterized by violence and with no regard for tradition, which, after all, is the memory of a people. In view of what was said above about the *residuum evangelium*, the word revolution is not properly used of anything concerned with the Christian faith and in any case, the theology of reconstruction is not to be confused with revolution.

Reformation has to do with making a person or institution better by removing perceived faults, defects, and abuses. Achieving reformation usually entails persuasion. But the sixteenth-century religious movement which aimed at reforming the Roman Catholic Church has given the word a special slant in Christian history. For one thing, it broke the *Una Sancta* and resulted in the establishment of Protestantism. The operative idea was to seek change for the better in public life by abandoning or removing imperfections or faults. The story of the Reformation churches, however, reveals that several of the very things the reformers railed against have persisted in the Reformed churches.

Reformed Judaism presents us with a parallel movement, one dedicated to normalizing and harmonizing rational thought with historical Judaism. That endeavor has placed its stress on Judaism's ethical aspects but has not demanded strict observance of traditional Orthodox ritual. Once again reformation resulted in sundering Judaism.

The two cases cited of reformation in Christianity and in Judaism suggest that reformation does not go far enough and that it leads to schisms, which do not speak well of the religion. Reformation is a kind of halfway house that does not reach the core issue. The Christian Reformation issued slogans such as *sola fidei* and *sola gratia*, that covered a multitude of sins but ultimately were not conducive to clarification of the residuum evangelium. Reconstruction is not reformation.

At its root, restoration means bringing something back to a former or normal condition, as by repairing, rebuilding, or altering. Restoration is an attempt to give structure to a vision. The question to be asked is whether the vision is consonant with the original idea that gave rise to the original artifact. Again, history supplies an example in the 1660 restoration of the monarchy in England under King Charles II (1660–1685). Today the monarchy continues to be an important part of English tradition. Needless to say, the monarchy in England today does not have the same force as the original design, however beloved the queen may be. Reconstruction may be related to restoration but is not identical with it. Restoring, with its emphasis on structure, emphasizes the framework and organization, aspects that do not necessarily touch the most essential part, namely, the Holy Spirit.

At root "renewal," which is the more biblical word and paradigm, means to make new again by refurbishing, restoring, and giving renewed functionality to what is old, worn, and exhausted in an endeavor to bring it back to a new condition. For example, mission at bottom is a movement of transformation and renewal. The ecumenical imperative is also about renewal. Renewal concerns arranging for continued validity. Renewal is not only about restoring to an original state; it is also about bestowing renewed functionality. More importantly, it is about viability and the ability to give life. Thus renewal is consistent with John 20:31 in which we see that the Scriptures and the incarnation are for the purpose of giving life in abundance.

A school of theology called Christian Reconstructionism could already be found in the United States and Switzerland of the 1960s. Founded by Rousas John Rushdoony, Christian Reconstructionism influenced the seminal evangelical writer Francis Schaeffer, an American who formed the Christian community known as L'Abri. Located in the Swiss Alps, L'Abri became a place where religious intellectuals gathered to study.[28] Christian Reconstructionism was, in some of its expressions, a very strict Calvinism, and with L'Abri as a base, Schaeffer became the apostle of hard right stances on political and social issues. Unlike Schaeffer, Rushdoony was postmillennial in theology, that is, his expectation was that Jesus would not return to earth until after Christians had established a thousand-year reign on earth. The important point is that reconstructionists wanted to build the kingdom themselves.

Of the movement, Charles Villa-Vicencio wrote, "The task of liberation theologians has essentially been to say 'No' to all forms of oppression. The prophetic 'No' must, of course, continue to be part of a liberating theology. As the enduring struggle for democracy in some parts of the world begins to manifest itself in differing degrees of success, however, so the prophetic task of the church must include a thoughtful and creative 'Yes' to options for political and social renewal."[29] Theology of reconstruction is an attempt to participate in building a just society, especially in light of the destruction that resulted from apartheid ideology. Such theology is possible in a *kairos*, a critical time.

The reconstructionist vision operates as a set of "middle axioms" or evolving principles of evolving society, that is, as a provisional definition of human society.[30] But Reconstructionism also endeavors to discover interdisciplinary collaboration. Middle axioms and interdisciplinary collaboration constitute the method of theology of reconstruction. The narrative of the return from exile and the rebuilding of Jerusalem provide the horizon for reconstruction. Similarly, the motif of new creation as reconstruction (2 Cor 5:17) can be a help in a theology of reconstruction.

Contextualization

In the 1970s the Theological Education Fund (TEF), with headquarters in Bromley, Kent, United Kingdom, acted as the high priest of contextualization. TEF was founded

---

28. Schaeffer, *Christian Manifesto*; Goldberg, *Kingdom Coming*, 7, 13–14, 37–38.

29. Villa-Vicencio, *Theology of Reconstruction*, 1.

30. José Miguez Bonino, "Middle Axioms," in Lossky, *Dictionary of the Ecumenical Movement*, 761; Visser 't Hooft and Oldham, *The Church and Its Function in Society*; Grenholm, *Christian Social Ethics in a Revolutionary Age*.

by the International Missionary Council (IMC) Assembly of December 28, 1957, to January 8, 1958, that met in Accra, Ghana.[31] The venue was not accidental, but intentional and significant. Ghana had gained independence from British colonial rule on March 6, 1957. The story of Ghana was symbolic of the growing nationalism and the movement toward independence throughout the Third World—India, Pakistan, Ceylon, and Burma had become independent in the years following 1948, and one African state after another was to gain independence in the 1960s. The venue also epitomized a growing consciousness of the necessity for colonial churches to shed their colonial image and to become churches of their respective soils. In that context contextuality came to the fore within theological education.

Charles Ranson became the first director of TEF. He had been a long-standing missionary in India before joining the IMC, and he had a sense of the way the situation in the mission field was changing as the independence movement in Asia gathered momentum. That consciousness led TEF to search for new models of church and theology so as to reflect the shift from colonialism to independence.[32]

The second director of TEF was Shoki Coe, an Asian theological educator from Formosa (Taiwan). With one exception, the staff consisted of a team of Third World theological educators: Aharon Sepsazian, an Armenian Brazilian; Desmond Mpilo Tutu, a South African; and Ivy Coe, also an Asian. One American, James Berquist, who had been a missionary in India, was the exception. This predominantly Third World staff was to socialize Third World theologians in contextual theology. The effort was ecumenical. The root word, context, concerns the interpenetration and interaction of text and context. In 1974, Shoki Coe wrote, "By contextuality we mean that wrestling with God's world in such a way as to discern the particularity of this historic moment; and by contextualization we mean the wrestling with God's word in such a way that the power of the incarnation, which is the divine form of contextualization, can enable us to follow his steps to contextualize."[33]

Contextualization, as James Burtness helpfully comments, "is a word which points to the demise of absolutes and the embracing of relativities, whether in physics or theology or politics. It is a reminder that the inductive method, whether in the chemistry laboratory or in a Bible study group, yields probabilities rather than necessities. It signals an eagerness to live with specifics rather than generalities, with particulars rather than universals. 'Context' is a word which fits naturally with such phrases as theory of relativity, scientific method, situational ethics, and statistical probabilities."[34] The significance of this quotation is that every theological construct is contextual and should

---

31. Orchard, *Ghana Assembly of the International Missionary Council*.

32. Ranson, *Christian Minister in India*; *A Missionary Pilgrimage*; and *Renewal and Advance*.

33. Coe, "Contextualisation," 7; Kinsler, "Mission and Context," 23–29; Lienemann-Perrin, *Training for a Relevant Ministry*; Russell, *Contextualization*.

34. James H. Burtness, "Innovation as the Search for Probabilities: To Re-contextualize the Text," in Theological Education Fund, *Learning in Context*, 10.

be so recognized. To call the language of normative theology into play is wrongheaded and misguided, if not imperialistic. Contextual theology has its own threefold critical principle by which it should be judged: integrity, authenticity, and creativity.

Ignited by the work of Ranson, the quest for contextual theology swept the Third World in the 1960s and 1970s. But particularly exciting experiments with it were made in South Africa, especially at the Institute of Contextual Theology, associated with the Dominican theologian Albert Nolan. His version of contextual theology was influenced by Latin American theologizing, particularly the hermeneutical circle of See-Judge-Act. The method began with sociological analysis, leading to reading of the text, and finally issuing in action.[35] Contextual theology in South Africa was rooted in a church and theology that had been sensitized to the cause of liberation from South Africa's oppressive, violent, and murderous apartheid system and was endeavoring to discern the meaning of the gospel and God for their circumstances. Nolan suggested that three streams were coming together for the transformation of South Africa: "an unrelenting popular movement of resistance; coordinated international pressure upon the government of South Africa; and religious legitimation for change."[36]

Contextual theology has developed in different ways, but in each case the social context was what determined which questions would be addressed to the biblical text. It was, first, undertaking the social analysis of apartheid and then appraising it in the light of reading Scripture that made it possible for people to rise to the challenge of opposing that dehumanizing political system. Because missionary and colonial measures in the rest of Africa had sought to make Africans into clones of the North Atlantic, contextual theologies there sought to engage the mind of Africans and Africa, that is, African cultural identity in its various forms.

Contextual theology worldwide developed its own momentum—as do all systems—leading a friend of TEF, the ecumenist Lesslie Newbigin, to provide a perceptive critique. He wrote,

> The word *contextualization*, coined originally by Shoki Coe, was very useful in shifting people's thinking away from the backward looking implications of "indigenization" and the covertly imperialistic implications of "adaptation," so as to direct attention to the task of communicating the Gospel in terms of what is really happening now in the cultures with which the church is involved. It has now become one of the slogan words of Third World Theology, and in the process seems to me to have changed its meaning. As now commonly used, it seems to me to refer to a kind of theology which starts from the problem which a community faces and then, with one's predetermined framework,

---

35. Speckman and Kaufmann, *Towards an Agenda for Contextual Theology*; Nolan, *God in South Africa*.

36. Nolan, *God in South Africa*; Nolan, *Jesus before Christianity*; De Gruchy, *Theology and Ministry in Context and Crisis*.

seeks to formulate the Christian message. The end result is, inevitably, a programme or a crusade rather than "good news," law rather than gospel.[37]

Taken as a characterization of all contextual theologies, I am not sure that this critique is wholly justified. But like Bernard Thorogood I appreciate the thrust of his concern: "His passion for the missionary engagement made him a critic of the more liberal theologies which have been influential in recent decades. Yet there was no anti-intellectual conservatism. Rather he sought a restatement of classic evangelicalism built on first-hand missionary experience, questioning all easy compromise with secularism."[38]

Liberation Theology

The phrase liberation theology was coined by Gustavo Gutiérrez, a Peruvian and a Franciscan Roman Catholic priest. The phenomenon became much in evidence and widely influential in the 1960s and 1970s. Its high priests, mostly but not wholly Latin American, included Juan Luis Segundo, Uruguayan Jesuit; Ernesto Cardenal, Nicaraguan priest; Juan Sobrino, Salvadoran Jesuit; Leonardo Boff, Brazilian Franciscan; Clodovus Boff, brother of Leonardo; Hugo Assmann, Brazilian theologian and sociologist; José Comblin, Belgian-born Latin American religious leader; and Carlos Alberto Libânio Christo (Frei Betto), Brazilian Dominican brother.[39]

Though detractors have dismissed liberation theology as being political theology or Marxism in religious (that is, Christian) guise, the movement has distant roots in the Christian humanism of the fifteenth and sixteenth centuries. Strictly speaking, however, liberation theology may be said to originate from the Assembly of Latin American Roman Catholic Bishops, in 1968, convened in Medellín, Columbia, though it owes something as well to *Gaudium et spes*, the Second Vatican Council's Pastoral Constitution on the Church in the Modern World, promulgated on December 7, 1965.

Liberation theology is a generic label that encompasses a number of varieties: Latin American liberation theology, North American feminist theology, black theology, Hispanic theology, First World eco-theology, and for good measure, African and Asian theologies of liberation. But whatever the manifestation, certain notes can be found associated with the movement.

First is the catch phrase "preferential option for the poor," which was a code for looking at things from the underside of history and therefore with a keen eye for engaging the excluded and marginalized of society.[40] In this regard, liberation theology borrowed from Marxist analysis and language, though it never bought into

---

37. Newbigin, *Theological Education and the Scientific Approach*, 67.

38. Bernard Thorogood, "James Edward Lesslie Newbigin," in Lossky, *Dictionary of the Ecumenical Movement*, 822.

39. Brown, *Gustavo Gutiérrez*; Brown, *Liberation Theology*; Gutiérrez, *Theology of Liberation*; Cook, *New Face of Church in Latin America*.

40. CELAM, *The Church in the Present-Day Transformation of Latin America in the Light of the Council, II: Conclusions*; Eagleson and Scharper, *Puebla and Beyond*.

the atheism of Marxism. The context that gave rise to liberation theology's distinctive stance was the presence in many Latin American countries of a certain sympathy and unholy alliance between church, state, and military. In that situation, liberation theologians championed the cause of the marginalized and excluded, a stance enshrined in the phrase "preferential option for the poor." In practice, preferential option for the poor often meant support—with the aim of building a just society—for leftist political movements, even for Marxists, as well as the use of violence to confront injustices. These consequences flowed from liberation theologians' conviction that theology must issue in action.

Second, with a view to the establishment of justice and dignity, liberation theology identified institutional violence as something to be engaged directly. In pursuit of this objective, liberation theologians sought to identify and articulate social arrangements that create hunger so that they could be engaged.

Third, liberation theology identified structural sin as an objective of correction. The concept of structural sin meant for them that sin, beyond being incontrovertibly personal, also had social dimensions, for example, as can be seen in neocolonialism and neofeudal relationships.[41] Redemption, a metaphor for salvation, is thus seen to be also a quest for transformation of the social realities of human life.

Therefore, fourth, liberation theology is intrinsically engaged in the endeavor of social analysis so as to identify and correct social mechanisms that lead to injustice.

Fifth, against the foregoing background, liberation theology was committed to orthopraxy, that is, correct action leading to human liberation. The commitment to orthopraxy obliged the theological enterprise to pursue a correlation between belief and practice.[42]

Sixth, liberation theology characteristically stressed the pastoral dimension of theology. For some time theology invested heavily in intellectual scientific analysis and ordering of reality, but it lacked immediate and adequate ties to the pastoral challenges of church and society. Indeed, pastoral theology had been, consciously or unconsciously, treated as unacademic and as a stepchild in theological circles.

A characteristic step accompanying liberation theology's rediscovery of the crucial role of theology was the formation of "basic Christian communities," which were social groups that engaged in Bible study for the sake of action. The basic Christian communities galvanized the poor, that is, the excluded and marginalized, to take charge of their own destiny. Liberation theology's embrace of the basic Christian community movement was read as taking a stance against the institutional church.

Liberation theology has been associated with not only Latin America, but also North America, where it is especially to be found among African Americans in the

---

41. Gutiérrez, *Power of the Poor in History*; Boff, *Faith on the Edge*; Mesters, *Defenseless Flowers*; Cook, *Expectation of the Poor*; Scharper and Scharper, *The Gospel in Art by the Peasants of Solentiname*; Brockman, *Romero*; Romero, *Voice of the Voiceless*.

42. Casas, *The Devastation of the Indies*; Shaull, *Naming the Idols*.

United States. It found its way to Africa because of a rather similar historical experience there of imperialistic colonial domination and concomitant economic exploitation, being particularly strongly represented in Southern Africa, that is, Tanzania and South Africa.[43] In this theological approach we find the Word of God engaging the challenges of the context. It addressed Third World experience by means of a holistic approach that was guided by some rules of textual analysis. Liberation theology's holistic approach entailed the integration of theology, anthropology, economics, and epistemology. Its textual analysis was a means of discovering the internal logic of the scriptural text as it related to the liberation theologians' own contexts.

Black Theology

In his poem *The Second Coming*, William Butler Yeats writes,

> Now I know
> That twenty centuries of stony sleep
> Were vexed to nightmare by a rocking cradle,
> And what rough beast, its hour come round at last,
> Slouches towards Bethlehem to be born?

This is an apocalyptic, rather sinister, and emotive expression of a reawakening after a long slumber. In the 1960s the image fitted the awakening of the Black Power movements.

Frederick Douglass was the first to use the term "Black Power." It features in his mid-nineteenth-century essay "The Doom of the Black Power," but there it stands in opposition to Negro interests, signaling the demonic force behind the slave trade. In 1954 the novelist Richard Wright used the phrase in a positive sense for the animating force behind the national independence movements in Africa. The phrase gained traction when Adam Clayton Powell used it at a rally in Chicago and at the commencement address he gave at Howard University on May 29, 1966. Black power became the rallying cry of radical black nationalist groups, as distinguished from the civil rights movements. Black power became a code for empowerment of black people, especially their empowerment as victims of racism.

Black power then became the political expression of black religions and black theology. It took diverse forms: independence from white control; black churches, prayer, symbols, and litanies as social expressions of black community; and black identity and self-expression.[44] Given the circumstances of blacks, liberation was

---

43. Nessen, *Orthopraxis or Heresy*; Frostin, *Liberation Theology in Tanzania and South Africa*; Katjavivi et al., *Church and Liberation in Namibia*.

44. Evans, *Black Theology*; Nicolson, *A Black Future?*; Cone and Wilmore, *Black Theology*; Cone, *Black Theology and Black Power*; Charles H. Long, "The Black Reality"; Roberts, *Liberation and Reconciliation*; Roberts, *A Black Political Theology*; King, *Stride toward Freedom*.

salvation. Race had become a tool for structural exclusion of blacks. The black consciousness movement fought against both the inferiority complex among blacks and the superiority complex among whites. It was an affirmation that blacks are as capable as any other group.

In South Africa black theology and black consciousness movements are tied together. The name of Stephen Bantu Biko is synonymous with black consciousness. "Black" as an epithet in black consciousness and black theology is not about color of skin; rather it is about a mental attitude. In Biko's rhetoric the epithet "black" signaled a strong solidarity among Africans, Indians, and Coloureds.

> Black Consciousness is an attitude of mind and a way of life, the most positive call to emanate from the black world for a long time. Its essence is the realisation by the black man of the need to rally with his brothers around the cause of their oppression—the blackness of their skin—and to operate as a group to rid themselves of the shackles that bind them to perpetual servitude. It is based on self-examination which has ultimately led them to believe that by seeking to run away from themselves and emulate the white man, they are insulting the intelligence of whoever created them black.[45]

Biko may not have been formally styled a theologian, but he was a landmark in the sense that his black consciousness movement was a catalyst in black theology's reframing of Christianity.

Social analysis leading to reflection and action was a critical tool for engaging with the social and political reality of South Africa. The country was in the grip of pathological fear, and those who dared to stand up to be counted were sent into detention or had to go into exile or had to acquiesce in being restricted to Bantustans. Each of these was an attack on the dignity and humanity of black people. By default, resistance, with its emphasis on black solidarity in the face of oppression, became the most humanizing response available. It held out hope for a future with a vision of a common humanity and a society founded on justice.

God the Creator must have had deliberate reasons for creating blacks and, therefore, blacks must be consciously proud of themselves, their religion, and their outlook on life. Pride in being African may seem to deny Biko's religiosity, but he believed that "man's internal insecurity can only be alleviated by an almost enigmatic and supernatural force to which we ascribe all power, all wisdom and love."[46] Barney Pityana carries the point further: "Biko built his political system on a spiritual foundation . . . spiritual . . . concrete, holistic, bringing the fullness of humanity to bear on the material and objective world."[47]

---

45. Steve Biko, cited in Aelred Stubbs, "Martyr of Hope: A Personal Memoir," in Biko, *I Write What I Like*, 92; Biko, *Black Consciousness and the Quest for a True Humanity*; Mangcu, *Biko: A Biography*.

46. Lindy Wilson, "Bantu Stephen Biko: A Life," in Pityana et al., *Bounds of Possibility*, 43.

47. Graham Duncan, "Steve Biko's Religious Consciousness and Thought . . . ," in Du Toit, *Legacy*

Since religion is fundamental to Africans, theologians cannot claim to have a monopoly on theological discourse. Biko was holding out for the democratization of theology. Theology is the worship of God. It is the work of the people, and it emerges from suffering people's daily struggles.

Black theology holds on to Jesus, but its Jesus is one who, in a situation of oppression, is endeavoring to liberate the oppressed peoples. For black theology Isaiah 61:1–4 and Luke 4:18–19 were key Christological texts. Jesus saw his ministry of being in solidarity with humans as a pointer to his eschatological role as savior and judge.

Other blacks and whites in South Africa have contributed to the articulation of black theology, including Itumelang J. Mosala and Takatso A. Mofokeng.[48]

African Theology

Black theology and African theology have often been mislabeled as African nationalism donning religion and theology. But they follow the logic of the Christian theology of the incarnation and the record of the church throughout history as she has followed her mission to the ends of the world. In their day the Ethiopianists understood the way that Christian missions from Europe were holding the theology of the African church and African church models in a North Atlantic captivity. David Brown Vincent, also known as Mojola Agbebi (1840–1917), wrote, "To render Christianity indigenous to Africa it must be watered by native hands, pruned with the native hatchet, and tended with native earth. . . . It is a curse if we intend forever to hold at the apron-strings of foreign teachers, doing the baby for aye."[49] Church, like theology, must be in consonance with the natural and relative habitudes of the African and with the harmonization of native institutions with biblical Christianity.

Many African theologians have endeavored to write African theology, among them John S. Mbiti (Kenya), Harry Sawyerr (Sierra Leone), K. A. Dickson (Ghana), Bénézet Bujo (Democratic Republic of Congo), Charles Nyamiti (Tanzania), Hilary B. P. Mijoga (Malawi), Jean-Marc Ela (Cameroon), Kä Mana (Democratic Republic of Congo), John S. Pobee (Ghana), Mercy Amba Oduyoye (Ghana), and Musimbi Kanyoro (Kenya). Expatriates too—Diane Stinton, for example—have written on African theology.[50]

In 1971 James Cone and Gayraud Wilmore organized a consultation (held in Dar es Salaam, Tanzania) between African theologians and African American theologians. In the paper they presented there, they observed, "African theology is concerned with

---

of Stephen Bantu Biko, 115–40.

48. Mosala, *Biblical Hermeneutics and Black Theology in South Africa*; Mofokeng, *The Crucified among the Crossbearers*.

49. D. Brown Vincent, *Africa and the Gospel* (1889), cited in Ayandele, *Missionary Impact on Modern Nigeria*, 200; Ayandele, *African Historical Studies*, 107–36; D. Brown Vincent, "Hamites General Economy" (1881), summarized in James Johnson to Laing; John S. Pobee, "Good News Turned by Native Hands . . . ," in Phiri and Werner, *Handbook of Theological Education in Africa*, 13–27.

50. Gibellini, *Paths of African Theology*; Stinton, *Jesus of Africa*.

Africanization. Black theology is concerned with liberation. But Africanization must also involve liberation from centuries of poverty, humiliation and exploitation. A truly African theology cannot escape the requirement of helping the indigenous churches to become relevant to the social and political ills of Africa, which are not unrelated to Euro-American imperialism and racism."[51] Their words remind us that theological construction is time bound and contextual. For while both African and black theologies concern African identity and social-political challenges, they are on the agenda and may be stressed at any point in time because of the challenges faced at that time.

African Personality and Négritude

During Africa's age of independence, politicians there gave expression to ideas that ran parallel to the yearning for African authenticity and identity that Christians were expressing. Two such ideologies were the ideology of African personality, which Ghana's Kwame Nkrumah and the Convention People's Party (CPP) touted, and négritude, which Senegal's Léopold Sésor Senghor proclaimed.

In 1958, in a speech at the fifteenth Annual New Year School of the University of Ghana's Institute of Extra-Mural Studies, K. A. Gbedemah, minister of finance in the administration of Kwame Nkrumah, articulated the ideology of African personality forcefully: "African Personality means that Africans should be able to stand up to any person, no matter his colour of skin; this is not necessarily looking upon others with disdain, but to think of ourselves as equal." This statement was a direct disavowal and rejection of the European assumption of the childlikeness of Africans. African personality was a call for African identity and culture to be taken seriously on the world stage, and it sought to inculcate black awareness along with pride in black race, history, and heritage. The movement and concept were positive efforts to undergird black pride.

Kwame Nkrumah himself sometimes spoke of it as the African genius. He wrote,

> When I speak of the African genius, I mean something different from *négritude*, something not apologetic, but dynamic. *Négritude* consists in a mere literary affectation and style, which piles up word upon word and image upon image with occasional reference to Africa and things African. I do not mean a vague brotherhood based on a criterion of colour, or on the idea that Africans have no reasoning, but only sensitivity. By the African genius I mean something positive, our socialist concept of society, the efficiency and validity of our traditional statecraft, our highly developed code of morals, our hospitality and our purposeful energy. . . . It is only in conditions of total freedom and independence from foreign rule and interferences that the aspirations of our people will see real fulfillment and the African genius find its best expression.[52]

---

51. See *New Christian*, November 17, 1971, 1347.

52. Kwame Nkrumah, *Speech at the Opening of the Institute of African Studies*, in Nkrumah, *Axioms of Kwame Nkrumah*, 3–4.

As an ideology, African personality sought to foster for Africans a face and identity in the parliament of the peoples of the world—and unapologetically so.

Léopold Sédar Senghor's ideology of négritude grew from the same West African coast. As a movement négritude—the name was coined by Aimé Ferdinand Césaire, a Martinique-born poet, playwright, and politician—was a combined ideological and aesthetic concept that strongly affirmed the independent validity of black culture. Needless to say, négritude stood in opposition to colonialism. For his part, Frantz Fanon, the philosopher-psychiatrist and revolutionary thinker, rejected the language of négritude and advocated black revolution.

A poet, philosopher, and politician, Senghor appropriated the concept of négritude, which, he stated, "is not simply a question of resuscitating the past or trying to live *dans le muse Négro-Africain*; but of animating the world of today with the values of the African past."[53]

He embraced African socialism but he was religious, a believer in God, though he could refer to God using terms such as "that ultra-consciousness" and "the ultimate goal of our progress." Senghor sought to build this earth "out of earth," so as to attain fullness of well-being and pursue programs against disease, poverty, and ignorance. Fanon's publications, by contrast, became the handbook of the black revolution, profoundly influencing the revolutionary movements of the 1960s.[54] "Each generation," Fanon insisted, "must out of relative obscurity discover its mission, fulfill it, or betray it."[55]

Aborigines Rights Protection Society

Long before African politicians stepped forward to trumpet the nonnegotiable necessity that African identity be projected on the world stage, similar tendencies were finding expression in church circles. The Aborigines Rights Protection Society (ARPS), Ethiopianism, and African Initiatives in Christianity provide three examples.

ARPS, founded by chiefs and literate Africans, was launched in the Gold Coast in 1897. Its purpose was to defend Gold Coast land rights. At first a nationalist body, it was "dedicated to promote and effect unity of purpose and of action among all aborigines of the Gold Coast."[56] Several of ARPS's stalwarts were churchmen. For example, Samuel Richard Brew Attoh Ahuma (1864–1921) was a minister of the Methodist Church. George Kuntu Blankson (1809–98) was also a Methodist as well as a founding member of the Society for Promoting Christian Knowledge in the Gold Coast.

---

53. Léopold Sédar Senghor, speech given at Oxford University, October 1961, in Senghor, *On African Socialism*, 141–48; Léopold Sédar Senghor, speech given at Howard University, Washington, DC, Sept. 28, 1961; Ansah, "Aspects of Negritude," 66–78; Cox, *Socialist Ideas in Africa*, 27–30.

54. Fanon, *Black Skin, White Masks*; Fanon, *Wretched of the Earth*; see Gibson, *Fanonian Practices in South Africa*.

55. Fanon, *Wretched of the Earth*, 206.

56. Ward, *History of Ghana*, 357; Kimble, *Political History of Ghana*.

In addition to its attention to land rights, ARPS critiqued the missionary methods of the churches founded by Christian missions from Europe. ARPS's critique of Christian missions and education received classic expression in the words of J. S. Casely Hayford: "The methods of the pioneers of civilization among us were peculiar. They were even dangerous. They tended to destroy African nationality."[57] Attoh Ahuma concurred and described missionary methods as leading to "the denationalization of African converts."[58] In place of that result, ARPS proposed the "Doctrine of the Return to Things Native" or "Gone Fantee," which sought a "fusion of what is good in the traditions and customs inherited from our ancestors with the adaptation of what is good—and only what is good—of what we learn by contact with Europeans."[59] John Mensah Sarbah extended the thought by writing, "To be wholly African in outlook is not incompatible with being a good Christian. . . . Pride of race in the African is not a sign of disloyalty [to the Crown]."[60]

Ethiopianism

Ethiopianism was a nineteenth-century development that first flourished in West Africa and then spread to Southern Africa. It was a protest movement against the North Atlantic or European captivity of the church and the gospel. According to George Shepperson, underlying motives for the protest included "the stimulus of European ecclesiastical secession; reaction against over-strict disciplining of African converts by European missionaries; the desertion of some African separatist ministers to increase their personal power and status by administering church property and monies; the creation of tribal churches in which due respect was paid to African customs; and a rejection of the colour bar [present] in many European-controlled churches."[61] This list of motives and sources of the Ethiopianist movement signals a very complex story. But it represents a deep yearning on the part of Africans to stand around the throne of God as Africans and not as Caucasian clones. The words of Mojola Agbebi quoted above are fully germane on this point.

Ethiopianism represented a blend of several African aspirations. First, it incorporated an appeal to the early African church heritage, especially during the early centuries of the church. Second, it expressed a yearning for an African spirituality, for the spirituality inherited from the missionaries was foreign to Africans. Third, it asserted the validity of African cultural identity in the church; Africans were tired of

---

57. Hayford, *Ethiopia Unbound*, 100.
58. "Editorial," *Gold Coast Leader*, April 20, 1907.
59. Ibid.
60. Sarbah, *Fanti National Constitution*, 256.
61. George Shepperson, "Ethiopianism: Past and Present," in Baëta, *Christianity in Tropical Africa*, 251.

being cast in the image of European and American missionaries. Fourth, this search for African cultural identity was also in varying degrees a quest for pan-Africanism.[62]

Many Designations, One Gospel

The plethora of designations for human attempts to dialogue about engagement with the Word of God and about human encounter with the Numinous in the real world is a reminder that theological constructs do not descend from heaven like a bride adorned for her husband. A theological construct is a dialogical engagement between the Numinous—especially as made manifest in the revealed Word of God—and the experience(s) of people, as well as the culture of a particular people, including the socio-political-economic challenges they face. In the early church, personal issues, nationalisms, social and economic strains, rivalries between sees, liturgical disputes, problems of discipline, and puritan ideas of church not only caused schisms, but they also formed the background of theological and doctrinal statements forged by the early church.[63] Theology in Africa is not and could not be any different. The epithets black, African, liberation, and reconstruction in theology are reminders of the contexts that spawned particular formations of theology and that, as mentioned, sometimes ran parallel to the agendas of politicians.

The manifold yearnings for African identity in the encounter with the gospel are long-standing. Not only are they consistent with the gospel's core message of the incarnation and with the practice of the church as it has spread around the globe, but they also express a desire to take lessons from the fate of the church in the Maghreb. A thriving church was present in Roman North Africa from as early as AD 180. It produced theologians such as Tertullian, Cyprian of Carthage, and Augustine of Hippo Regius, whose theological production indelibly influenced the Church of the West. But the North African church fell before the Muslim onslaught because North African Christianity did not engage the native Berbers. Prefabricated imported standards are insufficient for judging theological excellence; in Africa, theological excellence must also be judged by what speaks to the condition of homo africanus.

---

62. Pobee and Ositelu, *African Initiatives in Christianity*, 23.
63. Greenslade, *Schism In the Early Church*.

7

Is There an African Theology and What Is It?

CHRISTIAN THEOLOGY CAME TO Africa via the missionary movement and was implanted in conjunction with the various phases of the North Atlantic incursion into Africa. Those who came to Africa brought what they had and knew, including both peoples and cultures. Consequently, structures and uses were planted in Africa that had their raison d'etre in Europe, and Africans became caught in a North Atlantic captivity. They could ingest and regurgitate the foreign theological artifacts, but they were never at home in those constructs. An earlier chapter mentioned the highly critical reception that the Aborigines Rights Protection Society of the Gold Coast and also Ethiopianism afforded to theological constructs imported from Europe. Expressions of dissatisfaction with what the missionaries assumed were "normal" arrangements for mission, theology, and theological education were voiced quite early. In expressing their discontent, Africans were raising the question, "How might Africans *feel at home* in the construction of theology, theological education, and mission?" By implication, a vision of the possibility of an African style and approach in theology can be seen to have been present very early. Perhaps more surprising was the absence of an outright rejection of Christianity and its constructs per se.

At one time, using the language of African theology was dismissed by some as merely African nationalism donning the clothes of religion and theology. But the fact that the proponents of African theology did not reject Christianity outright as being only a face of the colonial onslaught on Africa, coupled with the fact that Africa has today become the heartland of world Christianity, suggests the inadequacy of that thesis.

Before independence, African peoples were oriented more to the colonial metropoles than to the African countries next door to them. The colonial languages—especially English, French, and Portuguese—formed part of the metropole-periphery complex and proved to be obstacles to free communication between African countries. The independence movement, when it came, threw open the gates and created opportunities for communication between Africans and across Africa. The new situation made possible not only movements across borders but also the translation of works in French into English and vice versa. Thus the writings of Bénézet Bujo and

Jean-Marc Ela in French have appeared in English translations to the enrichment of studies in our respective corners.

In the 1980s African American theologians at times expressed dissatisfaction with African theology, criticizing it for being held in dialogue with African cultures. They wanted us to show greater appreciation for their version of black theology and liberation theology. Some of us, however, were not satisfied with the idea of placing African theology and black theology in opposition to each other, for all theologies are responses to the challenges posed by their context, as the earlier chapter "What Is Theology?" attempted to argue. Because of the missionary practice of treating the African as a tabula rasa, Africans felt themselves entangled in captivity to North Atlantic theological constructs. In its own way, African theology was an attempt to become freed from that North Atlantic captivity. African theology sought to translate the logic of Christianity's core message of the incarnation into an African idiom. Throughout history Christianity has taken on the color and hue of the places it has gone. The Semitic, Latin (Roman), Greek, and many other forms of Christianity are each statements of the one gospel. No apology needs to be made for the fact of African theology, as its development is consistent with the core of Christian faith and the historical practice of the church. I used to enjoy reminding my Latin American and African American colleagues verbally that any attempt to cajole African theologians into giving up African theology for their mintings of the gospel was imperialistic.

The life and the teaching of Jesus supply the impetus for pursuing African theology. His use of parables to inculcate spiritual truths gives an example of teaching that starts from the known, everyday things, and proceeds to the unknown and mysterious challenges. Following Jesus' example, African theologies start from African epistemology, ontology, and challenges so as to address them in the light of the gospel.

African Epistemology and Ontology

My use of the language of African epistemology and ontology is by design. The terms refer not only to culture—which provides Africans' identity and their wavelength for engaging in communication—but also to their social, economic, and political circumstances and challenges. Politicians in Africa have been known to consult spirit-beings and spirit-agents to seek protection, guidance, and success in their political ventures. In modern economic ventures Africans of all manners of description have been known to consult spiritual beings and gods in their quest for success. The same African politician or economist who piously speaks of keeping religion out of economics and politics may be consulting shrines. I refer to this phenomenon as "double insurance," a practice that is not uncommon in African societies.

African theology, whatever else it does, is an attempt to accompany homo africanus in an informed and critical way as Africans negotiate their religious-spiritual epistemology and ontology in the arenas of social, economic, and political life. This pastoral effort gives significance to publications by African theologians such as Laurenti Magesa and Jean B. Zoa, archbishop of Yaounde, Cameroon.[1]

The communitarian epistemology and ontology of African societies—that binds together the present (that is, the living), the dead (the living ancestors), and the future (the yet to be born or posterity)—has been creatively used by the Sierra Leonean Anglican theologian Harry Sawyerr as an avenue for understanding the Christian doctrine of *communio sanctorum* (communion of saints).[2] Sustained by the communitarian principle of the church, the living and the dead are made one through fellowship with God and the life of the Spirit.

Similarly, the Tanzanian Roman Catholic Camillus Lyimo pressed the communitarian epistemology and ontology of homo africanus into the service of *ujamaa* theology. *Ujamaa* is a political ideology associated with Mwalimu Julius Nyerere, founding president of Tanzania, that articulated five basic tenets of African belief: equality of all humans, sense of community, freedom, sharing, and real love. Lyimo writes that ujamaa theology "is not meant to be a theology of *ujamaa* politics or *ujamaa* economics. Yet, certain overtones of *ujamaa* politics will prevail, because we are never completely free from the ties of our political and economic environment. An *ujamaa* theology, therefore, is an attempt to consider how man, in his capacity to share as a being-in-community, ordered by divine will, can truly make life worth living on this earth of grass and dust, thus answering God's call on creation: 'Fill the earth and conquer it' (Gen 1:28)."[3] This statement by Lyimo is candid and it in some ways answers the ready dismissal offered by some, especially non-Africans, who scorn African theology as politics masquerading in the garb of theology.

In light of the foregoing, Lyimo continues,

> Theology is born of ideas and reflections. Unless the intellectuals of Africa in all fields share ideas and enrich each other there will scarcely be creativity. Shared reflections give way to a system of patterned thought. This in turn gives way to conviction and conviction to action. *Ujamaa* theology calls the politician, the theologian, the philosopher, the poet, the musician, the rural farmer, the tribal idler and the women, indeed everybody, to the sharing of ideas. Perhaps it is due to the inadequate sharing of ideas among ourselves [Africans] that renders us silent and dependent on the thoughts of others such that there is no mutual, spontaneous enrichment.[4]

Again, Lyimo strikes a sobering chord of warning when he states that all processes for constructing human community are subject to error and to fostering aberrations.

---

1. See the articles by Magesa, "Return to the World: Towards a 'Theocentric Existentialism' in Africa," 277–84, and "Catholic Yet African," 135–39, as well as Zoa, "Committed Christian Building a New Africa," 99–104.

2. Sawyerr, *Creative Evangelism*, 93–96, 111–12.

3. Lyimo, "The Quest for a Relevant African Theology," 141; see 140–43.

4. Ibid., 142.

He therefore calls on theology to be prophetic and practical: "The task of an *ujamaa* Christian, in building of human communities, is to criticize, not as an onlooker, but rather as one consciously and deliberately working hard, here and now, to share with others and bring about the transformation truly desired by God."[5]

Some African theologians have also argued for Christianity to be a unifying factor in a developing Africa.[6] In the later chapters "The Altar and the *Polis*" and "The Altar in the Marketplace," I will attempt to sketch examples of constructive Christian theology that extend the contribution of theology beyond the classroom or academy.

Experience shows that in Africa the churches have, time and again, picked up the casualties of bad economic and political adventures. Such moves are easily swept from view under the rubric of social welfare activity or as part of the social responsibility of the churches. But at the end of the day, the churches' shouldering of these responsibilities has a theological rationale. For they are attempts by the church to model the gospel of hope in very difficult and trying circumstances and to shore up the fundamental concern of religion and theology for humankind made in God's image and likeness.

Fear of Syncretism

The failure, if not the refusal, of Western missionaries to take the African context and reality seriously in theologizing was in part influenced by an almost pathological fear of syncretism and polytheism, which seemingly lay near the heart of African religion and society, and so of paganism. But here Max Warren's insightful critique of Western secular society is worth pondering.

> Without realizing it we have drifted back into the old polytheism against which the prophets of the Lord waged their great warfare. The real essence of paganism is that it divides the various concerns of man's life into compartments. There is one god for the soil; there is another god of the desert. The god of wisdom is quite different from the god of wine. If a man wants to marry he must pray at one temple; if he wants to make war, he must take his sacrifices elsewhere. All this is precisely where the modern paganism of our secular society has brought us today. Certain portions of our life we call religious. Then we are Christians. We use a special language.[7]

African theology, following the holistic epistemology and ontology of Africans, forms a kind of protest against opposing the sacred and the secular to each other, and it embraces a commitment to the recovery of a holistic understanding of society, reality, and life. Seen in that light, African theology has no apology to make; it is staking a

---

5. Ibid., 142.
6. See, e.g., Omoyajowo, "Christianity as a Unifying Factor in a Developing Country," 74–79.
7. Max Warren, as cited in Lehmann, *Ethics in a Christian Context*, 85.

claim to a place around the throne of grace where all peoples are invited to take their place to sing the Creator's praise and glory.

The attempt to hold catholicity/universality and incarnation/contextuality together is often bedeviled by a pathological fear of syncretism. The issue is to distinguish the kernel of the basic Christian revelation and faith from their husk or incarnated form, difficult as that is. When the kernel and the husk have been identified and isolated, the agenda is to seek for dynamic equivalents and to pursue a dynamic understanding of tradition. Lamin Sanneh writes, "Biblical material was submitted to the regenerative capacity of African perception and the result would be Africa's unique contribution to the story of Christianity."[8]

Excessive fear of syncretism overlooks the fact that religion is a cultural product. But bearing the impress of our culture is not something to be feared, especially when we remember that full embedment in culture is affirmed by the incarnation of Christ—the very place where God intervened decisively. Indeed, as Boff reminds us, "The Church as a structure is as syncretistic as any other expression. Pure Christianity does not exist, never has existed, never can exist.... What exists concretely is always the Church, the historical-cultural expression and religious objectification of Christianity.... Catholicism is a grandiose and infinitely complex syncretism.... Syncretism, then, is not necessarily evil nor does it represent pathology of pure religion. It is a normal condition of the Incarnation, expression and objectification of a religious faith or expression."[9] Before becoming singularly exercised about syncretism, let us all—as Christians, churchmen, and theologians—remove the beam from our own eyes.

---

8. Sanneh, *West African Christianity*, 180.
9. Boff, *Church, Charism, and Power*, 92–93.

8

Multitudes before the Lamb: Pluralism and Theology

THE TITLE OF THIS chapter is in part a paraphrase of Revelation 7:9–11 (MSG): "I saw a huge crowd, too huge to count. Everyone was there—all nations and tribes, all races and languages. And they were . . . standing before the Throne and the Lamb and heartily singing [praise to God]." The book of Revelation is an apocalypse, a type of writing that abounds in symbolism so as to reveal an eschatological message. In Revelation with its context of persecution, two contrasting groups are immediately distinguished. On the one hand, those who will not accept pain and discomfort quickly become apostates, "profaning the Holy name" YHWH (*Hillul-Ha-Shem*; see Lev 22:32). On the other hand are those who refuse to deny their faith commitment—"sanctifying the Holy Name" (*Hallul-Ha-Shem*)—and who are ready to pay the price of faithfulness. Those who have held on through thick and thin become the multitudes who stand before the Lamb, praising God. Theology, like worship, bears testimony to the subject of study found in the Word, namely God. Bearing testimony is an obligation from which no force majeure could absolve a believer.

The multitudes who are faithful in bearing testimony about God and the Lamb are strikingly diverse. Not only are large numbers of people present, but also, and perhaps more striking, the multitudes include persons from all nations, all ethnicities, all races, all cultures, all languages, all identities—and we may add, all genders, all ages, and all religions. The ecumenical vision and imperative bear the mark of this inclusive vision. Indeed, as the Deutero-Pauline Letter to the Church of Ephesus articulates it, this inclusive vision was God's "long range plan in which everything would be brought together and summed up in him [Christ], everything in deepest heaven, everything on planet earth" (1:10 MSG). In this vision we see ultimate convergence in God, giving recognition to the Creator of all as the sovereign Lord of all life and history.

Rainbow Nation

Preceding chapters have discussed various designations for theological construction in Africa. Each of them presupposes the world of peoples, who all are obliged to give account of faith, not losing sight in the process of the common worship of the one Creator of all and the common humanity of all. The immediately preceding chapters drew attention to the way pathological fear of and obsession with polytheism and syncretism undermine ability to have a holistic vision of life. The crowds that are emphasized in Revelation 7—in which all nations, tribes, and so forth have their place at worship around God's throne—provide another option for a holistic epistemology and ontology. In that light, Desmond Tutu's use of the language of the "rainbow nation" in speaking of South Africa, his native land, is most appealing; it is consistent with and corroborates the plea for holism.

In the name of the ideology of apartheid, South Africa had introduced a law that forcibly separated peoples into four racial categories: White, African, Indian, and Coloured, with the fourth group including the original natives, the Khoisan. On December 5, 1991, while preaching in Tromsö, Norway, north of the Arctic Circle, Tutu said,

> At home in South Africa I have sometimes said in big meetings where you have black and white together: "Raise your hands!" Then I've said: "Move your hands" and I've said "Look at your hands—different colours representing different people. You are the rainbow people of God." Remember, the rainbow in the Bible is a sign of peace. The rainbow is a sign of prosperity. We want peace, prosperity and justice and we can have it when all the people of God, the rainbow people of God, work together.[1]

The language of the rainbow nation has caught on in post-apartheid South Africa. When Tutu introduced the phrase, it was a dream. It was an eschatological vision that, in religious language, yearned for realization of the vision of a common humanity made in God's image and likeness. It was a vision in which all together enjoy peace and prosperity, dignity and justice. It was a statement of ecumenical theology.

If Tutu used rainbow language of South Africa, we dare to extend it to Rainbow Africa and even Rainbow World.

There Is Something in a Name

When I entered the University College of Ghana in 1957 to embark on the scientific study of the phenomenon of religion, the department within the Faculty of Arts in which I enrolled was styled the Department of Divinity. Upon graduation, students were awarded the Bachelor of Divinity (BD) of the University of London, with which the University College of Ghana had a special relationship. When I returned to it as

---

1. Cited in *African Ecclesiastical Review* (AFER) 16, no. 3 (1973) 278–80.

a lecturer in 1966, after completing graduate studies at the Divinity School of the University of Cambridge, the department had been redesignated as the Department for the Study of Religions. Was the change a cosmetic one or a telltale? Elsewhere the same discipline is styled theology. What prompted the change of designation? What story does it tell? At the very least, it adumbrated a vision of an inclusive society, the need for theological study to foster the building of a community of communities.

African culture, like the Christian faith tradition, is replete with names that tell a story, such as Immanuel (God with us, Matt 1:23). Names tell a story; they state a fact as told from a particular perspective. And that fact or history or story as it is retold is shaped by other factors such as nationalism and even fantasies. And so, the name *ecclesia anglicana* reminds us that whatever the truth and historical facts, the Anglican Church is the English minting of the one holy, catholic, and apostolic church. That observation brings us back to the word "context" and to a reminder that changes to particular expressions indicate that something else is also going on.

Significantly, the Department of Divinity at Legon was renamed the Department for the Study of Religions after the Gold Coast became the independent nation-state of Ghana and the University College of the Gold Coast became the University of Ghana. As C. G. Baëta, a principal architect of the new designation, puts it, Nkrumah, the nationalist leader of Ghana who described himself as a "Marxian and non-denominational Christian," engaged the staff to express his unease and unhappiness with the department's name. The designation inherited from colonial days sounded sectarian, focusing on the Christian religion. His government would find it difficult and unjust to continue supporting a sectarian department.[2] Critics interpreted this statement as the antireligion attitude of a Marxist. But the critics' response missed the real point of Nkrumah's stance. For one thing, the Constitution of Ghana avowed the nation to be a secular state in the sense that no one religion could be considered the official religion of the state. It was an option for freedom of conscience and of religion. It was an option for recognizing the truth of the facts on the ground in Ghana—both religions many and no religion. Pluralism characterized the religious scene in Ghana and, for that matter, in Africa as a whole, which features African Traditional Religions in their pluriformity, Christianity in its pluriformity of the sundered *Una Sancta*, Islam in its pluriformity of Sunni tradition (89 percent of the world's Muslims), Shi'i tradition (10 percent), and Kharijis and Ahmadiyya (together 1 percent), plus Hinduism and some Buddhism.

Let Baëta speak again, giving the rationale for establishing the Department for the Study of Religions at the University of Ghana. He writes, "It is not religions at all that were being placed side by side under one roof . . . [but] people, men of different faiths. . . . What are the fundamental assumptions . . . underlying schemes of study in which Christian and Muslim themes, as well as topics from Primal Indigenous African religions are arranged to correspond with one another according to the sub-areas in which they arise and interlace with the same syllabuses? What is the basis of

---

2. Baëta, *Relationships of Christians with Men of Other Living Faiths*, 2.

this symbiosis of persons and subjects of study? Since the three religious traditions in question claim so widely divergent truths, what philosophy of Truth is here in play?"[3]

The change of name was not cosmetic. It reminds us that in discourse about the God-Word, in Africa at any rate, we must be mindful to take the plurality of religions seriously, and that theology as a discipline or institution must aim at developing human beings as God, the Almighty, Creator, and Savior, has designed them to live in this one world. God created, and none may dare to disenfranchise the other. As we face religious pluralism, we are obliged to be in dialogue with other human beings, even if our faith persuasions and commitments differ. An attitude that reflects humble, personal, human engagement and relevance is the bottom line of the encounter. African countries are religiously pluralistic. Acknowledgedly, in some cases religious pluralism has worked out to be religious syncretism.[4] That aspect of religious pluralism need not detain us here.

Pluralism is identified by Gerald Lenski as a "situation in which organized groups with incompatible beliefs and practices are obliged to co-exist within the framework of the same country or same society."[5] The accompanying table provides a snapshot of religious pluralism in Africa today.[6]

Country	Christianity	Islam	Traditional religions and other religions
Algeria	1.0	99.0	0.0
Angola	95.0	0.5	4.5
Benin	42.8	24.4	32.8
Botswana	71.6	0.3	28.1
Burkina Faso	23.0	61.0	16.0
Burundi	75.0	5.0	20.0
Cameroon	69.2	20.9	9.9
Cape Verde	99.0	0.0	1.0
Central African Republic	80.3	10.1	9.6
Chad	34.0	53.0	13.0
Democratic Republic of the Congo	95.8	1.2	12.9
Djibouti	6.0	94.0	0.0
Egypt	10.0	90.0	0.0
Equatorial Guinea	93.0	1.0	6.0
Eritrea	62.5	36.5	1.0
Ethiopia	62.8	33.9	3.3

3. Ibid., 8.

4. Pierce, "Restless Spirits," 68–77.

5. Lenski, "Religious Pluralism," 25.

6. The table "Religious Affiliation in Africa by Country as Percent of Population" has been adapted from "Religion in Africa," http://www.wikipedia.org/wiki/religion_in_Africa.

Country	Christianity	Islam	Traditional religions and other religions
Gabon	73.0	10.0	17
Gambia	9.0	90.0	1.0
Ghana	71.2	17.6	11.2
Guinea	10.0	85.0	5.0
Guinea-Bissau	10.0	50.0	40.0
Kenya	78.0	10.0	12.0
Lesotho	90.0	0.0	10.0
Liberia	85.5	12.2	2.2
Libya	1.0	97.0	2.0
Madagascar	41.0	7.0	52.0
Malawi	79.9	12.8	7.3
Mauritius	32.2	16.6	51.2
Mozambique	56.1	17.9	26.0
Morocco	1.1	98.7	0.2
Namibia	90.0	0.0	10.0
Niger	5.0	90.0	5.0
Nigeria	50.8	47.8	1.4
Réunion	84.9	2.1	13.0
Rwanda	93.6	4.6	1.8
Sahrawi Arab Democratic Republic	0.0	100.0	0.0
São Tomé and Príncipe	97.0	2.0	1.0
Senegal	5.0	94.0	1.0
Seychelles	93.1	1.1	5.8
Sierra Leone	21.0	77.0	2.0
Somalia	0.0	100.0	0.0
South Africa	79.7	1.5	18.8
South Sudan	60.5	6.2	32.9
Sudan	3.0	97.0	0.0
Swaziland	90.0	1.0	9.0
Tanzania	61.0	35.0	4.0
Togo	29.0	20.0	51.0
Tunisia	1.0	98.0	1.0
Uganda	84.0	12.0	4.0
Zambia	87.0	1.0	12.0
Zimbabwe	84.0	1.0	15.0

Table 8.1 Religious Affiliation in Africa by Country as Percent of Population

Muslims outnumber Christians in several West African countries, not to mention the countries of North Africa. I suggest that the principle that should guide and inform the encounter of religions is the Golden Rule; we should do to others as we would have them do to us. This stance requires us to go beyond dogma and to see religion as fundamentally about commitment to what is human, or, to use biblical language, to view humanity as made in God's image and likeness and therefore entitled to dignity and honor.

Allow me to unpack the implications of pluralism. First, there is one, single, same, and common space, be it community, society, country, or world. Second, present in that one space are different, divergent, and even incompatible beliefs and practices. Third, the foregoing scenario imposes on everyone the duty to consciously and conscientiously manage pluralism in such a way as to secure the humanity, dignity, and well-being of each and all who answer to the description of "human in the image and likeness of God." Management of religious pluralism, however, is often waylaid by power games, with ensuing tensions and violence, as, for example, in Sudan. For convenience, the following discussion will be limited to African Traditional Religions, Christianity, Islam, and Judaism.

Often discussions of religious pluralism have not taken African Traditional Religions as seriously as they should. In part this neglect has been a consequence of the fact that African Traditional Religions have not been as well written about as the other religions. This lacuna has led many observers to miss the important truth that in traditional African societies "there is little or no differentiation [between religion and ordinary life]. The familial, political, educational/economic spheres of life were part and parcel of the whole social fabric."[7] The Enlightenment's separation of religion from social life simply does not fit the traditional African's life story. African Traditional Religions "serve to create a 'cosmos' and a sacred canopy overarching all the affairs of human life."[8] In consequence, Africans have a religious epistemology and ontology; their African identity, including its religious aspects, has been taken in with their mothers' milk. That identity has lasting priority. Even when an African welcomes another religion, it is truer to describe the situation as "I am first an African and, second, a Christian."[9] This statement should not be surprising for it is consistent with the picture given in Revelation 7:9–11. Therefore, quick resort to the label of syncretism for describing the welcome given by Africans to other religions is a judgment that is not helpful. In any case, Christianity itself—because of its core message of the incarnation—has a track record of being syncretistic. That is what incarnation entails.

---

7. Hodges, *Conflict and Consensus*, 373–74; J. Max Assimeng, "Historical Legacy, Political Realities, and Tensions in Africa," in Rajashaker, Pobee, and Schön, *Encounter of Religions*, 3.

8. Berger, *Sacred Canopy*.

9. Pobee, "I Am First an African and, Second, a Christian," 268–77.

The Threat Posed by Access to Political Power

To speak of "giving an account of our faith and hope" is to describe theology as acting in service to the mission of the community of faith. But the history of missions suggests that cultivating the gospel in a particular context is done in company with some ideology or other. One such ideology is that of power, namely, Christendom. During her first three centuries, the Christian church underwent persecution time and again. When Constantine the Great, the Roman emperor from 306 to 337, following an ecstatic experience at the Milvian Bridge in 312, acknowledged Christianity as part of a "joint system," Christianity became a *religio licita*. By this pronouncement it gained the status of being one of the licensed or permitted religions of the empire. Emperor Theodosius I (379–95) advanced Christianity's standing in the Roman Empire further by making it the empire's sole authorized religion.[10] Emperor Justinian I (483–565) developed the idea further in *Res publica Christiana*, which enunciated a vision of one empire, one ruler, one religion.[11]

These developments led to arrogance and intolerance on the part of the Christian ruler and the Christian church. Constantine's experience at the Milvian Bridge claimed the sanction of Christianity for warfare, rather a departure from Jesus' teaching that "all who take the sword will perish by the sword" (Matt 26:52 NRSV). The overall effect was to deny freedom of conscience to non-Christians. In 415 Christian mobs tore Hypatia, at the time the world's leading mathematician and a Neoplatonist lecturer, to pieces in Alexandria. By allowing the emperor to meddle in internal church affairs, Christians mortgaged the future of Christian liberty. State protection of the church was simultaneously terrible, onerous, and embarrassing.[12] The ideology of Christendom allowed the secular ruler to interfere in the affairs of the church, including in doctrinal disputes. The spirit of establishment to which the Christian church became accustomed informed Christian missions and theology when they were brought from Europe to Africa.

Two examples can serve to show the spirit that an establishment ideology generates. The first example comes from St. Cyprian (d. 258), who declared that "*extra ecclesiam nulla salus est*" (there is no salvation outside the church).[13] Stated crudely, non-Christian religions were dismissed as non-religions that were to be suppressed, if not eradicated. The same attitude marked the launch of Protestant Christian missions. Richard Sibbes (1577–1635), a founding father of Protestant missions, asserted that "the Spirit of God does not dwell in unregenerate nature, in men who are not men."[14]

---

10. Meyendorff, *Imperial Unity and Christian Divisions*, chap. 1; Reston, *Defenders of the Faith*; King, *Emperor Theodosius and the Establishment of Christianity*.

11. Reston, *Warriors of God*; Reston, *Dogs of God*.

12. Jones, *Constantine and the Conversion of Europe*; Baynes, *Constantine the Great and the Christian Church*.

13. Cyprian, *Letter 73*; Cyprian, *On the Unity of the Church*; see Augustine, *De Baptismo*.

14. Sibbes, sermon at Cambridge University, quoted in Rooy, *Theology of Missions in the Puritan*

What this attitude meant on the ground was made manifest in the missionary practice of the ideology of the tabula rasa.

Taking such a stance makes it impossible even to attempt to dialogue with adherents of non-Christian religions. It also issues in violence, something that was recognized and sanctioned by the *doctor communis* and *doctor angelicus*, Thomas Aquinas (1225–74). He stated,

> From the point of view of heretics themselves there is their sin, by which they have deserved not only to be separated from the Church, but to be eliminated from the world by death. For it is a far graver matter to corrupt the faith, which is the life of the soul, than to falsify money, which sustains temporal life. So if it be just that forgers and other malefactors are put to death without mercy by the secular authority, with how much greater reason may heretics be not only excommunicated but also put to death, when once they are convicted of heresy.[15]

Intolerance and even violence against schismatics, heretics, and people of other faiths has a long history in the church. During the Donatist controversy, Augustine of Hippo argued that the use of violence against heretics and schismatics was justified.[16] Indeed, Pope Innocent II (1198–1216), in a letter to the magistrate of Viterbo, March 25, 1199, wrote, "*Longe sit gravius aeternam quam temporalem laedere majestatem*" (it is infinitely more serious to offend against the Divine majesty than to injure human majesty).[17] In this way the stage was set for abuse of human rights and acts of violence against those who did not accept the normative or dominant statement of the Christian faith. Such thinking provided the rationale for the Inquisition and the Crusades.[18]

Within the ideology of Christendom everything is seen and defined in terms of dogma, which divides. Those who do not subscribe strictly to some particular doctrinal statement or formula are viewed as outsiders and possibly as enemies who must be compelled to comply. It is striking how church leaders have used the biblical phrase "compel them to come in" (Luke 14:23 KJV) to justify the use of force and violence against those who do not subscribe to their particular statement of belief. For example, in addressing the Donatist schism, Augustine cited the passage to justify using force against the Donatists.[19] Such an outlook shifts from seeing religion as being about what is fundamentally human to being consumed with affirmation of a dogma.

A similar close linkage between religion and politics is to be found in Islam as far back as the Prophet Muhammad himself. In Mecca his attempts to create a frame of mind receptive to his teaching had been frustrated. Then in 621, he was invited

---

Tradition, 30.

15. Aquinas, *Summa Theologica*, 2.2, 14, qu. 2, art. 3.
16. Augustine, *Epistle* 93 5.17; *Epistle* 175 17.
17. E. Vacandard, "Inquisition," in Hastings, *Encyclopaedia of Religion and Ethics*, 8:330.
18. Greenslade, *Schism in the Early Church*.
19. Augustine, *Epistle* 93 2.5.

to Medina. It looks, however, as though ulterior motives were involved in the invitation: two warring clans, the Aws and Khazraj, needed his influence. Muhammad was designated Prophet (of God) and Ruler. The "house of Islam," comprising immigrants from Mecca, Aws, Khazraj, and Jews, was ruled by "God and His Apostle." The head of state was Allah, but he ruled through an executive who enforced the law. That was a political and social necessity. The "house of Islam" was at once a religious, political, economic, and legal entity. When Muhammad died, a caliph was installed, who served as the secular and religious head of the Muslim state.

Historically, Islamic religious opinion and authority have weighed heavily on the character of secular or civil authority. In the Sunni tradition the institution of the *ulama* has been composed of religious teachers and jurists who, though having no direct power, have exercised influence by force of personality and persuasion. In Shi'i Islam the equivalent of the ulama have been known as the *mujtahide*.

The development in both Christianity and Islam of strong linkages between religious and secular authority has meant that the two religions have encountered each other not only as faith traditions but also as rival power blocks. Thus the Theodosian arrangement of 380 set the stage for epochal conflicts twelve centuries later between Islam, led by Suleyman I, and Christendom, led by Charles V. It was a collision of two worlds, Islamic and Christian, with skirmishes and epic sieges from Hungary to Rhodes—and ultimately to Vienna, which, if Suleyman had won, would have caused Europe to become Muslim as far west as the Rhine. In all these the embrace of Islam was as much political as religious. Rulers were considered to be sinless and infallible by divine right, and down the line Baghdad became the Rome of Islam.

Attention was drawn earlier to traditional African society's religious and spiritual epistemology and ontology. That epistemology and ontology, as would be expected, became manifest through African sociopolitical organization. Traditional African systems are of roughly four types: acephalous societies (ethnic groups without chiefs) such as the Dagaba of Ghana and the Igbos and Tiv of Nigeria; centralized societies (ethnic groups with kingdoms ruled by chiefs) such as the Akan of Ghana, Yoruba of Nigeria, Buganda of Uganda, Swazi of Swaziland, and Zulu of South Africa; "politics as kinship writ large" (the clan leader is head of the polity), for example, the Kojokrom of Western Ghana; and age-based societies such as the Maasai and other peoples in East Africa. [20] Clearly the religious situation of African societies is complex and much too broad to be addressed in a single chapter. But the one case of a single people, the Akan of Ghana, may be illustrative.

Among the Akan, chieftainship was a composite role; the same person was at once judge, commander-in-chief, legislator, executive, and administrative head of

---

20. Igbos were overwhelmingly acephalous, but not all were, for "a few notable Igbo towns such as Onitsha . . . had kings called Obi, and places like the Nri Kingdom and Arochukwu . . . had priest kings" (https://en.wikipedia.org/wiki/Igbo_people#cite_note-society-38). See Fortes and Evans-Pritchard, *African Political Systems*; Middleton and Tait, *Tribes without Rulers*; Richards, *East African Chiefs*; Smith, *Government in Zazzau, 1800–1950*.

the community. The most important role was a sacred one because mystical values intruded into the systems for administering law and order. The chief represented the community, its permanence, solidarity, and continuity.[21] Akan society's encounter with the Christian church took the form of an engagement between traditional religion and the foreign religion along with that religion's practice of the missionary ideology of the tabula rasa. Thus the challenge of pluralism was not only a three-cornered engagement of African Tradition Religion, Christianity, and Islam; it also entailed sociopolitical engagement. Such engagement cannot be limited to doctrinal or dogmatic issues. It also requires sensitivity to other religionists, who at the end of the day must be recognized as fully human, just as are any others.

Clash of Civilizations

In 1993 Samuel P. Huntington, Eaton Professor of the Science of Government and director of the John M. Olin Institute of Strategic Studies, Harvard University, introduced the phrase "clash of civilizations" into political discourse.[22] His article was not first of all a study in religion or theology; it was a project addressing "the changing security environment and American national interest." But, he argued, coming clashes would not be the result of rivalries between nation-states or be occasioned by the rise of tribalism at the expense of nation-states. "The great divisions among humankind and the dominating source of conflict will be cultural," he predicted; they would, therefore, be between civilizations.[23] Such civilizations are many: Chinese, Anglophone, Western, Latin American, and Arab among them. Islamic civilization has Arab, Turkish, and Malay subdivisions.

The great divisions between civilizations relate to basic differences of history, language, cultural traditions, and views on relations between God and humanity. They are tied to "appropriate" relations between individuals and the group, citizens and the state, parents and children, husbands and wives, and to differences in how responsibility, liberty, authority, equality, and humanity are perceived. Against the backdrop of today's globalized village, consciousness of particular identities becomes heightened. Hence we encounter talk of Asianization in Japan, the Hinduization of India, Westernization, Russianization, and so forth. Huntington suggests that "even more than ethnicity, religion discriminates sharply and exclusively among people."[24] Religious identity is sometimes mixed up with economic factors, as we find with the Economic Cooperation Organization Free Trade Agreement of 2003 among ten Muslim countries: Afghanistan, Azerbaijan, Iran, Kazakhstan, Kyrgyzstan, Pakistan, Tajikistan, Turkey, Turkmenistan, and Uzbekistan.

---

21. See Busia, *The Position of the Chief in the Modern Political System of Ashanti*.
22. Huntington, "The Clash of Civilizations?," 22–49.
23. Ibid., 22.
24. Ibid., 27.

With all these developments go fault lines. Thus Europe is divided between Western Christianity, on the one hand, and Orthodox Christianity, on the other hand. It would not be surprising if the clash between the West and the Muslim world that has been identified were to take a violent form. This analysis suggests that religion, more than being a faith tradition, is a culture and a civilization—and encounters between religions and cultures and civilizations can issue in violence. "Such clash as exists because of a world of clashing civilizations . . . is inevitably a world of double standards: people apply one standard to their kin countries and a different standard to others."[25]

The situation is roiled further by the character of the relationships between the West (allegedly Christian) and the rest of the world (often similarly thought of as being coterminous with non-Christian religions). Huntington writes,

> The West dominates international political and security institutions. . . . Global political and security issues are effectively settled by a directorate of the United States, Britain and France, world economic issues by a directorate of the United States, Germany and Japan, all of which maintain extraordinary close relations with each other to the exclusion of lesser and largely non-Western countries. Decisions made at the U.N. Security Council or in the International Monetary Fund that reflect the interests of the West are presented to the world as the desires of the world community. The very phrase "world community" has become the euphemistic collective noun (replacing "Free World") to give global legitimacy to actions reflecting the interests of the United States and other Western powers. Through the IMF and other international economic institutions, the West promotes its economic interests and imposes on other nations the economic policies it thinks appropriate.[26]

The language of a clash of civilizations, whatever its original meaning, has been heard as a clash between Christian civilization and Islamic civilization. In this regard three expressions have arisen that muddy the waters: Islam, Islamism, and Islamist extremists. Islam refers to the religion. And so Donald Rumsfeld states that Islamism "is not a religion but a totalitarian political ideology that seeks the destruction of all liberal democratic governments, of our individual rights, and of Western civilization. The ideology not only excuses but commands violence against the United States, our allies, and other free people. It exalts deaths and martyrdom. And it is rooted in a radical, minority interpretation of Islam."[27] It hardly needs to be pointed out that as a political statement, Rumsfeld's comment is economical with the truth.

Again, Rumsfeld writes,

> According to their own utterances, writings, and propaganda, Islamists seek to reestablish the caliphate, an empire that stretched from Spain to India in

---

25. Ibid., 36.
26. Ibid., 39.
27. Rumsfeld, *Known and Unknown*, 353–54.

the tenth century, and expand it around the globe. The network of our terrorist enemies comprises a diverse group of people, but what links them are totalitarian, expansionist, and revolutionary distortions of Islam. Some Islamist ideals are represented by Shia ayatollahs in Iran; others by bin Laden and Sunni al-Qaida terrorists in Pakistan. All Islamists, however, promote replacement of the world's international system of nation-states with a single theocratic empire that imposes and enforces sharia (Muslim holy law). Islamist ideology rejects democracy, civil liberties, and laws made by men. Those of us who embrace such practices are despised and detested as an insult to Allah. Though his statement was mocked and ridiculed by some, President Bush was correct—profoundly so—when he said the terrorists who struck on 9/11 "hate our freedoms—our freedom of religion, our freedom of speech, our freedom to vote and assemble and disagree with each other."[28]

It is perhaps not without interest that Rumsfeld should choose to use the term "Islamist" rather than the word "Muslim," the proper name for an adherent of the religion of Islam. Use of the term "Islamist," which sounds rather like the name of the religion of Islam, not only signals the ideologization of Islam but also guarantees hostility and peddles enemy imagery against Muslims. For in the United States, perceptions of the religion of Islam are not infrequently confused by Islamophobia and mixed with images of violence. Added to that, a palpable suspicion exists of anything that sounds Muslim or Islamic.

In negotiating religious pluralism we are to be warned against anything that may look or sound like peddling of enemy-images. Characterizing someone as an enemy does not make for peace, nor does it deeply know and recognize the other person as also bearing the image and likeness of God. It fosters alienation. In any case, the teaching of Jesus to love our neighbor as ourselves is at no point exclusive of the other. We may dislike and even disapprove of a particular religion or its manifestations. But we are not allowed to hate the person who holds a particular belief.

In this regard, I turn to Emmanuel Lévinas (1906–95), a Lithuanian Jew, who took French citizenship in 1930 and taught philosophy at the Universities of Poitiers, Nantes, and Paris. In a book written in French and later translated into German as *Die Zeit und der Andere*, he introduced an expressive phrase: "to heed the heteronomous call."[29] We are called to feel the cry and the pain of the other person, whatever his or her identity. In an interreligious encounter, all participants must endeavor to hear the cry and pain of the other person, whatever the religion.

I have intentionally dwelt at length on plurality of religions as enmeshed in plurality of cultures and civilizations and not consisting simply of a certain number of faith traditions so as to draw attention to the fact that religion is part of a complex

---

28. Ibid., 721–22.

29. Lévinas, *Die Zeit und der Andere*; Lévinas, *Humanisme de l'autre homme*; El-Bizri, "Uneasy Meditations Following Lévinas," 293–315.

whole. What may be paraded as an encounter between religions often contains other strands, economic and political. Seeing religion as entwined with multiple other cultural strands, however, fits well with an understanding of culture as a composite construct of values and customs. The view of religions and cultures as composites helps us to clarify fundamental differences between an individualistic as distinct from a communitarian epistemology and ontology—and the consequences that flow from each for liberalism, constitutionalism, human rights, equality, liberty, rule of law, democracy, free market, and separation of church and state.

Despite all good intentions, acts of interreligious violence have taken place all over the world. India, which prides itself on being the world's largest democratic nation, has experienced horrific interreligious strife and violence. The destruction of the Mosque of Babur, in Ayodhya, Uttar Pradesh, in December 1992, in this predominantly Hindu nation, is a key example. In Africa, Egypt, Nigeria, and Sudan have experienced interreligious strife and violence. So part of the agenda for African theology is to explore ways of cultivating interreligious peace, while being mindful of the non-specifically religious components that are present, and ways to give practical meaning and expression to Lévinas's instructive phrase.

To suggest that Islam qua Islam is violent and averse to peace is a caricature, if not a falsification, of true Islam. A Muslim begins encounters with other humans with the greeting "*Al-Salaamu alaikum wa baraka tahu*" (peace be upon you and the mercy and blessings of God). If Muslims have been violent, it is not because Islam as a religion is violent; other factors have intervened, for instance, the political solvent in which Christianity, like Islam, has been soaked. One need only call to mind Christendom and the memory of the Crusades, with the sense of exclusion and marginalization they conveyed.

Some, however, would contest the position just enunciated on two grounds. The first relates to the traditional greeting of "*al-salaamu alaikum*" (peace be upon you). When the greeting is uttered, the full response or returning greeting is "*al-salaamu alaikum wa rahmatullahi wa barakatahu*" (peace be upon you and the mercy of Allah and blessing). It has been argued that originally use of these greetings was restricted and that they were only licit for exchange between Muslims. On the question of exchanging *salaam* with non-Muslims, the Prophet said, "Do not greet the Jews and the Christians with *salaam*. However, if they *salaam* first, we may reply by saying *wa alaikum* (and upon you)."[30]

Second, if as argued earlier, that (following Constantine's conversion and after he had ordered and supervised the Council of Nicea) it was the political solvent that made Christians violent, in a similar way, Islam was marked politically by the *hijra* when Muhammad fled Mecca in 622. On this reading, the political element appears to have been at the heart of Islam from its foundation. Further, Islam has never been a minority religion except at its margins, as, for example, when Muslims trade or live in

---

30. See http://www.missionislam.com/knowledge/salaam.htm.

a *kafir* country (land of nonbelievers). Examples would be the Mande-Dyula traders in precolonial Asante and the Muslim diaspora now living in Europe and the United States. It can be argued, therefore, that the political solvent seems to have belonged to Islam's inner core from its very beginning. The jury still seems to be out on the question of whether or not Islam as a religion is violent, but in several West African countries Muslims have not been violent.

The Particular and Peculiar Case of Siblings

Judaism and Christianity are connected if for no other reason than that Jesus, whose ministry brought Christian faith into existence, not only started in the Jewish synagogues of Nazareth and Capernaum but also articulated the connection as follows: "Do not think that I have come to abolish the law or the prophets. I have come not to abolish but to fulfill. Amen, I say to you, until heaven and earth pass away, not the smallest letter or the smallest part of a letter will pass from the law" (Matt 5:17–18 NABRE). Alan Segal writes, "So great is the contrast between previous Jewish religious systems and rabbinism, that Judaism and Christianity can essentially claim a twin birth. It is a startling truth that the religions we know today as Judaism and Christianity were born at the same time and nurtured in the same environment."[31] For these reasons they have been called Rebecca's children. For its part, Islam identifies Jews and Christians as *ahl-ul-kitab*, people of the Book. Along with Islam the two religions have their roots in the Scriptures of the Old Testament, which for each of them is a basic resource. According to the Quran, Judaism and Christianity are also *ahl-al-adhimma*, that is, people under protection.

Presently a special relationship exists between Islam and both Judaism and Christianity. Jews and Christians have, therefore, full rights of protection in Muslim society. Historically, a relationship has existed between *Muslim ummah* (Muslim community), *ahl-al-dhimmi*, and *ahl-al-kitab*. During the Middle Ages, socio-spiritual and intellectual interaction took place among the three. Judaism, Christianity, and Islam all take Abraham for their hero, and when the prophet Muhammad began his prophetic ministry, he claimed to be repeating the message God revealed to Abraham, Moses, and Jesus. That there should be some differences is not at all surprising, for various strands of Abrahamic tradition are apparent in Scripture itself. According to the tradition, God called Abraham with a grant or promissory covenant, to wit, that against all odds Abraham would take possession of Canaan and beget progeny who would dwell in Canaan (Gen 12:1—25:11). But within this overarching biblical tradition, we see differences between the Yahwist tradition (Gen 12), the Elohist tradition (Gen 15), and the Priestly tradition (Gen 17). Whatever the differences, however, they

---

31. Segal, *Rebecca's Children*, 1. See also William C. Chittick, "The Role of Love in the Qur'anic Worldview," cited by Amir Hussein, "Law and Love," in Ryan, with Setzer and Hussain, *Law and Love: Jewish, Christian, and Muslim Attitudes*, 34–41.

each speak of a national and religious identity, and Abraham emerges as the progenitor of Israel.

The Christian texts represent explanatory and exegetical commentary on the Old Testament with emphasis on Abraham as one justified by his profound faith in God to provide him with future progeny (Gal 3:6–9). The Quranic texts focus on Abraham as the model of a monotheistic gentile, a quintessential opponent of the false notion of plurality in the Godhead. Quran 3:65, 67–68: "People of the Book; why will you debate about Abraham when the Torah and the Gospel have not been sent down until after him? Can't you understand . . . Abraham was neither a Jew nor a Christian but a Gentile monotheist (*haniff*), surrendering (Muslim) to God, nor was he one of those who ascribe portions (to God). Indeed, those (are) the people with Abraham or the ones who followed him and this prophet and those who kept faith. God is the friend of those who keep faith."

Thus even though Judaism, Christianity, and Islam each honor Abraham as their hero, differences in emphasis are present. That is why Patrick Ryan is persuasive when he argues that the three religions "may live together more fruitfully and more peacefully if we recognize the polyvalence of Abraham, the polyvalence of great concepts like faith and revelation, community and the path of righteousness. Once we have learned how we all creatively reinterpret what may seem to be the same stories, how we all work out varying types of midrashim on common themes, we may learn to live together in peace."[32]

The Abraham motif shared by Judaism, Christianity, and Islam is not a matter of mere references to texts; more importantly, it is a celebration of a life that was marked by Abraham's willingness to sacrifice his only son. To celebrate is to dare to imitate and to accept what is celebrated as a model for life, represented in the case of the faith of Abraham as willingness to make a sacrifice of what is most dear and precious to us. Of the uniqueness of Abraham's faith, Danish philosopher and theologian Sören Kierkegaard (1813–1855) states:

> Abraham believed, and [he] believed for this life. Yea, if his faith had been only for a future life, he surely would have cast everything away in order to hasten out of this world to which he did not belong. But Abraham's faith was not of this sort. . . . Yet Abraham believed and did not doubt, he believed the preposterous. . . . Venerable Father Abraham! Second father of the human race! Thou who first wast sensible of and didst first bear witness to that prodigious passion which disdains the dreadful conflict with the rage of the elements and with the powers of creation in order to strive with God.[33]

But the common tradition of Abraham unites the three religions only if they dare to live his faith. As Kierkegaard put it, "Forgive him who would speak in praise of thee,

---

32. Ryan, with Polish and Hussain, *The Faith of Abraham: Bond or Barrier?*, 19.
33. Kierkegaard, *Fear and Trembling*, 34–35, 37.

if he does not do it fittingly. . . . He will never forget that in a hundred and thirty years thou didst not get further than to faith."³⁴

Another area that may be flagged is the attitude of Judaism, Christianity, and Islam toward marriage. In Christianity, marriage is integral to the Divine plan, a sacred bond. It is monogamous and exclusive. In Judaism marriage is more than a contract; it is *kiddushun* (sanctification). In both religions, marriage is vested with sanctity by its tie to divine authority. So marriage is not just a positive contract; it is vested with morality. While Christianity has focused on monogamy, Islam approves of polygamous arrangements in the belief that polygamy is sanctioned by God. This polygamous arrangement is justified with a statement attributed to the Prophet Muhammad, "Marry and increase in number because with you I increase the nation [of Muslims]."

Alas! All positive relationships between Islam and Christianity went wrong and did so in part because of the two religions' politicization. As mentioned earlier the ideology of Christendom as an ideology of power made Christianity first and foremost a political entity that could rival other political entities and then secondarily a religious-spiritual institution. Islam, soon after the death of the Prophet Muhammad, was accommodated to the caliphate, which meant that Islam also had become politicized. In spite of—as children of Abraham—coming from the same stock and sharing a common heritage and similar values that could have been a source of unity and strength and have brought the two faiths together, they began to see each other as rivals for power. Thus a choice was made for the way of political and ideological conflict rather than for cultural or spiritual development.

Plurality with its diversity—ethnic, racial, cultural, religious, denominational, gender, age—is a natural phenomenon. Plurality and diversity represent different identities. They are a gift of beauty from God, saving us from boredom. But diversity and plurality become a problem when natural distinctions are interpreted ideologically, especially when used to exclude others. Experiences in our time as well as in recent memory signal the awful consequences of ideologized identity, which can erupt with explosive intensity—for example, the communal conflicts between Hindus and Muslims in India. Obviously, this topic has implications for theology and theological education, if they are to serve the well-being of humans.

Three Traditional Models of Dealing with Religious Pluralism

With regard to building a community of religious communities, historically three models have been proposed. The first is to create a synthesis of religions by means of adding. The approach was pioneered by the Mogul Emperor Akbar in the sixteenth century when he attempted to create a "divine religion" out of Hinduism, Islam, and Christianity. He sought to put together the most important features of the most important religions

---

34. Ibid., 37.

to create a new uniform world faith in which persons of different backgrounds could feel at home. The attempt proved impractical; religions are living organisms. They are animated by the faith of believers who express themselves in forms and symbols that cannot be simply transferred from one setting into a different one.[35]

The second model is that of synthesis by reduction. This approach to the plurality of religions has attempted to reduce each religion to its smallest possible denominator. The weakness of this approach is that the resulting abstract constructs satisfy no one, particularly no one's spiritual needs.[36]

The third approach, which seems to be the only realistic or viable one, follows the path of interreligious and interfaith relations and dialogue. The approach via dialogue and relationships calls for realism that accepts existing religions "as they are, in their particularity and peculiarity, and the shock of secularism which is leading the religions to a reappraisal of their heritage which, again, will bear the peculiar stamp of the respective religion. This, after all, is what is primarily meant by the principle of tolerance; that people in other religions are taken seriously as adherents of that particular religion, without forcing them into decisions which they themselves are not prepared to take."[37]

Search by Each and All, Not Just the Specialist

Interfaith relationships must not be left as the preserve of specialists; rather, they should consist of encounters between adherents of different faith traditions that come about as people live together in meaningful religious coexistence. Cross-questioning and even controversy are part of the fabric of interfaith encounter and dialogue that, nevertheless, respect the rightful claims of religious truth and commitment. Interfaith encounter and dialogue require the effort of critical self-appraisal rather than mere self-defense. At base, interfaith dialogue is a joint pilgrimage rooted in the idea that all humans share common origins and common goals.

Dialogue signals talking through issues with no holds barred. It entails bringing all sides of an issue under scrutiny. Everything must be put on the table, all must be free to participate in the conversation, and each must feel listened to. Dialogue is not undertaken first of all to convert or proselytize, but to articulate and express the respective and even divergent positions of the different religions. If possible, dialogue may seek to come to a convergence. Dialogue implies a willingness to take risks, because in dialogue, there is the possibility of being convinced and converted to the other position. Such risk is consistent with faith. Conversion is the prerogative of God.

---

35. H.-W. Gensichen, "World Community and World Religions," in Pobee, *Religion in a Pluralistic Society*, 33.

36. Ibid., 34.

37. Ibid., 35.

As Paul states, "Neither the one who plants nor the one who waters is anything, but only God, who causes the growth" (1 Cor 3:8 NABRE).

The dialogue challenges us to see religion not so much in terms of dogma as in respect to what is human. At the climax of the creation, God created humans, male and female. Interreligious dialogue has the aspiration of refurbishing human beings and what is human. That is its goal and destination.

The theology of Karl Barth (1896–1968) forms a prominent landmark in the formulation of confessional theology. He argued that God's *sole* revelation is found in Jesus Christ and that the Word of God is God's one and only revelation. Barth denied that any natural revelation of God can be found in creation outside of Jesus Christ.[38] Barth's position—denying a point of contact for the Word of God in humankind—suggests a debatable discontinuity between grace and creation. Such extreme neglect of humans' own capacity necessarily neglects pastoral care; what shall be said to someone lying on his or her deathbed?

The first affirmation of the Christian Scriptures—namely, that God is the Creator of all and everything—is the basis of the ecumenical imperative. And it supplies us with proper perspective for engaging pluralism. As Psalm 24:1 (NABRE) reminds us, "The earth is the Lord's and all it holds, the world and those who dwell in it." Beyond being an affirmation that God created all that is, the psalm was used in temple worship. It signaled the entrance of God into the temple alongside the concomitant moral requirements that fell upon the congregation as they entered to dine with the Lord. The psalm's teaching claims everything for God, for all belongs to God. Juxtapose this language with that of the Letter to the Ephesians: the Christian life and teaching is about "summing up of all things in Christ, things in heaven and things on the earth" (Eph 1:10 NASB). Theology in Africa just as anywhere else should be an agent in spearheading the uniting of all things to God. It is necessarily missiological. But it is mission in the sense of building a community of communities, devoted to the marks of God's sovereign rule. This building together cannot be compelled or extracted; it has to be a dialogue, a cultivation of we-feeling in a family.

The World Council of Churches' Programme on Dialogue with Other Living Faiths and Ideologies expounded some theological virtues for interreligious dialogue:

- To be convinced that inspiration from God may not be finally closed.
- To consider the possibility of the need, in concrete situations, to discover complementary truths.
- To abstain from passing negative judgments on people of other faith traditions.
- To work together, wherever we may be and whenever possible, in definite areas from a theological and political perspective.[39]

38. Karl Barth, quoted in Thomas, *Attitudes toward Other Religions*, 96.

39. That is, areas of cooperation need to be defined and carefully spelled out by representatives of each of the parties' theological and political perspectives.

- To explain to each other in a frank manner our respective positions. This step calls for mutual witness and readiness to listen to the other's critique.
- To allow ourselves to be enriched by others.
- To so work that religious communities become a community of communities.
- To work for a world in which there is peace with justice and which, therefore, avoids mental and physical conflict and tension.
- To orient ourselves toward the rule of God.[40]

Some consequential issues flow from the vision just mapped out. First, we may dare to believe that the inspiration of God may not be finally closed. If the end waits for God, then we must be open to the possibility that God may continue to reveal himself and things to us. We may dare to believe that the scientific, technological, and communications revolutions of our time owe their impulse to God. Taking African cultures on their own self-understanding has initiated us into new and enriching vistas, for example, the religious and spiritual epistemology and ontology of homo africanus, the communitarian epistemology and ontology which the nations of the North need so badly today.

Second, under the ecumenical perspective, we dare to be open to the possibility, in concrete situations, of being faced with the need to discover the complementariness of truth. Black and white categories may not supply the most rewarding, enriching, or renewing approach. Third, the ecumenical perspective requires us to be slow to pass negative judgments on other faith traditions. Biases must not be paraded as gospel truths. Even though we may disagree on aspects of a faith tradition, the dignity and well-being of persons of other faith traditions are nonnegotiable, because those people too are created by, and in the image and likeness of, the one and same Creator God.

Fourth, under the ecumenical canopy, all are obliged to work together, wherever we may be and whenever possible, with careful attention given to the differing theological and political perspectives of those involved. The Life and Work Movement, one of the streams of the ecumenical vision, ventured the axiom "Doctrine Divides, Service Unites."[41] The slogan encapsulates the quest for an inclusive society from which no one may be excluded and it establishes an option for creating a spirit of brotherhood. Worship, service, and solidarity are closely related. Along the way,

---

40. World Council of Churches, *Guidelines on Dialogue with People of Living Faiths and Ideologies*; Hallencreutz, *New Approaches to Men of Other Faiths*; Ariarajah, *Not without My Neighbour*; Griffiths, *Christianity through Non-Christian Eyes*; Sheard, *Interreligious Dialogue in the Catholic Church since Vatican II*; Samartha, *Living Faiths and the Ecumenical Movement*; Newbigin, "The Basis, Purpose, and Manner of Inter-Faith Dialogue," 253–70.

41. Sundkler, *Nathan Söderblom*; Oldham, *The Churches Survey Their Task*; Bennett, "Breakthrough in Ecumenical Social Ethics," 132–46; and Paul Abrecht, "Life and Work," in Lossky, *Dictionary of the Ecumenical Movement* (1991), 691–92.

conflict inevitably arises—and often enough social catastrophe—with which we must conscientiously engage as we seek for its resolution.

Religious pluralism challenges us to be fundamentally concerned, to cultivate our capacity for a overall view of the whole, and to seek sure judgment on all possible questions, large and small. Rather than pursue abstract theoretical discussion, we should pray for prophetic insight. Above and beyond that, we should be committed to joy in our service and to being used to the full. Theology, worship, service, and solidarity must be held together. Theology dare not be relegated to the scholar's study or the lecture room; it should be a public matter and foster practical Christianity. Working with a sense of pluralism, theology must endeavor to stimulate thought among church persons who seek to own their social and political responsibility.

Uniqueness of Christ

A Christian theologian who engages in interreligious dialogue has ultimately to face the question of where Jesus, Christ and Lord, fits into the dialogue. Indeed, the Lamb in the title for this chapter is a reference to the crucified, risen, and ascended Christ and Lord. Concepts such as uniqueness, finality, and absoluteness have been used in speaking of Christ. But the terms "finality" and "absoluteness" carry a lingering air of or strongly presuppose some ideologies and principles that are inimical to mutual respect. As the various religions seek after the Numinous, it is least offensive for us to think in terms of Christ's uniqueness vis-à-vis all the other religions on offer. Because what Christ offers is new, other religions may be deemed to be preliminary, anticipatory, and preparatory to the Christ event. What makes Christ unique is the human emphasis and not an idea or philosophy.

An earlier chapter outlined the residuum evangelium. Here we are concerned to attempt a restatement of Christian truth now that we have been exposed to other new truths. But we do well to heed the caution voiced by Stephen Neill that it is possible to restate Christian faith in such general terms that it is reduced to a vague theosophy from which the particular challenge presented by Christian faith has been eliminated.[42] Certain basic convictions must be maintained if Christianity is to remain recognizably Christian. Of these I list seven.

- There is only one God and Creator, from whom all things take their origin.
- This God is a self-revealing God, and he himself is active in the knowledge that we have of him.
- In Jesus the full meaning of the life of humanity and of the purpose of God for the universe has been made known. In him the alienated world has been reconciled to God.

---

42. Neill, *Christian Faith and Other Faiths*, 231–32.

Multitudes before the Lamb: Pluralism and Theology

- In Jesus, Christians see the way in which they ought to live; his life is the norm to which they are unconditionally bound.
- The cross of Jesus shows us that to follow his way will certainly result in suffering; this suffering is neither to be resented nor to be avoided.
- Christian faith may learn much from other faiths, but it is universal in its claims. In the end Christ must be acknowledged as Lord of all.
- The death of the body is not the end. Christ has revealed the eternal dimension as the true home of man's spirit.

To make these affirmations is not to deny the right of any of our interlocutors to challenge or criticize any one of them. It is simply to state the limits of concession. If any one of these cardinal points were to be seriously modified, Christianity would become—as Neill warns—something unrecognizably different from what it is.

To this point Hendrik Kraemer adds a codicil on how Christians should go about entering into dialogue with other persons. "Christ's ambassadors in the world, in order to preach the Gospel, can and must stand in the world of non-Christian religions with downright intrepidity and radical humility. And the same applies to the Christian standing in the world of culture, wherever it may be."[43]

Implications of Pluralism

In closing this chapter, I wish to lift up for consideration two implications of the ground that has been covered: first, the dichotomy between "faith" and "cumulative tradition" and, second, the topic's institutional implications for the study of theology.

On faith and cumulative tradition, Wilfred Cantwell Smith writes:

> It seems quite evident, and readily demonstrable to the sensitive and informed, that what used to be called the religions are finite, human and historical—as well as infinite, divine, and timeless. This applies to one's own, as well as to others.
>
> Each is a divine-human complex in motion. That is why careful historical scholarship separates each into two component elements: ones that I have called respectively "cumulative tradition" and "faith." In faith, we are in touch with God. Or seen more largely, God—if we are to use the theistic term—is in touch with particular men and women and children, at particular times and places, through particular mundane forms. Human history is and always has been in part mundane, transitory, finite; and in part, transcendent. For human beings, each in a particular earthly context, are in relation to God; faith is my name for that relation, wherever, and in whatever form, it occurs. More precisely, it names the human side of the relation. The cumulative tradition, however,

---

43. Kraemer, *Religion and the Christian Faith*, 335.

> historical awareness is increasingly able to see, is finite, human, and historical. It is in constant process. To imagine that any [cumulative tradition] is stable is now seen as an historically conditioned, [albeit] historically understandable, error. Christian doctrines have evolved. They are still evolving. None is finally true. The Torah and the *shari'ah* (Jewish and Islamic "Law") came into historical existence slowly; and today they are in process of revision.[44]

This rather long quotation is a warning against fundamentalism and proof-texting and is a call to humility. For God's revelation is not complete, and awareness of that fact must be reflected in all engagements between religions. All our interreligious encounters must be imbued with the sense that each faith tradition has been, and should attempt to continue to be, in touch with God.

The institutional dimension of the relation between faith and cumulative tradition demands of us sensitivity to the contextual coloring of the faith, which must be renegotiated as new times bring new and different challenges. That demand imposes in essence an agenda of distilling the essential faith that lives between the poles of contextuality and catholicity, the local and the universal.

Islam, Violence, and the Quest for Unity and Peace

Africa has been plagued by violence initiated by so-called Muslim groups. At the time of writing, Boko Haram was active in Nigeria; the Islamic Movement for Oneness and Jihad in West Africa (MUJAO) in Mali; Al-Shabaab in Somalia along with its attacks in Kenya, for example, its September 21, 2013, attack on the Westgate Mall; and for good measure, the violence in the Central African Republic between the primarily Muslim rebel coalition, Seleka, and the Christian Anti-Balaka militia. Since these cases have been read as evidence of Islam's inclination to violence, some comment on them is necessary.

Boko Haram—after attacks on Chibok in Nigeria's Borno State (on April 14, 2014), Maidugri, Damaturu, Abuja (the national capital), and Lagos (the commercial capital)—is establishing a caliphate in Northern Nigeria. The group was founded in 2002 by Muhammed Yusuf who named it *Jama' at ahl as-sunnah li-d-da'a wa-l-jihad* (The Community of Sunni People for Propagation [of Islam] and Struggle [for the Faith]). In short, the founder understood the group to be a Sunni Muslim movement with a tendency to extremist militancy. When Abu Bakr Shekkau succeeded to leadership after Yusuf was killed in 2009, the group assumed an even more militant stance. This phase of increased militancy is what has been captured by the group's new name of Boko Haram, a mixture of Hausa and Arabic that means literally "book education is forbidden." Their signal kidnapping of some 200–300 girls from a church school seems to give substance to the new name.

44. Wilfred Cantwell Smith, "History in Relation to Both Science and Religion," in Smith and Burbidge, *Modern Culture from a Comparative Perspective*, 16.

At the very least, the kidnapping of the schoolgirls bespeaks a group culture that disempowers women. Patrick Ryan has argued that the group has its roots in the early-nineteenth-century Fulani jihad as well as the teaching of the fifteenth-century extremist North African scholar Muhammad al-Maghīlī.[45] The fact of declaring a caliphate, however, is itself evidence of the politicization of the religion. The declaration that the group would marry off the young girls and sell them in the market is evidence of sex trade and a resurgence of slavery, which have nothing to do with authentic Islam. Therefore, a real issue exists regarding the authenticity of Boko Haram's religious claims and the integrity of the group's purported Muslim identity.

The social factors and challenges that created the persons who are attracted to Boko Haram—namely, tyranny, economic and social dysfunction, unemployment, rural underemployment of youth, and the numbers of floating or itinerant students of the Quran in the decades of Nigeria's oil boom (1973–92)—form another issue. On the one hand, Boko Haram's ability to carry out acts of violence with impunity speaks of a governmental void. The lack of any effective response from the government, especially the security services, may be symptomatic of the government's incompetence and inadequacy. The appearance of incompetence raises questions of corruption and lack of political will. On the other hand, a ready resort to describing the movement as (Muslim) terrorists often hides a narrative of jihad and an enemy image, both of which often serve the political agendas of outsiders. For example, the Nigerian government has had to resist attempts to use Boko Haram as a smoke screen that would provide cover for sneaking through US yearnings to have an African High Command as part of its global security strategy.

In 2012 West Africa saw violence in Mali which featured the Islamic Movement for Oneness and Jihad in West Africa (MUJAO), with support from Al-Qaeda in the Islamic Maghreb (AQIM) and from the Tuaregs. Among other violent acts, MUJAO destroyed historic Islamic literature of great importance in Timbuktu, the celebrated Muslim city and center of learning in central Mali. It is telltale that MUJAO and its allies could even consider destroying these historic Islamic documents, sacred to Islam, which have made Timbuktu a Mecca for Islamic scholars. The group's agenda obviously went beyond shoring up the faith of Islam. In any case, from what religious threat was MUJAO going to defend Mali? Mali is 90 percent Muslim with only 5 percent Christian and 5 percent adherents of African Traditional Religions. It therefore had no reason to feel threatened by either Christians or followers of the traditional religions. The intervention led by France is also telltale, as is the fact that the Tuareg—a Muslim Berber-speaking people from Central and Western Sahara—have never felt at home among the natives of Mali. The narrative of Islamic resurgence and militancy served to hide the real causes of the eruption, namely, the economic and military interests of France and the disenchantment of the Tuareg.

---

45. Ryan, *Boko Haram*.

September 21, 2013, saw the horrendous seizure of the Westgate Shopping Mall, Nairobi, Kenya, in East Africa, by Al-Shabaab, a self-styled Islamic group. In addition to the loss of some sixty lives—persons whose only crime was to be shopping at the mall at the time—and the wounding of more than 175 others, was the terrorizing of many more innocent persons. Even more baffling is that the attackers were from Somalia. The apparent cause of the incident was that the Kenyan government had, in the name of East African community, contributed resources to intervene in the long-standing chaos within Somalia. Within their homeland of Somalia, Al-Shabaab had made a name for itself by beheading people, recruiting boys to fight (infant/child soldiers), and forcing girls into marriage. The group was running a parallel administration with strict discipline and greater efficiency than the official government of Somalia. According to the United Nations, Al-Shabaab has revenue streams amounting to US$100,000,000. Additionally, Al-Shabaab engages in illicit ivory trade, conducts illicit charcoal trade, and expropriates cash intended for genuine and respectable Islamic charities. In sum, Al-Shabaab's activities suggest that more than strictly religious considerations are present in the factors that play a role in its social construction.[46]

The Central African Republic saw, in 2013, the unleashing of bloodletting between the primarily Muslim rebel coalition called Seleka and the largely Christian militia called Anti-Balaka. The conflict resulted in much carnage on both sides, and people were uprooted from their homes, with many becoming refugees in the Democratic Republic of the Congo. Though the religious labels of Christian and Muslim have been attached to the factions, it is not insignificant that the Roman Catholic Archbishop of the Central African Republic and the country's Chief Imam teamed up to travel through the country to seek peace. Quite plainly, the friction and violence had no official sanction. The reasons were social, political, and economic. The adversarial relationship between Christians and Muslims does not give cash value to the Christian affirmation of God as creator of the whole world or to Islam's concepts of *ahl-ul-kitab* (people of the Book) and *ahl-al-adhimma* (people under protection). The unity of humankind and the unity of all creation as created by God must be made central and become the very foundation for all our evaluations and judgments. This criterion of unity must in turn be buoyed up by that of peace, which is a characteristic of the kingdom of God.

Unity, like peace, time and again proves elusive, despite our agendas for the renewal of humanity and the rest of creation for the sake of achieving peace and unity. Despite living in an age of unprecedented revolution in communications, our ability to understand one another is often undermined by suspicion, fear, and mistrust. A Pentecostal experience can help us to overcome these barriers. As Pope Benedict XVI stated in his homily for Pentecost, May 27, 2012, "Unity can only exist as a gift of

---

46. David Smith, "Al-Shabab's Hold on Somalia Rules Out a Purely Military Solution," *Mail and Guardian*, South Africa 29, no. 44 (November 1–7, 2013) 22; see http://mg.co.za/article/2013-10-31-al-shababs-hold-on-somalia-rules-out-a-purely-military-solution.

God's Spirit who will give us a new heart and a new language, a new ability to communicate.... [At Pentecost] the Holy Spirit... settled on each one of them, and kindled within them the divine fire, a fire of love capable of transforming them. Their fear evaporated, they felt their hearts filled with new strength, their tongues were loosened and they began to speak freely."[47] For replacing division, alienation, and hatred with unity, understanding, and love, a Pentecost experience is necessary.

As a sine qua non of the search for unity and peace, the Pentecost experience imposes a demand that we walk in the Spirit. That walk is a denial of selfishness, enmity, discord, jealousy, and disagreements that subvert our living as humans and in community. Let us underline that religion ultimately is about what is human and not primarily about doctrine and dogma—and what is human must recognize that pluralism and diversity are part of God's order of creation. In Africa, acknowledging the reality of pluralism is not only to be done for the sake of living at peace, but also so that we can construct a theology that will be life affirming and to honor our vocation to worship God.

---

47. Benedict XVI, "From Babel to Unity," *L'Osservatore Romano*, no. 22 (May 30, 2012) 5.

9

I Am an African Christian

THIS BOOK IS AN attempt by an African theologian to articulate the key affirmation of the religious group known as Christians. It is the affirmation of an adherent neither of African Traditional Religion nor of Islam in Africa. So the epithet "Christian" is important and to be taken seriously in the exercise. At one time juxtaposition of the words "African" and "Christian" would have been frowned upon. The missionary practice of tabula rasa (building as if on a clean slate), which started from a very negative appraisal of African culture, did not consider anything good and beautiful to be present in African cultures on which Christianity and Christian theology could be built.[1]

No apology needs to be made, however, for maintaining that my identity is that of an *African* Christian. For one thing, in sober fact, before I became a Christian by baptism and confirmation, I was ensouled with Africanness, which was taken in with my mother's milk.[2] Africanness is more than color of the skin; it is culture and worldview-taken-for-granted, which cannot be erased. Second, use of the adjective "African" is consistent with the core biblical message of the incarnation. Third, the history of the church demonstrates that Christianity, wherever it has gone, has taken the color and hue of the locale.

From "The Way" to Christian Church

The appearance of the word "Christian" occurs in the literature only after a delay. Initially those who were to acquire the epithet "Christian" were styled "those who belong to the Way" (see, e.g., Acts 9:2), a phrase that pinpoints the earliest self-understanding of the believers as a movement. Only when the gospel spread to Antioch were the disciples for the first time called "Christians" (Acts 11:26), that is, followers of Christ or persons who imitate Jesus of Nazareth, Christ and Lord. The epithets "Christ" and "Lord" are interpretative epithets, signaling his followers' commitment to the life, story, and teaching of Jesus of Nazareth. For that reason articulation of what one believes

---

1. Pobee, *Toward an African Theology*, chap. 4; Pobee, *The Word Became Flesh*.
2. Pobee, "I Am First an African and, Second, a Christian," 268–77.

about Jesus is central to any theology that claims to be Christian. The New Testament comes at this idea by inviting people to be *imitators*—of God (Eph 5:1; Matt 5:48), imitators of Christ (1 Cor 11:1; 1 Thess 1:6), imitators of the apostles (1 Cor 4:16; 2 Thess 3:7), imitators of the churches of God (1 Thess 2:14), and imitators of those who through faith and patience inherit the promises (Heb 6:12). The invitation is a charge to imitate a lifestyle and values that are consistent with the values of the kingdom of God. To be a Christian is to be committed to a way of life that conforms to the teachings and standards of Jesus, who is both Christ and Lord, so as to be conformed to "the Way" and to Christ's image.

Confession of What a Person Believes

The title of this chapter declares, "I Am . . . ," for the chapter is a statement of what the writer believes and affirms about Jesus and the movement Jesus initiated. Beyond being an intellectual and academic exercise, a theological statement is fundamentally a confession of faith that Jesus is Christ and Lord, exercising the functions of God in a unique way. The statement is as well an act of worship, for confession and worship are intertwined. This study may pay its dues to scholars and scholarly works, but at the end of the day its affirmations arise from the writer's personal struggles and experiences with God and God's Word in the world. At its root theology is and must be confession of faith.

A faith tradition normally has antecedents. In the case of Christianity, those antecedents lie within Judaism and Greco-Roman ideas. The language in which early Christian confession is couched borrows from the idiom and worldview of the context in which the first Christians lived. Christ's followers today, wherever they are located, do not come to faith *de novo*. A living tradition goes before us that must be reckoned with, translated, and interpreted across time and space to new times and new places. In this case, the context and idiom(s) are those of Africa, bearing in mind her hopes and fears. Thus the issue of how tradition should be received and treated is real and must be considered.

Received Traditions

African Christians are heritors to at least two streams of tradition that have gone into making Christian identity: the biblical sermon and the Chalcedonian definition. Under the heading of the biblical sermon fall the language and statements of the Synoptic Gospels (Mark, Matthew and Luke), the Johannines, the Pauline, Petrine, and Jacobian Epistles, and the Epistle to the Hebrews. These works are replete with language such as Son of Man, Son of God, Wisdom, and Light—with the Johannines verging on the language of Neoplatonist philosophy. Whatever judgment one makes regarding that last assertion, the "Gospels voice the confession: Jesus the Christ, the unity of the earthly Jesus and the Christ of faith. By this the Gospels proclaim that faith does not begin with itself but lives from past history."[3]

The dialogue between the high priest and Jesus at the latter's interrogation paints another picture. Here the key phrases are "Son of the Blessed," "Son of the Most High," and then Jesus' own preferred self-designation, "Son of Man." The juxtaposition of Son of God and Son of Man affirms that "the messianic King, God's Son, coincides in a remarkable way with the frail human figure, 'the Son of Man,' whose vulnerable, martyr-loyalty has brought him through death to this position of glory and dominion before the aged 'President of the immortals.'"[4]

At this point two key themes may be delineated. The first is whether, in the language used by the New Testament, the thrust is not so much on the being or ontology of Jesus, as on Jesus' work and function. Oscar Cullmann writes, "The New Testament hardly ever speaks of the person of Christ without at the same time speaking of his work.... When it is asked in the New Testament 'Who is Christ?,' the question never means exclusively, or even primarily, 'What is his nature?,' but first of all, 'What is his function?' Therefore, the various answers given to the question in the New Testament visualize both Christ's person and his work."[5]

For an African attempting to articulate the common or core message of Jesus, Christ and Lord, therefore, the bottom line issues are: Who is this Jesus Christ and what does he mean for me? The African context has other beings on offer, such as traditional deities and the ancestors, as well as the offering of Islam. Why therefore the preference for Jesus and no other being? And how exclusive is acceptance of and allegiance to Jesus, Christ and Lord?

The range of Christological titles available emphasizes the contextual nature of every religious and theological statement. As Christianity moved into the Greek and Latin heartlands, other languages came into use, and other Christological formulations, such as the classical Chalcedonian definition, emerged. The stream of tradition that issued from Chalcedon appears to reduce the person of God to propositional phrases. In using the philosophical language of *ousia* and *phusis*, *substantia*, and *persona*, Chalcedon takes a markedly different tack than does the functional approach of Scripture.

The otherness of the Chalcedonian definition reminds us of another important element or ingredient to be found in statements of who Christ is. Not infrequently, times of controversy have become the occasion for seeking appropriate language in which to formulate a definition of who Christ is. Personal and human considerations; nationalistic, social, and economic factors and challenges; rivalries among the Great Sees of Jerusalem, Alexandria (Egypt), Rome, Antioch, and Constantinople (the New Rome); liturgical disputes, Puritan tendencies, and disciplinary problems: all have in

---

3. Bornkamm, *Jesus of Nazareth*, 23.
4. Moule, *The Origin of Christology*, 26.
5. Cullmann, *Christology of the New Testament*, 3–4.

varying degrees influenced particular statements about and perceptions of the one and same Jesus, Christ and Lord.

It is salutary to remember that a Christological statement is, of necessity, a contextual statement. Each emerges from the worldview and challenges of its context. Unsurprisingly, therefore, even on the continent of Africa no one statement can answer to the needs of every context. For example, under the oppression of apartheid South Africa, Christ was characterized as the Liberator. In West Africa the honorifics of a Chief have been used of Jesus Christ. Challenges imposed by necessity lead theologians to new ways and new language for articulating the identity and significance of Jesus and his meaning for humanity.

Two Immovable Poles of Christology

Attempts to articulate Christology differ, but the humanity and divinity of Jesus remain immovable: to use the language of Chalcedon, he is "truly human, truly divine." That is what is meant when the titles "Son of Man" and "Son of God" are applied to Jesus. These titles signal, on the one hand, unconditional dedication to the purposes of God no matter the cost and, on the other hand, the extraordinary intimacy between God and Jesus.

For all the humanness of Jesus, he also exuded authority such as no mortal seemed to have had—authority to perform miracles (which is God's prerogative) and to wage a crusade against Satan (Mark 3:23–30), authority to forgive sins (Mark 2:1–12; Matt 9:1–8; Luke 5:17–26), and an authoritative way of teaching the message of God (Mark 1:22; Matt 5:21–22, 7:29).[6]

As African theology, in its turn, endeavors to address the essential core Christian affirmation of Jesus as human and divine, it necessarily seeks to find within the African story the language and experience with which to articulate and illustrate homo africanus's sense of and experience with Jesus of Nazareth. To speak of the divine underlines the unique relation of Jesus of Nazareth to God as the very facsimile of God, corresponding to the glory, character, and nature of God.

The Essentially Contextual Nature of This African Statement

The formulation of a contextual African theological statement may benefit by learning from other contextual statements. In chapter 5 above, I quoted comments made by the African church father Augustine of Hippo Regius on the Fourth Gospel's use of "*logos*," a word that owed much to the Neoplatonists.[7]

---

6. See Schweizer, *The Good News according to Matthew*, 118.
7. Augustine, *Confessions*, 7.9.

For all the affinities between the language of the Fourth Gospel's exordium and that of the Neoplatonist Plotinus, the Stoics, and even Judaism (Prov 8:22–36; Sir 24:1–22; Wis 7:22—8:1), the Fourth Gospel still has something unique to say. The revelation in Jesus as God's *Word* (John 1:1) has a personal character to it in much the same way that salvation involves a personal relationship. Salvation is projected in terms of relationships, namely, sonship. In Christ, as Barnabas Lindars states, God's glory "kept breaking through in human life, in the words and deeds which will form the substance of the narrative of the Gospel."[8]

But there is always an *extra*, to which no one language by itself can do justice. Therefore, the only wise course to follow is to be open to complementary truths. No single statement, however eminent, has the stature to be deemed to be *the truth* captured and encoded for all time. Because of the ever-widening experience of humans, we must be open to and leave room for other portraitures of the Christ.

The Finality, Absoluteness, Uniqueness, Ultimacy of Christ?

The biblical records give the impression of a special relationship between Jesus and God, especially in the claim that salvation is possible for those who believe in Jesus, the only begotten Son of God. In the ongoing and widening experience of human beings, is the incarnation still the fullest expression of God for modern society? How plausible today are the claims Christians make about Christ? To consider these concerns adequately requires us to introduce several theological terms into the discussion—finality, absoluteness, uniqueness, and ultimacy of Christ—terms that carry philosophical presuppositions and implications with them.

Two statements by Charles F. D. Moule articulate so well the position that I wish to espouse that I feel compelled to cite them at length. The first states,

> The question is whether God's continuing revelation of himself in man's constantly widening experiences may still be meaningfully described as "in Christ." Can it be reasonably maintained . . . that, in progressively learning more about man and his psychology, about his personality and his mutual relations, about society and the corporate character of human life, and about the universe, we are only finding a "developing" insight into what, all along, has been in Christ? Is the understanding of Jesus as more than an individual, as transcendent and eternal and all comprehensive, which already emerges in the New Testament, valid for all time? Does the Christ of the New Testament keep pace, so to speak, with new discoveries? It seems to me that modern psychological and sociological research does often confirm insights already gained through Christ; and conversely, that New Testament insights into the meaning of human life and of community do often illuminate modern investigation into psychology and sociology. But can one generalize and say that this is always so, and will always be so? The study of

8. Lindars, *The Gospel of John*, 80.

> Christology needs must take account of modern insights into personality and society; but will the result be only a developing insight into what was, from the beginning, implicit in Christ, or will Christ be left behind and Christology cease to be a relevant term? That is at least part of what is meant by asking about the ultimacy of Christ.[9]

This quotation poses more questions than it answers. That appeals to me because of my conviction that theology must be a resource to help seekers as they struggle to find their own answers. Prefabricated answers may not always be conducive to renewal, which is the goal of theology.

Moule's second statement addresses the issue of clarity and focus when Christians make claims about Christ's absoluteness, finality, uniqueness, or ultimacy, especially in a pluralistic context such as in Africa. He writes that the New Testament evidence

> does not point to any exclusive claims for Christianity, in the sense of excluding all other ways to God as invalid. Rather the distinctiveness of earliest Christianity is found in a Person whose achievement includes the hopes and expectations of the Judaism and paganism of his day, but does so in paradoxical and distinctive ways, so as greatly to transcend them. And this pattern, *mutatis mutandis*, seems to me to be applicable also in what I have deliberately omitted from this paper, namely the relation of Christianity to other faiths today. If Christianity claims to be not merely one religion among others, but uniquely all-inclusive, its origins certainly do not belie the claim. It arose in a Middle East compound of Greek and Jew, but its derivation seems to be not wholly explicable in terms of Jew or of Greek, but only in terms of an event inclusive, but without parallel. In reply to the time-honoured question, "But does not such a claim imply the denial that there is 'salvation' in any other?," one may say that, on the contrary, it is precisely because God is revealed by Christ as a God who became incarnate that he is able to save those who sought or who seek him in other ways, whether before the Incarnation or beyond the range of its acknowledgement. But, equally, this implies no slackening of the "missionary" motives; for if God is, indeed, the God of all because he is the God and Father of our Lord Jesus Christ, then it follows that those who know him by his incarnate name must long for and be committed to the bringing of all men, so far as in them lies, to the fullest possible understanding of him in this way.[10]

Moule's statements give helpful insight for the way forward in articulating Christ. The Christ of Palestine who came on the scene in the fullness of time in Judea (Gal 4:4–5) must become the Christ of all nations (Col 1:15–20), in whom, in the words of the Christmas carol, "the hopes and fears of all the years are met." Jesus represents the fulfillment of time in a way that steps decisively beyond the Jewish view.[11] Of the

9. Moule, *Origin of Christology*, 142–43.
10. Ibid., 158.
11. Bligh, *Galatians*, 331; Lightfoot, *St. Paul's Epistle to the Galatians*, 166–68.

four terms given in the subheading to this section—finality, absoluteness, uniqueness, and ultimacy—I am inclined to regard the issue of Christ's ultimacy as the topic with which at present African theology ought to engage.[12]

Christology in the Third World

Because Africa in particular and the Southern Hemisphere in general were evangelized from the North, statements found in the South about the heart of the Christian message have been North Atlantic artifacts. As a result the theology of the church as being one, holy, catholic, and apostolic has been shortchanged. Artifacts peculiar to the Latin and Greek traditions have been paraded as universal and, in the process, the universality of the church and Christian faith has been denied. Full incarnation of the church of Christ in the cultures of the world is not possible without a real incarnation of Christ in all the varieties of human existence. And this ongoing incarnation is happening. In the wisdom and design of God, Africa, Asia, Latin America, and the Pacific have become the heartlands of world Christianity.[13]

In India, Raja Ram Mohan Roy (1773–1833), Kesbab Chandra Sen (1838–84), Swami Vivekananda (1863–1902), Mahatma Gandhi (1869–1948), Vengal Chakkarai Chettiar (1880–1958), and Sarvepalli Radhakrishnan (1889–1975) represent some from India who have attempted to add an Asian etching to the oikoumene's theological and Christological mosaic.[14] For all of these, speaking the Christological language of "nature" and "person" is not a natural preference; Indian Hindus instead stress the ethical and mystical unity between Jesus and the Father. For them, Jesus' living for others becomes an example of renewal with national relevance.

Latin America has stressed the way that social challenges impact a culture's framing of Christology.[15] Christology necessarily reflects and influences the life and praxis of an ecclesiastical community. Latin American efforts in constructive Christology project the primacy of the utopian element over the factual, the primacy of the critical element over the dogmatic, the primacy of the social over the personal, and the primacy of orthopraxis over orthodoxy.

---

12. In making this recommendation, I recognize that the Latin origins of "finality" (*finis*, that is, boundary, limited end, object, aim highest) and "ultimacy" (*ultimum*, that is, the greatest, the final, the last) are essentially different.

13. Andrew F. Walls, "Towards Understanding Africa's Place in Christian History," in Pobee, *Religion in a Pluralistic Society*, 180.

14. Boyd, *Introduction to Indian Christian Theology*; Thomas, *The Acknowledged Christ of the Indian Renaissance*; Samartha, *Hindus vor dem universalen Christus*; Samartha, *Hindu Response to the Unbound Christ*; Wolff, *Christus unter den Hindus*; Camps, *Partners in Dialogue*, 200–215; Balasuriya, *Jesus Christ and Human Liberation*.

15. Hugo Assmann, "The Power of Christ," in Gibellini, *Frontiers of Theology in Latin America*, 133–50; Sobrino, *Christology at the Crossroads*; Boff, *Jesus Cristo libertador*.

Africa! Who Do You Say I, the Son of Man, Am?

Jesus, after a time with his disciples, asked them, "Who do you say that I am?" (Luke 9:20 NABRE). Discipleship and commitment to Jesus are not possible without some response to this question. Africans are obliged to face it at two levels: What do African theologians say? And what do mere "mortals" say of Christ? Of the scholars we may draw attention to Elizabeth Amoah (Ghana), Kwame Bediako (Ghana), Bénézet Bujo (Democratic Republic of Congo), Kwesi A. Dickson (Ghana), John Mbiti (Kenya), Jesse Mugambi (Kenya), Mercy Amba Oduyoye (Ghana), John Pobee (Ghana), and Gabriel Setiloane (South Africa)—and for good measure the Canadian Diane Stinton (Canada and Kenya).[16] Christological statements in Africa tend to be in line with the God of the Old Testament. The particularity of such African constructs needs to be complemented by a universality that is informed by the New Testament so that particularity and universality can be truly complementary.

Plenum and Plurality of Christological Images and Symbols

All language is figurative and symbolic, using familiar things to "capture" and articulate deep and significant experiences. The act of choosing a particular image to communicate is contextual in the sense that the speaker selects a familiar image from the array of possible images on hand in the setting or context. In the nature of the case, the selection of any particular image is bound to be partial, varying with the context, for no image is an exact fit for what it is trying to communicate. Therefore, it is more realistic to see individual images as snapshots of the same object that other snapshots may complement. In this sense, statements of Christology may be likened to a gallery of paintings of the same object.

Diane Stinton has helpfully gathered into a single chapter such a gallery of African Christologies, for example, Jesus as Leader or Chief, Jesus as Liberator, and Jesus as Elder Brother.[17] The idiom is African but the imagery is filled with biblical insights.

Shaped as they are by their communitarian epistemology and ontology, Africans have a need for leadership. They would use different words, but by and large African societies would affirm the biblical statement that because "there was no king in Israel;

---

16. See, e.g., Setiloane, "Christus Heute Bekennen aus der afrikanischen Sicht von Mensch und Gemeinschaft," 21–32; John S. Mbiti, "Some African Concepts of Christology," in Vicedom, *Christ and the Younger Churches*, 51–62; Mugambi and Magesa, *Jesus in African Christianity*; Bujo, *Christmas: God Becomes Man in Black Africa*; Oduyoye, "An African Woman's Christ," 119–24; Elizabeth Amoah and Mercy Amba Oduyoye, "The Christ for African Women," in Fabella and Oduyoye, *With Passion and Compassion*, 35–46; Kwame Bediako, "Biblical Christologies in the Context of African Traditional Religions," in Samuel and Sugden, *Sharing Jesus in the Two Thirds World*, 115–57; Bediako, *Jesus in African Culture*; Kuma, *Jesus of the Deep Forest*; Pobee, *West Africa: Christ Would Be an African Too*; Pobee, "Jesus Christ—The Life of the World: An African Perspective," 5–8; Pobee, *Exploring Afro-Christology*; Stinton, *Jesus of Africa*.

17. Stinton, *Jesus of Africa*, 177–218.

everyone did what was right in his own eyes" (Judg 21:25 NASB). In their struggle to obtain power and exercise leadership, African nationalists often threatened to destroy the institution of chieftaincy. But in the end they appropriated the honorifics of the chief and king to themselves. The actions of Kwame Nkrumah in Ghana are a case in point.[18]

This example suggests that the imagery of the chief remains an institution at the heartbeat of the Ghanaian social structure. Therefore the imagery of chieftaincy remains appropriate and useful for capturing the idea of Christ.[19] Against that background the psalmists' exclamation that "the Lord is King" has resonance. The Christian feast of Christ the King also takes on special meaning when Africans view it through the lens of their sense of kingship.

Composite Personality

In Akan society the office of chief is a composite office: judge and peacemaker, commander-in-chief in times of war, and priest. Of all the chief's functions, the religious and spiritual functions are the most important. This truth becomes especially evident during the *Akwasidae* festival when the *Asantehene* (the king of the Asante) enters the stool house on behalf of the nation to offer sacrifice to the ancestors, on whom, it is believed, the well-being of the living depends. Thus the chief is more than simply a human person; sacral qualities attach to his person and to the stool of the ancestors on which he sits. Applying the epithet "chief" to Jesus, therefore, is an affirmation of Jesus' social and divine character. The starting point of a Christian's confession is the claim that Jesus is chief, but unlike other chiefs, he is unique and stands as the king of kings.

As a religious and social celebration, writes Johann Christaller, the *adae* festival "is arguably the most important festival celebrated in honour of the ancestors by the Akan. These are days set aside for the remembrance of late rulers, to honour them, pour libation to them, 'give them something to eat and drink,' and ask for their favours and blessing."[20] A striking point of the adae festival is the opportunity it offers for public participation.

As chief, the ruler leads the celebration. In addition to being both chief and priest, the chief is a leader. In that sense the Christological epithet *archègos* (pioneer; Heb 2:10, 12:2) comes into its own. But Jesus is "pioneer" with a difference; he is pioneer by virtue of confessing God by his life and work and death on the cross. Through these he expresses a living faith; in obedience to the will of God, he pays the ultimate price of death on behalf of humanity, thus becoming an example to be followed by all who confess him as leader.

---

18. Pobee, *Kwame Nkrumah and the Church in Ghana, 1949–1966*, 142–51; Pobee, *Politics and Religion in Ghana*, 23–37; Yankah, *Otumfuo Osei Tutu II*, 62.

19. Williamson, "The Lyrics of the Fanti Methodist Church," 128; *AMECEA Documentation Service* no. 11 (1974): 2.

20. Christaller, *Dictionary of the Asante and Fante Language Called Tshi (Twi)*, 226.

I Am an African Christian

In popular imagination the Asante have been a warlike nation, and in the past the Asante conducted wars against the Denkyira and others. During those wars the asantehene acted as commander-in-chief. But this picture needs to be set beside another important role of the chief, that of peacemaker and reconciler, for an essential aspect of the chief's role is to exercise judicial power and to administer justice and peace.

Focusing on use of the word "chief" to signal leadership, however, introduces more subtleties, for among the Asante, "leadership" itself represents a multifaceted concept. The honorifics used of chiefs—*kantamanto*, *kasapreko*, and *asomdwehene*—spell out aspects of what leadership entails. *Osagyefo kantamanto* is the traditional praise name of the *ohene*, that is, the chief styled as *kataman* (nation-coverer, from ökataömann, "the one who covers the whole nation or world").[21] The nearness or likeness of the two words *kantamanto* and *kataman* to each other may suggest that the chief is called to be as God, that is, as one who covers the nation. Another etymology, however, derives *kantamanto* from *ka* (say), *ntam* (oath/vow), and *onnto* (does not break), that is, one who never goes back on his oath or on his word. By this etymology the term becomes almost synonymous with *kasapreko*—the second praise name of Osei Tutu I (1697–1731)—which means "he who speaks once and for all," that is, a determined person. A third praise name is *asomdwehene* (prince of peace). Another praise name of Osei Tutu I, as also of Ofori Atta I of Kibi, is *osagyefo*, which means literally "one who obtains allies for winning a war (*osa*)," "the collector of an army," or "one who hires an army to join his own."[22] Christaller adds that in Fante, the language of another Akan group, the word means "deliverer."

The title "chief" or "king" is a composite idea, encompassing a number of character traits and qualities. Some of them—such as determination, honesty, being an instrument of deliverance, and being an instrument of peace—can be related to Christian ideas and can serve as models for Christians. Further, citizens were expected to model or emulate the qualities of the chief. Borrowing praise names used of the chiefs in Ghanaian lyrics still leaves room for upholding the uniqueness of Christ.[23]

Other West Africans, however, are dissatisfied with using the titles of the chief as Christological titles. Kwame Bediako, also a Ghanaian, stresses the fact that Christ is proclaimed in the context of poverty, powerlessness, and religious pluralism. He holds, therefore, that the image of the chief may not be appropriate for speaking of Christ.[24] The chief represents power and authority while Jesus is servant. Also, Bediako suggests that in the context of religious pluralism, the idea of chief may not be obvious or readily understood by many participants. He suggests a different epithet, *nana* (elder), though chiefs are also called nana.

---

21. Ibid., 416, 421.
22. Ibid.
23. Williamson, "Lyrics of the Fanti Methodist Church," 128.
24. Kwame Bediako, "Biblical Christologies in the Context of African Traditional Religions," in Samuel and Sugden, *Sharing Jesus in the Two-Thirds World*, 81–121.

Harry Sawyerr, also a West African but from Sierra Leone, uses as a point of departure the observation that the religious and spiritual epistemology of homo africanus has within it a strong strain of anthropomorphism. Drawing in turn on the anthropomorphic imagery of the Great Family in which Jesus Christ is the head and universal elder brother, the firstborn of the family of God (Rom 8:29; 1 John 3:2), he stresses the humanity of Jesus, "the man in whom God lives." Sawyerr adds, however, the idea of the mystical relationship between Christ and those who would follow him as disciples (Eph 2:19–22; 3:14—4:16), insisting on their obligation to be conformed to and shaped in Christ's likeness.[25]

A related Christological image that also arises from the anthropomorphism of African cultures is that of Christ Our Ancestor. The strong family sense of homo africanus, with its communitarian epistemology and ontology, leads some African theologians to place emphasis on the image of Christ as our ancestor.[26]

Building on the kinship imagery that is characteristic of African societies and using the unjust sociopolitical challenges of the African context as a point of departure, Chukwudumu Okolo constructs a Christology of the Black Christ.[27] Needless to argue that this is a case of African theology that has learned from liberation theology the crucial role played by the starting point in theological construction, namely, the historical and concrete situation of the context. The Christological statement that "Christ is Black" articulates that Christ is on the side of Africans pommelled and oppressed by the violence, brutality, and even segregation of apartheid.

The Christology of the Black Christ raises some poignant questions. Is Christ limited or trapped in the plight of oppressed Blacks? Do aberrations from Christian principles, evident in some cases, necessitate the rejection of accompanying authentic Christian teaching? Whatever judgment is made on these questions, Christ's witness of love and suffering remain part of the cost of the *residuum evangelium*.

At present a plethora of African Christologies are available to us. For at least three reasons, it would be an error to feel compelled to choose only one of them. First, the New Testament attests that several Christological titles were present from the very beginning. Second, every image and all imagery is by definition partial truth and never the whole truth. Finally, we have learned from liberation theology the importance of taking seriously the context from which we theologize.

Multiple Approaches within African Christology

At least five different approaches can be discerned in contemporary African Christology, each seeking to answer the question: Who do Africans say that Christ is? The first

25. Sawyerr, *Creative Evangelism*, 72–74.

26. Pénoukou, *Églises d'Afrique*; Pobee, *Toward an African Theology*, 94–98; Bujo, "Pour une éthique africaine Christocentrique," 4–52; Nyamiti, *Christ as Our Ancestor*.

27. Okolo, "Diminished Man and Theology: An African Perspective," 83–86.

is the incarnational approach, articulated in Rome in 1974 by the Synod of Bishops of Africa and Madagascar, in which the mystery of the incarnation becomes the model for Christology.[28] The eternal Word taking human form in Jesus in Palestine is a warranty for Christ taking human form in African nations. This incarnational approach takes something from the statements of Vatican II, especially *Ad gentes* (3.22), and Pope John Paul II's encyclical letter *Slavorum apostoli* (June 2, 1985) and his address to the Kenyan bishops, *Catechesi tradendae*, no. 53 (May 5, 1980).

The second approach is that of the *logos spermatikos* (the seed of the Word). It employs the idea of the L\logos to argue that Christ the Word pervades all human beings and, therefore, all cultures must be open to the gospel.[29] This approach can be traced to early church fathers such as Justin Martyr and Clement of Alexandria.

Third is the functional analogy approach, which, for example, depicts Christ as the greatest Ancestor.[30] Properly understood, followers of this approach include Bénézet Bujo, Charles Nyamiti, and John Pobee. Advocates of the approach find parallels in biblical Christological titles.

Fourth is the Paschal Mystery approach. For it the death and resurrection of Jesus forms the center of Christology. Jesus as human is limited, but the resurrected Christ belongs to all cultures and identifies with them through the proclamation of the gospel. This approach seems to follow the articulation of the mystical body of Christ in Ephesians 1:22-23.

The fifth approach is biblical, basing its exposition on the universal dimension of Christ and on Jesus' identity with the Father (John 8:58, 12:27-50). Therefore, Christ transcends every historicization of him, a fact that opens the door to the idea of the possibility that Christ was present in African cultures before he was proclaimed there.

I Am an African Christian

The title of this chapter, "I Am an African Christian," is a confession of faith signaling my allegiance to Christ; nevertheless, I share a common humanity with other persons who do not make the same confession. Our common humanity entails that none of us may disenfranchise the other. Together we share this world created by God, not by some human being. The most challenging part of my confession is how to share God's Word and world with other persons and other confessions.

One of the convictions of a Christian is that life is more than the purely physical and that we are in the final analysis accountable to the One who created us. As human beings, we are ultimately accountable for the character of our relationships with our fellow humans and for our use or misuse of creation. The parable of the sheep and

---

28. See *AMECEA Documentation Service* no. 11 (1974) 2.
29. Shorter, *Toward a Theology of Inculturation*, 79-82.
30. John S. Mbiti, "Jesus Christ in African Religion?," in Pobee, *Exploring Afro-Christology*, 21-29.

goats, found in Matthew 25:31–46, is a message of the last social judgment. Our final accounting as portrayed there is inextricably linked with relationships in this life.

To be a Christian is at once to treasure the Word of God, to live a life of faith, and to commit to a moral life, which become raw material for accountability to the Creator. Our commitment to eradicating famine, suffering, and disease—all of which are found in Africa in abundance—is a matter for which we will give account before the Creator.

Augustine of Hippo, in his Sermon 103, fittingly encourages Christians: "Do not grieve or complain that you were born in a time when you can no longer see God in the flesh. He did not in fact take this privilege from you. As he says; 'whatever you have done to the least of my brothers, you did to me.'"

10

God and the Social Order

IN 1968, TWO YEARS after the coup d'état that removed Osagyefo Dr. Kwame Nkrumah from office and power, I, then a young lecturer, set a question for the BA Honours degree in New Testament as follows: "Critically examine, in the light of the New Testament, the coup d'état in Ghana in February 1966." The external examiner, a distinguished New Testament scholar from King's College, University of London, remarked that the question in that form was not appropriate in a New Testament examination. Whatever the issues, the response signals some long-standing stances found in Christian thinking. They often find expression as "Keep religion out of politics" or "This is economics—keep religion out." Such a stance reflects the atomization of theology and life that is axiomatic in our time and that carves up life into autonomous and independent units.

Two considerations, however, should caution us against atomization of scientific study and theology. First, we should consider the significance of the fact that Adam Smith (1723–90), the person who gave us the first academic statement of economic theory, was an ordained minister of the Church of Scotland as well as being a Scottish political economist and philosopher.[1] At that time, knowledge was still one and not compartmentalized. Indeed, theology was styled the Queen of the Sciences.[2] As convenient as the atomization of knowledge is—and indeed of theology as well—compartmentalization should not be allowed to obstruct a holistic view of life.

The saga of creation and the biblical perspective on life demand that we resist compartmentalization of life and knowledge, for everything was created by God. I use the word "saga" advisedly to signal that the creation account is not to be taken as a scientific account of the origins of the universe. Rather, the creation story utilizes the language of mythology to express the faith of the Hebrews that the one God created heaven and earth and everything in it. It is an assertion that all human labor has been dignified by virtue of being a collaboration with God to perfect the garden he planned.

---

1. Smith, *An Enquiry into the Nature and Causes of the Wealth of Nations*.
2. Newman, *The Idea of a University*.

Understood in this way, everything in the world—including social order—possesses a divine reference and can fit into a holistic religious understanding of reality.

Homo Socialis

The saga of creation asserts that God reasoned that "it is not good for the man to be alone. I will make a suitable partner for him" (Gen 2:18 NAB). Male and female were created to complement each other as partners and are by implication equal. The language used to express how the woman was created, "bone of my bones and flesh of my flesh" (Gen 2:23 NAB), signals that the two parties are of the same nature and same dignity. Humans are created to be *homo socialis*, that is, social beings marked by equality of the sexes, interdependence, mutual respect, and harmony. These attributes form the contours that give integrity to community and society. Marriage and family life are part of the design established at creation (Gen 2:24). In Africa, marriage is the union not just of a couple but also of their respective families. Here again, we see that humanity is created for sociability, and to live is to live in community—whether as family (nuclear or extended) or as clan, tribe, nation, or race.

The family constitutes the prototypical community. At the most basic level, "community" describes a collection of people residing within a geographical area.[3] But at their best, communities are conscious of being a social unit and they have a measure of group identification.[4] At their best, communities constitute a system of interdependent relationships and interaction. Members of communities have a substratum of shared meaning or, as W. I. Thomas puts it, a We-Feeling and a sense of community.[5] A sense of community implies an awareness that whether we like it or not, other people's lives will influence ours for good or for ill, and ours theirs. It further implies a sense that we need others to help us to define ourselves as well as our problems.

Community relationships are modeled in a whole range of ways—patrons, benefactors, partners, and siblings. For healthy modeling one needs the sense that each person bears the *imago Dei* as well as recognition that the other person is a fully human being and not a *res* (a thing). The *imago Dei* and recognition of the humanity of others provide a moral substratum for addressing social order. For that reason, what is human is the measure of social order, and social order serves what is human and the well-being of humans.

The ideology of globalization and the emergence of groupings, local, regional, and international—for example, the United Nations Organization (UNO), the United Nations Educational, Scientific, and Cultural Organization (UNESCO), World Health

---

3. Theodorson and Theodorson, *A Modern Dictionary of Sociology*, 63; Abercrombie et al., *Penguin Dictionary of Sociology*, 47–48.

4. Durkheim, *Elementary Forms of Religious Life*; Durkheim, *Division of Labor in Society*, chaps. 2–7; Tönnies, *Community and Association*.

5. Thomas, *Social Behavior and Personality*.

Organization (WHO), the Food and Agriculture Organization (FAO), the Africa Union (AU), Economic Community of West African States (ECOWAS), the South African Development Community (SADEC), the community of Brazil, Russia, India, China, and South Africa (BRICS), the World Council of Churches (WCC), and the All African Conference of Churches (AACC)—signal both the sense of and need for a larger community than one's own.

As M. M. Thomas puts it, "There is growing sense of common humanity or human solidarity in the world which finds its expression in mutual concern, a sense of participation in the struggles of others for their fundamental rights, and a common endeavor in building structures of a world community and searching for an ethos to make them stable. This 'secular ecumenical movement' may be only beginning, but it is already a genuine movement of human solidarity which we must recognize as a new factor of no small significance in the world today."[6]

Our discussion to this point presents two poles for negotiating social order. One pole consists of the individual and his or her particular identity; the other pole consists of corporate and group life and their identity. The measure of either pole is what is human. Two particular documents based on human experience give us some of the contours of the task.

The first is the United Nations charter which states:

> We, the peoples of the United Nations, determined to save succeeding generations from the scourge of war, which twice in our lifetime has brought untold sorrow to mankind, and to reaffirm faith in fundamental human rights, in the dignity and worth of the human person, in the equal rights of men and women and of nations large and small, . . .
>
> And for these ends to practice tolerance and live together in peace with one another as good neighbours, and to unite our strength to maintain international peace and security, . . .
>
> Have resolved to combine our efforts to accomplish these aims."[7]

The foregoing text is based on a draft by South African Jan Christian Smuts (1870–1950). This text emerged, of course, from a particular context. But the fact that the United Nations, the worldwide body that to our day affirms this charter, exists is evidence that all right-thinking persons and nations hold to these principles for creating a healthy social order.

The insights of the UN charter were informed by two world wars (1914–18, 1939–45), which issued in enormous carnage and massive destruction. What is often not given serious consideration is that these two wars, in which colonial people

---

6. M. M. Thomas, "The World in Which We Preach Christ," in Orchard, *Witness in Six Continents*, 15.

7. Charter of the United Nations, "Preamble," June 26, 1945.

of color joined white colonial masters to face a common danger, also exposed and removed the veil of mystery that had accorded superiority to whites. People of color learned that whites died just as they did. They discovered that blacks too were able to make sacrifices for the cause of freedom, security, and peace, and that they could be as heroic as whites.

The UN charter represents a convergence and concurrence on the part of all people to strain toward and make sacrifices for peace and security for each and all. Elements essential to that goal include the dignity and worth of each human person, equal rights for male and female, tolerance, and good neighborliness. These provide the contours of individual life and social order.

The second important document is a section of Thomas Jefferson's First Inaugural Address, delivered in 1801, in which he articulates the freedom that social order must pursue:

> Equal and exact justice to all men, of whatever state or persuasion, religious or political; peace, commerce, and honest friendship of all nations, entangling alliances with none; . . . freedom of religion, freedom of the press, and freedom of person under the protection of the habeas corpus, and trial by juries impartially selected. These principles form the bright constellation which has gone before us and guided our steps through an age of revolution and reformation. The wisdom of our sages and the blood of our heroes have been devoted to their attainment. They should be the creed of our political faith, the text of civil instruction, the touchstone by which to try the services of those we trust; and should we wander from them in moments of error or of alarm, let us hasten to retrace our steps and to regain the road which alone leads to peace, liberty, and safety.[8]

Admittedly this statement is an artifact of the United States. But not only has it been tried and tested and found helpful for renewal of social life, but it also has proven creative around the globe.

It is tempting to offer extended commentary on these texts, but later chapters will provide occasion to address some of the pertinent issues. For now, I put forward three comments. First, the tenets these texts enumerate are the wisdom of the ages. Roman coins bore the inscription *Pax et Securitas* (peace and security). Social order is about peace and security, which the Roman head of state represented.[9] The two quotations detail some aspects of that goal.

Second, we must not expect to see all details of the ideas fully present and active in every place because of differences in contexts and experiences. Though the statements are helpful guides, each place must translate and interpret them in light of its own context, circumstances, and challenges. As always, the principle of contextualization

---

8. Thomas Jefferson, First Inaugural Address, March 4, 1801, http://avalon.law.yale.edu/19th_century/jefinau1.asp.

9. Stauffer, *Christ and the Caesars*.

underlines that each construct yields probability and, therefore, must be adapted to the local setting.

Third, the missionary and colonial practice of tabula rasa ignored the fact that homo africanus also brought experiences and ideas, ones colored by having been minted in African circumstances and challenges, to the table of discussion.

An African theologian's work, therefore, is to engage in and sustain, in a rational manner, a trialogue between inherited models, Christian insights, and ideas particular to Africa.

Some Traditional African Hints

Social order represents the confluence of sociocultural, economic, political, and ethical issues and challenges. We dare ignore or exclude none of these elements, for what may look like a straightforward economic issue has, time and again, been found to be enmeshed in cultural factors. Issues of development have been, time and again, tripped up and trapped by cultural habits and factors. Therefore, it is necessary to attempt a holistic approach to all issues of social order.

Social order represents a people's hopes and fears with regard to their well-being, that is, their wholeness, which is not unrelated to the theological term "salvation." The Akan of Ghana express that *summum bonum* with the word *ahoto* (literally, the *tō*—or peace, rest, and security—of *aho*, that is, the self). In short, well-being encompasses the peace, restfulness, contentment, and security of people, individually and corporately. It expresses inner/internal and outward/external peace, both material and spiritual.

The Akan also prayed for *nsare-nson*, that is, for the seven graces:

1. *Nkwa*, long life, vitality, felicity, prosperity.
2. *Adom*, the favor of the world of spirits on whose favors the living depend.
3. *Asomdwee*, peace of mind, peace of society/community, freedom from perturbation.
4. *Abawotum*, fertility and ability to procreate (for the great responsibility is to foster the growth of the clan).
5. *Anihutum*, the ability to see, good eyesight.
6. *Asotatum*, good hearing.
7. *Amandore*, growth and development of society, its vitality and greatness.

Vis-à-vis the social order, the *summum bonum* is a multifaceted hope. As I wrote a quarter century ago, "It includes diverse items of divine grace, material prosperity, good health, [and] peace of soul [and mind] and surroundings [as well as] descendants through whom the continuity, security, and well-being of the individual as of the clan are maintained, especially given the high mortality rate of the tropics."[10]

Theology Engages the Social Order

The social order challenges theology to desist from roaming in the heavens, to come down to earth, and to engage peoples for their well-being. In the interface between the Word of God and the realities of the social order is the locus in which theology and the community of faith find their proper meaning. The word Pope John Paul II spoke to journalists as he was en route to Chile in 1987 speaks meaningfully to this point: "To the Gospel message belong all the problems of human rights, and if democracy means human rights, then it also belongs to the message of the Church."[11]

Christian theology, being committed to the Christian core-message of the incarnation, will engage the condition of homo africanus and of Africa, which has become synonymous with poverty and with those who too often are excluded, ignored, and marginalized. Thus Leonardo Boff offered the church an important insight when he argued for poverty as the prism of liberation theology. He insisted that the church herself should be poor when she reflects on living experience, "the stuff" of history. It is in that context that she can discover God's will for the church and theology.

Academic theology and so-called normative theology represent top-down sources and methods of guidance to long-neglected people at the bottom. Boff's approach, located within the lowest tiers of society, pursued the study of Scripture from within those contexts and gave impetus to grassroots political movements. In this way theology became an attempt to read the life and message of Jesus through the eyes of those who have customarily been excluded.

Solidarity with the excluded touches on two terms, peace and love, that are of key significance for Christian theology. The pursuit of love is given concrete expression when people of privilege attempt community, including spiritual community, with "the other" by living and sharing with people who are excluded. In this way theology is written in their lives together. Such activities endeavor to bridge the gaps that exist between rich and poor; as an ideal of Christian life, they offer an opening for beginning to discover people. Peace with justice is what Martin Luther King Jr. (1929–68) described as "love in calculation."[12] Scripture is replete with statements that enunciate the crucial importance of social responsibility as essential to living faith and spirituality. Jesus' teaching includes that of the last social judgment, spelled out in the parable of the sheep and goats (Matt 25:31–46). The judgment of God encompasses everyone,

---

10. John S. Pobee, "An African Christian in Search of Democracy," in Witte, *Christianity and Democracy in Global Context*, 280.

11. Weigel, *Witness to Hope*, 53.

12. Martin Luther King Jr., Speech to Montgomery Improvement Association (MIA) Mass Meeting, December 5, 1955, http://www.digitalhistory.uh.edu/disp_textbook.cfm?smtid=3&psid=3625.

not only those who believe and have signed up as followers of Christ, but also unbelievers and those who have not yet come to know the only true God, the Creator and Father of all. The former will be judged according to the measure of revelation they have received and made avowals of. The principle of judgment for nonbelievers will be acts of mercy they have or have not chosen to perform.

The imagery of separating between the sheep (the good) and the goats (the evil) conveys a message of our moral responsibility for actions we take in the social order, actions that place us or do not place us on the side of the Creator. The human power to choose between good and evil lies at the very heart of social order. Hunger, thirst, the "poor," and the most vulnerable such as the naked, the stranger, the outcast, the sick, and those in prison are matters of social concern. True generosity, loving deeds, and humanity are standard components of social order.

God's Preferential Option for the Poor: Ideology for the Social Order

The description in Matthew 25:40 and 25:45 (NABRE) of the most vulnerable of society as the "least brothers" of Christ and "these least" is striking. Such language travels in the same boat with liberation theology's language of "God's preferential option for the poor." Harvey Cox sums up the development of liberation theology:

> In their famous meeting at Medellín, Colombia, in 1968, the Latin American bishops proclaimed that the church should exercise a preferential option for the poor. Liberation theology is an expression of this preference. It is the attempt to interpret the Bible and Christianity from the perspective of the poor. It is in no sense a liberal or modernist theological deviation. Rather, it is a *method*, an effort to look at the life and message of Jesus through the eyes of those who have normally been excluded or ignored. . . . [Liberation theologians] work closely with the burgeoning "Christian base communities" of Latin America. These are local groups of Catholics, most of whom are from the lowest tiers of society, whose study of the Bible has led them to become active in grassroots political movements. Thus liberation theology provides both an alternative to the top-down method of conventional academic and ecclesial theology as well as a source of guidance to the long-neglected people at the bottom.[13]

In Africa—which in the aftermath of its experience of slavery, colonialism, and mercantile domination from the North has become synonymous with poverty—a strong argument exists for using the preferential option for the poor as an ideology for organizing the continent's social order.

It hardly needs to be argued that family life dwells at the core of social order, and so Scripture, after moving in the heavens, comes down to earth and family life. At the very heart of the Christian gospel stands the incarnation: "The Word became

---

13. Cox, *Silencing of Leonardo Boff*, 11; see also Boff, *Church, Charism, and Power*, 38.

flesh," that is, became human (John 1:14). Christ's incarnation took place in a specific, particular Semitic culture (Gal 4:4). In this fact we see that the Word of God and history are inseparable. Jesus has a mother, Mary. That note underscores the normalcy of the social order; it is not to be despised or underrated. Characteristically, African societies, like the societies we observe in the Bible, are communitarian. They have a communitarian epistemology and ontology, and the family constitutes the prototypical society and community.

Mencius (372–289 BC) spoke the wisdom of the ages when he asserted: "The root of the kingdom is in the State. The root of the State is in the family. The root of the family is in the person *of its Head*."[14] Thus a healthy family is a sine qua non for a healthy social order. As a gift from God, the family must be treasured and it must be shored up for the sake of a healthy social order. When Scripture states that "it is not good for the man to be alone" (Gen 2:18 NABRE), we hear expressed an option for a healthy family and, through that, for a healthy nation and a healthy world.

The health of social life must not be taken for granted; it must be cultivated intentionally and conscientiously. Values that make for sound and healthy family life must be inculcated. As the book of Proverbs puts it, "Train up a child in the way he should go: and when he is old, he will not depart from it" (22:6 KJV). Further, the worth of a sound value system is underscored: "A good name is rather to be chosen than great riches" (Prov 22:1 KJV).

The New Testament's household code of conduct (Eph 5:21—6:9) enjoins all members of the household to submit to one another. This code envisions reciprocal roles and a mutual obligation of love and self-giving as shown, for example, in the relationship between father and children and that between husband and wife. The fourth commandment, to honor one's father and mother, is fundamental to the social order (Exod 20:12; Deut 5:16; Prov 30:17). Parents are to be honored and respected as God's instruments in bringing about life and order (see Mal 1:6; Sir 3:1–16); in return, children honor their parents by looking after them. According to Akan wisdom, "The old woman looks after the child to develop and grow teeth, and the child in turn looks after the old lady when she has lost her teeth." Mutual caring and responsibility for each other form the basis of social order.

Similarly, in relationship with their children, the New Testament charges parents with the responsibility to bring up their children (Eph 6:4; Heb 12:6–8), to meet their basic needs (1 Tim 5:8), to create a spiritual atmosphere (2 Tim 3:15), and to practice such values as love, gentleness, trust, friendship, and understanding (Rom 14:17; Gal 5:22–23). Significantly, in bringing them up in the fear of the Lord, parents are warned against provoking their children to anger (Eph 6:4). Children have rights and are entitled to be treated humanely and with dignity.

The various races and nationalities as well as natural and legitimate ethnic identities are part of the social order and of legitimate social relations. These natural social

14. Legge, *Works of Mencius*, 4.1.5.

distinctions are not a criterion of either inclusion or exclusion or, in a healthy social order, a barrier to relationships. Unfortunately, natural social distinctions have sometimes been treated as phenotypes and have been made a source of great violence and distress.

Paul teaches that in the Christian fellowship, discrimination and treating people as inferior is impermissible whether on grounds of gender, race, color of skin, nationality, or class (Gal 3:28; Rom 10:12-13; 1 Cor 12:12-13; Col 3:11). At bottom the issue is how each identity enriches the social order in a positive and healthy manner. Patriarchal and gender stereotypes are not to be translated in a negative or oppressive way.

In the United States and South Africa, racism has wrought much havoc and destruction. US civil rights leader Martin Luther King Jr. spoke a Christian word when he said, in his speech during the August 28, 1963, March on Washington, "I have a dream that one day on the red hills of Georgia the sons of former slaves and the sons of former slave owners will be able to sit down together at the table of brotherhood.... I have a dream that my four little children will one day live in a nation where they will not be judged by the color of their skin, but by the content of their character."[15]

Earlier that year, in his "Letter from Birmingham Jail," King had identified how order is sometimes misused. He wrote: "The Negro's great stumbling block in his stride toward freedom is not the White Citizen's Councilor or the Ku Klux Klanner, but the white moderate, who is more devoted to 'order' than to justice . . . who paternalistically believes he can set the timetable for another man's freedom."[16] Social order must include justice and freedom, both of which are biblical values and marks of God's kingdom.

If King, a Christian minister, represents the struggle for social order with peace and justice within the US context, Nelson Rohihlaha Mandela (1918-2013) represents an essentially Christian view from the African continent. In the face of the violent ideology of apartheid present in the Republic of South Africa, he stated, "I have fought against white domination, and I have fought against black domination. I have cherished the ideal of a democratic and free society in which all persons will live together in harmony and with equal opportunities. It is an ideal which I hope to live for and to achieve. But if needs be, it is an ideal for which I am prepared to die."[17]

Just and free social order is hardly ever given on a silver platter. Each person must be willing to "risk martyrdom in order to move and stir the social conscience of his community and the nation . . . [to] force his oppressor to commit his brutality openly—in the

---

15. Martin Luther King Jr., "I Have a Dream," August 28, 1963, http://www.americanrhetoric.com/speeches/mlkihaveadream.htm.

16. Martin Luther King Jr., "Letter from Birmingham Jail," April 16, 1963, http://coursesa.matrix.msu.edu/~hst306/documents/letter.html.

17. Nelson Mandela, "An Ideal for Which I Am Prepared to Die," April 20, 1964, http://www.theguardian.com/world/2007/apr/23/nelsonmandela.

light of day—with the rest of the world looking on. . . . Non-violent resistance paralyze[s] and confuse[s] the power structures against which it [is] directed."[18]

In Africa, not infrequently, Scripture has been used indiscriminately, right and left. That approach, if not irrelevant, is not satisfying. Christian theologians addressing the social order must engage in dialogue between the gospel and the social order and the reality of pluralism. Issues of social order are also religious and spiritual issues.

Environment: A Measure of the Social Order

The argument as developed thus far has suggested that humans and their well-being are the measure of social order. But in the biblical and therefore the Christian view, humankind is not to be separated off from the rest of creation and treated in isolation. Human beings, male and female, the crown of God's created order, were placed in that creation, among other reasons, for the purpose of managing it—presumably doing so well and in accordance with the will and purpose of the Creator. Creation is composed of interrelated facets, one of which is the firmament, God's second act of creation. Composed of the skies and the environment—the atmosphere—the firmament is part of what God pronounced "very good" (Gen 1:31 KJV). So a good firmament is one of the things humans must manage.

From all over Africa come reports of environmental pollution and environmental degradation. For example, in Ghana the city of Tema has dark clouds of smoke hanging over it from oil refining and other industries. Parallel to the buildup of this smoke is an increased incidence of cancer. The discovery of oil in Ghana's Western Region has been a cause for rejoicing with much talk of the economic benefits. The implications and consequences for the environment are hardly mentioned. But if the experience of oil rich Eastern Nigeria is anything to go by, the consequences can be disastrous. In that instance, humans have not proven to be the measure of the social order. Religious groups and institutions that claim to be dedicated to human well-being must have the environment on their agenda as they work at securing the social order. To preach to persons who have been hit negatively by environmental degradation is to lock the door of the barn of well-being and order, after the horse of a good and sound and healthy social order has bolted away.

The measure of good theology—and a good sermon—is: What fosters and secures good, sound, and healthy order in which humanity can thrive? Such theology will have a pluralistic and ecumenical perspective, for others address the subject of the environment with different interests at stake and from diverse perspectives, whether from economic interest, especially that of the profit motif, scientific curiosity, or another angle of engagement. All of these ventures must be judged or measured

---

18. King, *Why We Can't Wait*, 28, 30.

according to values that promote the well-being of people. On that point religion and ethics have much to say.

Related to environmental security is environmental encroachment, which is part of the huge problem of land. In Southern Africa, Central Africa, and Kenya, contests over control of land have been the cause of much pain, destruction, and inhumanity. In Ghana peoples have fought over land. In African epistemology and ontology, to be denied one's ancestral land is to be denied one's human dignity, integrity, and identity. People's dignity is rooted in their land; therefore, we are presented with the need for a theology of *humus* (the Latin word for "soil" is also the root word for humanity).[19] Land is to be treated with respect. Access to land is one measure of a good social order.

The area of social order is where nature and nurture coincide. A sense of social order is acquired, in part, through a combination of experience and learned traits. In other words, nature and nurture, biology and culture need to be held together. Early social experiences such as educational opportunities or their lack, poverty, malnutrition, and child abuse are demonstrably related to specific kinds of cultural activity. Biosocial science—a synthesis of natural and social sciences—is key to developing a sound and realistic social order, as it is to our understanding of humanity. It is essential to advancing sound public policy and improving public health. Biological understanding and behavioral understanding should be pursued in tandem. Humans are fully part of nature; consequently, we dare to suggest that biosocial science is key to improving human welfare.

Pope Leo XIII's encyclical *Rerum novarum* (1891) marked a most significant turning point in Roman Catholic—and wider Christian—thinking regarding economics. While conservative Protestant churches' approach to the subject of economics maintained a sharp distinction between the spiritual and the secular, the eternal and the temporal, *Rerum novarum* introduced the concept of the "common good." The efforts of God's people in support of the social order are to be guided by a sense of the common good. The encyclical defined the right of workers to unionize, to receive just wages, and to work under humane conditions. The secular state, Tom Stransky summarizes, "has positive moral responsibilities and is the ultimate guarantor of the rights of the person in society." Against the background of industrial society's wage economy, "Leo XIII began the papal teaching tradition on the rights and duties of management, workers and the state, the protection of workers against exploitation, their right to just wages, and their right to organize themselves for protection and representation. He also introduced into social ethics the principle of *subsidiarity* in the society-state relationship: to preserve as much freedom as possible, the responsibility for social needs should begin with the local and smallest institutional authority, and be referred to the state only when other institutions cannot meet those needs."[20]

---

19. John S. Pobee, "An African Christian in Search of Democracy," in Witte, *Christianity and Democracy in Global Context*, 280–82; Edwards, "The Irrelevance of Development Studies," 116–35.

20. Tom Stransky, "Roman Catholic Social Encyclicals," in Lossky, *Dictionary of the Ecumenical*

What Leo XIII wrote is so clear that it hardly needs comment. It is a tall order, but happily it provides a starting point. Pope Pius XI, in his encyclical *Quadragesimo anno* (1931), carried matters further, stating that social justice and social charity are essential for constructing society. Even more striking is the encyclical's insistence that the laity have an integral role in the construction of society. *Summi pontificatus* (1939), an encyclical published by Pope Pius XII, also denounced denial of unity and solidarity of the human race as heresy. In this encyclical we see Roman Catholic social doctrine beginning to go beyond the nation to juridically established international relationships.

Pope John XXIII's *Mater et magistra* (1961) added another line to the etching: prosperity is at once wealth—national and international—*and* just distribution. Further, human freedom and dignity function as bases of world order and world peace. Pope John XXIII's *Pacem in terris* (1963) placed poverty and wealth on the agenda as an issue of social conscience.

The foregoing encyclicals were directed largely to the theme of development. Beginning in the 1970s, the focus of papal encyclicals shifted from development to human rights, for example, John Paul II's *Redemptor hominis* (1979) and *Laborem excercens* (1981). Interestingly, as in liberation theology at this stage, the language of "structural sin" and a preferential, but not exclusive, "option for the poor" became loud and clear in Pope John II's *Sollicitudo rei socialis* (1987).

Finally, as stated by Pope John XXIII, people and persons are "the foundation, the cause, and the end of all social institution," because God created human beings as social beings and above nature.[21]

Choosing to map out Roman Catholic insights on God and social order has been deliberate on my part, not from sectarian motivation but to signal that the subject of God and social order is so vast that no single theological statement can encompass it all. The social teaching of the church must be perceived as being in the process of ongoing development. Further, all of us are well advised to be open to the gains and contributions made available to us by other traditions.

Movement, 394.

21. John XXIII, "*Mater et Magistra*," May 15, 1961, para. 219, http://w2.vatican.va/content/john-xxiii/en/encyclicals/documents/hf_j-xxiii_enc_15051961_mater.html.

11

Sex: Uncovering the Nakedness of the Other

ALL OVER THE WORLD, Africa included, interest in sex runs high. Movies make much of sex. Sex scandals dominate the airwaves. In the United States, Senate hearings prior to confirmation of African American Clarence Thomas as a justice of the US Supreme Court were dominated by allegations of sexual harassment brought against him by another African American, university professor Anita Hill.

The attempt of another African American, Herman Cain, to become the flagbearer of the Grand Old Party (GOP, that is, the Republican Party in the United States) was derailed in 2011 because of allegations of sexual harassment. A sitting US president, Bill Clinton, was pulled here and there for philandering with an intern at the White House. In the United States a poll that appeared in *Time* magazine reported that 73 percent of the populace care somewhat or a great deal when a public figure is accused of sexual harassment. Only 18 percent said they did not care very much and 7 percent not at all. In Ghana, sex scandals, including those of religious personalities, are forever in the headlines. These reports signal deep moral questions and issues that affect the health of the nation. At the personal level, sex scandals are often seen as supplying an important window into someone's character. Sex is unquestionably placed squarely on the agenda of theology.

The English word "sex" is used in two senses: first, it indicates gender, male or female; and second, coitus. Both senses belong to the order of nature, and yet in Ghana we find what appears to be some embarrassment in talking openly about this natural order of creation. Thus the word sex is usually preceded by "excuse me to say" or "*sèbi*" (with humility and deference). This chapter addresses sex in the sense of coitus.

As a Christian, my primary resource is Scripture; for me, recourse to Scripture is both primary and inescapable. But as in all study of Scripture, we must be attentive to the principle of text and context. Engaging in dialogue between the Scripture text understood in its original context and the reader's context and situation is what can lead to conviction. A people's context includes their worldview (which is their "wavelength" and code) as well as their socioeconomic and political circumstances and challenges. Let us look to biblical insights under five headings that form a lexicon of coitus of sorts.

Lie With

Lot's two daughters devised a scheme to lie with their father. The elder of the daughters said to the younger, "Our father is an old man, and there is no one here to marry us in the normal way of the world. Come on, let us ply our father with wine and sleep [lie] with him. In this way we can preserve the race by our father" (Gen 19:31–32 NJB). To "lie" with in this context is not just a posture; it is to lie down in sexual relationship, sometimes spoken of as carnal knowledge (Gen 19:32–36; see also Gen 4:1 KJV "knew" and Lev 19:20 KJV "lieth carnally").

Leviticus 15:16–18 (NJB) goes further to say that such lying together goes with and issues in emission or ejaculation of semen: "When a man has a seminal discharge, he must wash his whole body with water and will be unclean until evening. Any clothing or leather touched by the seminal discharge must be washed and will be unclean until evening. When a woman has had intercourse with a man, both of them must wash and will be unclean until evening." Some of the details may be debatable, but for now our concern is to establish that the language of lying together refers to more than a posture; it encompasses a mysterious encounter and engagement between two persons, normally male and female. It is a means of intimate knowing (Num 31:17 NRSV), such that one would not normally lie with a stranger, someone we do not trust.

The biblical references suggest that coitus is more than an act of pleasure. It is an act of carnal knowledge for the sake of preserving the race. It is an act of intimacy.

To Know

"To know" was a biblical euphemism for sexual intercourse. "Adam knew Eve his wife; and she conceived" (Gen 4:1 KJV; see also Gen 19:8; Num 31:17, 35; Judg 11:39; 21:11; 1 Sam 1:19; 1 Kgs 1:4). To know in this sense is more than knowledge by the mind; rather it is insight of the heart, gained through lived experience. Its dynamics are love and response. Sex signals intimacy of knowing. It reveals the heart of the one seeking to know. Sex that does not express and foster intimacy of relationship between the couple shortchanges the act. Sexual intercourse is thus a responsible step, carrying with it concern and care—and responsibility—for the well-being of the partner.

Uncover Nakedness

The book of Numbers contains a list of sexual prohibitions, one of which begins "none of you shall approach anyone near of kin to uncover nakedness . . . of your father . . . your mother . . . your father's wife . . . your sister" (Lev 18:6–9 NRSV). The root verb means to uncover, leave destitute, discover, empty, raze, or pour out. In Leviticus 18:6 the word is used within a prohibition against incest; marriage as well as sexual relations between certain degrees of relationship are forbidden. The difference between flesh and flesh (Gen 2:23 NAB; that is, body of Adam and body of Eve) is a reminder that beyond their apparent similarity they represent more than the corporeal and that they may not be carelessly violated. Though literally bodies are alike, "flesh" signals a private and secret part of one's life which may be exposed only to the one you trust, love, and share a deep relationship with. After the fall, our experience of nakedness and sex—good gifts from God—become cloaked by a pall of shame, an evil fruit of sin (Gen 3:7). Nakedness (either in the sense of sexual relations, that is, coitus, or of exposure of the genitals to sight) cannot be tolerated outside proper relationships or settings (see Ex 20:26, 28:42), confidence, and mutual trust.

All these euphemisms suggest that coitus reaches beyond biological function; it also has deeper psychological and security implications. Therefore, sexual relations are not to be embarked upon casually and carelessly. Extramarital sexual relationships are frowned upon. Coitus is restricted to particular relationships and in particular is reserved for a couple duly married. Adultery, the word used by the priest to signal the seriousness of an extramarital relationship, is helpful: "May Yahweh make you the object of your people's execration and curses, by making your sexual organs shrivel and your belly swell. May this water of cursing entering your bowels, make your belly swell and your sexual organs shrivel!" (Num 5:19–22 NJB; see Lev 20:10).

Together with a high view of sex and sexual relationships, the Mosaic law articulates sexual (and therefore also) marital relationships that are forbidden; see Leviticus 18:6–18 and 20:10–21. Prohibited degrees of sexual relationship include that of a man with his father's wife, that is, his step-mother (Lev 20:11; Deut 22:30), his father's sister or mother's sister (Lev 20:19), or his uncle's wife (Lev 20:20). Also prohibited are sexual relations with a sister or half-sister (Lev 20:17), a sister-in-law (Lev 20:21), a daughter-in-law (Lev 20:12), or a granddaughter (Lev 18:10). Marriage to a woman and her daughter (Lev 20:14) or two sisters at the same time (Lev 18:18) is prohibited. Sexual relations with the wife of another man are also forbidden (Lev 20:10; Deut 22:22). These prohibitions hint that the proper context for sexual intercourse is within a properly contracted marriage between a man and woman. Violation of that relationship constitutes adultery.

Coitus is a means of knowledge. The saga of the garden of Eden contains a dialogue between God and Adam in which coitus was key to eliciting moral cognition. A particular tree in the garden symbolized knowledge of good and evil (Gen 2:9, 17). By disobedience to the divine prohibition of the fruit of the particular tree, humanity came to objective awareness of good and bad in a way comparable to the knowledge God has. Without that experience they were as children, innocent, not knowing what was around them. Whenever the language of "sleeping with" is used, it signals illicit sexual relationships: "If a man seduces a virgin who is not betrothed and lies with [sleeps with] her, he shall pay her price and make her his wife" (Ex 22:16 NAB).

In modern times same sex relationships have been projected as a human right and an expression of human freedom, but this outlook is contrary to the biblical position. Leviticus 18:22 and 20:13 prohibit a man from lying with—that is, having sexual intercourse with—a male as a man would with a woman. For those who transgress this prohibition, Leviticus 20:13 pronounces a punishment of death. In short, the Scriptures inveigh forcefully against unnatural sexual relationships. They do so in protest against the surrounding cultures in which prominent religious practices and sexual practices and expressions were one and the same thing. In the New Testament same sex relationships are not only stated to be unnatural, but are also said to be an expression of idolatry. Idolatry is to confuse the glory of the immortal God with an imitation of God; in consequence, God is said to give humankind over to degrading passions (Rom 1:21–28).

In Genesis 19:30–38, Lot's daughters made their father drunk so as to sleep with him. Their behavior was inappropriate. Even if their intentions were passable—to secure the continuation of the family—their actions were improper.

In the Scripture two words, fornication and adultery, are used to describe inappropriate use of sex. Adultery refers to illicit sexual relations between a married person and another person who is not his or her certified wife or husband. The implication is that coitus or sexual intercourse is to be reserved to express the union that exists between a married couple. The commandment is clear: Do not commit adultery. The context for the prohibition of adultery is the last part of the Ten Commandments which spells out duties to one's neighbor in order to secure life, marriage, and property against invasion or attack from others. The deed is not to be separated from the thought (as Jesus notes in Matt 5:28).

The word "adultery" (*na'ap*) is used in relation to both men and women (e.g., Lev 20:10). Adultery is sexual intercourse of a husband with the wife of another male, or of a wife with the husband of another woman. Fornication (*zanah*) is sexual intercourse of two persons—whether married or not—who are not married to each other. The prohibitions against adultery and fornication suggest that coitus is most appropriate when reserved to the intimacy of a conjugal relationship. The prohibition of adultery, write Keil and Delitzsch, is "directed against any assault upon the husband's dearest possession . . . [and also] upholds the sacredness of marriage as the divine appointment for the propagation and multiplication of the human race."[1]

Free Love?

Some persons have at times advocated for free love. They have done so on the basis of their understanding of what it is to be human and of the rights that attach to being human. For them the sexual urge, present from the age of puberty, is wholly natural. Natural urges are further understood as needing satisfaction. In a further step, that

---

1. Keil and Delitzsch, *Pentateuch*, 124.

logic is combined with an emphasis on human freedom as beings made in God's image and likeness.

Our understanding of freedom, however, must be checked against the description in Scripture of humans as beings made in God's image and "after our likeness" (Gen 1:26 KJV). Keil and Delitzsch comment,

> Man is the image of God by virtue of his spiritual nature, of the breath of God by which the being, formed from the dust of the earth, became a living soul. The image of God consists, therefore, in the spiritual personality of man, though not merely in unity of self-consciousness and self-determination, or in the fact the man was created a consciously free *Ego*; for personality is merely its basis and form of the divine likeness, not its real essence. This consists rather in the fact that the man endowed with free self-conscious personality possesses, in his spiritual as well as corporeal nature, a creaturely copy of the holiness and blessedness of the divine life.[2]

That being the case, humans are not simply to yield to animal instincts.

The prohibition against adultery is part of the Decalogue, the terms of the covenant between God and his people. The sum total of the individual laws is to love God and neighbor (Deut 6:4–9; Lev 19:18; Rom 13:8–10; Matt 22:37–40; Mark 12:29–31; Luke 10:25–28). This love encompasses our total being—the totality of our heart and soul and strength and mind. It is covenantal love—in Jonathan Sacks's words, "the redemption of solitude, the bridge we build across the ontological abyss between I and Thou."[3] Coitus then is not just a casual fling nor yet simply an act of pleasure. In Scripture, faithfulness in marriage becomes an image of the bond of loyalty present between God and his chosen people as well as between Christ and the church. In regard to faithfulness in marriage, biblical faith and African tradition converge, for the latter describes a man who chases after everything in a skirt as *bodom* (a dog). Dogs are not known to stick to one partner. When the female is in heat, the male dog's only concern is to mate with her, and he does not care where the coitus occurs.

Coitus Is Good and Not Intrinsically Bad

In his early life the church father Augustine of Hippo Regius lived riotously. He records in his *Confessions* that at a certain point he prayed, "Give me chastity and continence, but not just now" (8.7). When he did make a turnaround, sex became for him a great sin. His influence on the development of Christianity ensured that sex became a major sin and preoccupation. The emergence of monastic life contributed to the exaltation of celibacy as better than a relationship involving coitus. But that God created coitus

---

2. Ibid., 63–64.
3. Sacks, *To Heal a Fractured World*, 47.

is in itself a statement that coitus as such is good. The end to which it is employed is what determines its moral quality.

In pornography, sex has been trivialized by the god of our times, namely, pleasure. More and more people are acquiring pornographic videos or actually engaging in a career of pornography. Shelley Lubben, a porn actress, states,

> You have to do what they want on the sets. There's much competition. They can always find other girls. Girls bring in their friends and get kickbacks. They feel like stars. They get attention. It's all about the spotlight. It's about me. They have notoriety. They don't realize the degradation. Besides, this is a whole generation raised on porn. They're jaded and don't even ask if it is wrong. They fall into it. They get into drugs to numb themselves. They get their asses ripped. Their uterus hemorrhages. They get HPV and herpes, and they turn themselves off emotionally and die. They check out mentally. They get PTSD like Vietnam vets. They don't know who they are. They live a life of shopping and drugs. They don't buy real estate. They party, and in the end they have nothing to show for it except, like me, genital herpes and fake boobs.
>
> Porn is like any other addiction. . . . First, you are curious. Then you need harder and harder drugs to get off.[4]

In pornography with its depictions of "gang bangs and bestiality and child porn," sex in contemporary society has been trivialized with far-reaching consequences for the affirmation of the salvation of humankind. As porn star Lubben states, "Porn gets grosser and grosser. . . . Porn destroys intimacy."[5] This testimony from an insider is frighteningly clear: the rampant porn of our time disengages sex from love. Porn holds up an illusion that is beholden only to pleasure; it is a hive of dysfunction and destruction.

Changes in legal and social mores seem to have allowed the culture of porn to go mainstream. The embrace of an illusion of intimacy says much about an emerging culture that also finds it easy to market cruelty, another measure of the depths to which humans can descend when they lose sight of the obligation to love. Robert Jansen comments, "What is the difference between glorifying violence in war and glorifying the violence of sexual domination? . . . Our culture is saturated with sex. . . . We accept a culture flooded with images of women who are sexual commodities. Increasingly, women in pornography are not people having sex but bodies upon which sexual activities of increasing cruelty are played out. And many men . . . like it."[6]

If the boot were on the other foot, with women treating men the way that men are treating women, the men would not like it. And no normal man would be in the least amused to have his daughter be caught up in the culture of porn just presented. The perversions of pornography challenge Christianity's fundamental affirmation

---

4. Shelley Lubben, quoted in Hedges, *Empire of Illusion*, 60.

5. Ibid.

6. Robert Jansen, *Getting Off: Pornography and the End of Masculinity*, cited in Hedges, *Empire of Illusion*, 61.

regarding sex. Christian theology—honed in on wholeness and salvation as it is—has to have modern culture's deification of sex as part of its agenda. On the ethical principle of "what you do not want done to yourself, do not do to others," the Christian church is obliged to work against the culture of pornography.[7]

The story of the pornographic industry may be coupled with that of US women torturers at Abu Ghraib prison in Iraq to demonstrate the spread of the culture of pornography around the world. The marks of that culture include sexual humiliation, abuse, and rape. Some would argue pornography is a matter of freedom and the right of consenting adults to watch whatever they desire. Such an attitude reflects warped desires and painful and degrading attitudes toward sex and especially toward women. Not only does the porn culture glorify sex; it also peddles other worrisome things. Hedges again writes, "Porn is overtly racist. Black men in porn films are primitive animals, brawny and illiterate studs with vast sexual prowess. Black women are filled with raw, animalistic lust. Latina women are hot and racy. Asian women are sexually submissive geishas."[8] This profiling of peoples is ugly and an affront to the values of the kingdom of God and to Christian values that are based on the fact that God created all humankind in God's own image and likeness.

A number of related issues should be of concern to Christian theologians. In the culture of pornography, men have been known to willfully and knowingly infect women with HIV. As if that were not enough, they have been known to go themselves to clinics using false names or even for anonymous testing, as if endeavoring to deny their victims any possibility of medical intervention and a cure. Women in this industry are put under pressure not to require condoms because knowledge of their use would allegedly damage the salability of the films. The women would be seen to be, not performers, but commodities, objects for making money. To reduce humans to the level of commodities is an infringement of their dignity as persons and treats them as either subhuman or nonhuman. The founder of Adult Industry Medical Healthcare Foundation commented in 2007 that "denial is the backbone of pornography when it comes to health care."[9]

What of Africa?

In Africa, speaking openly about sex is simply not done. But the facts that have just been presented challenge that silence; they demand that Africans address the subject of sex frankly in the light of God's truth. The porn culture is a hive in which cruelty is endemic; from it an undercurrent of sexual callousness and perversion courses through contemporary society. Fundamentally, the porn culture reduces human beings to squalid, submissive objects.

---

7. Confucius, *Analects*, 15.23; see Aristotle, *Nicomachean Ethics*, 79.16; Hillel, *Talmud*, "Sabbath," 106.1; Matthew 7:12.

8. Hedges, *Empire of Illusion*, 76.

9. Sharon Mitchell, cited in Hedges, *Empire of Illusion*, 79.

In an earlier chapter the point was made that theology is a "second step." In my life as executive director at the World Council of Churches, in Geneva, the then general secretary, Emilio Castro, used to tease me saying, "Everybody says that John Pobee is a sharp theologian. But I will not recognize that he is until he takes his Bible to engage the prostitutes in the red light district on his way to and from the Anglican Church." At the time, I was also an assisting priest at the church, but I would not be found even talking to a prostitute. This was all too true even though, as a New Testament scholar, I was completely familiar with the Johannine (8:1–11) story of the woman apprehended in the act of adultery, in which Jesus did not draw his garments about him in holy wrath or embarrassment or fear. Therefore the current wisdom that vibrant theological construction starts with consciousness of the social circumstances already present in the context challenges us to make sure that sex has a place on the agenda of theology. The summons issued by the Holy Father, Pope Francis, to the Synod on the Family in October 2014 underscores the same demand: that we have the subject of sex on our theological agenda.

As guidance for the course African theology should pursue in the future, I would like to call upon three important streams. First, though it is impermissible to go so far as to claim that sex is evil, we dare not shrink from declaring that the porn culture is evil. We can, however, commend the epigram that states that theology is grace and ethics is gratitude. A clear understanding of the grace offered by the gospel encourages me not to become stuck on the evil misuse of the gift of sex but challenges me to live a moral life in tune with God's holy ways.

Second, while not condoning porn culture, Jesus' responses to the woman caught in adultery and to the woman at the well in Samaria (John 4:1–42) are instructive. In the case of the adulterous woman, Jesus did not deny that adultery can be enslavement to evil and lawlessness and constitute following the devil (John 8:1–11, 34; 1 John 3:4; 5:17). He is neither indulgent nor self-righteous. Presenting grace or representing grace may involve addressing the circumstances that have held the sinner in their grip.

In the case of the Samaritan woman, she not only suffers the "double jeopardy" of being a woman and a Samaritan, but she also has had five husbands (John 4:18). Some interpret the verse as "You (Samaritans) have had five *ba'alim* (gods). And your present god is not your real *ba'al* (owner)."[10] Whatever the translation should be, the woman is a sinner. Jesus, however, does not just write her off; he engages her, seeking through pastoral ministry to lead her to a Christ-centered and life-centered life. Even a sexual deviant can be led to Christ. The test of the conversion is when the pervert turns seriously to proclaiming and living life according to the standards of Christ.

---

10. We may well be given pause in embracing this interpretation, for in John 4:18 only the Samaritan woman is addressed; Samaritans in general are not addressed. The text mentions neither a *ba'al* (lord) nor five *ba'alim* (owners, by extension "gods"), but refers only to "your five men" (πεντε ἄνδρας or in the Latin Vulgate *quinque viros* "your five husbands").

Third and even more astounding is when Jesus jeered at those who believed themselves to be religious, stating that "harlots" would precede them into the kingdom of God (Matt 21:31–32). Jesus was by no means justifying the sexual acts of the prostitutes, but he could not damn them forever. If they responded to his message and his call to repentance, there could be hope for them. We see once more that ministry is to be exercised in the direction even of harlots. Moral character consists of action on God's side, following the commandments of God and walking in God's holy ways (cf. Deut 23:18; Jer 5:7–8; Hos 4:14; Amos 2:7). Moral character and God's holiness require that we avoid *porneia*, that is, fornication, adultery (Matt 5:31–32), unchaste and illicit behavior, premarital sexual relations, and illicit unions that can be incestuous. What Jesus demands is a state of heart and mind completely devoted to God. To reach out missionally to sexual deviants is our obligation; their faith is entirely in God's hands.

12

Our Mothers and Sisters

Fellow Citizens in the Human Community and Church

As we approach this chapter, I wish to relate a bit of my own personal evolution as it relates to the chapter's topic. During this book's planning stage and even some three years into its writing, the title for this chapter was simply "Our Mothers and Sisters and Theology." As I suggest later in the chapter, that title reflected the way my early family life and upbringing had shaped me. Experience, as noted in an earlier chapter, is a formative factor in theology. But I was exposed to more than the experience of my family. I also learned of men who had sisters, yet who nevertheless beat their wives. I woke up to the possibility that having siblings was not sufficient to ensure a level playing field for women and men.

Much further down the line, in late 2012, an awful rape—indeed a gang rape—and murder of a young medical student occurred on a bus in India. About that same time I joined my wife in Pretoria, South Africa. There too, time and again, rape cases filled the news headlines. Then in February 2013 the South African Paralympian Oscar Pistorius killed his girlfriend, Reeva Steenkamp. Reports of these events elevated my level of conscientization related to the rights, and too often plight, of women. Beyond recognizing women as siblings, men should be deeply and sensitively conscientized and be fully convicted that women are fellow citizens in the human community. Recognizing God's wisdom in choosing to make some male and others—our mothers and our sisters—female, men must acknowledge that women are and must be esteemed as fellow humans and full citizens of the human community.

Several consequences follow from this point. First, if women are fellow human beings, then ill treatment of them by men is also an indication of how men understand themselves as human beings. Second, if women are as human as their male counterparts, then women, too, are entitled to all that is invoked by the phrase human rights and are to be treated with dignity and accorded the rights of citizens.

And so, the title of this chapter in its current form reflects an evolution for me from seeing women as family members and as mothers and sisters and daughters, to a deeper and richer view of women as fellow humans, co-endowed with essential and nonnegotiable rights and entitlements.

The story just told—of the way my experience within my parents' home shaped and colored my view of gender—points to a typological reenactment on my part of my experience growing up within my family. In effect, I sought to emulate my parents' provision of a framework for understanding the past, negotiating the present, and discerning the will of God for the future. In theological construction, our interpretive framework does not come solely from the Word of God. Our experience of and in the family also supplies a "handle" for discerning the present in God's light.

Terminology

To speak the language of "our mothers and sisters and God-talk" is to enter the terrain of gender and theology, feminism, feminist theology, the feminist movement, and womanist theology. My psyche is averse to and uncomfortable with all words ending in "-ism," such as capitalism, communism, imperialism, racism, and hedonism. All-isms signify the politicization of the root word. Time and again, the result obfuscates the fundamental issues needing serious attention and makes some people unduly defensive or overly aggressive.

The title of this chapter, "Our Mothers and Sisters," seeks to underline the fact that feminist issues—whether the unemployment and inequality of women, systematic and systemic imbalances responsible for women's continual unequal social and economic status, or violence against and sexual harassment of women and girls—are also men's issues. The women, that is, the mothers and sisters, daughters, and wives, are our relations, not things. They are our kith and kin, fellow humans without whom our own humanity is imperfect and suffers in one way or another. As Akan wisdom puts it: "When a sharp instrument is sticking out of another person's side, it is tempting to suggest it is something sticking into and out of a tree." Reports of rape relate not just the experiences of women; they also record our own human challenges and failings as men.

The United Nations' Fourth World Conference on Women was convened in 1995 in Beijing, China, to "promote women's opportunity and equality." Thousands of delegates gathered from 180 countries. At that conference, Hillary Clinton, then first lady of the United States, said, "If there is one message that echoes forth from this conference, let it be that *human rights are women's rights and women's rights are human rights once and for all.* . . . As long as discrimination and inequities remain so commonplace everywhere in the world, as long as girls and women are valued less, fed less, fed last, overworked, underpaid, not schooled, subjected to violence in and outside their homes—the potential of the human family to create a peaceful, prosperous world will not be realized."[1] I say amen to Mrs. Clinton's message; the situation and circumstances of women raise political issues that theologians cannot avoid. As Karl Barth noted, prayer itself is a political act; the church must take concrete steps to address women's issues. But I remain a theologian, not a politician, and so I seek to bring a theological perspective to this topic.

Gender

The English word "gender" derives from Middle English *gendre*, which is related to the French word for "kind" and the Latin word *genus* (descent, origin). Gender has come to mean sexual identity, the condition of being male or female, man or woman. It is used to signify females or males as a group.

Feminism

According to the *Encyclopedia of Feminism*, "Feminism originates in the perception that there is something wrong with society's treatment of women: it attempts to analyze the reasons for and the dimensions of women's oppression, and to achieve the women's liberation."[2] The word is derived from the Latin *femina* (woman) and signifies a person who has the qualities of a female. As a label, "feminism" encompasses issues of sexual equality, women's rights, and advocacy of women's rights. The word feminism—first used in April 27, 1958, in a book review published in *Atheneum*—describes a movement.[3] As a movement, feminism resonates well with the description of the earliest Christian community as "the Way," that is, as a movement (Acts 9:2). By definition a movement has political implications; further, social matters are simultaneously spiritual and political concerns for they involve allocation of power and consequently give rise to ethical issues.[4]

Backdrop of Injustices

The suffragette movement that emerged in late nineteenth-century England is a reminder that women were discriminated against and were debarred from voting. Indeed, even into the 1960s, women in some European countries were not entitled to receive pay equal to what men received for the same job—if they were allowed to be employed at all in jobs and positions that were customarily reserved for men. In

---

1. Hillary Rodham Clinton, remarks to the UN 4th World Conference on Women plenary session, Beijing, September 5, 1995 (italics added), http://www.americanrhetoric.com/speeches/hillaryclintonbeijingspeech.htm.
2. Tuttle, *Encyclopedia of Feminism*, 107.
3. See Rossi, *The Feminist Papers*, 27–64.
4. Van Baal, "The Political Impact of Prophetic Movements," 68.

the not too distant past, for a woman to acquire a passport or open a bank account required that a man act as guarantor. Clearly, women did not receive equal treatment with men. These facts indicate a culture of injustices.

Unfortunately, gender-based activism, which frequently takes the form of feminist rhetoric, often leaves men defensive and unreceptive, creating enemies in our own societies. Acknowledging that fact in no way serves to condone the sickening attitude of male chauvinists. Misogyny is symptomatic of a larger malaise underlying the general need to struggle for safety, justice, public health access, and education.

Gender is tied to culture expectations and roles. In hunter and gatherer societies, gender roles evinced a particular logic. Because hunting required a physique adapted for running and muscular strength, the male of the human species appeared to be cut out for that responsibility and role. The anatomy and physiology of women did not appear to be geared toward sustaining high levels of strenuous physical demand. Physically women appear to be better suited, in hunter and gatherer societies, to roles commonly assigned to them nearer the homesite. That women are fitted physiologically to follow up conception with gestation, birthing, and nurturing—all of which center around the home—is not in dispute.

The difference, therefore, between men and women is not primarily about superiority or inferiority. Nor should it be seen in terms of competition and rivalry; rather it is best understood in terms of equipage for roles and responsibilities. In Africa, culture, history, and traditional norms of conduct have been highly hierarchical. Since culture constitutes the environment within which religion takes shape, religion, including the Christian religion, has most often been patriarchal, and the essence of religion must be disentangled from what is cultural. To attempt this intricate work necessitates fresh perspectives on distorted images and representations. It entails a conversation or even conversations between cultures. The rhetoric and implications of corresponding and complementary gender roles call for discernment: what works within a society's value framework for governance and fullness of life—personal, professional, and political? The answers to that exercise are critical to happiness, self-actualization, and self-fulfillment.

Story, Biography, and God-Talk

In an earlier chapter I argued that stories mediate meaning and possibly truth. It is hardly necessary to argue that in Scripture, truth, message, and meaning are mediated through stories. Biography is a connected narrative that tells a story and thereby mediates a message.[5] At bottom, biography is grounded in simple facts of history: I was given birth by a mother to whom my umbilical cord was attached, and I was

---

5. John S. Pobee, "Theology as Biography," in Trompf and Hamel, *The World of Religions*, 31; Graham Hayes, "Interviewing the Past, Wulf Sachs for Instance," in Denis, *Orality, Memory, and the Past*, 53.

brought up in a family of three girls and two other boys. The relationships between my parents, sisters, and brothers were part of nurturing me into becoming the person I have become. They were persons in reference to whom I was able to define myself, my being, and my identity. Needless to say, that experience has gone into how I talk theologically, especially about women. My God-talk is in part a reflection of the story of the relationship between my mother, father, siblings, and myself.

Preference for "Mothers and Sisters"

Students are wont to devise names or nicknames for their professors. My students at the University of Ghana used to call me *mama-ba* (mammy's baby). According to them, I was forever taking examples and giving illustrations based on experiences in my natal family, especially my experiences with my mother and sisters. In other words, my experience of family life has contributed to shaping my theology and its thrust. My rational processes do not begin *ex nihilo* or *in abstracto*; my perceptions of and sensitivity to women have been influenced by my experience with my mother and sisters. From this experience comes my preference for the language of "mothers and sisters" rather than for gender or feminist theology.

For some people, the language of mothers and sisters may be offensive, because such language *seems* to put a glass ceiling over the heads of females, confining them to the home as wives, mothers, homemakers, and home managers, roles often buttressed by patriarchal cultural stereotypes.

At times categorical statements are made of women as the weaker sex, allegedly emotional and prone to panic in difficulties. My experience is different. My mother was a teacher who chose to stay back at home, when six of us arrived on the scene, to see to our nurture. The nurture of children into vital and vibrant persons in society is too serious a business to be played with the backhand. The end result has been something we are proud of as each one of us, the girls included, has risen to the top in his or her profession; each one has been mentioned in dispatches as a model for the next generations.

The eldest of the three girls became the headmistress of a celebrated school founded and led by nuns of the Order of the Holy Paraclete. She was the first African to head the celebrated school. The second girl rose to be head of the largest midwifery training school in Ghana. The third sister became a medic who studied medicine at the University of Giessen, Germany, and therefore did her studies in German. The three boys in turn became a professor of medicine, a celebrated lawyer, and a professor of theology. Being a mother and homemaker was a choice on my mother's part, and the end result well justifies that choice. But it was a choice, not something forced upon her.

There is another dimension of this experience. Our mother, in addition to staying back at home to nurture wholesome children, also took to baking bread in commercial quantities. From that business she, with our father, supported the education of my doctor brother and lawyer brother, training for which professions was not available in Ghana in those days. The doctor sister was the last of the siblings. She was afforded every opportunity the same as the boys, such that she was able to earn a scholarship to do her medical studies abroad in Germany. The curious thing is that my siblings' generation has been repeating the model we learned from our parents.

With such experience, I see motherhood and sisterhood as most serious charisms that are not to be pooh-poohed. Needless to say, I am inclined to be suspicious of easy dismissals of the language of motherhood. My plea is for us to pay more attention to the content and model of motherhood and sisterhood. In my family experience, mother like father, sister like brother, have exhibited what is entailed by the biblical assertion that God created male and female in God's own image and likeness. Ideology is in part what makes or unmakes motherhood or sisterhood, not just the biological fact of motherhood or sisterhood.

Gender Issues: Neither Crusade nor Cases

Musimbi Kanyoro, a Kenyan female theologian and linguist, has written that to "many men and women, inside and outside the church, the words feminist/feminism continue to invoke fear, inspire controversy and to arouse a visceral response. Feminism/Feminist are therefore dangerous words representing dangerous concepts and dangerous people."[6] Men have no reason to be defensive or negative; theological constructs offered from the perspective of women are gifts that enrich the community of faith. The memories and stories of my mother and sisters (as of my brothers) are, in the words of Graham Hayes, "universe constructing, foundation laying, certainty guaranteeing, and goal clarifying means of understanding reality."[7]

Ideology and Stereotyping

Claims made in the name of gender give me pause. For example, is it the simple truth that "women are willing to consider options more carefully for a longer period of time than men until the right route for action is found"?[8] I will not dispute that *some* men jump straight into action. But some women, also, are overly hasty. Do men exhibit impetuous behavior because they are men or because of their particular individual character? Again, is Harvard psychologist Carol Gilligan correct, pure and simple, that "women have greater moral strength . . . higher ethical standards and a particular ability

---

6. Kanyoro, "Challenges of Feminist Theologies to Ministerial Formation," 16.

7. Hayes, "Interviewing the Past, Wulf Sachs for Instance," in Denis, *Orality, Memory, and the Past*, 53.

8. Talyn Rahman-Figueroa, "Women in Diplomacy: An Assessment of the Role of British Diplomatic Service in Overcoming Gender Hierarchy, 1990–2010," cited in Martha Pobee, "Gender Issues in the Ghana Foreign Service," 13.

to establish and maintain good relationships with people . . . [and so] have the qualities of a contemporary political actor"?[9] I do not dispute that some women exhibit moral strength. But is that because they are women? Or is their character to be credited to their moral upbringing? Have there not been men who also have shown moral strength?

Raising these critical questions is in no way to contradict Shoma Chatterji's statement that "because women as a gender have been structurally disempowered, excluded and subjugated, they provide different perspectives and acute insights into situations where unequal power relationships exist."[10] For one who accepts the ideology of God's preferential option for the poor as articulated by liberation theology, Chatterji's assertion is incontrovertible. But even here, I have in my profession encountered women senior administrators who failed to empathize with women in distress, and I, a man, had the humble privilege of identifying the problem and helping to resolve it. Beyond gender lies the more fundamental issue of being human. Time and again, gender issues are compounded and confounded by non-gender accretions.

The Role of Experience in Augustine's Theology

Certain aspects of Augustine of Hippo's biography, that is, his life experience, were decisive for his theological writings—namely, being an African, living during the barbarian threat to the Roman world and to Christianity, and the shifts he underwent in his philosophical anthropology. That his nine years' experience (373–82) with the dualism of Manichaeism had an enormous effect on his thought has long been recognized. His mother Monica, especially her death at Ostia in October 387, demonstrably had a tremendous impact on his theology. The theology that he developed thereafter can be crudely laid out as "church = Catholic orthodoxy = Monica." The church is the "true mother of all Christians" and enjoys full disciplinary powers to correct those who prove recalcitrant and to bring back the wayward.[11] Each person's theology emerges in dialectical dialogue with that person's circumstances and biography—nor can it be otherwise for faithful women who desire to theologize. No apology needs to be made for the fact that women's theology bears the impress of their identity and experiences.

Feminist Theology and Womanist Theology

The quest to claim space for women's legitimate place and experience in theology has two designations: feminist theology and womanist theology.[12] The label of womanist theology is used for theology crafted in the crucible of non-Western, nonwhite

---

9. Carol Gilligan, cited in Rahman-Figuaroa, 13.

10. Shoma Chatterji, cited in Martha Pobee, 14.

11. Augustine, *De Vera Religione*, 4.6; see Frend, *Rise of Christianity*, 662–63; Pobee, "Theology as Biography," in Trompf and Hamel, *The World of Religions*, 316–19.

12. Ruether, *Sexism and God-Talk*; Grant, *White Women's Christ and Black Women's Jesus*.

experience with the implication that nonwhite experience lies outside the scope of feminist theology. Musimbi Kanyoro is helpful when she writes,

> For a start, feminist theologies dared to look at our histories as they are told in biblical texts, the teachings and practices of the church over centuries and in the present day. Sadly, women have found that our histories are deeply rooted in *Patriarchy, a legacy of African Culture, Judaism and Christianity*. Judaism and Christianity were shaped by patriarchy. Feminist theologies as influenced by patriarchy have affected our experience and naming of God. Patriarchy has shaped our structures of work, worship and decision-making. Feminist theologies rightly name the gender injustices to women in these areas. Yet gender alone cannot define the injustices that women experience globally. While women's theologies appeal to solidarity to combat the subordination of women, they also are capacious enough to include the concerns of women affected by social injustices such as racism, poverty, culture, etc. Those theologies open themselves to different concerns for different women: women who are married as well as those who are single, women who are mothers as well as those who are not (by choice or force of circumstances), poor women as well as wealthy women, women of various ethnic backgrounds and religious persuasions, and the list goes on. Difference is a reality. Difference can become a source of fear, bias, and ignorance that result in injustice, but it can also be a platform for celebrating variety and beauty. By affirming difference, women's theologies are striving to model the possibilities of celebrating difference.[13]

Experience of Double Jeopardy

African women are placed in a situation of double jeopardy, first externally, as Africans and therefore "primitive" in relation to the rest of the world, and then internally, as women in African cultures that privilege males over females. First as Africans: the ideologies of colonialism and racism have contributed to perceptions of Africa and Africans as a

> separate reality, light years away from the rest of the world; a conquerable land . . . whose people, for mysterious ancestral reasons, are instinctively averse to the rational mind and scientific thought. And it is with this mind-set where the usual stereotypes are found—atrocities, wars, famines, pandemics and permanent instability. In order to understand why the "Africas" are always perceived as being and remaining primitive, one must merely look at the media coverage of the self-seeking charity, which is widespread among the humanitarian organizations; in the best hypotheses the "Africas" are depicted as lush, exotic paradises and therefore as possible tourist destinations that defy the imagination.[14]

13. Kanyoro, "Challenges of Feminist Theologies to Ministerial Formation," 17–18.
14. Albanese, "Africa, Quo Vadis?," 10; see also Kunambi, "Women of Africa: Awake!," 302–4.

This parlous profile is shared by both African males and African females.

But a second jeopardy arises for African females. Traditionally, within African cultures women have not had equal status with that of men. For example, women could not have primacy of place vis-à-vis inheritance. As mentioned, a woman could not acquire a passport or open a bank account without the authorization of a man. Because their place was said to be the home and kitchen, that is, as homemakers and bearers of children, women were not encouraged to go to school, especially for higher education. The practice of denying educational opportunities to females has manifestly shown itself to have been due to prejudice. Today women have proven themselves and achieved excellence in all areas—such as medicine, engineering, mathematics, and astronomy—that used to be closed to them and held as a male preserve.

Christian theology is obliged to fight against the double jeopardy of injustice and discrimination under which African women labor. Enabling women to truly bear the image and likeness of God, as Scripture teaches, is a measure of the credibility of Christian theology. Can it fulfill its promises? As the Akan of Ghana put it, "When a naked person promises you clothing, you are advised to look at his condition to see whether he can deliver." Thus the issue of mothers and sisters and God-talk is a critical test of Christian theology's credibility. To put it bluntly, before theologians dare to preach to politicians about women's rights, they should ensure that their own credentials and credibility are unblemished.

Our Mothers and Sisters: A Critical and Vital Resource

As is well known, females constitute more than half of the population, whether of a society, a country, a continent, or the world. But this fact is not just a demographic and statistical issue. Demography has consequences, and sociologists have demonstrated the strong, irrepressible maternal component in African socialization.[15] States Jacques Giri, it is "African women . . . before men, before school, before radio, cinema, television who will form the Africa of tomorrow. After all, women in Africa produce more than 60 percent of the income and it is about time that they become more involved in the administration of the 'Res Publica.'"[16]

Basic Issues in Feminist Theology

I have drawn attention to the significant demographic disparity between men and women in society, which is even more marked in the church, as well as to the biblical affirmation that male and female alike are created in the image of God. I have noted that past and present social, economic, and political realities work to disadvantage

---

15. Todd, *L'enfance du monde*.
16. Jacques Giri, quoted in Albanese, "Africa, Quo Vadis?," 10.

women even though they constitute more than half of society. Cultural and religious presumptions also place women at a disadvantage. Therefore we may unashamedly and unapologetically apply liberation theology's insight of God's preferential option for the poor as a perspective from which to work for the reconstruction and renewal of the position of women in human societies. Leonardo Boff writes, "If by 'feminism' we understand whatever defends the basic equality of women to men, maintains that women are human persons and opposes any institutions that seek to reduce them to the status of objects, then Jesus was certainly a feminist. After all, the general tenor of his ethical teaching consisted in the liberation of human beings from a legalistic, discriminatory morality, in favour of a morality of decision, freedom and the communion of sisters and brothers.... The ethical revolution launched by Jesus created a space for the liberation of women as persons."[17] Feminist theology is a means to the end of enabling women to have a voice, to be themselves, and not to be treated as clones of men. This cause is not merely a quest for power or even equality. Hillary Clinton goes so far as to argue that it is an issue of national security. She states, "It is also a big deal for our security. Because where women are disempowered and dehumanized, you are more likely to see not just antidemocratic forces, but extremism that leads to security challenges for us."[18]

Because women are—by and large—universally disadvantaged, the agenda to strive for the health, well-being, and security of women must also be universal. But Christianity's core message of the incarnation mandates that the realities faced in the African context should be a particular focus of attention. How is the general injustice to women particularly manifested in Africa and African countries? What does the good news (the gospel) of the kingdom of God and his righteousness bring to bear on the challenging situation found on that continent?

Peculiar African Context

The situation found in Africa gives a peculiar slant to the subject. The responses and constructs found in Europe and America were developed within a context shaped by the Christendom ideology. In that setting Christian faith and theology were at an advantage over all other faiths and religions. Africa does not have that luxury; Africa lives in a context of religious pluralism, with African Traditional Religions, Christianity, Islam, and some Hinduism the most prominent. Theology in Africa vis-à-vis

---

17. Boff, *Ecclesiogenesis*, 79.

18. Hillary Clinton, cited by Gayle Tzemach Lemmon, "The Hillary Doctrine," http://www.newsweek.com/hillary-doctrine-66105. Resolution 1325 of the UN Security Council, October 2000, acknowledged for the first time the political contribution made by women to the search for peace and security. Before that, the United Nations in 1979 adopted the Convention on the Elimination of Discrimination against Women and thus made women's concerns a major issue on the UN agenda. A result was the formation of a legal framework for inclusion of women in decision-making and leadership at the national level.

women must work with a hermeneutic of pluralism and an ecumenical perspective. This means that while lessons may be learned from other religions and nations or continents, African theologians are obliged to look at the significance of individual contexts and the particular issues emerging from them and then to engage in *dialogue* in order to develop rational, viable responses.

The dialogue that is needed is both *ad extra* and *ad intra*. On the one hand, it is dialogue between women's experience and the male-dominant culture; on the other hand, dialogue must be carried out between women of different faith persuasions—for example, between Christian theologians and Muslim theologians. In Africa, Muslim women (and men) theologians must be sought as interlocutors to work with Christian women theologians in identifying the Word of God for Africans' renewal and transformation, exposing the cultural myths that have been axiomatic in society. Such theological labor should not be, first and foremost, a matter of reacting to received statements; much more importantly, it should be creative and constructive and complementary.

Construction Blocks

Removal of certain roadblocks was essential for progress to be made. Apart from the inherited mentality that women's role and place were in the home and kitchen and that schooling, especially to the highest level, was therefore not important or even appropriate for women, a common presumption was that "reading" theology (the academic study of theology) must lead to ordination to the priesthood or clerical ministry. Since women were excluded from ministry in some churches, reading theology simply was not an option for women. By default, men would speak for women. When the truth that God created humankind—male and female together—in God's own image and likeness (Gen 1:26–27) became more fully internalized, women were at last able to read theology and equip themselves to speak for themselves. They were able to prepare to give account at a new level of their faith and hope as enjoined by 1 Peter 3:15.

With its commitment to building an inclusive society, the ecumenical movement became a catalyst for the role of women in theology. Advocacy by the WCC reaches back at least as early as the 1970s. In response to an earlier consultation convened in West Berlin that was sponsored by the WCC's subunit on women in church and society, the 1974 meeting of the WCC's Commission on Faith and Order, held in Accra, decided to initiate study of the "theological and practical aspects of the community of women and men in the church."[19]

The 1974 Berlin conference "Sexism in the 1970s: *Discrimination* Against Women" shifted the discussion from "cooperation between women and men" to "social and economic justice for women."[20] Sponsored by the World Council of Churches, the

19. See Parvey, *The Community of Women and Men in the Church*.
20. Ibid.

"Ecumenical Decade of Churches in Solidarity with Women," 1988–98, had a fivefold thrust:

- empowering women to confront oppressive structures;
- affirming the decisive contribution of women;
- enhancing the visibility of women's perspectives vis-à-vis justice, peace, and integrity of creation;
- enabling the churches to free themselves from practices and teachings that discriminate against women;
- encouraging churches to live in solidarity with women.[21]

In this way, by intentionally exploring ecclesiological and theological challenges, theologians were seeking to develop authentic community composed of women and men together.

These conferences were not a rapid, revolutionary movement. They addressed issues such as Christian concepts of God, the authority of Scripture, diakonia, ordination of women, and the language, symbols, and imagery of Scripture as they influenced relationships between women and men. We do an injustice to the subject of women in church and society when we limit the topic to a single issue such as power or equity or the ordination of women. In my view, using the language of "community of women and men in church and society" leads to a truer and more fruitful description of the issue of gender and theology. It signals the plenitude of society and church as seen in the relationships that may exist between identifiable entities in the community. Using Bible studies as her lens, Wendy Robins in *Through the Eyes of a Woman* points out the breadth and seriousness of the subject. She addresses such issues as refugees, migrants, and asylum-seekers; women and poverty; women and health; women in God's image; and women and justice, peace, and an equitable world.[22]

My perspective in writing this book is that developments in Africa are moving in the right direction. From the womb of the WCC there emerged in 1989 the Biennial Institute of African Women in Religion and Culture, formed at the behest of the Circle of Concerned African Women Theologians. Again, the formative steps were taken in Ghana. The Biennial Institute of African Women in Religion and Culture was created "in response to the dearth of literature on African Women by African Women. The primary concern, however, [was] for theological literature created by African women."[23] It is significant that the publication that came out of the first conference had the title *Talitha Qumi!* (Young Girl, Rise!). Women had to be enabled to speak for themselves and to make their contribution to theology.

---

21. Aruna Gnanadason, "Ecumenical Decade: Churches in Solidarity with Women," in Lossky, *Dictionary of the Ecumenical Movement* (2002), 377.

22. Robins, *Through the Eyes of a Woman*.

23. Oduyoye and Kanyoro, *Talitha Qumi!*, 1; Oduyoye, *Who Will Roll the Stone Away?*

Subsequent publications from the conferences of the Circle of Concerned African Women Theologians include *Groaning in Faith: African Women in the Household of God* (1996) and *Her Stories: Hidden Histories of Women of Faith in Africa* (2002).[24]

One point merits to be stressed. It would have been easy for the Circle of Concerned African Women Theologians to have become a closed group of women. But from the first they took seriously the word "community," which signals inclusivity. Musimbi Kanyoro writes that, in behalf of the Circle, Mercy Oduyoye's

> net was cast far and wide, and not only to women but to some men of goodwill as well. John Pobee, then the Executive Secretary for the Program for Theological Education (PTE) at the World Council of Churches, was one of those whom Mercy convinced to invest in the Circle. He believed in the concept of the Circle and supported its efforts on a personal level and through his unit's work. He attended some of the planning meetings and shared his ideas freely. He helped raise funding for Circle women to attend international conferences, and he included Circle women in his program as resource persons or as sponsored participants to ecumenical events. He also encouraged the use of publications written by Circle women.[25]

I cite Kanyoro's statement to emphasize my conviction that theology created by women must not be ghettoized and my commitment to this idea. Building on my understanding of theology as wisdom, I am further instructed by the traditional African wisdom of my heritage that *adwen-wotoa-toa* (wisdom is pieced together by engaging different options and diverse insights).

In 1995 Mercy Oduyoye published a monograph entitled *Daughters of Anowa: African Women and Patriarchy*.[26] The cover of the book has two blurbs, which are instructive. In the first, Peter Paris of Princeton Theological Seminary writes, "Brilliant . . . book by a woman of faith and hope, one whose deep Christian convictions have inspired her to tell the truth about women's experience that they in turn might be freed from the spirit of submission." How can I not draw attention to Oduyoye's publication in this present book?

Rosemary Ruether's blurb is equally exciting: "Oduyoye cuts through the arguments about whether African women are oppressed or not, whether they should be 'feminists' or not, by detailing not only the realities of oppression, but also pointing toward a wholistic vision of justice and mutuality for the African community as a whole. . . . A most welcome contribution to the shaping of a literature on African women's liberation theology and ethics." The theology of our mothers and sisters is shaped by a holistic vision of justice, mutuality, liberation, and ethics.

---

24. Kanyoro and Njoroge, *Groaning in Faith*; Phiri et al., *Her Stories*.

25. Musimbi Kanyoro, "Beads and Strands: Threading More Beads in the Story of the Circle," in Phiri et al., *Her Stories*, 24–25.

26. Oduyoye, *Daughters of Anowa*.

Oduyoye was a contemporary of mine in the Department of Divinity, University of Ghana, and in the Divinity School, University of Cambridge. Though she was older than me, I was at each stage a year ahead of her in my studies. During those years we bonded and were influenced by the same professors, particularly by Noel Q. King and C. G. Baëta. They were our parents in the academy and we grew there as siblings. I learned to see Mercy Amba Oduyoye as my sister in theology in addition to seeing her as a sister in God's household and through creation.

The choice of the word "Circle" in the name Circle of African Women in Theology (CAWT) is pregnant with meaning, especially in the African context where traditionally those gathered for a meeting sat in a circle. The circle is a platform for dialogue. "It constitutes a level playing field that includes everybody and places everyone on the same plane, making eye contact possible. Circles also allow growth without disrupting form—one simply makes the circle bigger to embrace newcomers or additional entrants."[27] The word "circle" represents an option for collective action to address challenges that are larger than single individuals.

The label also meshes well with the locus of CAWT's birth, namely, within the Program on Theological Education (PTE; later the program of Ecumenical Theological Education or ETE), a subsection of the World Council of Churches which has its headquarters in Geneva and is the privileged instrument of the ecumenical movement. PTE/ETE's hermeneutic zeroed in on *koinonia*, that is, communion, community, solidarity, participation, inclusion, and inclusivity. The theme of *koinonia* at once reached out horizontally (building a community of communities) and vertically (fostering a spirituality that tunes into the Supreme Being and allows that experience to radiate out into everyday life and relationships).

As it turned out, CAWT became a model of the ecumenical vision. It created space for members of all religions—Christians, Muslims, and adherents of African Traditional Religions—to be in dialogue. Accomplishing that was a unique achievement, for other theological associations were often limited to followers of the Christian religion in its plurality and did not make room for the plurality of religions in their entirety.

I felt able to work with CAWT not only because I was director of PTE but also because of the Mama-ba complex that I mentioned at the beginning of this chapter. My embrace of CAWT was more than a pragmatic orientation; it sprang from conviction and commitment. But translating that commitment into reality met with some difficulties.

First, as an arm of the WCC, PTE was obliged to form partnerships with churches and theological institutions and associations in the various regions of the world. In practice the presence of these partnerships meant that applications to PTE had to come through member churches. But if truth may be told, the partnering institutions were at times infused with patriarchy and sexism and, time and again, were not keen to recommend women and their causes.

---

27. Ramphele, *Conversations with My Sons and Daughters*, 182.

On some occasions, interference rooted in family and ethnic considerations generated inconsistencies in the attitudes manifested within various regions. The logic of describing yourself as a council of churches meant that the power lay with the churches in the regions. Some described the relationship as one of bosses (the churches) and servants (bureaucrats in Geneva). I preferred a different image expressed in the slogan that "the customer is always right"; but the "bargain" had to be consistent with my moral/ethical principles. That set the stage for politicking.

Second, I was proactive in identifying competent potential female students and negotiated with institutions to suggest their candidature. In this regard, my having gone to the directorship of PTE with established professional credentials was a blessing and advantage. I was able to work toward placement of potential students in institutions where I knew the professors, who then took an interest in their development.

Third, I actively raised funds for the students' professional development. Our program gave heed to liberation theology's preferential option for the poor, and for a time women had an edge on men. The option was preferential but it was not exclusive. A related principle was that the churches had to make a commitment—before the female scholars went for advanced study—that, upon successful completion of the studies, they would use these women appropriately in some area of theological and ministerial formation.

As this outline of the mechanics of walking with the churches and theological institutions in the interest of women in theology may suggest, I was convinced that the Circle ought not to be a closed unit or system. It needed collaborators. Further, its story had to be shared widely; hence, PTE/ETE's help in publishing studies by women theologians. That effort too was consistent with the root word *koinonia*, which signals community building and communication and sharing.

Gender: A Function of Homo Socialis

In the biblical creation saga, the note of gender is struck from the beginning (Gen 2:18–25). While Adam and Eve are created by divine decree (Gen 1:26–27), further account is taken of Eve with the divine declaration: "It is not good that man [Adam] should be alone; I will make him a help of his like" (Gen 2:18; following Delitzsch). In other words, gender is primarily understood in social terms; each is to be a helpmeet of the other. Modeling of social relationships as a matter of being a helpmeet has been the subject of intense debate and, sometimes, pain.

The sequence of the creation, Adam first, Eve second, has been taken to mean the primacy—interpreted in terms of supremacy and superiority—of the man over the woman, or worse still, the inferiority of the woman before the man. Some find support for ideas of superiority and inferiority in terms of the second creation story's account of God, after causing a deep sleep to come upon Adam, performing an operation to remove a part of Adam's ribs and from it to create Eve (Gen 2:21–23). It is striking that Eve is taken from the ribs of Adam and not from the soil as Adam was. The story speaks to the inseparable unity and fellowship between Adam and Eve. The issue before theology in Africa, as elsewhere, is what unity and fellowship between male and female should look like in actual practice. Modeling the unity and solidarity of male and female is on the agenda of mothers and sisters and the God-Word.

Going further, gender as a means of unity and fellowship is read as the foundation for the moral order and the ordinance of marriage. Keil and Delitzsch write, "As the moral idea of the unity of the human race required that man should not be created as a genus or plurality, so the moral relation of the two persons establishing the unity of the race required that man should be created first, and then the woman from the body of the man. By this the priority and superiority of man, and the dependence of the woman upon the man, are established as an ordinance of divine creation. This ordinance of God forms the root of that tender love with which the man loves the woman as himself, and by which marriage becomes a type of the fellowship of love and life, which exists between the Lord and His Church (Eph 5:32)."[28]

Thus, according to the biblical faith tradition, gender is of an order of creation for the sake of the community and for fellowship characterized by a sense of the other as "bone of his bone and flesh of his flesh," as a suitable helpmate and helpmeet. Modeling this biblical insight, however, has been fraught with difficulties, especially in relation to issues of power. Already in the Semitic and biblical context, we see the primacy and priority of the male in creation modeled as hierarchy with God at the top, Christ below God, man below Christ, and woman below man. Ranking women at the bottom has been interpreted as signifying the inferiority of the woman to the man and a denial of her dignity and rights (see 1 Cor 11:1–16).

As stated in an earlier chapter, God has not ceased to reveal more about himself and his will with the conclusion of the writing of the Bible. We have much more to learn. Whatever we may have thought Scripture or the writings of Paul had to say may have to be revised. Experience is proving that women are capable of doing almost everything that men do. Women have become distinguished medical doctors, engineers, spacepersons and astronauts, lawyers and jurists, and even priests. Occupations and professions long thought to be the preserve of males are being ably performed by females. Time and again cultural biases have undermined the integrity of theological construction.[29]

Feminist God-Talk: A Life and Death Issue

The Bible claims that women are also bearers of the *imago Dei*. The demand made by feminist theology that this biblical claim be recognized and that logical consequences be drawn from it is no accident. Because the demand appears to make an assault on

28. Keil and Delitzsch, *Pentateuch*, 89–90.

29. Kanyoro, "Cultural Hermeneutics: An African Contribution," in Ortega, *Women's Visions*, 18–28.

the privileged position of men, some men have responded violently. For example, on December 6, 1989, Marc Lepine killed some fourteen women at the École Polytechnique, University of Montreal, Canada, because they were feminists. In January 1995 a group of women in a church in Africa were reprimanded for daring to articulate the problems of women in a Letter to Synod. In 1995 students attacked, harassed, and destroyed the property of a woman theologian and her family because of the lecturer's research on sexual harassment on the university campus.[30]

To embrace feminist theology can be and at times has been costly. But far outweighing considerations of comfort and convenience, what is at stake is whether Christian faith can be adjudged credible in its claims when the church represents itself as part of God's army whose mission is to seek justice and dignity for all since each person is made in God's image and likeness.

Beyond Patriarchal Constructs to Transformational Constructs

Theology in the service of mission faces a date, an appointment with repentance, change, transformation, and renewal. We cannot continue to do things in the same old ways and expect change. In this regard the phrase introduced by Letty Russell, "the church in the round," can be of great assistance to us. Russell used "church in the round" to describe communities that gather around the table to connect faith and life.[31] Her model is anything but patriarchal and hierarchical. She writes, "This education is feminist because it advocates the full humanity of all women together with all men. It is theological because it seeks to understand and live out ways of participating in God's agenda of mending the creation. It shares a common, Christian feminist conviction that theologians must be 'intrinsically relational' and 'justice oriented,' if they are to be life-giving for women together with men" and to foster personal, social and ecclesial renewal.[32] Engaging other feminist networks, including those outside the church, is necessary in prosecuting such an agenda.

The citation given earlier from the Fourth World Conference on Women, held in Beijing in 1995, is evidence of my commitment to such dialogue. Broadly conceived, dialogue is essentially cross-cultural encounter and, to that extent, inherently ecumenical. Ecumenical theological education and formation, states Letty Russell, includes "listening to difference and learning respect for differences; sharing a community of confrontation and struggle; learning about church doctrines and differentiation as they are lived out in vastly different political and cultural contexts; sharing in one another's spirituality and liturgical life; developing lifelong friendship as part

---

30. Phiri, "Women, Church, and Theological Education," 39–43; Mud Flower Collective, *God's Fierce Whimsy*, 141.

31. Russell, *Church in the Round*.

32. Russell, "Education as Transformation," 23; Russell, *The Future of Partnership*.

of an ecumenical network."[33] In all the foregoing what is at stake is "the possibility of Christian transformation for tomorrow."[34]

African women have entered the field of theology; things can never be the same again. As Nyambura Jane Njoroge writes, "The entry of African women theologians into the discourse has challenged the male-articulated scholarship as being gender specific and, therefore, ignoring and rejecting women's experiences and perspectives on African reality. Women contend that ethics constructed by male scholars do not go deep enough to confront and dismantle both Christian and African traditional values, attitudes, beliefs and structures which are life-threatening to women. To a large extent, African theology and liberation theology have been uncritical of cultural values that appropriate sexism in church and society. It appears as though the men assumed that to attack Western imposed values and structures will be enough to transform African communities."[35] This statement suggests that God-talk by our mothers and sisters is not just reactionary; it is creative and constructive, aimed at securing women's inclusion and participation in the academy, church, and society.

For a last word on this subject, let us drink from the wisdom of a great son of Africa, James Kwegyir Aggrey (1875–1927). He wrote: "The surest way to keep a people down is to educate the men and neglect the women. If you educate a man you simply educate an individual, but if you educate a woman you educate a family."[36] Not only do women constitute more than half of society numerically, they also are a critical and strategic agency for formation and transformation of church and society.

A Nilotic proverb states a similar insight: "In Africa, if you educate a boy, you educate a man; if you educate a girl, you educate a nation." Albanese comments as follows: "It is because of the youth and because of women that civil society is a maturing one composed of Christian communities, environmental associations, movements working to defend human rights with the declared intent to create affection towards the *res publica* (the common good) in opposition to the promoters of the Nation-State."[37] If we ignore or shortchange our mothers and sisters in theological and ministerial formation, we do so to our own harm and impoverishment.

A Personal Reflection

In 1967, as a youngish lecturer but also as coordinator of the New Testament program of the Department for the Study of Religion at the University of Ghana, I reorganized the program along three major lines: biblical languages, introduction to New Testament studies, and theology and ethics of the New Testament. As part of the theology

---

33. Russell, "Education as Transformation," 24; Ortega, *Women's Visions*.
34. Russell, "Education as Transformation," 30.
35. Njoroge, *Kiama Kia Ngo*, 124.
36. Smith, *Aggrey of Africa*, 139.
37. Albanese, "Africa, Quo Vadis?," 34.

and ethics focus we tackled issues of gender and sex. As we did so, I invited psychologists, biologists, lawyers, and doctors to come in and give us perspectives from their disciplines so that theological wisdom could be nurtured in dialogue between biblical faith and other sciences that affect human well-being.

That year the best student was a young female whom we later sent to Cambridge for further study. In one discussion on gender, an older male who had come to the status of pupilage after long years as a teacher asked the prized lady, "Do you think being an extraordinary student makes you equal to your future husband?" I was personally shocked, not only because the questioner acknowledged the academic excellence of the woman student, but more so by the brazen attitude the comment exuded.[38] That experience registered on me how deep the issue of sexism went, and it became one of the wellsprings for my commitment to gender studies and gender issues.

As my oldish student waxed eloquent, I noticed that he seemed to base his positions on Scripture. In consequence, I have been minded to look at issues of gender and Scripture. That is why the creation narratives have been important for me in the classroom. What does it mean when Genesis 1:26–27 (NAB) states, "Let us make man in our image, after our likeness. . . . God created man in his image; in the divine image he created him; male and female he created them." At the time of creation, the two sexes were created together, thus implying their correspondence. Their closeness is reflected in the Hebrew words "*ish*" (man) and "*ishah*" (woman). Both enjoy life from God and, therefore, have serious responsibility for God's creation and for creating life. These are some considerations exemplary of the equality of male and female.

A further striking thing about the first creation saga is the charge given in Genesis 1:28 to "have dominion over the fish of the sea, the birds of the air, and all living things that move on the earth." First, the charge is given to "them," to humanity. Second, women are not included as entities over which man may in the genuine sense have authority and dominion. That power is given to male and female together, because both of them bear the image of God. Humanity, along with the rest of creation (Gen 1:24–25), is entitled to respect and protection.

Juxtaposing the first creation story with my male student's comment reveals that a supposedly Christian theological position has been affected by additives and influences that may not be Christian at all, but rather have come from his experience within his natal home, culture, power complex, and so forth. The incident serves as a reminder that in reading Scripture, translation plays a role; so does interpretation, which always is shaped by some ideology or other.

---

38. Pobee, *Culture, Women, and Theology*.

Some Apparent Biblical Difficulties

It may be helpful to look briefly at two passages of Scripture that are often cited by those who wish to import patriarchy into Christianity.

1 Corinthians 11:1–16. In a section addressing organization of the church, Paul outlines a hierarchy: God-Christ-husband-wife. It is striking that church leadership or priesthood nowhere appears in this hierarchy. Clearly Paul is making use of accepted customs of his time. His concern at the moment is with functional relationships and not so much with issues of superiority and inferiority. Function is an aid to order because God is believed to be a God of order.

The additional comments on women's headdresses evidently echo the style of the time, for at other times and places in Scripture, men also could wear long hair (Judg 13:5; Num 6:5). The insights of this paragraph suggest that ideas regarding women underwent evolution, and they warn us against proof-texting.

The argument about men not covering their heads on the grounds that males bear the image and likeness of God (1 Cor 11:7) is rather strange, because the creation story is clear that male and female together were created in God's image and likeness (Gen 1:26–27). *The African Bible* adds, "Women should wear veils, not as a sign of subordination to men, but as a sign of their authority to pray and to prophesy precisely as Christian women, not as imitations of men."[39] To read patriarchy into the text of 1 Corinthians 11:1–16 is impermissible.

Ephesians 5:21–33. The injunction of deutero-Paul that "wives should be subordinate to their husbands" (Eph 5:22 NAB) is often treated as sanctioning the ideology of patriarchy. The whole section, however, composes part of a discussion of the idea that the unity of the church finds concrete expression in the integrity of each Christian family. The language is not that of power and patriarchy; it is the language of mutual love, obedience, tolerance, and forgiveness in the household.

We would be remiss not to take notice in passing of women in the ministry of the church. First Peter 2:1–15 is unequivocal about the priesthood of all believers. This priesthood is a matter of divine election, and the heart of that priesthood is "to announce the promise of him who called us" (1 Pet 2:9).

African Cultural Heritage

As I mentioned, my students called me *mama-ba*. In African culture, especially among the Akan of Ghana, it is said that "only a woman/mother knows who is the baby's father." Consequently, the concept of bastard is meaningless. If the mother identifies the father of the baby, it is a shame on the man if he does not accept his role in the pregnancy and also his obligation to name the child upon birth.

---

39. *The African Bible*, 1927.

Conversely, a child is styled the mother's child, and the Akan ethnic group identifies a child by its mother. The Akan are a matrilineal society, which means that for inheritance purposes one belongs to the mother's family and lineage. By virtue of being descended from a particular woman, one has identity and standing in her kinship group. For a person's identity to be defined and shaped through the woman/mother says something positive about the place of women in Akan society.

Among the Akan, biological motherhood is expressed in a name that shows the reverence with which mothers are regarded in African society. Similarly in isiXhosa a mother may be called *NoPhumzile* (mother of Phumzile) or *NoSiziwe* (mother of Siziwe). Similarly, in Sepedi (a Northern Sotho language), a mother may be styled *MaTlou* or *Makarabo*. *Ma* in Sepedi is equivalent to *No* in Xhosa; both honor the mother of someone. An adult woman is addressed as *Bomme* or *Omama*, thus showing reverence. Even adopted children address their adoptive mothers as *Motswaledi w aka* (the one who gave birth to me). In this way they honor both motherhood and the woman who nurtures the child into becoming a mature and healthy person.

These titles of respect remind us that gender relationships involve intimacy and the management of power relationships. Gender relationships are, above all, about intimate social relationships and the beauty of togetherness. They are also at their root about the young finding ancestors or role models. Children do not grow up rootless; parents, especially mothers, are called upon to teach insights into the secrets of life to their children.

In family discussions in southern Ghana, especially when there is an impasse, the Akan say, *yere ko abrewa hö*, literally we are going to the old lady (*abrewa*). The old lady represents a fund of wisdom and of knowledge of the traditions of the clan. A man will not be called *abrewa*; the term is reserved for a seasoned old woman. In spite of women's public invisibility and a seeming culture of patriarchy, when the chips are down, the woman of experience and wisdom is the final arbiter.

But as a matter of fact, in both culture and religion, a culture of patriarchy has too often been all too evident. Christian theologians, however, will align their stance with the Pauline affirmation that "all of you who were baptized into Christ have clothed yourself with Christ. There is neither Jew nor Greek; there is neither slave nor free person, there is not male and female; for you are all one in Christ Jesus" (Gal 3:27–28 NAB; see Acts 16:11–15; Rom 16:1–16; 1 Cor 7:1–40; 14:33–36; Phil 4:2–3). Race, ethnicity, culture, and gender are but accidental differences among us, for at bottom all humans are to be seen in the light of the image and likeness of God and, therefore, as possessing inherent dignity. This means that male and female, once incorporated into Christ, share spiritual unity and equality.

This outlook is consistent with the way that Jesus, the founder of the Christian faith, in addition to all his male disciples also had around him ministering women. They also learned at his feet and, therefore, they cannot legitimately be excluded from discipleship and all that it entails. Significantly it was a woman, Mary of Magdalene, who first experienced that something had happened to Jesus, that is, his resurrection.

She was the one who first announced Jesus' resurrection to the disciples (John 20:1–18). In this way, a woman became—so to speak—the first missionary and initiated a revolution in which women could no longer be kept in the background and barred from proclaiming the gospel.

Although the position and practice of Christ and his disciples ran counter to the gender practice of the time, a full-fledged frontal attack on institutional injustices may not be the wisest and most useful approach. Still it is important to make one's position clear, even to dig in one's heels so as to inculcate justice and charity and to give the words cash value. In approaching this theme through mothers and sisters—and I may add daughters—I am at the same time asserting that as much as I desire justice and charity for my mother and siblings, I also desire the same for women who may not be my kith and kin.

Ordination of Women

Before concluding this chapter on gender issues, some reference to the long-standing issue of women in ministry is necessary. I have purposely left the topic to the end so as to avoid the temptation to let discussion of gender in relation to ministry seem to be the only issue. There are women who engage in advanced study of theology without necessarily seeing it as preparation for ministry in the narrow sense of becoming a church liturgical functionary. And they have good warrant, for 1 Peter 2:5–10 plainly teaches the priesthood of all believers, as a matter of divine election. All are summoned to "announce the praises" of him who called us. In my own case, I came to the priesthood after I had become a full professor of theology.

Various arguments have been advanced for outlawing the ordination of women, but gender should not be the primary consideration. The critical issue is whether the community of faith can humbly discern signs that God in his wisdom is choosing to call a particular person into his service. I am persuaded that there are no arguments in Scripture against the call of women to God's service. The story of the ministering women who accompanied Jesus during his ministry should put the quietus to such arguments.

Several strands of Scripture make me want to be attentive to the call of God case by case. First is the consistent evidence of Scripture that God, time and again, does not conform to human styles. Thus we find that God calls those who are "no people" to be "his people." It is God's style to include those who are excluded and marginalized.

Second is the story of the encounter between Jesus and the Samaritan woman at the well at Sychar (John 4). As a "twofold outsider"—both a Samaritan and a woman—this woman represents "double jeopardy." Yet at the climax of the story, in that village "many of the Samaritans . . . began to believe" in Jesus. They did so "because of the word of the woman who testified" (John 4:39). Thus the woman represented what defines the church, namely, mission. If a woman has embodied in herself what defines the church, no reason exists for excluding women from the essential ministry of the church.

A third strand is what may be called the Gamaliel Principle: "If this endeavor or this activity is of human origin, it will destroy itself. But if it comes from God, you will not be able to destroy [it]; you may even find yourselves fighting against God" (Acts 5:38–39). We are not allowed to play God. We should be mindful of the fact that human motives are often mixed and, therefore, should seek to hear the still small voice of God in spite of the din around us.

As we negotiate the story of our mothers and sisters in church and society and theology, two biblical words become the hermeneutical key to the process: freedom or liberation and the cross. On the positive side, freedom, one of the values of the kingdom of God, demands that we identify and name the ways that the well-being and dignity of women refract in life, society, and church. On the negative side, not only do we need to identify the pain of women but also we need to be conscious that our task is counter-cultural and, therefore, may bring to us the cross. The ridicule and other suffering of the cross is the price to be paid for obeying the gospel as we seek to build inclusiveness in community, society, and the church as the household of God.

13

The Altar and the *Polis*

AN ALTAR IS A religious artifact, an elevated structure before, at, or upon which religious ceremonies are enacted. In Christian circles it is the place for enacting the sacrifice of the Eucharist. An altar, therefore, signifies religious worship, especially when it entails a rite of sacrifice that sanctifies or makes a seemingly material substance holy. "*Polis*" is the Greek word for a city, a conurbation, or a community. It is the root of our word "politics," the art or science of government, which deals with the organization of a society or nation, presumably to secure its peace and security.

Politics in community life is as old as human existence. Long ago Aristotle (384–322 BC) correctly stated that "man is by nature a political animal."[1] To recognize that we are surrounded by politics all the time and that politics ultimately is about power and power relationships is a mark of wisdom. For its part, community life exists in different shapes, forms, and levels—for example, people can live and be organized as families, clans, peoples, nations, and states. As cited earlier, Aristotle's younger Chinese contemporary, Mencius (372–289 BC), observed that "the root of the kingdom is in the State. The root of the State is in the family. The root of the family is in the person of *its Head*."[2] A community reflects family relationships, on the one hand, and the person of the leader of the community, on the other hand. Countries and states serve as living social laboratories as they experiment with new ideas and theoretical perspectives and as they implement new policies for restructuring and developing economic and other state assets for the transformation of society.

The modern concept of the nation-state is a nineteenth-century invention. For example, what became Prussia had formerly been the regions and small states of North Central Europe, including present-day northern Germany and northern Poland. What became the Gold Coast had been a congeries of indigenous societies, sometimes warring against each other. Long before modern times, Aristotle had recognized that "a state is not a mere society, having a common place, established for the prevention of mutual crime and for the sake of exchange. These are conditions without which a state cannot

---

1. Aristotle, *Politics*, 1.2.
2. Legge, *Works of Mencius*, 4.1.5.

exist.... The end of the state is the good life, and these are the means towards it.... [A] political society exists for the sake of noble actions, and not of mere companionship."[3] What distinguishes a state from any other collection of human beings is its goals, namely, avoidance of crime, sharing of life together, and provision *for noble actions*.

Corruption, violence, unconscionable power and use of force, and selfishness cannot lead to a sound state or sound political organization. Political life at its best is motivated by a desire for a better life for one's country and its people. But the wisdom of the ages records that humans are tempted to do what is not good. As the Roman poet Publius Ovidius Naso (43 BC–AD 18) put it, "*Video meliora, proboque, deteriora sequor*" (I see and approve better things, but follow the worse).[4] The Apostle Paul also articulates this sentiment well: "The willing is ready at hand, but doing the good is not. For I do not do the good I want, but I do the evil I do not want" (Rom 7:18–19 NAB).

As humans we live in moral ambiguity. Therefore, humans must intentionally strive for moral perfection, and we need a structure of laws that keep us in check (cf. Gal 5:14–26). Life without strong government, states the English philosopher Thomas Hobbes (1588–1679), is "nasty, brutish, and short." He continues, "During the time men live without a common power to keep them in awe, they are in that condition which is called war; and such a war, as is of every man against every man."[5]

Because of the contradictions inherent in political life, Augustine of Hippo Regius (354–430) posited two cities: the earthly and the heavenly. The two cities, he said, "have been formed by two loves: the earthly by the love of self, even to the contempt of God; the heavenly by the love of God, even to the contempt of self."[6] Christians see political engagement as an attempt to give godly structure to life on earth. As Augustine spelled out, "The peace of all things lies in the tranquility of order; and order is the disposition of equal and unequal things in such a way as to give to each its proper place."[7]

Throughout Christian history, especially in streams descending from Eusebius's theology of the empire, the empire has been seen as an instrument of a divine power. Though the emperor, as the face of the empire, is elevated into being a quasi-messianic figure with a transcendent mission, this stance does, in fact, sound a biblical note (Rom 13). Viewed against that background, church and state are understood to be aspects—only provisionally distinct—of a single divine and therefore Christian polity, and the state is held up as the vehicle of divine purpose in history.[8]

---

3. Aristotle, *Politics*, 3.9.

4. Ovid, *Metamorphoses*, 7.1.20; see Petrarch (ca. 1327), "Sonnet 225" and "Canzone 21," in his *To Laura in Life*.

5. Hobbes, *Leviathan*, 1.13.

6. Augustine, *De Civitate Dei*, 14.28.

7. Ibid., 19.13.

8. Augustine, *Epistle* 93, 3.9; *Epistle* 97, 2–3. See also Markus, *Saeculum: History and Society in the Theology of St. Augustine*, 133–53; Baynes, *Political Ideas of St. Augustine's "De Civitate Dei."*

Adam Smith, Scotch economist and moral philosopher, argued that for the development of a more free and prosperous society, government is necessary and that it must carry out three functions: national defense, administration of justice (law and order), and provision of certain goods (transportation, infrastructure, and basic and applied education). Smith's third element forms one aspect of state building. Government does not exist for itself; it exists for a purpose and function. That purpose and function in turn become the test by which the integrity of political activity and the identity of legitimate government are measured.

Politics for Development

Politics, so as to have integrity and identity, must have a vision of development. According to Pope Paul VI, "Development is the new name for peace."[9] Yet the attainment of peace, one of the values of the kingdom of God, constantly proves elusive, beset by economic irrationality and insecurity. One component aggravating this irrationality and insecurity has been the use of constructs and models of development based on artifacts and cultures of foreign lands. In this way, the legitimate hopes and fears of the local people have too often been ignored.

Development studies have been scholarly but irrelevant, in part because the victims of development have not been involved in defining the subject and because of the imposition of prefabricated theories by so-called specialists.[10] The need is for contextuality in the task. We need to ask what excites people. What issues do local persons across all natural divides—young and old, women and men, all ethnicities and religions, and so forth—speak about with excitement, hope, fear, anxiety, and anger?

Modern concepts of development have characteristically led to the building of cities. The cities' bright lights are an attraction for many from the rural areas whose populaces are synonymous with the disadvantaged, the marginalized, and those excluded from the artifacts of modernity. While the bright lights of the city attract people, the rural areas are neglected and facilities found there are inadequate. Thus the city is not just a place to live; it is also, and perhaps more importantly, the place to go to school, hospital, and work. This disparity in opportunity is a recipe for uneven development.

Wholesome Ideology for Nation-State Building

The organizing principle of modern governance is ideology. According to Andre Dumas, "Ideologies are blueprints of the future made by a certain ideologue or group of elites within the community to move the masses."[11] An ideology requires a set of

---

9. Pope Paul VI, *Populorum progressio*; Byers, *Justice in the Marketplace*.
10. Edwards, "Irrelevance of Development Studies," 116–35.
11. Verkuyl, *Contemporary Missiology*, 374. See Dumas, *Die Kirche als Faktor einer kommenden Weltgemeinschaft*; André Dumas, "The Ideological Factor in the West," in de Vries, *Man in Community*,

strategies and methods by which, hopefully, a bridge can be built between an idea and its fulfillment. Further, ideologies possess a strong collective stamp and are a way of achieving social consensus.

Throughout world history there have been many and diverse ideologies. Time and again, Christianity and democracy have been alleged to be bedfellows, if not siblings. Partly because Christians were persecuted in Communist Russia under the Soviet leader Josef Stalin (1879–1953), the suggestion has often been voiced that Christianity and Communism or Christianity and socialism are enemies. But Christianity has no particular ideology. As in the story of the heavily-laden donkey that was offered a choice: "Which do you prefer, going uphill or going downhill?" to which the donkey piped back, "What of the road in the valley?" There are always alternatives and additional options. Our African continent has seen several ideologies, as mentioned earlier: African socialism (Ghana), ujamaa (Tanzania), négritude (Senegal), pan-Africanism, Nkrumaism, conscienscism, colonialism, apartheid, communism, democracy, globalization.[12] All the foregoing have been implemented in one African state or another. There is no one single African story; there are multiple African stories. For the moment the important point is that as a religion Christianity does not embrace or endorse or depend on a particular ideology. Since the church is present within the state, it can comment on aspects of the regnant ideology and its practices as judged on the basis of the church's nonnegotiable principles and its vision of human and societal well-being.

Politics for Nation Building and State Building

Politics concerns two things, nation building and state building. Because modern nations have been built out of congeries of peoples—some of whom had at one time or another been at war with each other—a fundamental question on the agenda of nation building has been how to build a sense of belonging for each and all. How can a sense of inclusion be cultivated rather than pursuing dogma—which has the capacity to divide and regrettably does so? The task is one of fostering a sense of common humanity and of being each other's keeper, for which Christians use the words "love" and "common good." As I see it, at root African traditional cultures, Christianity, and Islam are fundamentally about what is human. Africans' basic epistemology and ontology arise from their sense of community. This sense of community is an option for solidarity across race, ethnic, class, gender, and religious lines. It enjoins collective efforts and supports an engaged citizenry that is committed to walking together and working to secure the sense of self-worth of every person. The African conception of humanity has a sense of interconnectedness that seeks to build a just, participatory, and sustainable society. That was the agenda after freedom was gained from colonial rule, and

---

57–78; Mannheim, *Ideology and Utopia*.

12. Sigmund, *Ideologies of the Developing Countries*; Nkrumah, *Conscienscism*; Senghor, *On African Socialism*; Baako, "Nkrumaism—Its Theory and Practice," *Evening News*, June 27, 1960.

it remains on the agenda of nation building. But time and again in Africa recidivist tendencies toward separatism, enmity, and violence have been manifest. For example, we have seen Luo versus Kikuyu conflict in Kenya, Akan versus Ewe in Ghana, Zulu versus Xhosa in South Africa, and Hutu versus Tutsi in Rwanda. The ethnic problem is further confused by religious pluralism. Managing religious pluralism for the well-being of all is a significant agenda item for nation building.

If nation building is the task of enabling people to feel that they belong together, the other item on the agenda of politics is that of state building. To state building fall the tasks of providing health care, trade, and education for all citizens and of securing the coherence and well-being of the country and society. However, religious bodies, especially Christian churches and missions, from their beginnings, saw the social services of education and healthcare as handmaidens of mission. Thus they became collaborators with political actors, by which process the Christian churches earned the accolade "Church, the guardian angel of African nationalism."[13]

Two phases may be discerned in the process of nation and state building. The immediate independence agenda often was ensnared by a cult of heroism. Heroism, says Prince Mashele, is "a way of thinking that makes multitudes of people believe that their social, political and economic fates depend on the actions or benevolence of special individuals in society who possess extraordinary abilities and powers that are beyond ordinary citizens."[14] Nkrumah was the hero of the struggle for independence in the Gold Coast/Ghana. Nnamde Azikiwe was the hero in Nigeria's struggle for independence. Jomo Kenyatta was the hero of the struggle in Kenya. Julius Nyerere was the hero of the struggle in Tanganyika/Tanzania. But the cult of the hero disturbs and postpones a necessary element of the democratic processes, namely, development of willingness to take the risk of transcending liberation politics. Taking this risk requires vision and the courage to forge new paths. But if the process is put off, transition to a credible democratic machinery of governance is shortchanged. The cult of the hero quickly becomes a personality cult that in turn translates into marginalizing of opinions at variance with those of the hero. That path has emptied onto the slippery slope descending to the dictatorships that have plagued Africa's independent countries.[15] Lack of attention paid to coordination, administration, and time management issues in poor execution of the will of the people.

---

13. Sithole, *African Nationalism*, 55.

14. Mashele, *Death of Our Society*.

15. Ocran, *A Myth Is Broken*; Mazrui, "Nkrumah: The Leninist Czar," 9–17; Dennis Austin, "Strong Rule in Ghana," *The Listener* 67 (January 25, 1962) 157–57; Tibor Szamuely, "The Prophet of the Utterly Absurd," *Spectator* no. 7185 (March 11, 1966) 281.

Charismatic Leadership

The phenomenon of the hero and the cult of personality bear some relation to Max Weber's idea of the charismatic leader. As used by Weber, charisma signals a hero of the moment, especially in emergencies. The charismatic leader's credentials for authority derive from other than human sources and his authority is "a gift of grace."[16] To that extent the charismatic leader is like a judge in the Old Testament.

The charismatic leader may be distinguished from a chief, king, or traditional ruler by virtue of the fact that the authority of the latter rulers is sanctified by long-held custom and by the fact that their authority is located in a family to which one must belong in order to qualify for exercising authority.[17] In the rise of a charismatic leader, therefore, the stage is set for a struggle between the traditional leader and the political or nationalist leader who does not come from a royal home.

A third category of leadership is that of the person whose qualifications for leadership and authority derive from possession of particular skills—for example, a teacher, a professor in the academy, a doctor, or even some politicians.

The fundamental issue, however, is that of actual functional leadership. I suggest that authentic leadership is present when it is an embodiment of the dreams, ideals, and dilemmas of the people; it is not simply a matter of entitlement. That is a key issue as the altar and the polis—the church and the state—encounter each other. The question of leadership will not be settled by some vague, or even specific, theories and dogmas; it has to do with whether the leadership on offer fosters the legitimate dreams and ideals of the people.

Leadership, Power, and Authority

At the heart of the encounter between the altar and the polis lie the entwined issues of leadership, power, and authority. The altar and the polis are not enemies or rivals for power and authority. The issue is whether the complex bundle composed of leadership, power, and authority is vital and viable in the sense of serving to shore up the humanity of the citizens, their dignity, and their true freedom. The task is not just political. The promise of material blessing hoisted aloft by Nkrumah's famous statement, "Seek ye first the political kingdom and all other things shall be added to you," proved elusive and was hardly translated into the *Realpolitik* of the independent nation-state.

Other issues of the encounter between altar and polis include the clash between the politics of liberation and democratic governance; the mismatch between the skills necessary in prosecuting the struggle for independence and the skills required for governance of an independent nation; and the difficulty of establishing a clear vision,

---

16. Weber, *Theory of Social and Economic Organization*, 355; see 354–60.

17. N. Q. King, "Kingship as Communication and Accommodation," in Bruce, *Promise and Fulfillment*, 142–62.

held in common, of sustainable development for shared growth. The role of the altar is not one of working to advance some preconceived political theory; rather it stands guard over what will foster human dignity and freedom with justice and well-being, which, in biblical language, are synonyms for salvation.

No Theocracy

The idea of theocracy is present at the beginning of biblical faith. Down through the years, however, we see the New Testament move beyond the model of theocracy to focus on the kingdom of God, which is not equivalent to theocracy. Already in the Old Testament, indications of dissatisfaction with the theocracy of Israel are evident (1 Sam 8). The people desired effective leadership to meet the challenges posed by other nations—presumably to lead them beyond the radical egalitarian social vision of tribal society and to allow them to pursue rational economics and politics so as to keep in step with the times.[18] But when God grants the request, the result is not an absolute monarchy, which would have translated as power at the top and poverty at the bottom. Each individual's identity is defined in terms of his or her membership in the covenanted people of Israel, with obligations stipulated by God.

If the Old Testament conceived of everything under the rubric of the lordship of God, the New Testament focused on the kingdom of God, that is, the reign of God in people's minds, hearts, and lives so as to redeem all life to God. In another chapter I approach the topic in terms of human rights. Here it is sufficient to identify the contours of God's kingly rule: truth and truthfulness (Eph 4:15; Col 3:9–10); love, mercy, and lovingkindness (Rom 13:8–10), the only true norm of social practice; justice and righteousness (Rom 14:17); peace (2 Cor 13:11); and reconciliation (2 Cor 5:11–21). These are the qualities that the altar demands of the polis. In this setting, capricious leadership is ruled out, as is enslaving the citizens of the polis. Appropriating or confiscating citizens' private property is also excluded. Shoring up the identity, dignity, and security of each identifiable group as well as of individuals as persons who bear the *imago Dei* is a priority.

However, "there's many a slip between the cup and the lip," states an ancient proverb; the pursuit of nation building in Africa has too often been tripped up by

18. Observant readers may have noticed a preference in this book for the words "ethnic" and "ethnicity" rather than "tribe" and "tribal." "Tribe" and "tribal too often serve to deprecate the societies they are used to describe. Use of the words in colonial times served that purpose, but prior use of the terms in the Middle East and Asia also had a negative connotation. The words express oppositions between urban and rural societies and especially between sedentary/agrarian and nomadic/pastoral societies, with denigration of the latter. Why should the mainly agrarian/partly nomadic Israelite society of 1100 BCE, itself in transition from a rural warlord type of society to a small incipient kingdom with a court at an urban center, be qualified as being tribal? Apart from the word's denigrating connotations, such qualification overlooks the society's natural historical complexities and transformations. The misleading and abusive ring of the word "tribal" is further underscored by the implication that pre-monarchic Israelite society is tribal whereas monarchic and later Israelite society is not.

corruption. Various Commissions of Enquiry have established catenas of corruption in the land of my birth, Ghana.[19] In South Africa, publications abound detailing reports of corruption at all levels of government—central government, city and municipal councils, and police services—as well as in business and more. African heads of state such as Mobuto Sese Seko of Zaire/DRC; Sani Abacha, the late military ruler of Nigeria; and Robert Mugabe of Zimbabwe have all been mentioned in dispatches in connection with corrupt practices. If truth be told, not only individual heads of state, but whole nations have been guilty. Business deals and national development projects have been, with corruption such as the infamous 10 percent cut taken by individuals for awarding public contracts. Companies and governments from the Northern Hemisphere have been accomplices in corrupt business deals. Corruption takes many and diverse forms, for example, bribery, nepotism, patronage, theft of state assets, evasion of taxes, diversion of revenue, and electoral fraud. Corruption and fraud occur when opportunity coupled with the absence of mechanisms of accountability and open review serve to distort choice.

Whatever form they may take, issues of corruption are moral and ethical issues and therefore have a place on the agenda of theology and of the faith community, which claims to be the conscience of society. Salvation, individual and corporate, and corruption do not blend well. Moral, political, personal, and social corruption subvert the promise of political freedom, for moral rectitude is essential to an equitable and peaceful nation and to globalization.

Political life can no longer be lived solely within the bounds of the national level. Globalization means that the stage has grown broader and that the politics of Ghana, for example, cannot be hidden away in a corner. Therefore, present at the heart of political debate must be a sense that political activities have an end or purpose that reaches beyond themselves and beyond the local national setting. They are to be carried out in behalf of human beings who share a common humanity with the rest of the human community, both at home and abroad, and they have an obligation for the well-being of those other humans—and not just that of politicians and public functionaries. The phrase quoted earlier from Levinas, "heeding the heteronomous call" (chap. 7), must be given cash value in political life as well. This call is consistent with the democratic option, and national interest can no longer be defined by a narrowly conceived Realpolitik.

---

19. Each of the following is a report submitted by a commission of enquiry duly appointed by the government of the Gold Coast or, after independence, of Ghana. All were published in Accra by the Government Printing Department or Ministry of Information in the years shown in parentheses: *Report of the Commission of Enquiry into Mr. Braimah's Resignation and Allegations Arising Therefrom* (1954); *Report of the Commission of Enquiry into Trade Malpractices in Ghana* (1965); *Report of the Commission of Enquiry on the Commercial Activities of the Erstwhile Publicity Secretariat* (1967); *Report of the Commission [of Enquiry] into Kwame Nkrumah Properties* (1967); *Summary of the Report of the Commission of Enquiry into Irregularities and Malpractices in Connection with the Grant of Import Licenses* (1967); *Report of the Commission Appointed to Enquire into the Functions, Operations and Administration of the Workers' Brigade* (1968); Eric O. Ayisi [Commission Appointed to Enquire into the Functions, Operation, and Administration of the Workers Brigade], *Minority Report* (1968).

A fundamental issue that transverses religion and politics is to discern the criteria, principles, values, and ideology by which we can organize and live together and by which we can engage each other peacefully and with dignity, both within individual nations and in one global village. What civilized, humane standards and principles will enable us to live together in peace, in dignity, and with self-fulfillment? We may have ideas, but such a vision is not something that can simply be done *for* the people or handed to them as a ready-made package. The people *together* must work at creating a national vision, must own it, and must endeavor to structure it on the ground.

A theologian should uphold what is human first of all, because of the biblical affirmation that God created male and female in God's own image. Second, the theologian should hold out for the values of the kingdom of God, which are the core of Jesus' teaching. These values include peace with justice and right relationships, truth with compassion and love, reconciling and reconciliation, and an all-inclusive society. Present cultures of poverty and persistent violence must be unmasked as being really cultures and structures of exclusion. A culture of violence is able to persist only because some feel entitled to exclude and marginalize others and to ignore their well-being. When exclusion in any form is allowed to fester, however, peace with justice is not possible. Theologians must join with persons of good will in other disciplines in searching for mechanisms for building a truly inclusive community, society, and country.

Politics is, at bottom, about power. Unconscionable use of power creates tremendous pain and suffering. Unconstrained power often creates greed. Naming and shaming the evil that militates against wholesome community is critical; doing so requires courage and boldness and must be on the agenda of the theologian. An Akan proverb likens power to an egg. If held too tightly and firmly, it may break. If it is handled carelessly, it may also break, for it may drop. Monitoring, challenging, and then affirming the rightful use of power and authority is the duty and obligation of religious persons, especially theologians.

In seeking to live out the foregoing principles, we should be proactive and not simply reactive. All too often, religious people are caught in the position of reacting to steps already taken. People should be so formed, however (and here the role of religion comes into its own), that the values described become a regulative mechanism in their consciences and lives and endeavors.

Organizing at the International Level

People come "packaged" in various shapes and arrangements such as nuclear families, extended families, ethnicities, nations, and world community. Church and theology are not alone in seeking, at the level of the world community, to address the issue of human rights. Through its various organizations, the United Nations especially has also endeavored to address this critical issue. While appreciating the contribution made by the UN, let us suggest for the moment that the United Nations is not perfect and that, therefore, it also must be engaged by the community of faith and religious institutions.

The United Nations should not be deemed wholly innocent and righteous in all it does or that transpires there; some steps taken at the United Nations by the United States, Britain, France, Russia, and China are cause for concern. Power exercised through the United Nations is unequal. The relationships that exist there between the great powers and the rest of the world, which had been colonies and are still developing, are symptomatic of the unequal power relations that exist between the victors and the vanquished. Therefore, theology's concern for the dignity of all humans requires it to critique the stress on power and influence and to work for the equal sovereign rights of all. Watchfulness is all the more urgent and necessary because, time and again, powerful nations have used their veto power to advance their own national interests at the expense of weaker nations.

Even more worrying is the fact that China, Russia, and the United States are not signatories of the Rome Statute which set up the International Criminal Court and, therefore, cannot be hauled before it for their misdeeds, such as crimes of genocide, crimes against humanity, war crimes, or crimes of aggression. When the rest of the world was crying foul because of the ideology of apartheid as practiced in South Africa, the United States under President Ronald Reagan and Britain under Prime Minister Margaret Thatcher would not even give audience to the victims of apartheid's cruel and inhuman policies. Worse still, they helped South Africa to develop weapons of mass destruction, including nuclear bombs, something in the name of which they elsewhere waged war on Saddam Hussein of Iraq. Ironically, recently the United States and Britain organized the world against Iran for attempting to produce precisely what they helped South Africa to acquire. The US prison at Guantanamo Bay Naval Base, in Cuba, where prisoners have been in detention for years without trial, sticks out like a infected sore thumb. Its gross injustice violates the kingdom value of justice. All the foregoing are on the agenda of any African theology that would be faithful in identifying and articulating a theology of the kingdom of God and its righteousness in Africa and the world.

On the continent of Africa, where African theology is also being minted, the African Union (formerly the Organisation of Africa Unity) has awakened to the necessity for renewal in Africa at the levels of global political and economic systems. In 2000 the Millennium Partnership for the African Recovery Program (MAP) emerged. Two components within MAP are the New Partnership for Africa's Development (NEPAD) and the African Peer Review Mechanism (APRM). The former seeks to address the need for a new paradigm of international cooperation based on equal partnership. The mandate of the latter is, within the framework of NEPAD, to "encourage conformity in regard to political, economic and corporate governance values, codes and standards, among African countries [as well as within their] objectives in socio-economic development."[20] And who or which discipline is better placed than theology to contribute values? Theology is equipped, almost by definition, it would seem, to be a public advocate for justice, peace, and reconciliation and to promote the common good of all peoples.

Deliberately I end with the question just posed, that of the contribution theology needs to make in African contexts to formation of a mind-set that can sustain viable political life. The theologian as pastor and leader must cultivate the presence of the Holy Spirit and a life of prayer so as to be able to successfully discern the mind of Christ. Amid the myriad of political challenges, theology must stay on course with God's help so that God's kingdom can come on earth as it is in heaven. The agenda for theology is not only an intellectual activity such as theologians are obliged to pursue. It also demands pursuit of the traditional sevenfold gifts of the Holy Spirit as equipment for the journey. They are essential for the task—with all the dangers attaching to it—of challenging and critiquing elements of the status quo that are not in accordance with the values of the kingdom of God.

When colonialism ended, building of nation-states became very much on the agenda. The key words of that time included freedom, liberation, and self-government. But such language could only serve as a prelude to the building of a just, participatory, and sustainable society—one that, while learning from elsewhere, had to be creative in its pursuit of contextual viability. Today, the agenda has moved to a more advanced stage, namely, going beyond building nation-states and confronting the corporate state in a globalized world where the market and profit motif reign supreme. That leads us to the next chapter: "The Altar in the Marketplace."

---

20. See http://aprm-au.org/pages?pageId=mandate.

14

The Altar in the Marketplace

AT FIRST GLANCE, ENCOUNTERING a chapter with the market as its theme might seem out of place in a book on theology, especially when one hears the mantra "This is economics. Keep religion out." But Scripture's declaration, "In the beginning God created the heavens and the earth"; the first affirmation of the Apostles' Creed, "I believe in God, Maker of Heaven and Earth"; and the ecumenical vision make an apology for touching on economics redundant. The prayer of Jesus that God would "give us . . . our daily bread" puts economics on Christians' agenda. Given the vastness of Africa and the widely divergent economic issues and challenges it poses, this chapter necessarily must be highly selective in the topics it treats, especially offering a critique of economic visions put forward and their consequences for the well-being of peoples.

The Two Altars

The title of this chapter comes from John Chrysostom (ca. 345–407). In his *Treatise Concerning the Christian Priesthood*, he suggests that two altars can be seen at which priests worship—one in the sanctuary church, the other in the marketplace. Reverence and respect must be exhibited at the altar in the sanctuary where God tabernacles. But the other altar, in the marketplace, demands equal reverence and respect, namely, service to the poor, those in need, the suffering, and the homeless.[1] These insights are Chrysostom's commentary on Jesus' parable of the sheep and the goats (Matt 25:31–46). Here we cannot limit the category "priests" to liturgical agents, for Christian faith teaches the priesthood of all believers.

The parable of the sheep and goats suggests that economic issues are more than abstract economic theories dealing with such topics as supply and demand or profit and loss. Economic issues are also about the power to choose good or evil, a matter that is within the reach of everyone. One does not respond to the economic plight of people only when asked and only by offering prayers. The good person is generous

---

1. See Bria, *The Liturgy after the Liturgy*; Ion Bria, "Liturgy after the Liturgy," in Lossky, *Dictionary of the Ecumenical Movement* (2002), 705–6; Pobee, *Worship of the Free Market*.

and therefore attempts to build community with those less fortunate, who are also God's creation.

The name "Africa" has proverbially been synonymous with poverty, and people in poverty have too often been pushed to the margins of the human community. The religious/theological offer of well-being and definition of what is human will be short-changed if theologians ignore economic issues and their consequences for what is human. We should note that religious communities and organizations they support have time and again picked up the casualties of political and governmental economic misadventures. So I make no apologies for including a chapter on the altar in the marketplace.

What Is Economics?

Though the establishment of economics as an academic discipline is relatively recent, practical economics is as old as when human beings with different talents and resources first began to live in communities. It took the simple form of barter. The Papyri of Zeno (ca. 260–230 BC), discovered in the early twentieth century, contain information on the economic and fiscal administration of the Ptolemaean state. Apollonius (ca. 261–245 BC), the finance minister, received reports based on yearly visits made by two royal functionaries, the *oikonomos* (economist) and the *strategos* (military official). The *oikonomos*, the role occupied by Zeno, reported on the administration of finance and commerce. The goal of the finance minister who received the reports was to secure the peace and security of the state by prudent and efficient management of resources. Arrangements in the Ptolemaean state remind us that the disciplines of economics and political science are inextricably involved with each other.

Economics is essentially about the management of the (global) household. The production, distribution, and consumption of goods and services on the part of all humanity fall within its purview. Among the objectives of economics are human well-being and a just, participatory, and sustainable society and world. In essence this description of economics is a claim that the ecumenical vision goes beyond the church. Perhaps not insignificantly, the words "economics," "economy," and "ecumenism" share the same Greek root, *oikos* (household). Creation as a whole is a vast public household, signaling the unity of humankind as well as systematic interdependence. Therefore, theology dares to engage with and comment on economic matters in the name of oikos-theology.[2]

At its most basic level, economics is the management of the home, the household, and the nation.[3] Today statistics and theories often serve to shroud the discipline of

---

2. Ernst M. Conradie, "Notions and Forms of Ecumenicity," in Conradie, *South African Perspectives on Notions and Forms of Ecumenicity*, 54; Mercy Amba Oduyoye, "Africa," in Briggs et al., *History of the Ecumenical Movement*, 471.

3. See, e.g., Rana Foroohar, "8 Questions with Joseph Stiglitz," *Time*, August 18, 2016, http://time.

economics in mystery. But if you press beyond the figures, economics is the story of a people's circumstances: who paid what, to whom, for what, why, and at what time. The statistics represent a narrative; the bottom-line issue of that narrative is how the economic activity fosters or does not foster the well-being (salvation) of peoples. The economy is organized according to an ideology. When Lenin claimed that "political institutions are a superstructure resting on economic foundations," he recognized the interpenetration of ideology and economics, though he saw the constraining influence running the other direction.[4] The management of a common home in a world of tremendous diversity demands sensitivity. The variety of the world's institutions must be suited and fitted to each other with appropriate structures, including appropriately integrated fiscal union. Appropriate political institutions must be melded with appropriate and relevant socioeconomic institutions.

Keep Religion Out of the Market

The dictum "Keep religion out of the market or economics" is a legacy of Enlightenment culture and ideology. It is rooted in the Enlightenment's characteristic privatization of religion.[5] Experience has abundantly demonstrated, however, that time and again religious communities and institutions have been the ones who have stepped in to pick up the casualties and broken bones of political and economic misadventures. Several other things should warn us against giving unquestioning credence to the notion that religion should be kept out of economics. First, past experience has shown that at times religious institutions and economic productivity have blended well. For example, during Europe's Middle Ages and in spite of vows of poverty, monastic institutions invested in breweries and wineries that yielded a handsome income. Medieval churches also controlled large expanses of land, which were significant economic assets. In Ghana, although the African Initiatives in Christianity are said to attract the poor, they nevertheless are adjudged not to be poor and are active in business. Second, the Christian churches in Europe and the United States have accommodated themselves to capitalist and colonialist ideologies. So the question is not whether economics and religious principles may ever mix, but which principles will be embraced and for what purposes or ends and with what safeguards.

Earlier I defined oikos (household) in terms of the home. But for biblical faith the whole world is God's creation—God's home and household. This means that the four corners of the earth—the nations in their variety and with their differences—together belong to that one household which is God's. So as a theologian sees it, economics must work to enable all peoples to find appropriate economic space in which to live decently, sharing the bounty of God. That vision gives religion a role in the market.

---

com/4457109/joseph-stiglitz-interview/.

4. Lenin, *Three Sources and Three Component Parts of Marxism* (1961).
5. See Bosch, *Transforming Mission*, 262–345.

Macro and Micro Economics

In the early stages of its development as a discipline, economics dealt largely with macroeconomic issues, such as capital accumulation and growth, population, diminishing returns in agriculture, and national policies. By the second half of the nineteenth century more attention began to be paid to microeconomics, that is, to narrower issues of economic choice in the context of relative scarcity.[6] The shift in focus to microeconomics brings the significance of the context to the fore, which in turn provides a test of the relevance of any economic theory or construct. Economic contextual realities are at bottom thoroughly human issues. Christian interpretations of economic activities are an exercise in seeking the human face of God, the heart of the theology of the incarnation.

As an illustration, let us consider the issue of layoffs. Layoffs cause discouragement and anxiety for workers, especially when efforts to secure new jobs prove fruitless. Job hunting that does not yield good results leads to deep anxiety and distress. If—as is commonly stated—people are a company's most important asset, why get rid of them? And if there is a reason for doing so, is it good enough and must the action be carried out at the expense of human beings? That question is at once a religious and a moral issue. An especially worrisome matter is that financial services businesses, retailers, and technology companies have been known to use temporary drops in demand as an excuse for downsizing—even when the businesses themselves were not under duress. The consequences of downsizing for the physical and psychological health of employees and their families hardly need to be stated. Theologians and religious institutions, in order to be faithful to their vocation, have an obligation to stand guard against anything that undermines the well-being of people and society.

Ever-Changing Economic Scenes

The economic scene is ever changing. For example, that economic giant, the United States, experienced recession at the beginning of the twenty-first century. At the time this book is being written, Ireland, Spain, Greece, and Cyprus are gripped in economic crises. Since the scenario undergoes constant change, there can be no once and for all economic model or solution. But through all the changes, the theologian's concern is whether the economic model in use fosters and undergirds what is human, supports true human dignity, enhances human rights, and is sensitive to the cries of the marginalized and the excluded. In other words, both cultic life in the sanctuary and secular economic activity in the market are lived under God. Both must be done in a way that honors and praises the Creator God. Writes Ion Bria, "Outside the temple, in the public market-place, compassion for the poor is a sacred liturgy in which the

---

6. See Jevons, *Theory of Political Economy*, n2; Marshall, *Principles of Economics*.

faithful are the priests."[7] The theologian's obligation is to be sensitive to economic developments so as to identify and speak for what fosters the well-being of human persons and to denounce what undermines human dignity.

Biblical Input

The Scriptures of the Old and New Testaments, which are the foundation documents of the church and theology, attribute religious and spiritual significance to the economy. The classic statement of this position is the parable of the sheep and the goats (Matt 25:31–46) that states that the physical actions of feeding the hungry, clothing the naked, and visiting the incarcerated are at the same time religious and spiritual acts done on behalf of Jesus, Christ and Lord. Sounding a similar note, the prophet Amos does not spare cheats in the marketplace.

> Woe to you who turn justice to vinegar
> and stomp righteousness into the mud.
> Do you realize where you are?
> . . . .
> People hate this kind of talk.
> Raw truth is never popular.
> But here it is, bluntly spoken:
> Because you run roughshod over the poor
> and take the bread right out of their mouths,
> You're never going to move into
> the luxury homes you have built.
> You're never going to drink wine
> from the expensive vineyards you've planted.
> I know precisely the extent of your violations,
> the enormity of your sins. Appalling!
> You bully right-living people,
> taking bribes right and left and kicking the poor when they're down.
> Justice is a lost cause. Evil is epidemic.
> Decent people throw up their hands.
> Protest and rebuke are useless,
> a waste of breath.
> Seek good and not evil—
> and live!
> You talk about God . . .

---

7. Bria, "Liturgy after the Liturgy," in Lossky, *Dictionary of the Ecumenical Movement*, 705–6.

being your best friend.

Well, *live* like it. . . .

Hate evil and love good,

then work it out in the public square." (Amos 5:7–15)

Experience from time immemorial has shown that human economic endeavor marginalizes some members of society. When that is the case, religious persons must become the voice of the voiceless, speaking up for the excluded and marginalized. It is interesting to compare other translations of Amos 5:15. The Revised Standard Version (1952) is pointed: "Hate evil and love good, and establish justice in the gate." The Knox Bible (1954) translates this verse as "shun wrong, cherish the right, justice enthrone at your judgement-seat." We see that economic issues are and fundamentally must be concerned about justice in society for all.

Africa: Rich in Natural Resources and Yet Poor

The nations of Africa, the world's second largest continent, are severally and individually well endowed with natural resources.

- First, in spite of its vast expanses of desert, such as the Sahara and Kalahari, Africa also boasts vast expanses of rich arable land. That land could be developed for the benefit of the peoples on the continent. The creativity that the nation of Israel has shown with desert land suggests that even a desert need not be a curse and a plague.
- A second resource in Africa is water; the continent has fifteen landlocked river basins. The north-flowing Nile River traverses eleven countries with a population of three hundred million people, making its way through Tanzania, Uganda, Rwanda, Burundi, Congo (Kinshasa), Kenya, Ethiopia, Eritrea, South Sudan, Sudan, and Egypt. Other rivers include the Congo, Zambezi, Niger, and Volta. Lakes Albert and Edward, which empty into the Nile River, and Kivu and Tanganyika, which flow into the Congo River, are part of the African Great Lakes. Lake Malawi, which is shared by Malawi and Tanzania, connects to the Zambezi via the Shire River. Lake Chad is shared by Niger, Chad, Cameroun, and Nigeria.

The foregoing information suggests the presence of issues related to equitable sharing of common resources which are not simply an economic consideration. They also bring to the fore convictions about the common good and common humanity, which extend their reach into the area of ethics and morality. Cross-border reserves and resources and border-demarcation issues need to be managed in ways that enhance the security of all parties.

- Third, the proverbially poor continent, Africa, is blessed with hydrocarbon resources. In West Africa, Ghana, Ivory Coast, and Nigeria have hydrocarbon resources both onshore and offshore. Angola, Democratic Republic of the Congo, Gabon, Kenya, Republic of the Congo (Brazzaville), Ruvuma Basin of Tanzania and Mozambique, Somalia, and Uganda also have hydrocarbon resources.

Being blessed with hydrocarbon resources is also proving to be a curse measured in terms of massive corruption in the management of those resources and in the labor of creating a business climate that will favor their just and honest development. Further, especially where hydrocarbon resource fields span international borders, the challenge is one of managing cross-border resources and demarcating borders in a way that will favor peace and security. In Congo (Kinshasa), significant environmental issues arise because some concessions intrude into national parks and world heritage sites. In some rich mining areas, such as Katanga Province, elites play a major role in Congolese politics, manipulating policies and thus creating threats to national stability and cohesion.

In short, abundant blessings raise the need for a just and equitable legal framework within which resources can be shared so as to secure hope for all persons. Unilateral decisions, such as Ethiopia's hydropower development, have significant implications for other countries that share the same river, and those concerns must be taken into account.

- Fourth, Africa is blessed with mineral resources such as bauxite, manganese, tin, uranium (Democratic Republic of the Congo, Niger, South Africa), coal (South Africa), cobalt (Zimbabwe), copper (Zambia), diamonds (Democratic Republic of the Congo, Ghana, South Africa), gold (Ghana, Mali, South Africa, and others), and platinum (South Africa).

The blessings and curses that economic affairs encompass suggest that economics cannot be treated as though it were a self-contained activity; other disciplines such as religion, ethics, and politics must necessarily be brought to bear on economic issues for at least three reasons. First of all, economic concerns are at the same time religious, spiritual, and ethical matters; indeed, treating issues as purely economic concerns—unleavened by religious, spiritual, and ethical considerations—may not make for cohesion, peace, and health within society and nation.[8] As the Russian Orthodox theologian and philosopher Nikolai Aleksandrovich Berdyaev (1874–1948) states,

> The question of bread for myself is a material question, the question of bread for my neighbor, for everybody, is a spiritual and a religious question. Man does not live by bread alone, but he does live by bread and there should be bread for all. Society should be so organized that there is bread for all, and then it is that the spiritual question will present itself before [humankind] in

8. World Council of Churches, *Christian Faith and the World Economy Today*.

all its depth. It is not permissible to base a struggle for spiritual interests and for a spiritual renaissance on the fact that for a considerable part of humanity bread will not be guaranteed.[9]

Second, the concept of a *free* market implies a moral substructure, constantly ignored though that substructure might be. Even the free market recognizes the need for some governmental structure to guarantee law and order, to enforce contracts, and to defend against aggression. Left to themselves, markets lead to inequalities of income and wealth. In addition, the idea of a free market implies some theology, some anthropology, and a view of human nature.

Third, economics as a discipline deals with the basic issue of choice in the allocation of scarce resources, and the issue of choice invokes ethics. Indeed, the idea of welfare itself involves wider political, philosophical, and theological considerations, whether articulated or implied. As Ronald Preston puts it, "Value free economics and value free markets presuppose not only a legal structure but a network of human communal values and obligations."[10] Again, Preston argues that "economics by themselves have little to say about policy, but the little they say is important. Beyond that, politics, sociology and other social sciences are involved, and so is ethics. Behind ethics is some view of the nature and significance of human persons, and of that, religions and philosophy have much to say."[11]

What Is Human: The Measure of Wholesome Economics

To refer to communal values is also to refer to human persons. At its best, economics serves human beings; in doing so it should foster and undergird human identity. At that point religion and economics converge. A review of African societies reveals a workforce that is largely nonliterate and people who live in areas of dirt paths. Most towns have no parks, no community centers, no public libraries; most homes have no access to electricity and telephones. These characteristics are signs of communities and societies that are not developed to the fullest. Economics should be engaged so as to secure the benefits associated with development—such as schools, housing, medical services, and the benefits of technology—for the underprivileged as well as for humanity in general.

An earlier chapter suggested that religion is not so much about dogma and doctrine as it is about development of humanity to the fullest. In the words of Pope John Paul II, the fundamental mission of the church is "to make man better, more conscious of his dignity, more devoted in his life to his family, social, professional and patriotic commitments, to make man more confident, more courageous, conscious of his rights

---

9. Berdyaev, *The Origin of Russian Communism*, 225–26.
10. Preston, *Church and Society in the Late Twentieth Century*, 45.
11. Preston, *Religion and the Ambiguities of Capitalism*, 34.

and duties, socially responsible, creative and useful."[12] My conviction is that not only do religion and theology converge with economics in relation to the ultimate goal of securing human identity and dignity, but also that religion plays the peculiar and particular role of contributing a *telos* (end, goal, or purpose) to the exercise. This telos stands superior to market share and economic clout. For example, even if the rampant porno culture of our times has considerable market, its low regard for humans, especially women, poses a challenge to the theological conscience.

African Contribution to the Telos

Africans approach delineation of the telos with certain values already in hand. The Akan of Ghana call these values *nsare-nson*, that is, the seven graces: *nkwa* (long life, vitality, good health, felicity, and prosperity); *Adom* (the favor of the spirit world, without which the living are helpless and hopeless); *asomdwee* (peace of society, peace of mind, freedom from perturbation); *abawotum* (power to procreate, potency, sexual fertility, through which the continuity, security, and well-being of individuals and of clans are assured); *anihutum* (good eyesight); *asotatum* (good hearing); and *amandoree* (increase in the prosperity, vitality, and greatness of the entire clan and ethnic society). Together these graces are called *ahoto* (peace and contentment within and around the individual, family, clan, and world). In concert the seven graces constitute the *summum bonum*, which determines the relevance, vitality, vibrancy, and viability of any economic construct in Africa. The traditional African summum bonum is not dissimilar to the yearnings expressed by Franklin D. Roosevelt, president of the United States, in his January 1944 State of the Union address. He spoke of an "economic bill of rights" that included, he stated, the right to a job, decent housing, food, clothing, education, and medical care; protection from fear of old age, sickness, accident, and unemployment; and freedom from unfair competition and domination by unfair monopolies.[13]

Ideology and the Economic Construct

If religion contributes a vision of the human—that which is to be secured by economic construction—ideology provides a means to organize economic activity. Significantly, economics as a discipline was initially known as "political economy."[14] And now Johns Hopkins University's School of Advanced International Studies, located in the United States, boasts a chair of International Political Economics. This step by Johns

---

12. Whale, *The Pope from Poland*, 7.

13. See http://www.fdrlibrary.marist.edu/archives/stateoftheunion.html.

14. Smith, *Enquiry into the Nature and Causes of the Wealth of Nations*, 1776; Malthus, *Essay on the Principle of Population*; Ricardo, *On the Principles of Political Economy and Taxation*; Mill, *Principles of Political Economy*; Jevons, *Theory of Political Economy*.

Hopkins reminds us of the close connection between politics and economics; it also reminds us that political ideology shapes how economics is perceived and structured. Thus a study of religion and economics must be a trialogue among theology, political ideology, and economics.

Ideologies: Many and Diverse

By virtue of its encounter with foreign religions and ideologies, if not subjugation by them, Africa straddles a number of religious and ideological divides: those of traditional African religion and culture; those of Christian religion and culture, especially as minted with a Christendom ideology; and those of ideologies such as democracy, socialism, capitalism, centralized or controlled economies, free market, and globalization. Today one hears talk of social democracy and democratic Marxism. China and Russia, whatever claims to Marxism they may make, have also given license to capitalist practices. These developments suggest that the old assumption that one has to treat ideologies as binary—as though one has to choose one or the other—is, in reality, passé.

North Atlantic Captivity and Legacy

An earlier chapter addressed the epochal significance of colonialism in Africa. Lugard's concept of a "dual mandate" in the colonies gave expression to the notion that colonialism served the goal of making money for the colonialist and not that of developing the colony for the benefit of the indigenous people. As he put it, "Let it be admitted at the outset that European brains, capital, and energy have not been, and never will be, expended in developing the resources of Africa from motives of pure philanthropy; that Europe is in Africa for the mutual benefit of her own industrial classes, and of the native races in their progress to a higher plane."[15] Indeed, Robert Gascoyne-Cecil, third Marquess of Salisbury and British prime minister, in a 1897 speech to Guild Hall, London, was even more blunt: "We wish that trade should pursue its unchecked and unhindered course on the Niger, the Nile and the Zambezi."[16] These statements indicate in no uncertain terms the culture of self-interest and national interest that informs much of economic political activity.

The entire project of colonialism was built on the premise that Africa was uncivilized and, being flooded with paganism and cannibalism, was in need of civilization. Disinterested service and devotion to Africa was not part of the package; on the contrary, the European drive to derive "some" benefit and power and influence was fully present. In consequence the resources of Africa were exploited and developed in the interest of Europeans. Africa became the producer of raw material for the benefit

---

15. Lugard, *The Dual Mandate in British Tropical Africa*, 617.
16. Cited in Hargreaves, *West Africa Partitioned*, 2.232.

of Europe and at low and noncommercial rates. Africa was made to be in effect an appendage of Europe and was to be remade in that continent's image and likeness. Europe's failure to develop, if not active steps to prevent the development of, on-site industries and factories became a drag on Africa's economic development. The omission of this crucial step is key to the proverbial poverty of Africa.

In response to the ideology of colonialism, Aimé Ferdinand Césaire enunciated the ideology of Négritude, or self-affirmation of black peoples. He articulated that a person's status depends, in part, on his or her economic position. Similarly, Frantz Fanon, while rejecting the concept of Négritude, pointed to the imposition of an existentially false and degrading existence on blacks, one that demanded conformity to distorted values, as the defining strand of colonialism.

The end result was that Africa found itself at a disadvantage, being on the receiving end of an unjust political and economic system. To this point both African politicians and white humanitarians bear witness. For example, a former president of Senegal, Abdulaye Wade, wrote in 2003, "African leaders want a new start. For the West, Africa has been a continent apart—a place to be discovered, a source of slaves, a subject of economic domination. As African leaders began to assert themselves, the West turned attention to Asia. Africa represents less than 1 percent of world investment and 1.4 percent of world trade. Shipping routes now run directly between Asia, United States, Europe, typically bypassing Africa. There is no clearer measure of how far Africa has been marginalized."[17]

The real significance of Africa's poverty is the continent's marginalization and the exclusion of its peoples. As one American business executive expostulated at a conference, "But Africa does not exist" in economic terms. That exclusion translates into poverty—according to the United Nations, "nearly half the world's population, 2.8 billion people, survive on less than $2 a day" and "about 20 percent of the world's population, 1.2 billion people, live on less than $1 a day"[18]—but also into devaluation of people that reaches deeper than economics and politics. Certainly, great numbers of the people living in poverty are located outside Africa, but the point is that the talents and creative genius of the economically disadvantaged are not as valued as are those of other humans, even though it is the poor who work hardest. The language of economic growth smooths over and shields from view the real social consequences of the yawning gap between the rich and the poor. The human, which should be the measure of economic growth, is shortchanged.

Bob Geldof, a musician and humanitarian who in February 2008 travelled with George W. Bush, president of the United States, through five African nation-states (Benin, Ghana, Liberia, Rwanda, and Tanzania), offers another telling comment:

---

17. Wade, "Plan to Mobilise Capital," *Newsweek*, special issue, December 2002–February 2003, 72.
18. See Hunger, http://www.un.org/en/globalissues/briefingpapers/food/vitalstats.shtml.

> Africa is the only continent yet to be built. It will be here that some of the great politics of our century will play themselves out. It's a continent of 900 million potential producers and consumers. There are more languages and cultural diversity in Africa than almost anywhere else. Many of the great rivers and resources on the planet are here.
>
> The Chinese and the Indians are massive investors in Africa, and so must the West be. The US gets 19 per cent of its oil imports from the continent, and the figure is rising; in China, it's 30 per cent and rising. Europe must look more to Africa to avoid Russian oil. Europe is a mere 8 miles (13 km) north of this vast continent, with all the tensions over security and immigration that implies.[19]

Geldof's analysis is fair, but I wish to highlight three points. He confirms that Africa is still excluded and marginalized. That is the significance of his statement, "It is still the only continent yet to be built." Second, Africa cannot continue to be excluded. The colonial mentality must be changed in order for Africa to be treated as a true partner in the economic quest being conducted in service to the well-being of humankind. At the least, the numbers suggest a potential market. But a market that is exploitative cannot make for the inclusion of Africans in the world community.

The third thing of note is Geldof's mention of the Chinese and Indians in Africa. The United States in particular has been very negative about the Chinese presence in Africa. The Chinese are by no means perfect; they too have been exploitative. But they seem to offer better terms than have the United States and Britain. The Chinese and Indian presence once more brings into view the importance of a level playing field that offers justice to all parties.

International economic arrangements have been a recipe for injustice and have contributed to the poverty of the peoples of the South. This assessment corresponds to the critique of capitalism expressed by Lenin, "Uneven economic and political development is an absolute law of capitalism."[20] All economic arrangements and ideologies must be subjected to critique by the gospel with its values of the kingdom of God and of what is human.

Commerce and Christianity

In the nineteenth century the slave trade was still rampant in Africa, in spite of protests by humanitarians and the Evangelicals. David Livingstone (1813–73), a Scottish missionary and explorer in Central and Southern Africa, identified the need for European capital if the resources of Africa, notably its minerals and extensive arable land, were to be developed. His arguments were to be summed up in the catchphrase of the Zambezi River as "God's highway for Commerce and Christianity."[21]

19. Geldof, "The Healer," *Time*, March 3, 2008, 73–74.
20. V. I. Lenin, "On the Slogan for a United States of Europe," in Lenin, *Collected Works*, 3.272.
21. Livingstone, *Missionary Travels and Researches in South Africa*.

The campaign for Commerce and Christianity was designed to undermine the heinous slave trade, replacing it with honest and honorable trade that would serve as a channel for integrating African societies and building a community of communities. The phrase was seen as defining the Christian mission. Soon, however, the motive of mission was outstripped by interest in trade. Instead of trader and missionary going hand in hand into the interior to provide opportunities for European trade, to relieve the poverty of the Africans, and to inculcate the best of European and Christian morals, the project of Commerce and Christianity fostered an ideology of power and exploitation. A healthy cup became a poisoned chalice.

In the project for Commerce and Christianity we see demonstrated once again that the best idea can be corrupted over time and in translation as it crosses borders. No ideology of the market can be a once-for-all construct and solution. Review and vigilance are required constantly to assess whether a project is on course to serve the good and well-being of humanity and society. Because of the human capacity to sin, pursuit of trade—if it is not rooted in religious and spiritual values—can become worship at the altar of Mammon. Also, because international and global economic structures do not present a level playing field, the nations of the Southern Hemisphere are at a disadvantage. This fact raises issues of justice and fair play, which religion must be concerned with correcting.

The ghosts of colonial practices continue to haunt Africa and all past colonial countries. Colonial economic practices included land enclosures and forcible removal of natives. That practice was particularly nasty in some parts of Africa such as Kenya, Southern Rhodesia (Zimbabwe), and South Africa. Sudan, also, has seen expropriation of the lands of minorities. West Africa's reputation of being the white man's grave, because of the high mortality rate, forestalled implementation there of those practices in their full viciousness.

Growth: Secure Property Rights

One of the canons of modern economic rhetoric is that secure property rights are vital to economic growth. This tenet has been used simplistically to guarantee the security of property rights of foreign investors and local elites. Evidence shows, however, that time and again the property rights of indigenous peoples have not been respected. Cause for further concern is misuse that some people make of data assembled in the Political Risk Services' International Country Risk Guide and the World Bank's Worldwide Governance Indicators.[22] These data have enabled interested parties to extrapolate from the experience of foreigners and elites as though they were evidence

---

22. Information on Political Risk Services (PRS) and the International Country Risk Guide (ICRG) can be found at http://www.prsgroup.com/about-us/our-two-methodologies/icrg. For the World Bank's Worldwide Governance Indicators, see http://data.worldbank.org/data-catalog/worldwide-governance-indicators.

of secure property rights and to treat them as proxies for individual countries' quality of governance and rule of law. Consequently, while there is a correlation between the level of economic growth and security of property rights for foreign and elite investors, no similar correlation exists between the property security of minority groups and economic growth. Neither is there a correlation between property security and a country's ranking on the United Nations Development Programme's Human Development Index.[23] Economic growth that does not secure the property rights of minorities is fraudulent.

Capitalism versus Marxist Socialism

Discussion of economic progress within African nations at independence was reduced to treating the capitalist economic system (which was equated with the practices of the colonial dispensation) and Marxist socialism as binary opposites—and the newly independent African states seemed to favor Marxist/socialist structures. The new leaders seemed to have imbibed the sentiment expressed in Lenin's statement quoted earlier that "uneven economic and political development is an absolute law of capitalism."[24] But my use of the word "seemed" to characterize the attitude of the African politicians is by design. Though they made noises using Marxist rhetoric, it is far from clear that the rhetoric expressed deep-seated convictions. The politicians' lifestyles did not bear this out. Besides, the Soviet Union quite evidently also exploited African governments. A case in point is the way that in the 1960s the Soviet Union sold snow ploughs to Ghana as agricultural implements. Identifying ideology that is authentic and creative in the African context and that is morally alert is crucial to sound economic life.

The Parable of the Two Elephants

According to African wisdom, "When two elephants fight, it is the grass that suffers." The uneasy relationship between capitalist and Marxist/socialist ideologies has nothing good to offer the poor nations of the Southern Hemisphere. In the rivalry between the two ideologies, the poor nations become entangled in their spheres of influence. The African nations of Angola, Ethiopia under Mengistu Haile Mariam, and Mozambique became proxies of the superpowers, leading to tremendous chaos and impoverishment. The bipolar world's Cold War did not help Africa, which played the role of a pawn in power games.

---

23. See http://hdr.undp.org/en/content/human-development-index-hdi.
24. Lenin, "On the Slogan for a United States of Europe," in Lenin, *Collected Works*, 3.272.

Ideology of Globalization

Laden as it is with a sense that the world has shrunk into a global village and that, therefore, we are inextricably bound together, the ideology of globalization has been paraded before us as the salvation of the world. Its high priests have been the World Bank and the International Monetary Fund (IMF), the Inter-American Development Bank, and G7 (which consists of the seven leading industrialized nations: Canada, France, Germany, Italy, Japan, United Kingdom, and United States). Because historically some of these countries have been colonial masters, the economies of the South have become appendages of the G7.

Globalization is a project of progress and development based on the foundations of science, technology, and human reason, presumably unifying humanity under the vision and canopy of progress. (As the saga of the Tower of Babel [Gen 11:1–9] shows, the human quest for progress has deep roots.) The emergence of the Economic Community of West African States (ECOWAS), the Southern Africa Development Community (SADC), the European Economic Community (EEC), and the Organisation of Petroleum Exporting Countries (OPEC) is a reminder that economic salvation and security may be best sought in collectivities and not as individual self-sufficient islands of humanity. The problem that arises, however, is that in the name of globalization, manipulation has been paraded as progress. Wrong things and wrong outlooks have been sold to the Third World in the name of development and progress. In the name of globalization, African countries have been forced to roll back social services and to scale down staff, thus undermining peoples' security.[25]

Globalization as an ideology of the market has been given the epithet "free." But the label of "free market" is a misnomer when large numbers of people are ill-fed, ill-housed, ill-clothed, undereducated—if educated at all—and prey to preventable diseases. In contrast, the rich are getting richer at the expense of the poor, who continue to become poorer and poorer. The privileged, evidence suggests, have the capacity and capability to protect and extend their privileges and the market mechanism that supports them. Charles Elliott perceptively comments, "Interest groups, institutions, and structures of all sorts—political, administrative, legal, tenurial, and industrial—combine to ensure that markets work imperfectly, if at all. [They] are manipulated, biased, and influenced to work in ways that do not conflict with the perceived interests of those in power."[26]

Political independence by no means meant that the balance ceased to favor Britain. The General Synod of the Church of England, commenting on world economic prices in 1968, stated, "The industrialized countries are able to build into the prices they charge for their exports a certain standard of living for those who produce their exports. The developing countries exporting cocoa or cotton or copper have to take

---

25. Yeebo, *Ghana: The Struggle for Popular Power*, 178.
26. Elliott, *Patterns of Poverty in the Third World*, 2.

what the market offers with no guarantee that will afford a reasonable standard of living to the producers."[27] As an idea, the free market is a falsehood. The ideology of the free market is based on self-interest, a euphemism for greed.

The IMF, "the caring but strict nanny of the financial world," comes to the aid of nations in difficulty, but only on the condition that they devalue their currencies and reduce budget deficits through higher taxes.[28] In 1982, when Ghana entered into negotiation with the IMF for a loan in the amount of 538.5 million US dollars, the IMF demanded that the exchange rate of Ghana's currency, the cedi (GH¢), be adjusted. In 1983 Ghana obediently placed the required multiple exchange rate in use, which in effect meant a currency devaluation of 99 percent. As a result, within a year and a half—from January 1982 to June 1983—the annual inflation rate rose from 32.8 percent to 174 percent. Wages failed to increase correspondingly, instead lagging behind the rate of inflation. On top of that—in accordance with the dictates and self-interest of the IMF—subsidies for public services such as water, health, education, electricity, and transport were removed. With the introduction of a petrol tax, fuel prices were revised upwards. Petrol climbed from GH¢ 12.50 a gallon to 21.45 in 1983, gasoil from GH¢ 8.50 to 15.90 a gallon; kerosene from GH¢ 5 to 13.20 a gallon. These increases had the expectable consequence of raising the cost of many other things—and did so in a continent identified as poor.

Another indication of the elephant's raw self-interest was the extraction from Ghana of a promise not to nationalize any foreign or transnational companies without compensation. The effect was to clip the wings of the self-confessed socialist government of Flt. Lt. J. J. Rawlings. The IMF exhorted poor countries to export more. The result was competition among poor countries to export commodities, with a consequent substitution of imported products for domestic products. The morass of measures imposed had the effect of creating a buyer's market motivated primarily by self-interest. Making self-interest central in human affairs is a matter of concern for religion and theology, because doing so puts poorer people at a further disadvantage. Overall, measures generated by free market ideology were not people friendly, particularly when they led to retrenchment and a sense of gloom and hopelessness. The demand to export more diverted attention from a search for truly viable economies.

One pillar of the ideology of globalization is that governments do not create wealth: business creates wealth. Another is that inflation should be controlled by monetary and fiscal management. All such steps gave government officials an excuse for not exercising the proper functions for which taxes are collected and for which the people elected them to office. The ideology of globalization also gave banks free rein in the economy. The difficulties experienced by the United States in the later years of George W. Bush's presidency and by Ireland, Cyprus (2013), Greece (2012), and Slovenia (2013) represent a judgment on the faith put in the banks. All these crises tell

27. Church of England, *Let Justice Flow*, 8.
28. See *Newsweek*, April 13, 1992, 25.

stories of bad loans and unpaid debts. Economics without moral conscience, sooner or later, leads to disaster.

The logic of banks can be summed up in two words: debt and profit. The self-interest of banks and their focus on profit lead them to be more focused on someone's ability to pay interest on a debt than on payment of the principal, because the longer the loan is outstanding, the higher is the profit margin. In effect the poor are enriching the rich. Susan George writes perceptively that debtor nations "are not earning a fair price for their goods. The world economy is enfeebled as a result. The debtors' only recourse is to cut imports drastically in a desperate attempt to create a trade surplus that will allow them to pay back the banks. Once they have cut the fat, they start depleting muscle and bone. Agriculture and industry must forgo vital needs like fertilizer, spare parts and machinery. Debtor nations must also deprive their people."[29]

Ethical Context of the Market

For the ideology of modern economics a key phrase is the "free market." Development and free markets, though economic matters, have an ethical context. Ethics are involved when taxes are taken from the rich so as to help the poor. Ethical values are involved in creating the understanding that the gains of modernization, land reform, employment, and literacy should be widely distributed, that self-help and human dignity should be esteemed and supported, and that societies should work to overcome homelessness. In spite of the privatization of religion, which is a legacy of Enlightenment culture, morality is and should in fact be the arbiter of economics, actively seeking to foster the interests and well-being of the masses of people.

Liberation theology identifies poverty as a social sin and a scandal. But Leonardo Boff goes further when he writes of a special strength the poor bring.

> The exact meaning of this [preferential option for the poor] is to recognize the privileged status of the poor as the new and emerging historical subject which will carry on the Christian project in the world. The poor, here, are not understood simply as those in need; they are in need but they are also the group with a historical strength, a capacity for change, and a potential for evangelization. . . . The Church is directed to all, but begins from the poor, from their desires and struggles. Thus arise the essential themes of the Church: social change creating a more just society; human rights, interpreted as the rights of the poor majority; social justice and integral liberation, achieved primarily through sociohistorical freedom and concrete service in behalf of the disinherited of the world, and so on.[30]

---

29. George, *A Fate Worse than Debt*, 59; George, *The Debt Boomerang*.
30. Boff, *Church, Charism, and Power*, 9–10.

Thus poverty may not be the last word. Aware of God's preferential option for the poor, religious persons and theologians are obliged to remint the words "politics" and "economics" and to engage in a conscientious, determined, and focused assault on the idols of the market.[31] Excessive preoccupation with the market carries with it the danger of an idolatry that edges the Creator God out of all reckoning in human life. Devotion to any system devoid of the human heart and spirit is idolatrous.

The Prayer for Daily Bread as the Focus of the Ethical Imperative

The second petition voiced in the family prayer that Jesus taught his disciples asks God for provision of daily bread: "Give us this day our daily bread" (Matt 6:11 KJV). Provision of adequate food, available for everyone, is of direct concern for religion, theology, and morality. Thus the second petition of the *Paternoster* takes us back to Levinas's phrase "heeding the heteronomous call." It is a call to understanding economic activity as service entered into in support of human well-being.

The economic endeavor to provide the necessities that will make for human well-being has, however, another side, to wit, provision of legitimate human needs when society is in a state of economic, ecological, and psychological bankruptcy. In their search for a way out of their mental distress, people are turning to psychiatrists and soothsayers. They have a sense that in unfettered pursuit of material prosperity and indulgence in unrestricted consumption they have lost their inner balance and would like its restoration.

Hidden Side of Globalization

Other aspects of the ideology of globalization also raise issues for theology. For example, the globalization of economics means that human trafficking, a modern version of slavery, is now global in scope. Preying on people in 120 countries and trafficking them to 130 countries around the world, the "business" of human trafficking poses a challenge for theology. Emma Thompson writes that according to an International Labour Organization report, at any particular point of time in 2008 at least 2.5 million persons were in the process of being trafficked. Human traffickers entice females from poor countries with promises of good jobs that never materialize. Often their passports are taken from them. Some are put in solitary confinement to break their will and worse still are subjected to sex-slavery in appalling conditions. Labeled by Thompson "the hidden side of globalization," this dimension of globalization is a "sickening business." Slave laborers are found working both in domestic service and in hazardous factories. The promise of good jobs proves a lie, and the dignity and well-being of those who are trafficked suffer.[32]

---

31. Bacon, *Novum Organum*, aphorism 39.

32. Thompson, "Emma Thompson on Human Trafficking," *Newsweek*, March 8, 2008, http://www.newsweek.com/emma-thompson-human-trafficking-84043.

In drawing attention to the underside of the culture of globalization, I do not intend to suggest that globalization—or for that matter any other ideology—is by definition wrong or immoral. I would simply remind us that to be fulfilling, every ideology needs a human and moral compass.

Critique of All Ideologies

For theologians wishing to engage economic issues, a critical element is to have a memory of the past. In the story of Africa, two ideologies in particular need to be engaged, colonialism and globalization. For its part, colonialism was practiced in the interests of the European nations. In 1918 Paul von Hindenburg (1847–1937), German general and statesman, articulated the point well: "Without colonies there can be no industry and without industry there can be no adequate prosperity."[33] Whose prosperity he had in mind seems fairly clear. And so, Africa produced raw materials for European industries and African economies became addenda of and support to North Atlantic economic well-being. Such an arrangement could not foster equity, justice, healthy international relationships, or a sound form of globalization.

Similarly, those with the upper hand have walked over the interests of the weak. As president, George W. Bush was demonstrably contemptuous of climate change, a factor that weighs most heavily on the so-called Third World countries. The Africa Growth and Opportunity Act (AGOA), passed by the US Congress in 2000, ostensibly seemed aimed at opening up US markets to sub-Saharan Africa's produce such as textiles and apparel exports. But a clause attached to the bill contained a long list of "Eligibility Requirements" if a country wished to be eligible for AGOA. Among them, "African nations are required to cut corporate taxes and price support, cut government spending and allow multinational corporations unlimited right to buy and control natural resources. Eligibility is determined by the US President, based on whether that country is making progress towards a market-based economy, the rule of law, the elimination of barriers to US trade, and towards internationally recognized worker rights and a system to combat corruption."[34] In the dance between the United States and Africa, some countries are more equal than others. Can the chicken dance with the elephant? Here is a question of morality, justice, and equity.

The truth is that systemic causes of growing unemployment, poverty, and inequality are inherent in the ideology of capitalism. The consequences of commodifying the most basic services—such as water, electricity, and healthcare—hit every normal person, but especially the poor.

The litany today is that South Africa, a member of the Group of Brazil, Russia, India, China, and South Africa (BRICS), is the strongest country economically in an

---

33. Hindenburg, cited in Neill, *Colonialism and Christian Missions*.

34. Butty, "Africa Trade Law: One Year After," 26; Irvine, "If We Want a Future, It Can Only Be a Green Future," 14.

otherwise economically lagging continent. That terms of praise such as social transformation, transformational project, ideological capacity, capable state, and balance of forces are accorded to South Africa, does not hide, obliterate, or even touch the fact of the continuing dominance of white capital, with the result that blistering poverty persists in the country.

Theology needs to critique slogans and sloganeering and to challenge nations to look beyond slogans, statistics, and theories to pursue the well-being of all, especially the poor.

Economic Expansion and Sustainability

The profit motif, as noted earlier, has been central to the ideology of globalization. That motif has often been implemented as rampant economic expansionism. In the process, natural resources—especially those of poor Third World countries—have been wantonly exploited, raped, and wasted. Unbridled globalization as a model of economic development is having drastic consequences for the integrity of creation. Sandy Irvine addresses this aspect of assumed economic orthodoxy in a sensitive way, stating, "The real issue comes down to the questions of whether human society can keep expanding or whether it must be stabilized and seek deeper harmony between people and the planet. . . . The richer parts of the world are consuming more than their fair share, so it is folly to promise people in these countries that we can keep on enjoying ever higher levels of consumption."[35]

Going beyond criticizing, Irvine recommends making sacrifices in the interest of preserving the environment. He writes, "We have to select much more carefully what technologies we use. . . . Some technologies are quite incompatible with environmental and human well-being and we have to say no to them. The obvious example is nuclear power. In terms of the seriousness of their impact, transport systems based on the motor car are fatal, and we must switch investment to alternatives like public transport systems."[36] The US environmentalist Lester Brown poignantly comments, "We can no longer separate the future habitability of the planet from the current distribution of wealth."[37]

Economic Groupings and the Danger and Threat of Self-Interest

Political and economic groups such as G7, G8, ECOWAS, SADC, and BRICS have all bought into a version of capitalism in which the market drives the allocation of

---

35. Irvine, "If We Want a Future, It Can Only Be a Green Future," 14.

36. Ibid., 12–15.

37. Lester Brown, "Launching the Environmental Revolution," *State of the World* 1992, 181; cited in Newsweek Staff, "Earth at the Summit," *Newsweek*, May 31, 1992, http://www.newsweek.com/earth-summit-199290.

capital, the pace and places of development, the direction of exports and imports, and an ethic of economic growth. The whole falls under the label of "trickle down economics."

The rationale given for the growth ethic is that the wealth of nations in dominant positions can stimulate crumbs to fall down from their overloaded tables to the poor. Bluntly put, gross inequity is alleged to be the foundation of prosperity. On the ground, however, this "growth ethic" has fueled the ever-widening gap between the rich and the poor. It has institutionalized systemic injustice. All such rationalizations include elements of self-interest that remind us of the human penchant for advancing a culture of dependence, something that must be guarded against. Self-interest is manifest in the fortress mentality evident in the nations of the North.

"Ethiopia, Stretch Forth Thy Wings and Fly"

African patriots have used the imagery of an eagle stretching out its wings and soaring to inculcate the idea that Africans can and should wean themselves off a strategy of "AID"; that is, they should overcome a mentality that waits for someone else to provide for them or to do things for them, so that they can take their life into their own hands.[38] If the genuine well-being of people is to be served, taking such a step requires clarity regarding the sacrifices that will have to be made and demands that priorities for development be set. It requires that policymakers and populace face the topic of population growth and its implications for well-being. We must ask how the population growth rate can be kept in pace with national and natural resources. The issue of population growth is not only an economic issue; it concerns social morality as well and reflects both social progress and social values.[39]

Africa must also get her priorities right. For example, most of Africa has brilliant sunshine 365 days of the year. It is beyond comprehension that solar energy on the continent has not been vigorously developed. Especially is this the case when energy from other sources—oil, gas, nuclear—is either crippling African nations or placing them in captivity to non-African nations and businesses.

Micro Credit: Right Architecture of Globalization

Today banks are vital partners to economic activity. But the recent economic crises in the United States and in Europe have shown that banks—often guided by a market ideology and a profit motive—can be implicated in unconscionable and dishonest practices. When that has happened, horrendous misery, human indignities, and inhumane

---

38. For background to the wording of the subheading, see Pobee, "Let Ethiopia Hasten to Stretch Out Its Hands to God," 416–26.

39. John S. Pobee, "Towards a Theology and Ethics of African Population Dynamics," in Pobee, *Religion, Morality, and Population Dynamics*, 1–16.

conditions have followed. The crisis spawned by the activities of banks confirms that economic activity without a moral compass leads to disaster.[40] Because inherited economic structures are not delivering well-being for people, especially the poor, Muhammad Yunus has argued that we need to discover the "right" architecture for globalization.[41] In this endeavor, we do well to learn from others. By embracing an ecumenical perspective, we can learn from experiments conducted in the Muslim context.

In 2006, Yunus was awarded the Nobel Peace Prize for setting up the Grameen Bank which gave poor people the power to help themselves and thus supplied them with security in a most fundamental form. His approach recognized and acted to affirm the vital role that women play in the economic, social, and political life of their respective countries. Microcredit has improved the circumstances of millions of people, including youth. As the comment from *Publishers Weekly* found on the cover of his book states, "Yunus shows that micro-lending can be much more effective than an unwieldy and expensive aid programme."

The form of microcredit pioneered by Yunus is so crucial for the Third World situation that it is well to allow Yunus, the pioneer, to speak for himself.

> When we want to help the poor, we usually offer them charity. Most often we use charity to avoid recognizing the problem and finding a solution for it. Charity becomes a way to shrug off our responsibility. But charity is no solution to poverty. Charity only perpetuates poverty by taking the initiative away from the poor. Charity allows us to go ahead with our own lives without worrying about the lives of the poor. Charity appeases our consciences.
>
> The real issue is creating a level playing field for everybody—rich and poor countries, powerful and small enterprises—giving every human being a fair chance. As globalization continues to encroach on our socioeconomic realities, the creation of this level playing field can become seriously endangered unless we initiate a global debate and generally agree on the features of a "right" architecture of globalization, rather than drift into something terribly wrong in the absence of a framework for action. This framework will no doubt have many features, but we can keep in mind the following: The rule of "strongest takes it all" must be replaced by a rule that ensures everybody a place and a piece of the action. "Free trade" must also mean freedom for the weakest. The poor must be made active players, rather than passive victims, in the process of globalization. Globalization must promote harmony and partnership between the big and the small economies, rather than become a vehicle for unhindered takeovers by the rich economies. Globalization must ensure the easiest movement of people across borders. Each nation, especially poor ones, must make serious and continuous efforts to bring information technology to the poor people to enable them to take maximum advantage of globalization.

---

40. Stephen Gandel, "After Three Years and Trillions of Dollars, Our Banks Still Don't Work," *Time*, September 26, 2011, 40–45.

41. Yunus, *Banker to the Poor*, 249; Yunus, *Creating a World without Poverty*.

> Social entrepreneurs must be supported and encouraged to get involved in the process of globalization to make it friendly to the poor. Special privilege should be offered to them to let them scale up and multiply.[42]

The microcredit approach offers practical steps to be taken, thus providing a strategy that goes beyond ideology and articulating a vision. Yunus enunciates sixteen points.

1. We shall follow and advance the four principles of the Grameen Bank—discipline, unity, courage, and hard work—in all walks of our lives.

2. Prosperity we shall bring to our families.

3. We shall not live in a dilapidated house. We shall repair our houses and work toward constructing new houses at the earliest opportunity.

4. We shall grow vegetables all the year round. We shall eat plenty of them and sell the surplus.

5. During the planting seasons, we shall plant as many seedlings as possible.

6. We shall plan to keep our families small. We shall minimize our expenditures. We shall look after our health.

7. We shall educate our children and ensure that we can earn to pay for their education.

8. We shall always keep our children and the environment clean.

9. We shall build and use pit-latrines.

10. We shall drink water from tubewells. If it is not available, we shall boil water or use alum to purify it.

11. We shall not take any dowry in our son's wedding; neither shall we give any dowry in our daughter's wedding. We shall keep the centre free from the curse of dowry. We shall not practice child marriage.

12. We shall not commit any injustice, and we will oppose any one who tries to do so.

13. We shall collectively undertake larger investments for higher incomes.

14. We shall always be ready to help each other. If anyone is in difficulty, we shall all help him or her.

15. If we come to know any breach of discipline in any centre, we shall all go there and help restore discipline.

16. We shall introduce physical exercise in our centres. We shall take part in all social activities collectively.[43]

---

42. Yunus, *Banker to the Poor*, 249.
43. Ibid., 135–37.

This long quotation is attractive because it clearly, boldly, and sensitively identifies the reality of poverty in the Third World. It does not resort to dramatic clichés but states things in a simple, practical, and understandable way that even the economically unschooled can understand. Further, it convincingly calls people to action.

Another reason for placing the microcredit experiment from the Third World on the agenda is that we have been beholden to the North Atlantic heritage and models for too long. In a world that has not only become globalized but has also been socialized in the ecumenical imperative of Scripture, we must be bold in considering other offerings. In this instance we must be bold to learn from Islamic practices as regards economics.

Corruption

While Africa is blessed with abundant natural resources, it has ironically also become synonymous with poverty. Two factors in the irony are financial and legal corruption, themselves manifestations of moral corruption. Corruption has been at once individual, personal, and institutional; it is also structural. It takes many forms: maladministration, misuse of public funds, violation of policies and procedures, a craven culture of fear, intimidation, victimization, and nepotism. If the Christian church has any rightful claim to be the conscience of society, standing guard over morality, then church and religion must be bold to name the devils and evils present in society and thereby to conscientize culprits regarding their need to repent and to do what is right. But even more worrisome is the reflection that corruption in African societies has been named for decades, with no signs of a change in course. Church and theology must redouble their efforts to conscientize all levels of society to the reality that integrity, honesty, and truth are critical necessities for nation building and for the economic life of society.

Corruption reaches deeper than simple malfeasance. In making appointments, African governments often give party affiliation precedence over competence. But economics is a discipline that requires knowledge and competence, and underequipped administrators are at a disadvantage, especially when they are placed in positions that pit them against more qualified personnel. The idea of the common interest of all in the nation is too easily shortchanged or rendered nonexistent. As a result, disequilibria are allowed to go unchecked and social conflict erupts. Corruption in a country leads to negative evaluations on the part of foreigners, harming the climate for investment and foreign aid. The idea of the common interest is not unrelated to the principle of the preferential option for the poor.

Theologians must engage those spearheading the political economy. Strategy must be created, articulated, and developed along some nine lines: (a) delineation of the productive sectors of society, such as agriculture and natural resources; (b) property rights; (c) viable and sustainable investment; (d) fiscal policy; (e) pricing policy; (f) reforms in public enterprise; (g) reforms in the banking sector; (h) monetary and credit policies; and (i) foreign debt and arrearages. Each productive sector should address Who, What, and When. Theologians may not be the initiators, but they should be attentive to these areas; otherwise they will be faced with picking up the pieces when calamity strikes. For this reason theology may not in good conscience accept proposals that religion be kept away from issues of political economy. Theology must supply a *vision* for our land, especially for political economy.

What the theologian happily calls a vision for our land will be called a manifesto by the politician. Every day it sits, the Ghana Parliament opens with the following Parliamentary Prayer.

> O God, grant us a vision of our country fair as it might be,
>
> A country of righteousness, where none shall wrong his neighbor,
>
> A country of plenty, where evil and poverty shall be done away with;
>
> A country of brotherhood, where all success shall be founded on service, and honour shall be given to the deserving;
>
> A country of peace, where government shall rest on the will of the people and the love for the common good.
>
> Bless the efforts of those who struggle to make this vision a reality.
>
> Inspire and strengthen our people that they may give time, thought and sacrifice to speed the day of the coming beauty of Ghana and Africa.
>
> AMEN![44]

In effect, this prayer offered daily in Ghana's parliament states that even if theology, economics, and politics are different disciplines, they are united in working for a just, participatory, and sustainable society. By implication, theologians may not be barred from making such intelligent comments on political economy as may secure the dignity and humanity of all members of society.

It is in the best interest of everyone to be closely attentive to the foregoing, for history is replete with evidence that financial collapse is a harbinger of political extremism. One needs only to think of the emergence of Adolf Hitler from the collapse of Weimar Republic, the emergence of Vladimir Lenin and the Bolsheviks from the breakdown of czarist Russia, the emergence of Slobodan Milošević out of the economic meltdown of Yugoslavia, the emergence of Flt. Lt. Jerry John Rawlings from the economic chaos and corruption of the administration of General Ignatius Kutu Acheampong of Ghana. Fear, despair (personal and economic), and instability create space for demagogues and self-styled revolutionaries. The victims of such iniquitous systems yearn for hope. Jared Diamond's *Collapse*, with its analysis of factors that make for social decay (as summarized by Chris Hedges), is to the point: "Corruption, mismanagement, and political inertia by an elite, which is beyond the reach of the

---

44. See the conclusion of "Kufuor's Speech at the 3rd Young Professional Conference," *Modern Ghana*, November 4, 2011, http://www.modernghana.com/news/359357/kufuors-speech-at-the-3rd-young-professional-conference.html.

law, almost always results in widespread cynicism, disengagement, apathy, and finally rage. Those who suffer the consequences of this mismanagement lose any loyalty to the nation and increasingly nurse fantasies of violent revenge. The concept of the common good, mocked by the behavior of the privileged classes, disappears. Nothing matters. It is only about 'Me.'"[45] Selfishness and greed, the outgrowth of preoccupation with "me," is the beginning of corruption and chaos. But in opposition to greed and selfishness, Christians and theologians have a word to speak, and rightfully so.

For several African peoples and nations, political chaos and harsh, even irrational, economic circumstances have been simply part of the story and a feature of headline news. But such stories are tragic, for the stories of African nations—which are rich, especially in national and natural resources—do not have to be ones of blighted hope and pain. Political vision and economic activity marked by creativity, integrity, and authenticity—and informed by ecumenical vision—have the capacity to engender an unshakable faith and to provide solid hope that can undergird world unity in troubled times. Much of the seepage that is evident from the "historic churches" to churches comprising the African Initiatives in Christianity is informed by the gospel of prosperity. The promises of the gospel of prosperity are often not sustainable and seem instead to be little more than "celestial dope" and "pie in the sky."

But the seepage itself is an index of dissatisfaction with what is on offer in the historic churches. The presence of that dissatisfaction is symptomatic of a "gospel" and a theology that have failed to engage and dialogue with the socioeconomic and political circumstances of the people, whether because of an ideology that says to "keep religion out of politics" or because the church has regurgitated foreign attitudes that fell short of the principle of contextualization. My argument is a plea for a gospel and a theology that take poverty and the circumstances of the context seriously. The gospel we proclaim and the theology we live and teach need to be marked by vibrancy and vitality for the sake of vital faith and hope in Africa.

---

45. Hedges, *Empire of Illusion*, 183; Diamond, *Collapse*.

15

Human Dignity—Human Rights

EARLIER CHAPTERS ARGUED THAT fundamentally religion and, therefore, theology are grounded in the reality that humanity bears God's image and likeness. As a consequence of this reality, humans are entitled to dignity and honor, and Christian institutions have been heralds of human dignity and human rights. Christian missions in Africa, for example, have been described as guardian angels of African nationalism because—through their use of health and education as handmaids of Christian mission—they gave increased impetus to the yearning present in African hearts for recognition of their rights and dignity in the face of colonialism and other ideologies that did not foster human dignity. In Akan wisdom, however, close linkage also brings a danger. As the Akan say, "The one who daily carries the earthenware vessel to fetch water for the household is the most likely to break the vessel." The person who carries the jar is the one most likely to stumble and let it break; in similar fashion, we find that the vision of human rights is often not honored even within the church, which should be its guardian. We dare not condone such failure. Invocation of human rights will be secure only when they are firmly linked to a clear sense of who and what is human. Sadly, signs are abundant of a need for clarity on this latter issue, especially in a pluralistic and globalized world.

Ideology of Slavery

The phrase "human rights" is invoked so often that it has almost been denuded of meaning. One source of confusion is the fact that the high priests of human rights have in practice done things that both seem to deny and in fact do deny recognition of the rights and dignity of persons not on their side or of the same mind. The so-called Christian nations sold Africans into slavery. As mentioned earlier, the first missionary of the Society for the Propagation of the Gospel in Foreign Parts to serve in the Gold Coast, Thomas Thompson, wrote a pamphlet, *The African Trade in Negro Slaves Shown to Be Consistent with the Principles of Humanity and Laws of Revealed Religion*, defending the slave trade. Indeed, some, such as the Right Reverend Tom Butler of

Southwark, South London, were clear that the profits from the slave trade formed part of the bedrock of England's industrial development. In the process, blacks were treated as tools in that development and not exactly as human beings.

Ideology of Colonialism and Racism

The ideology of colonialism that characterized the encounter between Europe and Africa has been covered in an earlier chapter. Its various manifestations certainly did not treat Africans as the Europeans' equal.

> Racial prejudice was a characteristic of Western man since the very beginning of the history of Western civilization. In Africa, Asia and the Americas, people of colour were treated by Westerners as inferior and were used as slaves and servants. It seems as if colour prejudice has in a very early stage of Western history become part of Western man's identity. As early as the 5th century AD, monks started painting images of the devil in black. The association of black being evil has remained with Western man and deeply penetrated his mind, influencing his attitude towards Black people. When at a later stage in history Western man came in contact with Blacks, the people were seen as the cursed sons of Ham and that it was God's will or predestination that the White race must have authority or guardianship over the coloured race.[1]

Uneven Playing Field

With that background, articulation of human rights was far from balanced or even-handed, for the ground was not level. No sense of what is human prevailed across the board; conceptions of the peoples of color were assimilated to the image of Western man. Even today the plurality of *homo sapiens* is not granted its full due in articulating human rights. But the sentiment articulated by the Native American, Chief Seattle, cited earlier, offers us a pointer toward wisdom: We are part of the same thread; damage to any part of the thread affects us all. Human interconnectedness and pluralism are simultaneously characteristic of both nations and the global village.

Activities around the globe carried out by the United States of America, the high priest of human rights, call into question the genuineness and viability of that country's commitment to human rights. An example is the drone strikes in Pakistan and Afghanistan. The United States claims that its strikes are targeted, but on the ground drones have killed hundreds of innocent people, including children. The drone strikes are said to be part of a perpetual war for peace and an unrelenting war on terrorism and terrorists, as identified and defined by the United States, often with no or only

---

1. N. J. Smith, "Apartheid in South Africa as a Sin and Heresy: Some of Its Roots and Fruits," in Hofmeyer and Vorster, *New Faces of Africa*, 143.

suspect evidence. The Guantánamo Bay detention camp holds people who have been in prison without trial for over a decade, a fact that seems to contradict the country's profession of support for human rights. The United States arrogates to itself the roles of accuser, jury, judge, and executioner. In this way, human rights are violated by the high priests of human rights, and the concept of human rights is correspondingly brought into disrepute.

South Africa, while claiming to be the last bastion of Christian civilization on the African continent, developed the inhuman ideology of apartheid and carried out many actions that destroyed human life. In 1982 the South Africa Defence Force made raids into Maseru, Lesotho, to deal with members of the African National Congress that they called "terrorists" but who called themselves "freedom fighters." In the raid, thirty ANC freedom fighters were killed. Matumo Ralebitso, a daughter of Lesotho's ambassador to Mozambique, was also killed. "Western nations condemned the attack but stopped short of calling for further sanctions against the apartheid state."[2] The condemnation was a mere slap on the wrist compared to the Western nations' response to black African nations in similar situations. The horrendous violence and human and material destruction that accompanied the US ventures in Vietnam in the 1970s; the US war in Iraq—or was it the war of the Coalition of the Willing (mostly Western nations)—against Saddam Hussein; the ventures of the Western powers in Afghanistan: all of these raised issues of human rights offences initiated by the high priests of human rights, suggesting the presence of a deep and ongoing crisis about who is human and what it is to be human.

The insights provided in the foregoing paragraphs regarding Jan Smuts and the United States as well as other violations of human dignity and rights not mentioned here remind us of the universal human tendency to be accomplices in violence, whether state-sponsored, systemic, or personal.

In addition to differences of political ideology that fuel violation of human dignity and human rights, nations need to engage the reality of pluralism. Pluralism represents the coming together of the souls of many cultures, each a priceless thread in the rich tapestry that constitutes both human society and the nation-state. This diversity is at once a strength and a challenge. In our pursuit of the human, we must acknowledge the reality of *homo pluralis* and hone the gifts of each people so as to unite the human community and the nation-state and to build a better life for everyone.

Consequences of Glossing over the Real Identity of the Other

Inadequate attention to the plurality of homo sapiens has led too many to exalt the artifacts of one strand of the human species, namely, Caucasians, as *the* exemplar of human rights and the mark of what is civilized. A case in point is the Charter of the

---

2. Smith and Tromp, *Hani: A Life Too Short*, 149.

United Nations, which had no input from the Negroid race. In a globalized world-village, it hardly needs to be argued that important as the UN Charter (June 1945) and the UN's Universal Declaration of Human Rights (December 1948) may be, they cannot be made into fetishes, nor are they sacrosanct. There must be ongoing debate that recognizes the need for changes that arises with the appearance of other actors on the world stage. The received summaries of human rights are not changeless constructs, immutable for all generations to come. They stand in need of revision in light of what non-Caucasians, who were not part of the original framing, bring to the table. Any other approach will necessarily distort homo africanus, and other peoples, into the image and likeness of Caucasians.

Ideology Necessary for Modeling a Culture of Human Rights

Modeling a culture of human rights requires an ideology, but all too often the ideology of democracy is invoked reflexively. The promoters of human rights have also been high priests of the ideology of democracy. The escapades of Western nations in Iraq, Afghanistan, Vietnam, and colonialist Africa—especially the exploitation of Africans and attempts to crush African resistance—have made Africans suspicious of blandishments from abroad. But it is not my desire to follow the well-traveled path of lambasting imperialists and colonialists. Rather I wish to delineate a basic truth about the ideology of democracy that is key to a culture of human rights, namely, that democracy requires active participation on the part of citizens. So part of the quest for human rights is the issue of whether the citizenry is engaged or disengaged, whether citizens are empowered or disempowered. I suggest that poverty, high levels of unemployment, exclusion of segments of society from education and good health care, and insecurity are indices of a jaundiced vision of human dignity and human rights as well as of a dysfunctional citizenry.

Preamble of UN Charter—A Help

The Preamble to the Charter of the United Nations may be regarded as a roadmap that also adumbrates an ideology for human dignity and human rights. It reads:

WE THE PEOPLES OF THE UNITED NATIONS DETERMINED

- to save succeeding generations from the scourge of war, which twice in our lifetime has brought untold sorrow to mankind, and
- to reaffirm faith in fundamental human rights, in the dignity and worth of the human person, in the equal rights of men and women and of nations large and small, . . .

AND FOR THESE ENDS

- to practice tolerance and live together in peace with one another as good neighbours, and
- to unite our strength to maintain international peace and security...

HAVE RESOLVED TO COMBINE OUR EFFORTS TO ACCOMPLISH THESE AIMS.[3]

As a Christian and a theologian I give a general assent to the insights expressed in the Preamble of the Charter. It was a sensitive response to two horrendous world wars (1914–18, 1939–45). Through those experiences the framers of the Charter came to underline the fundamental importance of securing the dignity and worth of every human person. The word "person" (from Latin *persona*) signals a human being whose identity and rights are enshrined in law. A person has legal identity and may never be treated as a thing (in Latin, a *res*, that is, something nonhuman or subhuman).

Among the contours of human identity enshrined in law are the worth of each person, equality of rights, gender equality, freedom to live in community, and entitlement to peace and security (*pax et securitas*). From an African Christian viewpoint, it is desirable to undergird these precepts with Christian religious principles and contributions from the African worldview.

The Preamble of the UN Charter is based on a draft by Jan Christian Smuts (1870–1950), a South African military and political leader. His nation—with its horrendous abuses of human dignity and denial of rights on the basis of skin color—took the cup for racism. As colonial secretary, Jan Smuts opposed the movement led by Mohandas Karamchand Gandhi for equal rights of South Asian workers. In his political life Smuts consistently excluded the African majority from democracy and was a vocal supporter of the segregation of races. In 1929 Smuts wrote,

> The old practice mixed up black with white in the same institutions; and nothing else was possible, after the native institutions and traditions had been carelessly or deliberately destroyed. But in the new plan there will be what is called in South Africa "segregation"—separate institutions for the two elements of the population, living in their own separate areas. Separate institutions involve territorial segregation of the white and black. If they live mixed together it is not practicable to sort them out under separate institutions of their own. Institutional segregation carries with it territorial segregation.[4]

Here Smuts does not articulate the full-blown ideology of apartheid, but his statement is well on the way to it.

---

3. See http://www.un.org/en/sections/un-charter/preamble/.

4. Jan Christian Smuts, "Native Policy in Africa," in *Africa and Some World Problems* (Oxford: Oxford Univ. Press, 1930), 92, https://archive.org/details/africaandsomewor027995mbp.

Further, Jan Smuts had a patronizing attitude toward Africans: "These children of nature have not the inner toughness and persistence of the European, not those social and moral incentives to progress which have built up European civilization in a comparatively short period."[5] In other words, Africans were immature and needed the superintendence of the whites.

These ideas were not peculiar to Jan Smuts; they were pervasive in South African society and undercut support for political rights for blacks equal to those of whites. They formed an option for white political privilege.

Whatever may have been Jan Smuts's role in crafting the Preamble of the UN Charter, because of the deeply rooted inability of whites to accept the full humanity of people of other races, the stage was set for contradictions and dissonance between the vision of the Charter and the reality on the ground.

Saints Are Not Made by Acts of Parliament

The inconsistency between the UN Charter and race relations on the ground brings to mind a biblical story relating to King Josiah of Judah (640–609 BC). With the disintegration of the Assyrian Empire after the death of Ashurbanipal in 633 BC, the kingdom of Judah sought to throw off Assyrian hegemony, which included getting rid of all Assyrian intrusions into Judah's monotheistic religion. The timely discovery of the Book of the Law (Deuteronomy) gave King Josiah a pretext and the courage to attempt to restore the purity of Judah's religious practices by the purification of the temple, destruction of pagan altars, outlawing human sacrifices, and renouncing his predecessor's malpractices (2 Kgs 22–23). But his successors, Jehoahaz (ca. 609) and Jehoiakim (609–597), returned to all these evil practices. The lesson is that saints are not made by acts of parliament. People's consciences also need to be touched so as to arouse a sense of commitment to the proposed new order and a sense of outrage at any step that undermines human dignity and human rights.

Need for Moral Conscience

In addition to an ideology and a legal framework, a moral code that articulates the values of the nation-state is needed. To be appropriate, a nation's architecture of morality and values needs to embrace inclusivity, efficiency, a caring environment, provision of opportunity, and safe surroundings. Right leadership is also important. To speak of "right" leadership is to grope after such virtues as magnanimity and generosity of spirit; humility, modesty, approachability, and respect for others; morality, that is, discernment of what is right and good from what is wrong and bad; unity in striving for common goals; inclusivity; equality; a reconciling spirit and compatibility;

---

5. Ibid., 76.

accountability; humanity; commitment to and ability in listening and hearing (the government must hear the people and vice versa); a pro-youth stance that invests in tomorrow; and a preferential option for the poor. For securing a culture of human dignity and human rights, moral, ethical, and just leadership is essential. The leadership that is needed is nothing less than the paragon of virtue and humanity.[6]

The Contribution of Psychology

Carl Gustav Jung (1875–1961), Swiss psychologist and psychiatrist, has argued that being human has to do with consciousness. That is why earlier I wrote of culture as being the identity and wavelength of a people. Jung asks, "Is a person connected with something that is infinite or not? That is the telling question of his life. In our relationships to other men too, the crucial question is whether an element of boundlessness is expressed in the relationship."[7] Thus the issue of being human and of human dignity is about whether one is allowed and enabled to have consciousness. The Akan of Ghana have a similar phrase. When one is treated badly, they say, "*Oreku me sunsum*" (he is killing my soul, my consciousness). Jung's insight strikes a chord familiar to homo africanus.

Consciousness is all too easily reduced to individualism, which has formed the bedrock of the epistemology and ontology of Western society. Homo africanus's epistemology and ontology may be expressed as *Cognatus sum, ergo sum* (that is, I have blood relations, therefore I am). For example, the Zulu concept of *ubuntu*—I am because we are—is a testimony that interconnectedness with one another defines African consciousness. Ubuntu is an option for being united, having responsibility for helping each other, and standing in solidarity, especially with those on the margins. The Akan describe one who shows solidarity with others as òyè nyimpa dè (he or she is a true human being).

The cantus firmus of Akan society is that humans are wired by interconnectedness. The Akan say, *Anko-nam yè yaw* (it is a pain to walk alone). The Akan see social connections and connectedness as basic human needs. Interconnectedness and the ability to communicate are characteristic of what it is to be human and lie at the heart of solidarity. Such interconnectedness entails trust. To put it another way, human rights are best seen in terms of solidarity ensouled with trust and with acceptance of one another.

Again, Jung writing as a psychologist makes a similar point: "Respect for the eternal rights of man, recognition of the ancient, and the continuity of culture and intellectual history are essential to understanding who we are and our place in the scheme of the universe, where we fit, so to speak, our roots as human beings are

---

6. Ramphele, *Conversations with My Sons and Daughters*, esp. 59–79.
7. Jung, *Memories, Dreams, and Reflections*, 357.

programmed in our genes; our physical and emotional characteristics tap into our ancestral roots as well as ways of knowledge."[8]

The same idea of interconnectedness infuses the philosopher Levinas's phrase cited in an earlier chapter, namely, "heeding the heteronomous call." That person is human who heeds the call of the other person. What this implies is that human beings cannot escape the demand for making ethical decisions, and therefore a sensitive conscience is a mark of being fully human. Rights when understood as being general human rights must be seen less in terms of laws and more in terms of conscience, morality, and manifesting human interconnectedness.

The Freedom Charter of the African National Congress

South Africa today represents an African attempt at establishing human dignity and rights. Earlier the natives had smarted in a crucible of fire and torment stoked up by the ideology of apartheid, which thrived on ethnic and racial differences. Seen in this light it is most remarkable that the Freedom Charter (available online) of the African National Congress (and later, the South African national constitution) upheld the principle of a nonracial and, I may add, nonethnic society. Well before the Charter was composed, Chief Albert Luthuli in November 1952 drafted his personal and biblical statement entitled "The Road to Freedom Is Via the Cross."[9] His was a political vision built upon biblical, theological, and homiletic foundations. The suggestion is that obeying the tenets of the Christian faith is of primary importance for the success or failure of a political strategy. Luthuli embraces the goal of holding together the human qualities of consciousness and interconnectedness. His vision is like a check for nation-state building. The ongoing agenda for South Africa is how to cash that check and to translate the vision and ideal of nonracialism into a national identity and a cohesive contemporary society, while avoiding contradictions and incoherence in the interpretation. The issue runs much deeper than mere sloganeering; it has to do with the practice of translation and interpretation and has implications and consequences for representation and interaction. It requires conscientious, dogged effort to translate nonracialism as an ideal into practice, both nationally and individually.

I have already mentioned the association of the South African statesman Jan Smuts with the drafting of the Preamble for the UN Charter. This book is dedicated to two Africans of South African origin, Desmond Tutu and Walter Makhulu, both churchmen of distinction. Another churchman and diplomat, Z. K. Matthews, preceded them and on July 13, 1953, played a key role in drafting the ANC Freedom Charter. As things happen, I was on sojourn in Pretoria, South Africa, on July 13, 2013, for the sixtieth anniversary commemoration of that Charter. For these reasons,

---

8. Ibid.

9. Luthuli, "The Road to Freedom Is via the Cross," in Couper, *Albert Luthuli: Bound by Faith*, appendix 2, 214–17.

if not for more significant ones, it would be remiss of me not to mention the Freedom Charter in this account.

The UN Charter emanated from outside Africa. The stories, for example, of Abu Ghraib and of Guantánamo Bay detention center in Cuba suggest that some high priests of the UN Charter have been playing fast and loose with the Charter. That reality poses a challenge for us to look for other attempts at conscientizing people about human rights, especially constructs originating from our own mother continent of Africa. Herein lies the need, even necessity, for a book on African theology to address the Freedom Charter.

I am also obliged to address the Freedom Charter because of its association with Zachariah Keodirelang Matthews (1901–68) who was the Africa secretary for the WCC's Division of Inter-church Aid, Refugee, and World Service in the 1960s. Among his numerous contributions in this period was "African Survey," a report that he edited as part of a wider study of segregation and refugees. The document opened the eyes of the United Nations to the extent and gravity of the refugee situation. Z.K., as he was popularly and fondly known, served as ANC provincial president in the Cape. He is on record as having asked the Craddock Congress of the ANC in 1953, "I wonder whether the time has not come for the ANC to consider the question of convening a national convention, a congress of the people, representing all the people of this country irrespective of race or colour, to draw up a Freedom Charter for the democratic South Africa of the future."[10] Z. K. Matthews and Lionel "Rusty" Bernstein followed up the question by preparing a draft of the Freedom Charter.[11] It was adopted by the Kliptown Congress of the People in 1955 and by the ANC as part of its official policy in 1956.[12]

I have intentionally stressed Z. K. Matthews's association with the World Council of Churches, which was the privileged instrument of the ecumenical movement. Like Tutu, Makhulu, and the present writer, he had been socialized in the idea that theology and Christian religious life are meant to go beyond identifying and articulating dogma. They place Christ's followers under constraint to model in their lives the biblical affirmations that the entire creation is God's and that all human beings are created in God's image and likeness. Therefore, the inhuman ideology of apartheid that was dispensing exclusion and marginalization had to be resisted. Without saying it, Z.K. and others were putting into practice the earlier insight of Martin Luther that theology is to be lived even if it results in suffering and martyrdom. Religion is more than worship and liturgical acts; it is also engagement in social, economic, and political activity to shore up human dignity.

---

10. Cited in South African History Online, http://www.sahistory.org.za/article/freedom-charter-norman-levy.

11. Mbeki, "He [Z. K. Matthews] Awakened to His Responsibilities."

12. John S. Pobee, "Matthew Zachariah Keodirelang," in Lossky, ed., *Dictionary of the Ecumenical Movement* (2002), 749–50.

Before we turn to the content of the Freedom Charter itself, a comment made by one of the key personalities of both the ANC and the Communist Party is instructive. In it Joe Slovo provides insight into how the piece was received and owned. He writes, "Literally tens of thousands of scraps of paper came flooding in: a mixture of smooth writing-pad paper, torn pages from blotched school exercise books, bits of cardboard, asymmetrical portions of brown and white paper bags, and even the unprinted margins of bits of newspaper."[13] This comment shows that, whatever role Matthews and Bernstern played, the Freedom Charter was a document of the masses: of the people, by the people, and for the people. The religious and theological insights in it can be described in the same way: theology of the people, by the people, and for the people. It is no wonder that the Rivonia Trial of 1963–64 and banning of the framers of the Freedom Charter by the apartheid regime were not able to eradicate the Charter.

It is also striking that the document was signed by five persons who were chairmen of five South African organizations: Albert Luthuli, president of the African National Congress (ANC); Leon Levy, president, South Africa Congress of Trade Unions (SACTU); G. M. Monty Naiker, president, National Indian Congress (NIC); Jimmy Laguma, president, South African Coloured People's Congress (SACPC); and Pieter Beyleveld, president, South African Congress of Democrats (SACOD). The five associations together constituted the South Africa Congress Alliance. This list of signatories underscores the fact that a wide spectrum of people—multireligious and multiracial—owned the Freedom Charter as speaking for them. It spoke especially to the condition in South Africa of people of color. Nelson Mandela spoke of it as "the most important political document ever adopted by the ANC," and Cedric Mason has described it as a "deeply spiritual document."[14] What is political can at the same time be religious and spiritual and be a test of the viability of basic religious and spiritual affirmations. Though Luthuli was not present at the Kliptown Congress of the People, a message from him was read out by Arthur Letele, treasurer general of the ANC. The Congress bestowed on Luthuli the honor of *Isitwalandwe* (the Xhosa name for the feathers of *indwe*, a legendary bird), an honor bestowed only on the bravest.

The Preamble to the Freedom Charter states unequivocally that "South Africa belongs to all who live in it, black and white, and that no government can justly claim authority unless it is based on the will of all the people." The document is forthright in declaring that peoples of color deprived by South African apartheid of their birthright of land, liberty and peace must be liberated. The phrase "all who live in it [South Africa]" is explained as including all colors, all races, all genders, and all beliefs. In sum, one's humanity was to be measured in terms of one's relationship with and treatment

---

13. Slovo, *Slovo: The Unfinished Autobiography*, 109.

14. Nelson Mandela, "Statement in the Dock," Rivonia Trial, South Africa, April 20, 1964, http://www.theguardian.com/world/series/great-speeches-nelson-mandela; see also Nzo, "The Freedom Charter: A Beacon to the People of South Africa," *African Communist* (Second Quarter 1980), 23–37; Cedric Mayson, "A Deeply Spiritual Document: The Freedom Charter," *Umrabulo* no. 11 (June–July 2006).

of the other person. All should be equals, siblings sharing a common humanity in spite of differences in people's circumstances. The desired liberation was to be effected by freedom volunteers, persons committed to using nonviolent means and who accepted the obligation to be soldiers of truth.

The contours of the common humanity that was to be owned, respected, and honored are enumerated under some ten headings: The People Shall Govern; All National Groups Shall Have Equal Rights; The Land Shall Be Shared among Those Who Work It; The People Shall Share in the Country's Wealth; All Shall Be Equal before the Law; All Shall Enjoy Equal Human Rights; There Shall Be Work and Security; The Doors of Learning and of Culture Shall Be Opened; There Shall Be Security and Comfort; There Shall Be Peace and Friendship. As Luthuli saw it, the Charter provided an option for a *nonracial* nation, rather than a multiracial nation. Education, competence, work ethic, and merit—not race—should be the primary determinants of a person's position and condition in life. The Charter embodied an option for equal rights for national groups and a united nonracial nation.

The sixth of the Freedom Charter's ten paragraphs, "All Shall Enjoy Equal Human Rights," is worth quoting in full.

> The law shall guarantee to all their right to speak, to organize, to meet together, to publish, to preach, to worship and to educate their children;
>
> The privacy of the house from police raids shall be protected by law;
>
> All shall be free to travel without restriction from countryside to town, from province to province, and from South Africa abroad;
>
> Pass Laws, permits and all other laws restricting these freedoms shall be abolished.

These few clauses etch out freedom of speech and communication, of assembly and association and organization, of travel and movement and religion. The emphasis on freedom to communicate is not unlike what obtains elsewhere in Africa. For example, the Akan proverb states, "He is a murderer who does not allow me to speak."

Chief Luthuli could not attend the National Conference of the African National Congress, held in Queenstown in December 1953. But he sent a paper, his presidential address, in which he talked about freedom. The attempt to deny Africans freedom of association and speech, he wrote, could never stop them from fighting for their rights, because "the urge and yearning for freedom springs from the sense of divine discontent and so, having a divine origin, can never be permanently gagged."[15]

The foregoing contours of human rights are considered to be a covenant with Divinity and with the human family. They are no fait accompli; they should be worked at consistently and assiduously. And so the Charter concludes, in bold capital letters: "Let all who love their people and their country now say, as we say here: "*These freedoms we*

---

15. Albert Luthuli, "Presidential Address," African National Congress Annual Conference, December 18–20, 1953, in Karis and Carter, *Challenge and Violence*, 1953–1964, 115–16.

will fight for, side by side, throughout our lives, until we have won our liberty." The call to fight for freedom is a call for a life of service and sacrifice for the larger good.

Not all African nations have had the same painful experience of racism. But many African states, which came to be nation-states at the behest of colonialism, did not pay enough attention to the implications of their being congeries of different ethnic peoples or societies thrust together. They are still struggling with ethnicity, for example, Tutsi versus Hutu, climaxing in the genocide of Rwanda; Ibo versus Hausa in Nigeria; and Nanumba versus Konkomba in Ghana. In those regions, the challenges to be faced are those of nonethnicity and nonsexism, which replace that of nonracialism. Often the struggle is accompanied by painful memories.

Thus on the agenda of human dignity and human rights is the difficult issue of reconciliation of memories, beyond reconciliation of ethnic groups. It is an option for a united, nonracial nation and society, rather than a multiracial society. It is an option for healing, reconciliation, and doing what it takes to secure South Africa as a land that "belongs to all who live in it." This is a remarkable vision from a liberation movement.

Allow me to interject a comment on Chief Albert Luthuli. At the time of the Kliptown Congress, Luthuli was under a ban by the apartheid government. Yet he was involved as his message and the honor bestowed on him suggest. At a special conference in Bloemfontein in 1955, Luthuli (through Z. K. Matthews) in his presidential address sounded forth the refrain "no cross, no crown." It was Luthuli's mantra to encourage Africans to accept the general and larger good without expecting a personal (and immediate) reward. Clearly, his Christian commitment as a Congregationalist had influenced him to attempt to live a life of sacrificial service and nonracialism in the national political arena. In Luthuli, political rhetoric doubled as homiletic oration. The Freedom Charter, though a political statement, bore the fingerprints of Christians who were endeavoring to live their faith through politics or to engage in politics with a religious conscience and alongside others.[16]

The issue of human dignity and human rights subdivides in terms of race, ethnicity, nation-state, and gender. To these divisions must be added that of religion. Africans have a religious and spiritual epistemology and ontology. African Traditional Religions have, on the whole, been hospitable to other religions. This hospitality was due, in part, to their status as ethnic religions that did not face challenges from outside religions. But because African religions are fundamentally about a search for power, they could welcome another religion that was adjudged powerful.

The story is probably more complex than just suggested. African Traditional Religions were hospitable to other religions because they were oral, preliterate, prereflective, and nonformalized religions. Traditional religionists did not articulate their beliefs in the form of doctrines or doctrinal teachings and, therefore, easily adopted

---

16. Albert Luthuli, "Special Presidential Address," African National Congress Annual Conference, December 17–18, 1955, in Karis and Carter, *From Protest to Challenge*, 213; African National Congress, *Selected Writings on the Freedom Charter, 1955–1985*.

and adapted whatever extraneous religious ideas neighboring indigenous religions, Islam, or Christianity happened to offer. Christianity came to their notice through trade and other contacts. Jan Platvoet has documented the spiritualization and transcendentalization of beliefs in Nyame among the Akan from about 1500 onwards through contacts with Muslim and Christian traders and with missionaries. From being considered in earlier traditional thinking as a touchable, audible, and visible rain and sky god, Nyame developed into a being conceived of as a purely spiritual Creator-God in Heaven behind the sky.[17]

Conversely, the guest religions that were missionary, that is, Christianity and Islam, have tended to be intolerant of other religions. The Christian missionary practice of tabula rasa castigated other religions as no-religions, fetishism, heathenism, and demonic. Ideologies of power, specifically, Christendom and Caliphate, colored the missionary religions' view of followers of other religions, and they came to see themselves as rivals for power and influence. A result of their rivalry was the Crusades, which have been strongly imprinted on the minds of various religionists. As if the foregoing were not enough, individual religions have been torn asunder by schisms, schools, and denominations. Thus Islam has Sunnis, Sufis, Shi'ites, and more. Christians have the Roman Catholic, Orthodox, and Protestant churches among other branches. Not only have relations between Muslims and Christians been fraught, but within each religion, coreligionists have not always been friendly toward each other. For example, the crisis and violence—accompanied by horrendous loss of human lives and the creation of many refugees—in Syria and Iraq are in part an outcome of the Sunni-Shia divide. In consequence, human rights have often been honored in the breach. Given the religions' historical record, they must couple contrition and humility together with their advocacy of human rights.

In regard to violations of what it is to be human and the rights of humans, religion has been part of the problem and it must be part of the solution. Through experience the ecumenical movement discovered that "doctrine divides, service unites." Service in common buttresses a common humanity and enhances human well-being, which is part of the DNA of human dignity and rights.

This is a book about theology, but in line with an insight from John Henry Cardinal Newman, we can aver that academic life aims to produce not only learned persons but also, and perhaps more importantly, gentlemen and gentlewomen. Newman states, "It is almost a definition of a gentleman to say he is one who never inflicts pain."[18] By definition theological students, and for that matter anyone else who crosses the threshold of the academy, are recruits for living out what it means to be human and for conscientizing others vis-à-vis human rights. In this way they can fulfill their calling to be gentlepersons and live up to their obligation not to inflict pain.

17. Platvoet, "*Nyame ne Aberewa*: Towards a History of Akan Notions of God," *Ghana Bulletin of Theology*, 41–68.
18. John Henry Newman, "Discourse 8," in Newman, *The Idea of a University*, 175–98.

Christian Input

For Christians the point of entry into discussion of what it is to be human and of human rights is the belief that humans are the summit of creation. In the first place, Adam, that is, collective humanity, is formed out of *adamah* (earth), and the creation of humans can be compared to the work of a potter—so close is the relationship between human beings and the earth. Second, according to biblical tradition, male (Heb., *ish*) and female (Heb., *ishsha*) were created at the same time (Gen 1:27); this implies an equality of male and female that includes, among other things, power to transmit the life that they received from God. But the power granted to them is fundamentally about stewardship and is not a power to perform at will whatever acts they may choose. Theirs is a creativity that is not exploitative, but is encapsulated in harmonious relationships that promote God's gift of life. Thus being human and human rights encompass the ideas of dignity and such authority as corresponds to the *imago Dei*, to the dignity of all genders, and to creativity. The idea of creativity includes the concepts of vision and knowledge. Psalm 8 throws further light on the biblical understanding of humanity. What is human is best understood in reference to divinity. God has divine glory; humans have dignity (not divinity). Humans are a seemingly insignificant part of the greatness and wonder of God's universe. And yet in relation to the rest of creation, humans have dignity almost equal to that of heavenly beings (Ps 8:5–8; see also Heb 2:9).

Psalm 15 paints a picture of a human being who truly bears the *imago Dei*, or image of God. First, justice and righteousness are intrinsic to that person's character. Second, so is truthfulness. Third, the truly human person does not harm another person, whether verbally or physically. Defamation and disdain of friends are not part of the human vocation, but the human shuns the wicked. Fourth, a person who is truly a human being avoids lending at interest. This idea poses a challenge to contemporary ideas of investment. Indeed, the Old Testament forbids charging interest (Exod 22:25; Lev 25:36–37; Deut 23:19–20). Fifth, a human being does not take bribes, especially against the innocent.

Further, Psalm 15 inculcates the idea that what is human is tied to one's neighbor; it is locked into our moral and social nature. The human is marked by an un-hypocritical piety and genuine lowliness of spirit—only such have access to God. Integrity ensures the dignity and upholds the rights of the other (Ps 15:1–5). No wonder Psalm 15 is called the gentleman's psalm; its tenets flesh out the quotation given above from Cardinal Newman, defining the gentleman as one who never inflicts pain on another.

Jesus himself makes similar assertions in Matthew 5:23–24. When at worship in the temple, if you recall that your brother has anything against you, "Leave your gift there at the altar, go first and be reconciled with your brother, and then come and offer your gift" (NABRE). Important as liturgical rites may be, the call to reconciliation stands higher. To bear the image of God through Christ is to be a human being committed to the reconciliation of human society (Rom 5:10–11; 11:15; 2 Cor 5:18–20; Eph 2:16; Col 1:22). True religion is denied when we do evil to another person bound to us by ties of kindred. Jesus' teaching on leaving a sacrifice to go and be reconciled with a wronged neighbor implies a fundamental overcoming of cultic ideology. Pursuing human rights amounts to pure and unsoiled ritual.

The Values of the Kingdom of God as a Test of Humanity in the Image of God

Through reference to several Old Testament passages, the preceding paragraphs identify characteristics of the human as perceived by those of the Judeo-Christian faith commitment. That perception is summed up in the values of the kingdom of God, which was the core message of Jesus, the Christ and the Lord. An earlier chapter, "*Residuum Evangelium*," outlined the Christian understanding of those values. Persons who bear the *imago Dei* and *imago Christi* bring the values of the kingdom of God to their articulation of human values and human rights: truth and truthfulness; justice and righteousness; love, loving-kindness, and mercy; freedom and liberty; and peace and reconciliation. The task is to translate and interpret these values in my African idiom.

Freedom, Liberty, and Peace

Because of African nations' experience of colonialism, the words "freedom" and "liberty" gained currency throughout the continent. Freedom is at once a religious and a political concept. Fundamentally, liberty is the right, and freedom the ability, to make free choices in life. The two words suggest that each society must endeavor to be united in its diversity. The oft-used word democracy must signify a society that is genuinely participatory, and the claim to be a democracy must entail tolerance of the views of others.

In a message to the Congress of the United States on January 6, 1941, Franklin Delano Roosevelt laid out some of the contours of freedom:

> We look forward to a world founded upon four essential freedoms.
> The first is freedom of speech and expression—everywhere in the world.
> The second is freedom of every person to worship God in his own way—everywhere in the world.
> The third is freedom from want . . . —everywhere in the world.
> The fourth is freedom from fear . . . —anywhere in the world. [19]

These words speak of a liberty and freedom that must be enjoyed by all humans, irrespective of race, gender, or creed, or of wherever those people might live. Human

---

19. See Kaplan, *Barlett's Familiar Quotations*, 698.

beings have an inherent right to freedom and liberty, but a word of caution is in order, for the quest after freedom sometimes becomes lawlessness. Charles de Seconder, Baron de Montesquieu, reminds us that "liberty is the right of doing whatever the laws permit."[20] Liberty is not lawlessness.

Next to freedom in our esteem is peace. Often reduced to the absence of war, peace in the biblical understanding is a richer concept. It is absence of anything that transgresses another person's dignity and personhood. Peace is well-being for all persons, for individuals as well as communities. Franklin Roosevelt in his Fourth Inaugural Address, given on January 20, 1945, states the matter of interconnectedness well: "We have learned that we cannot live alone, at peace; that our own well-being is dependent on the well-being of other nations, far away. We have learned that we must live as men and not as ostriches, nor as dogs in the manger. We have learned to be citizens of the world, members of the human community."[21] Peace is a metric by which to measure true humanity and truly human community.

Peace is not given on a silver platter, nor is it ever a fait accompli. It must be worked at constantly and demands the commitment of each person to maintain it. But maintaining peace does not fall solely to persons considered as discrete individuals; governments have a role to play. Roosevelt perceptively states, "The only sure bulwark of continuing liberty is a government strong enough to protect the interest of the people, and a people strong enough and well enough informed to maintain its sovereign control over its government."[22] Unfortunately governments—though charged with maintaining justice, peace, and security—are often undone by excessive love for power. As Augustine of Hippo Regius put it, "*Remota itaque iustitia quid sunt regna nisi magna latrocinia*," that is, a state that is not governed according to justice would be just a bunch of thieves.[23] Such a situation arises when peace is more politicized than it is valued as an ethical principle.

Discordantly enough, preoccupation with religious truth has at times been at odds with the pursuit of peace. In the face of religious pluralism, the claim has often been made that Christianity has totally clean hands and that other religions are the violent ones. But within Christianity there have been wars between Roman Catholics and Protestants, and the missionary ideology of tabula rasa has at times been the occasion of violence against "natives." Roman Catholic alignment with the Portuguese colonial government brought horrendous destruction at Wiriyamu.[24] The Christian churches were the ones that mounted the Crusades against Muslims and sought to capture the "Christian Holy Land."

---

20. Montesquieu, *De l'esprit des lois*, 11.3.
21. Kaplan, *Barlett's Familiar Quotations*, 698.
22. Roosevelt, *Fireside Chat*, April 14, 1938.
23. Augustine, *City of God*, bk 4.
24. Hastings, *Wiriyamu*; Hastings, *Igreja e Missões Cucujaes*.

On occasion the claim has been made that peace is to Christians as war is to Muslims. But the early Muslim greeting *Al-Salaamu alaikum* (Peace be upon you) and its longer form *Al-Salaamu alaikum wa rahmatullahi wa barakatuhu* (Peace be upon you and the mercy and blessing of God) both attest to the fundamental importance peace has for the Muslim. The militancy associated with current Muslim groups such as Al Qaeda, Boko Haram, Islamic State in Iraq and Syria, and Al-Shabaab is a politicization of religion and is not to be confused with authentic Islamic religion.

Traditional African Input: African Wisdom

African conceptions of human rights tend to resemble the Akan African wisdom that *Hèn yinaa ara yè Nyame-mba; obi ara mmfi asase* (We are all children of God; none is the child of the earth). This saying expresses African commitment to the well-being and dignity of every person. In God's world and God's household, all humans are siblings. With that recognition comes a moral obligation and a sense of the importance and necessity to secure the well-being and dignity of each person, irrespective of age, gender, creed, race, or ethnicity. Still another picture needs to be put alongside the insight expressed by the proverb just cited. Akan stories suggest that *tete* (that is, long ago) some first humans did proceed from the earth, while others descended from the sky. Therefore, human beings are not to be toyed with. All humans are of equal value and none are to be held in low esteem. Differences in origin are not to be taken as reason for violation of another person.

Second, we may consider the piece of African art called *sepow*, that is, a human head with a sharp instrument piercing through the jaw, from one side to the other. The sepow symbol teaches that the ability to communicate is a mark of the human and an intrinsic aspect of human dignity and rights. It may be seen as an indirect way of recalling to our minds the primacy of freedom of speech in the quest for peace, human dignity, and human rights. Time and again a myth is peddled that Africans have no culture of human rights. But in Akan culture, freedom of speech is *the* mark of the human and of human dignity and rights. Some interpretations of the sepow symbol might seem to lend credibility to the myth, for the sharp instrument through the cheeks and tongue is interpreted as a way of forestalling a doomed person from uttering the *ntam kése* (great oath) against the ruler who has condemned the person to death or sentenced him to serve his ancestors. This piece of art rather graphically symbolizes the suppression of free speech. Yet even this interpretation of the art suggests that denial of free speech is a denial of a person's humanity and human dignity.

In African culture, freedom of communication and self-expression are fundamental marks of human rights. Brutal dictatorships, when present, represent the denial of a fundamental element of the African understanding of human rights. Thus wielding power wantonly and in a conscienceless manner is a betrayal of human dignity and human rights. As I wrote elsewhere, "To be denied freedom of speech is to be denied one's humanity. To be able to share one's thoughts, emotions, want and weakness is to be human and to have dignity."[25]

Third, in addition to freedom of expression, traditional African society is suspicious of uniformity of thought, especially enforced uniformity of thought. According to another Akan proverb, "If thirty hunchbacks walk together, their bottoms point in the same direction." Having identical views and positions and postures may not be the yardstick of being correct or of human dignity. Respect for human rights must include respect for the legitimacy of pluralism. And so the Akan say *Adwen wotoatoa* (wisdom is pieced together from divergent views). As George Hagan comments, "Unity emerges when we discover and put together the different chips which make up the solution of the national jig-saw puzzles."[26]

There is a fourth strand in the traditional African perception of human dignity and rights. According to an Akan proverb, *Wonsom, wonsom, òyè dom; wonsom wonsom oyè nyimpa* (pulling together in numbers as human persons working together is the key to success). This flows from the characteristic African communitarian epistemology, an epistemology that eschews exploitation or squeezing out of any one individual. For as another Akan proverb puts it, *Nsa nyinara nsè* (the fingers are not all the same); the fingers and thumb have different but complementary contributions to make. For that reason each component of the group must not only be respected but also be given space and be enabled to make his or her contribution. In combination, the Akan wisdom of freedom of expression and the need to pull together added up to an option for mutual respect expressed in a culture of collegiality and discussion in which consensus was not imposed.

It will be noticed that I am placing emphasis on Akan culture and not on "African culture." Care needs to be exercised in deciding whether what can be said of Akan culture can be said to be true for all African cultures. By the same token, one should be slow to endorse sweeping generalizations to the effect that the incidence of dictatorship in post-independence Africa is rooted in alleged dictatorship associated with traditional chieftaincy. For one thing, a chief could be destooled (that is, deposed) for not consulting the Queen Mother and the courtiers as well as other chiefs in the kingdom. Further, the tendency toward dictatorship is not unrelated to the psychology of liberation movements, which thrive on discipline, loyalty, and uniformity of purpose and ideology. Moreover, traditional Akan society possessed a culture of accountability; that is the significance of the provision for destooling a chief who failed to heed the voice of the people. Thus traditional Akan society was inclined toward what has been described as democratic governance.

---

25. John S. Pobee, "An African Christian in Search of Democracy," in Witte, *Christianity and Democracy in Global Context*, 278.

26. Hagan, "Human Rights and the Democratic Process," Symposium on the Concept and Practice of Human Rights in Ghana (Accra: Ghana Academy of Arts and Sciences, Twenty-First Anniversary Celebration, November 1980).

Here the issue of power raises its head; two comments are appropriate. First, on ritual occasions the first action a chief takes is to raise his sword to the skies to acknowledge that he is who he is and what he is by the grace of the Supreme Deity. It is a dramatic statement that he holds and exercises power and authority by the grace of God and, therefore, that he must never forget that we are God's children and accountable to God. Those acknowledgments should powerfully counteract tendencies toward either dictatorship or unscrupulous wielding of power and authority.

Second, an Akan proverb says *tumi te sè kosua* (power and authority are like an egg). If you clasp an egg tightly and forcefully, it will break; if you do not hold it firmly, it may drop and break. The option held out is for power to be coupled with humanity, conscience, and civility.

Land as a Measure of Human Rights and Dignity

Everywhere in Africa and throughout its history, the issue of land has been a major cause of friction and violence. The Aborigines Rights Protection Society was established in the Gold Coast to protect land there from European encroachment and appropriation. In Kenya, the Rhodesias (now the sovereign states of Zambia and Zimbabwe), and South Africa, the appropriation of native lands by white settlers and governments led to wars of liberation, for example, the first and second *Chimurenga* (uprising) in 1880–96 and 1966–80. The result was much carnage and destruction with many people fleeing as refugees. Even without the intrusion and interference of foreigners, land in Africa has been a cause of interethnic wars and family disputes. Therefore, land is very much an issue in Africa the consequences of which cannot but offer spiritual and theological challenges to the church and theologians. African theology cannot avoid having land on its agenda, because access to land is an existential issue.

Foreigners' high-handed appropriation of land ran counter to African perceptions, for to be human is to have access to land as bequeathed by one's ancestors. Land links us to our ancestors; to be denied our ancestors' land is to be denied our inheritance of their human dignity, integrity, and identity—and our sense of belonging. Land and human beings are interconnected. What seems to be bashing of white settlers in Southern Africa by African politicians is, according to Sebastian Bakare, "rather correcting an injustice which has for centuries been perpetrated against Africans. Therein is their dignity; therein is their identity; therein is their belonging, humanness. . . . A theology of land is an important undergird of human dignity."[27]

The search after human rights and dignity in Africa must return to African springs; we drink deeply from our own cultural wells rather than always regurgitating foreign artifacts and constructs.

---

27. Bakare, *My Right to Land, in the Bible and in Zimbabwe*, 59.

The Universal Declaration of Human Rights

The Preamble of the UN Charter, addressed earlier, had some notes relevant to the culture of human rights. But the United Nation's Universal Declaration of Human Rights, adopted on December 10, 1948, went much further. It appeared as a common standard of human rights, a veritable Magna Carta of human rights for all of humanity. That the declaration could be adopted at all was well-nigh a miracle, for the fifty-eight nation-states constituting the United Nations at its beginning represented diverse ideologies, political systems, religions, and cultural backgrounds as well as different patterns of socioeconomic development.

The Universal Declaration of Human Rights notes that the inherent dignity and the equal and inalienable rights of all members of the human family constitute the foundation of freedom, justice, and peace in the world. It also refers to the fundamental human rights, dignity, and worth of each human person; equal rights of men and women; freedom of speech and beliefs; and freedom from fear and want. It is incisive in stating that "human rights should be protected by the rule of law." But, as suggested above, inconsistencies and contradictions are present even among those who subscribe to these insights, and since saints are not made by acts of parliament, education and formation in the culture of human rights is necessary. In this regard, religious institutions—along with other institutions—can be helpful colleagues in addressing what is a common concern (see Article 26 of the Universal Declaration of Human Rights). Though I have called the document a Magna Carta, it is not legally binding. That fact again suggests to me the need for partners, such as religious institutions, to help disseminate its tenets throughout society.

More than sixty human rights instruments exist; the International Covenant on Economic, Social and Cultural Rights (ICESCR) and the International Covenant on Civil and Political Rights (ICCPR) are two examples. The insights gathered in all these instruments must also be made a part of the process of education and formation. As was stated on the occasion of the fiftieth anniversary of the signing of the Universal Declaration of Human Rights, we must endeavor to identify the best ways to "mobilize all strata of society in a reinvigorated and broad-based human rights movement."[28]

Mary Robinson, the second UN High Commissioner for Human Rights, said in 1997 that "human rights belong to people; human rights are about people on the ground and their rights." People must take ownership of the project of developing a culture of human rights. No wonder the Charter begins with "We the people." This emphasis on "we the people" demands a bottom-up approach: people everywhere must demand human rights and lobby with the representatives of the people vis-à-vis peacemaking, child rights, health, economic development, social development, eradication of poverty, and education for indigenous people.

---

28. See http://www.mefacts.com/cached.asp?x_id=10460.

In opting for a bottom-up approach, we are attempting to place the role of government and politics in perspective. The informed rights of the people and the will of the people have primacy; the role of government and politics is to serve them for the common good. Article 21 of the UN Charter states the point clearly.

1. Everyone has the right to take part in the government of his country, directly or through freely chosen representatives.

2. Everyone has the right of equal access to public service in his country.

3. The will of the people shall be the basis of the authority of the government; this shall be expressed in periodic and genuine elections which shall be by universal and equal suffrage and shall be held to be secret vote or by equivalent free voting procedures.

A Testimony from an African Self-Styled Humanist Politician

Championship of human rights is not the exclusive preserve of churches or for that matter of Christian theologians. When we seek to bolster respect for human rights, we do so in the company of atheists, African Traditional Religionists, Muslims, humanists, and so on. Therefore, allow me to include mention of the perspective enunciated by Kenneth Kaunda, a self-styled African humanist and politician who, nevertheless, was a product of the Presbyterian Church of Zambia. Kaunda identifies a strong experience or sense of community as *the* characteristic feature of African societies. Kaunda argues that this important sense of community is the basis for envisioning the creation in each person of a sense of being brothers and sisters. From it flow appreciation of the varieties of humanity and reinforcement of the strength of other persons. The fundamental human right is to love and to be loved; this recognition serves to impel people to realize their common history and common destiny.

Kaunda insists, however, that humanism's prospect for success in serving human rights depends on a religious attitude, especially on an understanding of the soul as the center of a network of relationships. He writes,

> War, the needless taking of human life, cruelty of all kinds, whether committed by the state, or the individual, the degradation of any human being, class or race, under whatever specious justification, are intolerable crimes against the religions of mankind, abominable to its ethical mind, forbidden by its primary tenets, to be fought against always and tolerated not at all. Man must be sacred to man. The body of Man is to be respected, made immune from violence and outrage, protected by science against disease and preserved, ennobled and uplifted. The heart of man is to be held sacred also, given the scope of love, protected against dehumanizing influences that would turn it into some biological machine. The mind of man is to be released from all

bonds, given freedom and opportunity to the full range of its powers in the service of mankind.[29]

The quest for human dignity and human rights is pursued against the backdrop of multiple injustices, denials of freedom, and absence of reconciliation among peoples. The indices of injustice include Jim Crow laws, racism, prejudices, sexism, and ageism. Serving to thwart the legitimate aspirations and dreams of peoples, these injustices are issues of civil rights as well as of moral righteousness. The quest for human dignity and rights needs leaders who are both dreamers and equipped with political insight and moral vision, following in the footsteps of such icons as Archbishop Desmond Mpilo Tutu, Archbishop Khotso Makhulu, and Nelson Mandela. All perhaps will recognize in Martin Luther King Jr., leader of the US civil rights movement, and his famous "I Have a Dream" speech at the Lincoln Memorial on August 28, 1963, the contours of a theologian giving account of faith and hope. King's speech faced the reality of his context; his deep engagement with that context enabled him to dream and hope for his nation and the world.

> I have a dream that one day on the red hills of Georgia, the sons of former slaves and the sons of former slave owners will be able to sit down together at the table of brotherhood.
>
> I have a dream that one day even the state of Mississippi, a state sweltering with the heat of injustice, sweltering with the heat of oppression, will be transformed into an oasis of freedom and justice.
>
> I have a dream that my four little children will one day live in a nation where they will not be judged by the color of their skin but by the content of their character....
>
> I have a *dream* today![30]

To attempt to comment on King's dream of human dignity and human rights would be to ruin its beauty and the clarity, except to say that the imagery of all sitting together at one table of brotherhood is a pictorial statement—drawn with faith and hope such as a Christian theologian would hold out to people—of what is human and of humans' concomitant rights and dignity.

Especially to be noted is the fact that after laying out some of the contours of his dream and hope, King ends with the words "I have a dream today." Faith and hope are a journey; they are an exploration and never a onetime achievement. Following a dream, steps must be taken if the kingdom of God is to be established on earth as it is in heaven, a kingdom in which liberty and freedom, peace, reconciliation, truth and truthfulness, compassion, and love are innate and universal. The model of faith and hope held out by the theologian offers a standard against which we can measure ourselves and our lives in this imperfect and difficult to comprehend world. Further, it

---

29. Kaunda, *Letter to My Children*, 57–58, 103–7; Kaunda and Morris, *A Humanist in Africa*.
30. See http://www.americanrhetoric.com/speeches/mlkihaveadream.htm.

is well to remember that the theologian's task is not only *to tell* but also *to do* the truth (1 John 1:1–4; 2:3–5; James 1:22–25).

Enemy Images—Ideologies of Hate—Politics of Anger

An old adage avers that "the enemy of my enemy is my friend." The US government led by President George W. Bush displayed this mentality when on trumped-up charges he decided to wage war on President Saddam Hussein of Iraq.[31] Unable to muster a vote of support in the United Nations, Bush decided to assemble a so-called Coalition of the Willing. When France expressed misgivings, France was blacklisted. The ideology that might makes right indwelt this story and disagreement was not to be tolerated. Without the judgment being expressly stated, the weak were thought not to be entitled to a different viewpoint. Smaller and weaker nations such as Bulgaria were propelled, if not cajoled and bullied, into joining the war. Mostly Eastern European nations recently liberated from the Soviet Union, they were—as Senator John Kerry famously observed—a "coalition of the coerced and the bribed." To me as an Akan nurtured on the wisdom that "he is a murderer, who does not allow me to speak my mind," the traits displayed by President Bush were in effect a denial of the human dignity and rights of the other.

Another manifestation of the enemy image that often cloaks a military and crusader mentality is evident in West Africa today. The emergence in Nigeria of Boko Haram is being used by some nations as an excuse for setting up an African High Command or Rapid (military) Force. Such an approach presents two problems. First, African nations can ill afford such military ventures since funding for them would come at the expense of badly needed creative instruments of national development, namely, the social services of health and education. Second, such military ventures do not address the fundamental causes of discontent that have given rise to the rebellion, namely, pervasive poverty and lack of facilities that make for human dignity. Proposals for militarization ignore the wisdom that "force may subdue; love gains." Either way, the dignity and rights of the weak are trodden underfoot, sacrificed in the interests of the powerful. In developing nations, instead of arming to the teeth, the focus should be on people's security rather than national security.

In pursuance of human dignity and rights, law is a critical instrument, guaranteeing human rights across the board. It is therefore strange that the United States, a supposed icon of human rights, is not a signatory of the Rome Statute of the International Criminal Court (ICC) that set up the ICC. Nor is the State of Israel. This omission means they are not accountable to the principle of law that the ICC represents. In November 2014, the ICC decided that Israel had committed crimes of genocide when she attacked a humanitarian convoy on its way to Gaza. But because Israel is not

---

31. See, e.g., "The Chilcot Report, Iraq's Grim Lessons," *Economist*, July 9–15, 2016, 48–49.

a signatory of the Rome Statute, the ICC could not prosecute. Other cases of genocide by Israel against Gaza remain unprosecuted for the same reason, and the United States, which claims the role of honest broker, is unable to bring Israel to order. Even more mysterious is that in 2014 the United States, after much bragging about the rule of law, opposed Palestine's application for membership in the ICC, principally so as to defend Israel. It would seem that the United States and Israel play fast and loose with the rule of law, a key plank of the quest for human dignity, rights, peace, and security.

Similarly, the press has linked Russia under President Putin with the 2006 fatal poisoning in London—using a lethal dose of radioactive polonium—of Alexander Litvinenko, a former Russian spy. Putin has also been accused of mass murder in Chechnya, but Said-Emin Ibrahimov's attempts to get the ICC to investigate charges related to Chechnya have come to nothing because Russia is not a signatory of the Rome Statute.

Africa and the world scene at large manifest worrying, if not depressing, signs of violations of human rights; these stand alongside bright and heartwarming exhibitions of actions in behalf of human rights and dignity. The existence of the two manifestations side by side is a reminder that the search for human dignity and rights is never a finished product. Aberrations, however, must not be accommodated; they must be eliminated, including addressing their root causes. The task of fostering a culture of human dignity and human rights does not belong only to some; it is the task of all in society, all persons and institutions, even persons of different faith traditions.

Education about human dignity and rights is critical. The test is not a matter of rhetoric or of empty and vague slogans; terms such as common humanity, common citizenship, and universal franchise must be given vitality and cash value. Succumbing to enemy images takes our eyes off those critical issues. Though we may hate the evil, by God's grace we can love even the aggressor, who also bears the image and likeness of God. Placing the focus on human dignity and human rights is an option for prioritizing what is human and for taking steps to enhance human well-being. This agenda of religion and therefore of theology for prioritizing what is human underscores the proper role of theology in the university, which is at once a place for learning and knowledge, and a space for developing human potential.

16

African Initiatives in Christianity

MISSIOLOGISTS HAVE NOTED THAT World Christianity's center of gravity has shifted from the Northern Hemisphere to the Southern Hemisphere and that Africa, parts of Asia, Latin America, and the Pacific are Christianity's new heartlands.[1] The segment of World Christianity that I identify as African Initiatives in Christianity (AIC) constitutes a notable part of that new reality. The acronym "AIC" also stands for "African Independent Churches" and "African Instituted Churches." We shall return below to the meaning of the acronym but, for now, it will be well to clarify several other points of terminology. A distinction has been drawn, for instance, between the so-called historic or mainline churches and church bodies that are labeled "sects." In its use, however, this distinction is judgmental and needs careful review. By the logic of the core message of the Christian Church, namely, the incarnation, every Christian faith community that comes into being becomes historic and contextual. So it is not proper to limit the appellation "historic" to certain churches and to exclude others. If they exist, they are historic and are on the way to becoming contextualized.

The word "sect" also calls for clarification. Etymologically, "sect" can be derived from the Latin conjugation of *secare* (to cut), *secui* (I have cut), *sectus sum* (I have been cut). Hence to describe an ecclesiastical body as a sect would signal that it was a breakaway, a part that had cut itself off or been broken off from the main body of the church. The word "*secta*," however, is more accurately derived from *sequor* (I follow) and signifies a mode of thought or a mode of behavior. For example, it might signify adhesion to Stoic philosophy or to a religious teaching and, by extension, the group displaying such behavior or adhering to such beliefs.

Modern sociology, in drawing a distinction between church and sect as though they were in opposition, has shortchanged the word's Latin etymology. The church itself is *secta*, and *secta* is not a breakaway from the church. To place "church" and "sect" in opposition to each other is to use the word "sect" as a pejorative. Such use is

---

1. Barrett, *Schism and Renewal in Africa*, 98, table 2; Johnstone, *Operation World*; Barrett, *African Initiatives in Religion*; Andrew F. Walls, "Towards Understanding Africa's Place in Christian History," in Pobee, *Religion in a Pluralistic Society*, 180–89.

biased, depends on a deceptive set of theological concepts, and condemns rival groups of believers as schismatics. For these reasons I prefer not to use oppositional language that would place "church" in opposition to "sect."

As a parallel construction, we may consider the biblical use of the word "Gentiles." The word served as a collective designation for all peoples who were not Israelites, followers of Judaism, or of Jewish stock. They were foreign to the original Judeo-Christianity found in Jerusalem, and a particular group of Gentiles in Antioch were the first people outside the Jews to welcome the gospel. The conclusion reached by the Council of Jerusalem—not to put unnecessary burdens on the non-Jewish believers—was an appreciation of differentiation within the genre of Christ-followers. But it was differentiation *within* the church; differentiation did not place some of Christ's followers outside the church. Much later, the split between the Greek church and the Latin church in the eleventh century did not unchurch either one church or the other. Similarly, the splintering of the Latin church at the time of the Reformation did not unchurch either party. Therefore I do not view with favor theories that envision some sort of lockstep progression from sect to church.

In truth, focusing too closely on the fact or accompanying circumstances of a break in church fellowship makes us lose sight of the real point of the break. For example, whatever may be said concerning the adulterous life of King Henry VIII of England does not invalidate the presence of a real and genuine quest—initiated earlier by Wycliffe and the Lollards—for religious and spiritual renewal and for a return to Scripture.[2] I submit that the distinction between sect and historic church is emotive labeling and is better avoided. Below in discussing the marks of church, I will comment further on this topic.

The Unseemliness of the Recurring Tendency to Schism

Paul, in his first letter to the Corinthians, identified the human penchant for divisiveness and competition. Such a spirit should have no place in the Christian church (1 Cor 3:1-21). Much truer to the spirit of Scripture is to think in terms of being coworkers, co-missionaries, and servants together of Christ. We are to be focused on Christ, the one sure foundation of anything that bears the description "Christian" (1 Cor 3:11). To tilt discussion in a positive direction—toward African contributions to the church; to steer clear of assumptions that would see churches in Africa, to the degree that they are *African*, as less than fully church; and to place the AICs fully within Christianity and the church, I prefer to describe the AICs as African Initiatives in Christianity.[3]

---

2. See Pobee, *The Anglican Story in Ghana*, 9-32.
3. Pobee, *Skenosis*, 64.

The Significance of the Epithet "African"

The epithet "African" in "African Initiatives in Christianity" rankles with some people because it seems to suggest a politicization of the faith and of the church as an institution. A more true reading of the epithet, however, is to see in it that Africans are accepting ownership of the core message of the incarnation. The African church, as Harold Turner writes, "has been founded in Africa by Africans and primarily for Africans."[4] First, the epithet "African" identifies this church's African provenance—where it comes from and the character it bears as it goes forth in mission. Indeed, the AIC churches can be seen exercising mission and ministry outside Africa and among non-Africans (often termed reverse mission). The ministry of the Embassy of God in Ukraine, Eastern Europe, for example, has been documented by Kwabena Asamoah-Gyadu. Going beyond the ideas of reformation, renewal, and revival, the ministry of the Embassy of God both represents and, in its practice, demonstrates "the Christ of All Nations." It is an example of the AICs in mission and a powerful demonstration of the truth that "the crucial things in Christian history have often taken place through obscure people."[5]

Second, the word signifies the concern to culture or enculturate the gospel in the African context. Third, though the AICs are now also found outside Africa and also have non-African clientele, their primary clientele is Africans. The late Ghanaian sociologist and Methodist lay preacher Kofi Busia wrote,

> The concept of "African" Christianity does not mean that there is a version of Christianity that is African any more than there is European Christianity. Christ as the Truth and the Way belongs to all ages and climes. There are universal and eternal elements of Christianity that cannot be nationalized or regionalized: yet Christianity enjoins a way of life to be lived in society and this must find expression in human relations and institutions. It is this expression of Christianity in an African milieu that we are seeking. The search affords opportunities of co-operation and interchange between clergy and laymen, between different denominations of the Church.[6]

The AICs represent a modeling of the insights outlined in Busia's statement.

Search for an African Identity

Missionaries from the North naturally brought with them the incarnated constructs of the church as they knew them. Therefore, as Busia wrote, in spite of Christianity's

---

4. Turner, "Typology of African Religious Movements," 17.

5. Asamoah-Gyadu, "An African Pentecostal on Mission in Eastern Europe," 297–321, echoing Andrew F. Walls.

6. Busia, "The Commitment of the Laity in the Growth of the Church and the Integral Development of Africa," *Laity Today*, 241.

core message of the incarnation, those "responsible for the propagation of the gospel in other lands and cultures have not shown sufficient awareness of the need for an encounter between the Christian religion and the cosmology of people outside European culture and tradition. It is this which has made Christianity either alien or superficial or both."[7] This comment did not issue from some rabid African nationalist politician; it was the considered judgment of a celebrated African sociologist and staunch lay preacher of the Methodist church. Other commentators from other denominations—for example, Peter Sarpong, a bishop of the Roman Catholic Church—came to similar conclusions.[8] Churches founded in Africa by the missionary movement from the northern hemisphere have found themselves to be in a "North Atlantic captivity." They are at present endeavoring to break out of that foreign mold so as to be true to their African identity, even as they engage more fully the one and same Lord and Christ.[9]

Some observers might be inclined to dismiss the efforts of the AICs as sheer fundamentalism riddled with antiscientific convictions. Such a response seems to me to be oblivious to the similarities between the constructs of the AICs and the worldview of Jesus and the New Testament writers. The AICs' stress on the experience of the Holy Spirit reflects a sense among them of mission grappling with the realities of the spiritual world and the realities of authority and communion with God. Kwame Bediako, taking the Archbishop Milingo phenomenon, in Zambia, as an expression of an African Initiative in Christianity, makes a point that is applicable to all AICs. He writes, "It is quite clear from Cardinal Milingo's ministry and writings that he develops his theological ideas on healing, exorcism and pastoral care consciously in relation to the thought-patterns, perceptions of reality and the concepts of identity and community which prevail within the primal world-view of African societies. He does this, however, not as a mere practical convenience, but because he considers that the spiritual universe of the African primal world does offer valid perspectives for articulating Christian theological commitments."[10]

Endorsement of the quest for an authentically African expression of Christianity is in no way equivalent to saying that every African practice is acceptable. The missionary practice of the tabula rasa, however, labeled some African practices as unacceptable without trying to understand them. Deeper probing than mere dismissal is needed, for as Sarpong writes, "African practices have been considered outmoded, cruel, senseless, ridiculous, annoying, born out of pride, [and] meaningless." Yet those practices persist. Sarpong continues, "We take a stand from our experience; we do not

---

7. Busia, "Has the Christian Faith Been Adequately Represented?," *International Review of Missions*, 89; see also Busia, *Report on a Social Survey of Sekondi-Takoradi*.

8. Sarpong, *Odd Customs, Stereotypes, and Prejudices*; see also Sarpong, "Christianity Should Be Africanised, Not Africans Christianised," 322–28; Sarpong, "African Religion and Catholic Worship," 6.

9. Pobee, *Toward an African Theology*; Pobee, *Skenosis*.

10. Bediako, *Jesus and the Gospel in Africa*, 86; see Bediako, *Christianity in Africa*, 19–23.

go further; we do not try to explain the meaning the actors attach to whatever is at stake. We do not try to find out how on earth something that seems so clearly cruel could even have started."[11]

Inadequacy of the Term "African Independent Churches"

The ecclesial expression being discussed has also been grouped under the label of "African Independent Churches." Use of the epithet "Independent" is meant to signal independence from the so-called historic churches. The epithet, however, does not fit only this genre, for the churches that grew out of European missionary activities are now also independent of their mother churches. Indeed, they have been independent for at least fifty years by now.

African Initiatives

Two other expressions have been proffered: African Instituted Churches and African Initiated Churches. The term "African Initiated Churches" places the spotlight on these churches' African founders. But the vital role played by African agents has been true even in the historic churches, where they have been legendary for their establishment of congregations. Indeed, the catechist has been the unsung hero of African church history.[12] On this question, however, we do well to heed the words of the Apostle Paul: "What is Apollos, after all, and what is Paul? Ministers through whom you became believers, just as the Lord assigned each one. I planted, Apollos watered, but God caused the growth. Therefore, neither the one who plants nor the one who waters is anything, but only God, who causes the growth" (1 Cor 3:5–7 NABRE). On biblical and theological grounds, any designation that puts the spotlight on the person or the agent of mission is better avoided. That is why I prefer to see the focus be placed on African initiatives in Christianity rather than on those churches' initiators.

Sect, Movement, Church

Earlier I expressed dissatisfaction with some people's use of the word "sect" to refer to this genre of ecclesial tradition. Others would rather label these churches as a "movement," doing so with the implication that the AICs are not in the full sense "real churches." It may be sufficient to point out that the earliest Christian community was called "The Way" (Acts 9:2; cf. 18:25–26; 19:23; 22:4; 24:14, 22; John 14:6); that is, it was a movement. "Movement" is not a pejorative word. Rather it signals that Christianity is less a

---

11. Sarpong, *Odd Customs, Stereotypes, and Prejudices*.
12. John S. Pobee, "African Spirituality," in Wakefield, *Dictionary of Christian Spirituality*, 7; John S. Pobee, "The Anglican Church in Ghana," in O'Connor, *Three Centuries of Mission*, 415; Pobee, *The Anglican Story in Ghana*, 217–37.

set of beliefs and doctrines—and stresses that Christianity consists more in being a way of life lived after the example of Jesus Christ. The name Christian was first applied to the community of Christ-followers at Antioch (Acts 11:26).

Varieties in a Genre

Scholars of ecclesial tradition have given various labels to distinctive varieties apparent from time to time within the generic Christian tradition. Significant labels used in the African context have included syncretistic movements,[13] witchcraft eradication movements, separatist church movements,[14] prophetic movements,[15] and messianic movements[16] as well as spiritual/Pentecostal churches, nativistic churches, and Zionist churches.

These designations suggest that while the varieties belong to the same genre, they represent differences in emphasis. They belong to the same family, but are not identical. They represent different interpretations or judgments that issue in particular ways of being church. The designation "syncretistic," when applied to a church, is a judgment that it represents a mixture and confusion of Christian elements with African traditional values. In writing about AICs, Sundkler used the word "syncretistic" to suggest that they were "the bridge over which Africans are brought back to heathenism."[17] But Boff correctly observes that Christianity itself is a "syncretism *par excellence.*"[18] One can start with Scripture; for example, 1 Corinthians 13 demonstrates syncretism. The hymn on love quotes copiously from popular non-Christian religious sources and, interestingly, does not contain a single reference to Christ. Similarly, the church borrowed funeral rites from Germanic and Celtic ancestor cults. Christmas rites were a rebaptism of the feast of the pagan god of thunder, Thor.[19] Boff comments, "In reality, [Christian religion] is a cultural product, the activity of human beings influenced by God's intervention. On the one hand, it is a gift from God and so, rightly, has a supernatural origin; and on the other, it is a human construct, where

---

13. Sundkler, *Bantu Prophets in South Africa*.

14. Turner, *History of an African Independent Church*; Daneel, *Old and New in Southern Shona Independent Churches*.

15. Fernandez, "Rededication and Prophetism in Ghana," 228–305; Haliburton, *Prophet Harris*; Shank, "Prophet for Modern Times"; Baëta, *Prophetism in Ghana*.

16. Sundkler, *Bantu Prophets in South Africa*; Martin, *The Biblical Concept of Messianism and Messianism in Southern Africa*; Oosthuizen, *Post-Christianity in Africa*; Balandier, "Messianismes et Nationalismes en Afrique Noire," 41–65.

17. Sundkler, *Bantu Prophets in South Africa*, 297.

18. Boff, *Church, Charism, and Power*, 99.

19. For one version of the origin of the Christmas tree, see http://catholicstraightanswers.com/what-is-the-origin-of-the-christmas-tree/.

many steps and stages may be studied and described.... The Church as a structure is as syncretistic as any other religious expression."[20]

Another Roman Catholic scholar, Robert Schreiter, reminds us that words such as "syncretism" are one-sided judgments, describing a phenomenon from the side of the observer, especially one who is biased against it. But it is important also to understand how a speaker's message is received within and lodged in the universe of the hearer and actor. For "meaning is established in social judgment, in the intense and repeated action between speaker and hearer."[21] Schreiter's comment does not mean that syncretism is acceptable, but it does suggest, in the words of Walter Hollenweger, that "before we criticize the AICs because of their syncretism we examine our own praxis and then ask ourselves and each other, under which conditions and when is syncretism not only acceptable but necessary?"[22]

The description "nativistic" signals an understanding of the AICs as constituting a reestablishment or perpetuation of native cultural trends. The label focuses a spotlight on the practice of tabula rasa that characterized most missionary activities of the historic churches. It signals dissatisfaction with that practice, which in effect shortchanged the core Christian message of the incarnation. The practice of tabula rasa made homo africanus a clone of the Caucasian. Africans as Africans were not able to feel at home in a Christianity and church cultured in and imported from Europe.

Of the various terms used for describing African church movements, "nativistic" is the least helpful. Historically the term was not invented by or in common use among missionaries; rather it was coined and promoted by anthropologists. If authors with a mission background also use the term "nativistic," they do so because they have read earlier publications by anthropologists promoting that perspective.

The tabula rasa approach—which either ignored or was negative toward Africans' traditional spiritual epistemology and ontology and which sought to explain things along the lines of psychological cause and effect—was most unsatisfactory for Africans. As far back as 1940 Margaret Field warned that "though it is not difficult by warfare, foreign administration, modern industry and other means, to smash up an ancient religious organization, the ideas which sustained it are not easily destroyed. They are only disbanded, vagrant and unattached. But given sufficient sense of need, they will mobilize again."[23] The persistence in Africa today of ideas of witchcraft, even among some intellectuals, supports her analysis.[24]

---

20. Boff, *Church, Charism, and Power*, 92.
21. Schreiter, *The New Catholicity*, 70.
22. Walter J. Hollenweger, foreword to Pobee and Ositelu, *African Initiatives in Christianity*, xii.
23. Field, "Some Shrines of the Gold Coast and Their Significance," 138.
24. Debrunner, *Witchcraft in Ghana*.

Prophetic Movements

The designation "prophetic movement" derives from the fact that several of these churches were started by self-styled prophets. Thus Prophet William Wadé Harris (ca. 1860–1929) started the Church of the Twelve Apostles found in Côte d'Ivoire, Ghana, and Liberia.[25] Other prophets included Joseph Ayodele Babalola (Christ Apostolic Church or Aladura) and Garrick Braide (Christ Army Church), both of Nigeria.[26] Interestingly, the Harrist Movement was most active at the time of the World Missionary Conference held at Le Zoute, Belgium, in 1926. Some who were in attendance expressed the wish that Prophet Harris had been at the conference. The conference itself described Prophet Harris as "Africa's most successful evangelist." The *Lagos Weekly Record*, November 18, 1926, carried the following comment: "The God of the Negro, it would seem, has arisen as a strong man from a deep sleep and surveying the wreck and ruin — the physical and moral degradation of the dusky sons of Africa — has gathered up his loins together to redress the balance of the old regime and already has begun to raise up instruments of his sweet will. Prodigies like Garrick Brady or William Wadé Harris are neither imposters nor false prophets. They are merely temporary vehicles for some manifestations of the divine will." Africans were proud of their prophets raised up by God. But their presence was also a protest against the fabrications of the missionary churches, hence, the idea of them as "true prophets" raised up by God.

The story of the Harrist Movement in the Gold Coast is interesting for the light it throws on the failure of the historic churches, the Anglican Church in particular, to see the movement as it truly was. During the First World War (1914–1918), Harris's prophetic movement swept through the Gold Coast. An agent of the movement, John Swatson, who was accorded the accolade "Bishop of the Sanwi," approached Archdeacon Gresham W. Morrison at Easter 1916, offering the fruits of his mission to the Anglican Church. While Bishop Mowbray O'Rorke was accommodating, J. L. Trafford, acting district commissioner of Aowin, in an official letter said to the bishop, "I sincerely hope for the good name of the Church . . . that he does not intend to give this undesirable man any power in the Aowin District, or trouble will ensue almost for certainty."[27] In short, the historic church could not see the prophetic movement for what it was but rather allowed political influence to cloud its judgment.

Africans stress charismatic leadership, and prophets appeared to them to be of a piece with traditional African diviners and priests. Therefore Africans were much more comfortable with the prophets than with the middle class gentlemen clergy offered by the historic churches.

---

25. Haliburton, *Prophet Harris*; Shank, "Prophet for Modern Times"; Wilbert R. Shenk, "The Contribution of the Study of New Religious Movements to Missiology," in Walls and Shenk, *Exploring New Religious Movements*, 194.

26. Tasie, *Christian Missionary Enterprise in the Niger Delta, 1864–1918*.

27. For the further story, see Pobee, *The Anglican Story in Ghana*, 148, 154–56; the quotation is found on p. 155.

Some of the prophets were assimilated to the Apostles, for example, Prophet Wovenu, founder of the *ApostolwoFeDede Fia Hiabobo Nuntimya* (Apostle Revelation Society), that originated in Tadzevu, near Keta, Ghana.[28] Another example, from Zimbabwe, is Johane Maranke, founder of the African Apostolic Church. Interestingly, visions called Maranke to be a prophet, and the visions are codified in *Umboo utsva hwa-va Postorie* (The New Revelation of the Apostles). Interest in these ecstatic experiences led to his identification with such biblical figures as Joseph and Moses. A distinctive element in these African churches' understanding of the prophet is that it is linked with pastoral work in addition to biblical foretelling.

Ethiopian Movements

The Ethiopian churches are non-prophetic and often claim ideological and religious links with Ethiopia, the symbol of black peoples. Based in Zimbabwe, Chibarirwe (African Congregational Church), founded by Sengwayo, and the African Reformed Church, founded by Sibambo, are two examples.

Messianic Movements

The description "Messianic Movements" was introduced by Sundkler to designate groups with strong messianic expectations. The label further suggested that the messiah was not Jesus but the leader of the group, such as Engenas Lekganyane of Zion Christian Church and Isaiah Shembe of the Nazareth Baptist Church, both of South Africa. As Sundkler at first expressed his understanding of the movement, the messiahship of this group of churches was "a radical distortion of prophetically oriented Christianity, as a result of which the Christ of the Bible was more or less superseded."[29] He later dropped that description in favor of a more "iconic" understanding in which the prophet has roles that are a reflection of Christ without necessarily usurping Christ's place.[30] The leaders of these churches are seen as being in an iconic relationship to Christ. The epithet "messianic" has also been interpreted as being the church's response to the realities of its sociopolitical context, particularly racism and excessive oppression.[31] Thus the epithet forces us to deal with Christological questions. Inus Daneel is convincing when he maintains that the epithet "messianic" signals iconic leadership; it is a *"projection of a common social usage onto the unknowable realm of life after death, namely, the custom that an ordinary man must never approach an eminent person except through the agency of an officially sanctioned intermediary."*[32]

28. Baëta, *Prophetism in Ghana*, 62.
29. Sundkler, *Bantu Prophets in South Africa*, 323.
30. Sundkler, *Zulu Zion and Some Swazi Zionists*, 193, 310; Martin, *Kimbangu*.
31. Balandier, "Messianismes et Nationalismes en Afrique Noire," 41–65.
32. Daneel, *Quest for Belonging*, 191; Daneel's italics.

Pentecostal Churches

George Jeffrey founded the Elim Four Square Gospel Alliance in Monaghan, Ireland, in 1915. Adherents were committed to experiencing anew the Day of Pentecost in their own time and lives. With that orientation, they prized the charism of speaking in tongues. Some of the tradition came to Africa, patterned on the UK original.

Three groups may be identified under the caption of Pentecostal and charismatic churches. First are the classic Pentecostal churches that derive from the Azusa Revival of 1906–09. Second are the denominational charismatics, who derive from the renewal movements of the 1960s. Third are the independent and nondenominational movements. The charismatic movements in Africa are not all of one type.[33] The Pentecostal churches emphasize the receiving and conscious experience of the Holy Spirit, baptism in the Holy Spirit, glossolalia, healing, and exorcism in the power of the Holy Spirit. Emphasis on exorcism in some of these churches is at times excessive in the sense that they adopt automatic, mechanical, and magical attitudes toward the Holy Spirit.

In many cases African Pentecostal churches do not derive from roots based in the United Kingdom. Rather they are expressing the desire for experiences that correspond to their African spiritual epistemology and ontology. The cerebral cast of missionary Christianity does not appear satisfactory when viewed in light of Africans' epistemology and ontology. For them religion that is to be taken seriously must be made manifest in acts of power. The founder of Eden Revival Church, Accra, Ghana, had a visiting card imprinted with the words "Rev. Prophet Yeboa Korie, God's Man of Power." The great attraction of this genre of churches as a whole is indisputably the hope of experiencing some mighty act of God's power. As Emmanuel Kingsley Larbi has written, "The single significant factor that has given rise to a boom in Pentecostal activities in Ghana is that Pentecostalism has found a fertile ground in the all-pervasive primal religious traditions, especially in its cosmology and in its concept of salvation."[34] Africans join the Pentecostal and charismatic movement in search for a place to feel at home because they already have a religious and spiritual epistemology and ontology.

The language to be found in the Pentecostal, charismatic, and Spiritual movements overall emphasizes inner renewal and personal well-being rather than institutional structures and administrative forms. Passion and emotion are not to be despised, because without them renewal and transformation are not possible. In the words of Lamin Sanneh, "Biblical material was submitted to the regenerative capacity of African perception and the result would be Africans' unique contribution to

---

33. Lederle, "The Spirit of Unity," 279–87; Lederle, *Treasures Old and New*, 268.

34. Larbi, *Pentecostalism*, 3; Asamoah-Gyadu, *Contemporary Pentecostal Christianity*; Asamoah-Gyadu, *African Charismatics*.

the story of Christianity."³⁵ Significantly, AICs represent a sizeable part of the new reality of Africa as a heartland of World Christianity. Andrew Walls goes on to draw the conclusion that theology that is worth talking about arises from locations where Christianity—and Christian theology—has a "noticeable effect on the lives and minds of a significant number of people."³⁶

What May Be Learned from AICs

AICs represent an earnest attempt to develop authentic African Christian churches. The so-called historic churches have been, by and large, clones of their sending missions in Europe. But AICs are at once both Christian and African, which answers to the core message of the Christian faith, the incarnation. This effort gives rise to the attempt to distinguish between what is nonnegotiable in Christian faith and what can be negotiated. The significance of this endeavor can be illustrated in three ways.

First, because Africans have a religious and spiritual epistemology and ontology, they experience considerable dissatisfaction in encountering the separation of spirit and flesh that has characterized the Enlightenment culture through which Western Christianity has passed and which has colored it. For example, to limit the explanation of ailments to empirical causes and effects and to exclude the supernatural from the analysis of illness is a most unsatisfactory approach in the eyes of African Christians. As Hollenweger cautions,

> Perhaps we can learn that the separation of the "natural" from the "supernatural" is not a particularly biblical way of doing theology . . . all the more since *huperphusikos* (supernatural) is not a biblical category (try to translate "supernatural" into Hebrew). For the AICs, all of nature—that which we believe to understand and that which we believe not to understand—is God's creation and, therefore, open to unexpected and not yet understood phenomena. A deeper discussion with the leading physicists and scientists could have taught us this long ago.³⁷

Thus AICs are more tuned to the wavelength of homo africanus than are the historic churches. The critique that AICs are syncretistic is a red herring, for syncretism is *sometimes* necessary and acceptable. The Manifesto of the Organisation of African Instituted Churches (OAIC) expresses the AIC story in this way: "We show how focus upon the world as a whole, both spiritual and material, is possible in contrast to the dichotomous Western world-view that divides the sacred from the profane, the spirit

---

35. Sanneh, *West African Christianity*, 80; Sanneh, *Translating the Message*.

36. Walls, "Towards Understanding Africa's Place in Christian History," in Pobee, *Religion in a Pluralistic Society*, 180.

37. Hollenweger, "Foreword," in Pobee and Ositelu, *African Initiatives in Christianity*, xi.

from matter, the supernatural from the natural. Our relationships to God's creation are one of respect and gratitude."[38]

Second, the historic churches and their theology, even when interested in and sympathetic to the AICs, have been baptized in the rivers of Enlightenment culture—a culture that in its beholdenness to rationality has tended to exorcise spirit, passion, and feeling from the universe. African epistemology makes room for passion, emotion, and feeling. To despise emotion, feeling, and passion is not helpful, for no change is possible without emotion. This divide accounts for the success AICs experience in making converts, even when the pews of the historic churches become emptier and emptier. The AICs represent another style of doing theology, one that does not grant nearly exclusive priority to heavily rational processes; rather their theology is danced out, which corresponds to homo africanus's characteristic practice of dancing out his religion.

Third, historic churches and their theology, having been run through the prism of Enlightenment culture, have been hijacked by a culture of individualism that contrasts sharply with the communitarian epistemology and ontology of African cultures. In spite of the historic churches' formal theology of the church as *koinonia*, Africans do not feel at home in churches minted within the culture of individualism. The OAIC Manifesto again states, "Humans-in-community: We have a spiritual view of life that nourishes our sense of family and community." Another paragraph continues, "Communion of saints: The relationship between the living and the dead enriches our churches as the living nurture the memory of our predecessors who are still influencing our own lives by their contribution to the welfare of our communities when they were still alive."[39] As Daneel comments, AICs have become "truly African *havens of belonging*," something very much lacking in the historic churches.[40]

Revisiting the Time-Honored Marks of the Church

As noted earlier, various designations have been used in speaking of the genre of Christian communities. All of those designations, however, were *etic* designations—they came from outside—for the critics were beholden to the Niceno-Constantinopolitan Creed's statement of "one, holy, catholic, and apostolic church," for short, the *Una Sancta*. That definition or statement of the church's essential character was shaped by the imperial model of the Roman Empire: one empire (the Roman Empire), one ruler (the Roman emperor), one religion (Christianity). The formulation reflected a pattern

---

38. "A New Force of Christian Churches—OAIC Manifesto," *Baragamu: The African Independent Churches' Voice* 1 (July 1996); available in Pobee and Ositelu, *African Initiatives in Christianity*, 67–71.

39. "A New Force of Christian Churches," in Pobee and Ositelu, *African Initiatives in Christianity*, 71.

40. Daneel, *Quest for Belonging*, 101.

of alliance between the Empire and the Christian church, but that alliance was not exactly synonymous with the complete Christianization of society.[41]

The idea of the Una Sancta has been brought into question down through the ages. The Great Schism between the Church of the East (Greek) and the Church of the West (Latin) in 1054 represents a major sundering of the Una Sancta. Further sundering of the Latin Church took place in the sixteenth-century Reformation that divided the Western church into the Roman Catholic and Protestant churches (Lutherans, Calvinists, Anglicans, and so on). Protestantism's fissiparous nature may be regarded as a reminder that the idea of the Una Sancta needs to be probed further. It may not be the only model for or the last word on the nature of the church.

The description of the church as "holy" was challenged in the fourth century by the Donatist schism. The early church, because of the challenge Roman rulers posed to it, had come to value zeal for the Lord, especially as shown by martyrdom. "The blood of the martyrs," it was said, "is the seed of the church." Martyrdom, properly understood, consisted of zeal to witness to the Lord and was prized by the church. Following Constantine, with the coming of the ideology of Christendom, holiness became watered down.

The form taken by the Protestant Reformation brings the issue of apostolicity to the fore. Do the Protestant churches reach back to the apostles who were witnesses to the resurrection of Jesus, which constituted the church of Jesus Christ? The note of apostolicity continues to be questioned in some quarters.

The mark of catholicity concerns the local church and the global church. Schreiter writes,

> Catholicity has traditionally been understood as [the Church's] extension through the world and its fullness of the truth handed down from the apostles. Now communication—including issues of culture, identity and social change—becomes a third and necessary addition to the theological concept of catholicity. It is perhaps only by such an addition that some of the struggles so apparent in theology today—about concepts of the church, appropriate forms of inculturation, commitment to liberation and possible reconciliation—can be addressed effectively. This theological addendum gives the new catholicity concreteness.[42]

I would submit that the AICs represent an attempt at Schreiter's "theological addendum" along the lines of communication as well as a desire for church as the communion of the Spirit.

The vibrancy of the AICs suggests that the mainline churches are best seen as one model of being church and not as being the last word on the *notae ecclesiae*. Two statements from the Manifesto of the OAIC are instructive. The first says, "Most of

---

41. Schreiter, *The New Catholicity*, 70; Meyedorff, *Imperial Unity and Christian Divisions*.
42. Schreiter, *The New Catholicity*, 6.

us are stable, growing churches with a Christian doctrine based on the Bible as sole authority, a special dispensation of the Holy Spirit, faith in the God of the Bible and confidence in its promises. One can say with conviction that AICs are part of the universal church and have much to contribute to her life." The AICs' emphasis on the use of Scripture echoes Protestantism's return to Scripture.

The second statement from the Manifesto states, "We may not all articulate [our faith] in written theology, but we express faith in our liturgy, worship and structures. Our services are alive with warm expressions of joy as we clap and dance in rhythm with the new spiritual and indigenous songs. Needless to say, the people come because they feel at home." This testimony expresses the AICs' continuity with traditional African spirituality by delineating the joy that is characteristic of religious and spiritual experience. The exodus especially of the youth from the historic churches and their migration to the AICs suggests a yearning after the joyful religion living within the AICs.

What More Can Historic Churches Learn from AICs?

The church defines herself by mission, and therefore the Christian identity of the AICs can be judged by how central mission is to them. As is well known, the historic churches went into doldrums until the Evangelical Revival reawakened in them the sense of mission, which issued in several missions to Africa. The AICs' growth is evidence that they are very much alive to the church's enduring self-understanding, that is, the church's conviction that she finds herself and her soul in mission.

In regard to the aims of mission in the field, the names of two mission thinkers stand out: Rufus Anderson (1796–1880) and Henry Venn (1796–1873). Anderson was secretary of the American Board of Commissioners for Foreign Missions.[43] Venn, prebendary of St. Paul's Cathedral, was also secretary of the Church Missionary Society. Venn proposed the idea of the "euthanasia of a mission," namely, that missionaries should work toward the goal of establishing churches that are self-governing, self-supporting, and self-propagating.[44]

And yet even when Africans become the overseers and administrators of a historic church, the mentality and models that prevail in that type of church are those inherited from the churches from the North. Even when historic churches are self-propagating, they are mediating theological and ecclesial constructs from other regions. After years of intoning self-support, historic churches in Africa continue to suffer from a syndrome of dependency. Heads of churches are forever going to partner churches and agencies abroad to solicit resources and supplements for their budgets.

The AICs by contrast have blazed new paths: a self-governing church must also be self-critical, a step without which sustainable growth is sacrificed. A self-governing

---

43. See Anderson, *Outline of Missionary Policy*.

44. See Shenk, *Henry Venn: Missionary Statesman*; Yates, *Venn and Victorian Bishops Abroad*; Warren, *To Apply the Gospel*; Allen, *Missionary Methods*.

church must cease to recapitulate foreign models. The criterion of self-support must develop into a more dynamic concept of self-motivation. As Stan Nussbaum comments, "Motivation caused things to move rather than simply to stand still. A self-motivating church is driven by its past experience of God's action and pulled towards the work it is called to do."[45] The criterion of self-propagating must also become that of self-contextualizing. Taking this step demands a thorough revision of the inherited missionary method encapsulated in the tabula rasa model.

Nussbaum concludes, "The African Independent Churches have exposed the limits of the old three-self formula by achieving it without being complete models of mature churches. Their pioneering experiences after achieving it are experiments at the cutting edge of mission which point us towards a restatement of the three-self formula: self-motivating, self-contextualizing and self-critical."[46]

AICs are not, however, a perfect, finished product, for not all is well with the AICs. First is the quite noticeable fissiparous tendency present among them. They began by breaking away from the historic churches to establish their own churches. Thus the Musama Disco Christo Church broke from the Methodist Church, Ghana. But, time and again, they have not stopped at one schism; the schismatic group itself has experienced further schisms. In 1996, following a conference in Nairobi, the OAIC publication *Baragamu* wrote in its editorial: "We have, as Christians, unashamedly fought each other in the past. We have dwelt on trivialities at the expense of true mission. The time is now to start praying together without ceasing (Rom 12:1–13) and to admonish one another with love (Eph 4:15) until we arrive at a common point. The writing is on the wall, bold and clear. We have two options. One is to listen to the loving voice of God and to work as a team. The other is to fail to do that and stand condemned for posterity for creating loopholes for hostile religious cults and fundamentalisms of all shades to eat into the very foundation of the legacy bequeathed to us by our Master Jesus Christ. I doubt whether we have an alternative."[47]

The consultation in Nairobi was sponsored by OAIC, the Centre for Black and White Fellowship (Selly Oak Colleges), and the Catholic fraternity. The presence of multiple sponsors would indicate that input at the conference came from other sources as well as from OAIC. Nevertheless, the fact that the words just quoted come from an editorial in an OAIC publication would lead one to believe that the OAIC endorsed the insights expressed.

The key insights may be parsed as follows:

---

45. Stan Nussbaum, "African Independent Churches and a Call for a New Three-Self Formula for Mission," in Nussbaum, *Freedom and Independence*, 2.

46. Ibid., 7–8.

47. Onyango, "Dialogue—The Dialogue: The Holy Spirit on the Move," 2.

1. The call to unity—which reverses the fissiparous tendency—is a legacy from Jesus himself, the founder of the Christian faith. His mandate supersedes the word of any human founder.

2. The call to unity is a call from "the loving voice of God." In other words, it imposes an obligation from God; it is not an option.

3. The call to unity entails working as a team, something that implies the ecumenical vision.

4. The call to unity is a process and never a fait accompli. The Divine voice conveys urgency such that a start must be made now.

5. The quest for unity—and turning one's back on fissiparous thinking—includes praying together and worshiping together (shared spirituality) and admonishing one another in love (being our brother's keeper).

OAIC may not have overcome that movement's fissiparous tendencies, but an awareness is present in the movement that things as they stand are not right. Happily, institutions exist—including the OAIC itself—that stand as reminders of the ultimate goal of unity and are working toward that end, among them the Pentecostal Association of Ghana, the National Council of Pentecostal Churches, the Ghana Council of United Churches, and the Christian Brotherhood Council (Ghana); *Fambidzano no yama Kereka ava Tema* (African Independent Churches Conference), which brought together the Shona independent churches; Bantu Independent Churches Union of South Africa, which brought together Zulu independent churches; and African Independent Church Association (AICA), headquartered in Queenstown, South Africa.

Elsewhere I have pointed out three reasons for these attempts to counter the fissiparous tendency. "In the first place, they represented a striving for recognition from both the historic churches and the government. Second, they expressed a smouldering yearning for greater unity among the AICs. Third, [the attempts arise from] a desire for better theological education."[48]

Clientele of AICs

The historic churches love to make much of the fact that the leadership of the AICs is well-nigh illiterate and that it caters to the poor, that is, to those who are economically, politically, and emotionally disinherited and who are not well educated, if not wholly nonliterate. That characterization may have been accurate for the early stages of the AICs. It may even be a factor in the penchant of AIC leadership for titles—claiming doctorates (when they have not darkened the halls of a university) and bestowing other titles on themselves, such as Rev. Brother, Apostle, Prophet, and Bishop (even

---

48. Pobee and Ositelu, *African Initiatives in Christianity*, 58.

though they are the head of only one parish and no diocese)—and for donning high church garb.

The picture today, however, is more nuanced than before. The clientele of these churches now includes university professors and lecturers, medical doctors, and other professionals. AICs are establishing or patronizing theological institutions that cater to their brand of theology and style of churches. Examples include Fambidzano's thriving Theological Education by Extension program in Zimbabwe, the Christian Institute of South Africa in South Africa, the Good News Institute in Ghana, the seminary of the Church of the Lord (Aladura) in Nigeria, and the Kimbanguist university and seminary in Congo (Kinshasa).

We may conclude that AICs are still works in progress. They are different from the historic churches, which are clones of North Atlantic models of church, with all the historical accidents and accretions they represent. Beyond dispute the AICs are, heart and soul, attempts at culturing the gospel and church in Africa and thus at fulfilling or approximating the incarnation, which is the core message of the gospel. For these reasons, the AICs may not be unchurched or dismissed from the body of Christ. Their judgment must be by God, not by human evaluation. If there were no other consideration, the biblical injunction to be at peace with all persons would require each of us to eschew hatred and contempt even for those who differ from us. Any other attitude falls under the judgment of God.

This attitude is consistent with the church's self-definition as catholic. Andrew Walls sums up the matter well: "A Church that is catholic implies that the resources of all Christian ages and places are open to uninhibited exploitation by all Christians."[49] Catholicity is a call to openness to the other and willingness to learn from the other.

---

49. Walls, "Towards Understanding Africa's Place in Christian History," in Pobee, *Religion in a Pluralistic Society*, 183.

Bibliography

Abelard, Peter. *Abelard's Ethics*. Translated with an introduction by J. Ramsay McCallum. Oxford: Blackwell, 1935.
Abercrombie, Nicholas, et al. *The Penguin Dictionary of Sociology*. Harmondsworth, Middlesex, UK: Penguin, 1984.
Achebe, Chinua. *Arrow of God*. London: Heinemann, 1964.
———. *No Longer at Ease*. London: Heinemann, 1960.
———. *Things Fall Apart*. New York: Knopf, 1958.
Adams, William Y. *Nubia: Corridor to Africa*. Princeton: Princeton University Press, 1977.
Adels, Jill Haak, comp. *The Wisdom of the Saints: An Anthology*. New York: Oxford University Press, 1987.
The African Bible. Nairobi: Paulines Publications Africa, 1999, 2005.
African Ecclesiastical Review (AFER) 16, no. 3 (1973) 278–80.
African National Congress. *Selected Writings on the Freedom Charter, 1955–1985: A Sechaba Commemorative Publication*. London: African National Congress, 1985.
Ahuma, Samuel Richard Brew Attoh. *The Gold Coast Nation and National Consciousness*. Liverpool: Marples, 1911.
Ajayi, J. F. Ade. *Christian Missions in Nigeria, 1841–1891: The Making of a New Elite*. London: Longmans, 1965.
Ajayi, J. F. Ade, and Michael Crowder, eds. *History of West Africa*. Vol. 2. London: Longman, 1974.
Albanese, Giulio. "Africa, Quo Vadis?" *L'Osservatore Romano*, August 22, 2012, 10.
Alexandre, Pierre. *An Introduction to Languages and Language in Africa*. London: Heinemann, 1972.
Allen, Roland. *Missionary Methods: St. Paul's or Ours?* London: Scott, 1912.
AMECEA Documentation Service no. 11 (1974) 2.
Amirtham, Samuel, and John S. Pobee, eds. *Theology by the People: Reflections on Doing Theology in Community*. Geneva: World Council of Churches, 1986.
Amu, Ephraim. *Twenty-Five African Songs in the Twi Language*. London: Sheldon, 1932.
Anderson, Rufus. *Outline of Missionary Policy*. Boston: American Board of Commissioners for Foreign Missions, 1856.
Ansah, Paul. "Aspects of Negritude." *Universitas* (Univ. of Ghana), n.s., 1, no. 4 (1972) 66–78.
Arendt, Hannah. *Between Past and Future: Eight Exercises in Political Thought*. New York: Penguin, 1993.

Ariarajah, S. Wesley. *Not Without My Neighbour: Issues of Interfaith Relations*. Geneva: World Council of Churches, 1999.

Armah, Ayi Kwei. *The Beautiful Ones Are Not Yet Born*. New York: Macmillan, 1968.

Asamoah-Gyadu, J. Kwabena. *African Charismatics: Current Developments within Independent Indigenous Pentecostalism in Ghana*. Leiden: Brill, 2005.

———. "An African Pentecostal on Mission in Eastern Europe: The Church of the 'Embassy of God' in the Ukraine." *Pneuma: Journal of Pentecostal Studies* 27, no. 2 (2005) 297–321.

———. *Contemporary Pentecostal Christianity: Interpretations from an African Context*. Oxford: Regnum, 2013.

Austin, Dennis. "Strong Rule in Ghana." *Listener* 67, no. 1713 (1962) 156–57.

Ayandele, Emmanuel Ayankanmi. *African Historical Studies*. London: Frank Cass, 1979.

———. *The Missionary Impact on Modern Nigeria, 1842–1914: A Political and Social Analysis*. London: Longmans, 1966.

Ayisi, Eric O. [Commission Appointed to Enquire into the Functions, Operation, and Administration of the Workers Brigade]. *Minority Report*. Accra: Ministry of Information, 1968.

Bacon, Francis. *Novum Organum*. Edited by James Spedding. London: Longman, 1857–1859.

Baëta, C. G., ed. *Christianity in Tropical Africa*. London: Oxford University Press, 1968.

———. *Prophetism in Ghana: A Study of Some "Spiritual" Churches*. London: SCM, 1962.

———. *The Relationships of Christians with Men of Other Living Faiths*. Accra: Ghana Universities Press, 1971.

Bakare, Sebastian. *My Right to Land, in the Bible and in Zimbabwe: A Theology of Land for Zimbabwe*. Harare: Zimbabwe Council of Churches, 1993.

Balandier, Georges. "Messianismes et Nationalismes en Afrique Noire." *Cahiers internationaux de sociologie* 14 (1953) 41–65.

Balasuriya, Tissa. *Jesus Christ and Human Liberation*. Colombo, Sri Lanka: Centre for Society and Religion, 1976.

Balcond, Anthony. "Narrative: Exploring a New Way of Doing Theology in the New South Africa." *Journal of Theology for Southern Africa* 101 (1998) 11–21.

Barr, James. "The Pelagian Controversy." *Evangelical Quarterly* 21 (1949) 253–64.

Barrett, David B., ed. *African Initiatives in Religion*. Nairobi: East African Pub. House, 1971.

———. *Schism and Renewal in Africa: An Analysis of Six Thousand Contemporary Religious Movements*. London: Oxford University Press, 1968.

Barry, F. R. *What Has Christianity to Say?* London: SCM, 1937.

Bartle, Philip F. W. "The Universe Has Three Souls: Notes on Translating Akan Culture." *Journal of Religion in Africa* 14, 2 (1983) 85–114.

Bass, Diana Butler. *Christianity after Religion: The End of Church and the Birth of a New Spiritual Awakening*. New York: HarperOne, 2012.

Baynes, Norman Hepburn. *Constantine the Great and the Christian Church*. Oxford: Oxford University Press, 1929.

———. *The Political Ideas of St. Augustine's "De Civitate Dei."* London: Bell, 1936.

Bediako, Kwame. *Christianity in Africa: The Renewal of a Non-Western Religion*. Maryknoll: Orbis, 1995.

———. *Jesus and the Gospel in Africa: History and Experience*. Maryknoll: Orbis, 2004.

———. *Jesus in African Culture: A Ghanaian Perspective*. Accra: Asempa, 1990.

Bellah, Robert N. *Beyond Belief: Essays on Religion in a Post-Traditional World*. New York: Harper & Row, 1970.

Bennett, John C. "Breakthrough in Ecumenical Social Ethics." *Ecumenical Review* 40, no. 2 (1988) 132–46.
Berdyaev, Nikolai A. *The Origin of Russian Communism*. London: Centenary, 1937.
Berger, Peter L. *The Sacred Canopy: Elements of a Sociological Theory of Religion*. Garden City: Doubleday, 1967.
Bernstein, Basil B. *Pedagogy, Symbolic Control, and Identity: Theory, Research, Critique*. London: Rowman & Littlefield, 2006.
Best, Thomas F., and Günther Gassmann, eds. *On the Way to Fuller Koinonia: Official Report of the Fifth World Conference on Faith and Order*. Geneva: WCC, 1994.
Beti, Mongo. *The Poor Christ of Bomba*. London: Heinemann, 1971.
Biko, Steve. *Black Consciousness and the Quest for a True Humanity* [London: Christian Institute Trustees, 1977].
———. *I Write What I Like*. Edited and with a personal memoir by Aelred Stubbs. London: Bowerdean, 1978.
Birmelé, André. *La communion ecclésiale: Progrès oecuménique et enjeux méthodologiques*. Paris: Cerf, 2000.
Blakely, Gloria. "Giving a Voice to a Dream: Martin Luther King Jr. in Words and Music." *Costco Connection: A Lifestyle Magazine for Costco Members* 23 (2008) 27.
Bligh, John. *Galatians*. London: St. Paul, 1969.
Blyden, Edward W. *Christianity, Islam, and the Negro Race*. Edinburgh: Edinburgh University Press, 1887.
Boff, Leonardo. *Church, Charism, and Power: Liberation Theology and the Institutional Church*. London: SCM, 1985.
———. *Ecclesiogenesis: The Base Communities Reinvent Church*. Maryknoll: Orbis, 1986.
———. *Faith on the Edge: Religion and Marginalized Existence*. Maryknoll: Orbis, 1991.
———. *Jesus Cristo libertador: Ensaio de Cristologia critica para o nosso tempo*. Petrópolis, Brazil: Vozes, 1972.
Bonhoeffer, Dietrich. *Letters and Papers from Prison*. London: SCM, 1971.
Bornkamm, Günther. *Jesus of Nazareth*. London: Hodder & Stoughton, 1960.
Bosch, David J. *Transforming Mission: Paradigm Shifts in Theology of Mission*. Maryknoll: Orbis, 1991.
Boulding, Kenneth E. *The Image*. Ann Arbor: Univ. of Michigan Press, 1956.
Boyd, Robin H. S. *An Introduction to Indian Christian Theology*. Madras: Christian Literature Society, 1969.
Bria, Ion. *The Liturgy after the Liturgy: Mission and Witness from an Orthodox Perspective*. Geneva: WCC, 1996.
Briggs, John H. Y., et al., eds. *A History of the Ecumenical Movement*. Vol. 3, *1968–2000*. Geneva: WCC, 2004.
Brockman, James R. *Romero: A Life*. Maryknoll: Orbis, 1989.
Brown, Lalage J., and S. M. Olu Tomori, eds. *A Handbook of Adult Education in West Africa*. London: Hutchinson, 1979.
Brown, Robert McAfee. *Gustavo Gutiérrez: An Introduction to Liberation Theology*. Maryknoll: Orbis, 1990.
———. *Liberation Theology: An Introductory Guide*. Louisville: Westminster John Knox, 1993.
———. "My Story and 'The Story.'" *Theology* 32 (1975) 166–73.
Bruce, F. F., ed. *Promise and Fulfillment*. Edinburgh: T. & T. Clark, 1963.

Brueggemann, Walter. *The Land: Place as Gift, Promise, and Challenge in Biblical Faith.* Philadelphia: Fortress, 1977.

Buah, F. K. *A History of Ghana.* Revised ed. London: Macmillan, 2003.

Bujo, Bénézet. *Christmas: God Becomes Man in Black Africa.* Nairobi: Paulines Publications Africa, 1995.

———. "Pour une éthique africaine Christocentrique." *Bulletin de théologie Africaine* 3 (1981) 4–52.

Bulhan, Hussein Abdilahi. *Frantz Fanon and the Psychology of Oppression.* New York: Plenum, 1985.

Burridge, William. *Destiny Africa: Cardinal Lavigerie and the Making of the White Fathers.* London: Chapman, 1966.

Busia, Kofi A. *Africa in Search of Democracy.* London: Routledge & Paul, 1967.

———. *The Challenge of Africa.* New York: Praeger, 1962.

———. "The Commitment of the Laity in the Growth of the Church and the Integral Development of Africa." *Laity Today* (1972) 239–46.

———. "Has the Christian Faith Been Adequately Represented?" *International Review of Missions* 50 (1963) 86–89.

———. *The Position of the Chief in the Modern Political System in Ashanti.* London: Cass, 1968.

———. *Purposeful Education in Africa.* The Hague: Mouton, 1968.

———. *Report on a Social Survey of Sekondi-Takoradi.* London: Crown Agents, 1950.

Butty, John. "Africa Trade Law: One Year After." *West Africa*, no. 4278, June 4, 2001, 26–27.

Byers, David M., ed. *Justice in the Marketplace: Collected Statements of the Vatican and the United States Catholic Bishops on Economic Policy, 1891–1984.* Washington, DC: United States Catholic Conference, 1985.

Cacioppo, John T., and William Patrick. *Loneliness: Human Nature and the Need for Social Connection.* New York: Norton, 2008.

Cairns, H. Alan C. *Prelude to Imperialism: British Reactions to Central African Society, 1840–1890.* London: Routledge & Paul, 1965.

Campenhausen, Hans von. *Tradition and Life in the Church: Essays and Lectures in Church History.* London: Collins, 1968.

Camps, Arnulf. *Partners in Dialogue: Christianity and Other World Religions.* Maryknoll: Orbis, 1983.

Carson, Ben. *Take the Risk: Learning to Identify, Choose, and Live with Acceptable Risk.* With Gregg Lewis. Grand Rapids: Zondervan, 2008.

Carter, Stephen L. *Civility: Manners, Morals, and the Etiquette of Democracy.* New York: Basic Books, 1998.

Cary, Joyce. *Mister Johnson.* New York: Harper, 1939.

Casas, Bartolomé de las. *The Devastation of the Indies: A Brief Account.* Translated by Herma Briffault. Baltimore: Johns Hopkins University Press, 1992.

CELAM. *The Church in the Present-Day Transformation of Latin America in the Light of the Council, II: Conclusions.* Bogota: CELAM, 1970.

Césaire, Aimé. *Discours sur le colonialisme.* Paris: Présence Africaine, 1950.

Chabal, Patrick. *A History of Postcolonial Lusophone Africa.* London: Hurst, 2002.

Chikane, Frank. *The Things That Could Not Be Said: From A(IDS) to Z(imbabwe).* Johannesburg: Picador Africa, 2013.

"The Chilcot Report, Iraq's Grim Lessons." *Economist*, July 9–15, 2016, 48–49.

"Chinois Rites." *Catholicisme.* Paris, 1930. 2.1060–63.

Christaller, Johann G. *A Dictionary of the Asante and Fante Language Called Tshi (Twi)*. Basel: Basel Evangelical Missionary Society, 1933.

Church of England, Development Affairs Committee. *Let Justice Flow: A Contribution to the Debate about Development*. London: Church House, 1986.

Cochrane, Charles Norris. *Christianity and Classical Culture: A Study of Thought and Action from Augustus to Augustine*. Oxford: Clarendon, 1940.

Coe, Shoki. "Contextualisation." *Theological Education* 11, no. 1 (1974) 5–7.

Commission Appointed to Enquire into the Functions, Operation, and Administration of the Workers Brigade. *Report of the Commission Appointed to Enquire into the Functions, Operations, and Administration of the Workers' Brigade*. Accra: Ministry of Information, 1968.

Commission of Enquiry into Irregularities and Malpractices in the Grant of Import Licenses. *Summary of the Report of the Commission of Enquiry into Irregularities and Malpractices in Connection with the Grant of Import Licenses*. Accra: Ministry of Information, 1967.

Commission of Enquiry into Kwame Nkrumah Properties. *Report of the Commission [of Enquiry] into Kwame Nkrumah Properties*. Accra: Ministry of Information, 1967.

Commission of Enquiry into Trade Malpractices in Ghana. *Report of the Commission of Enquiry into Trade Malpractices in Ghana*. Accra: Ministry of Information, 1965.

Commission of Enquiry on the Commercial Activities of the Erstwhile Publicity Secretariat. *Report of the Commission of Enquiry on the Commercial Activities of the Erstwhile Publicity Secretariat*. Accra: Government Information Services, 1967.

Cone, James H. *Black Theology and Black Power*. New York: Seabury, 1969.

Cone, James H., and Gayraud S. Wilmore, eds. *Black Theology: A Documentary History*. Vol. 2, *1980–1992*. Maryknoll: Orbis, 1993.

Congar, Yves. "Christianisme comme foi et comme culture." In *Evangelizzazione e culture: atti del Congresso internazionale scientifico di missiologia, Roma, 5–12 ottobre 1975*, 1:83–103. Rome: Pontificia Universita Urbaniana, 1976.

Congress for Cultural Freedom. *Science and Freedom: The Proceedings of the Conference Convened by the Congress for Cultural Freedom*. [London]: Secker & Warburg, 1955.

Conradie, Ernst M., ed. *South African Perspectives on Notions and Forms of Ecumenicity*. Stellenbosch, South Africa: SUN, 2013.

Cook, Guillermo. *The Expectation of the Poor*. Maryknoll: Orbis, 1985.

———, ed. *New Face of Church in Latin America*. Maryknoll: Orbis, 1994.

Couper, Scott. *Albert Luthuli: Bound by Faith*. Scottsville, South Africa: Univ. of KwaZulu-Natal Press, 2010.

Cox, Harvey. *The Silencing of Leonardo Boff: The Vatican and the Future of World Christianity*. Oak Park, IL: Meyer-Stone, 1988.

Cox, Idris. *Socialist Ideas in Africa*. London: Lawrence and Wishart, 1966.

Crollius, Ary A. Roest. "Inculturation and Incarnation: On Speaking of the Christian Faith and Cultures of Humanity." *Bulletin: Secretariatus pro Non Christianis* 12 (1978) 138–40.

———. "What Is So New about Inculturation? A Concept and Its Implications." *Gregorianum* 59 (1978) 721–38.

Cross, F. L., ed. *Oxford Dictionary of the Christian Church*. London: Oxford University Press, 1958.

Cullmann, Oscar. *The Christology of the New Testament*. London: SCM, 1963.

Daneel, Marthinus L. *Old and New in Southern Shona Independent Churches*. Vol. 1, *Background and Rise of the Major Movements*. The Hague: Mouton, 1971.

———. *Quest for Belonging: Introduction to a Study of African Independent Churches.* Gweru, Zimbabwe: Mambo, 1987.

Davies, William David. *The Gospel and the Land.* Berkeley: Univ. of California Press, 1974.

Day, Laura. *Practical Intuition: How to Harness the Power of Your Instinct and Make It Work for You.* New York: Broadway, 1996.

De Gruchy, John W. *Doing Christian Theology in the Context of South Africa, or, God-Talk under Devil's Peak.* Cape Town: Univ. of Cape Town, 1986.

———. "Quality, Authenticity, Creativity, and Ecumenical Theological Education." *Ministerial Formation* 67 (1994) 46–49.

———. *Theology and Ministry in Context and Crisis: A South African Perspective.* London: Collins, 1987.

De Gruchy, John W., and Charles Villa-Vicencio, eds. *Apartheid Is a Heresy.* Cape Town: David Philip, 1983.

De Vries, Egbert, ed. *Man in Community: Christian Concern for the Human in Changing Society.* New York: Association, 1966.

Debrunner, Hans W. *Witchcraft in Ghana.* Accra: Presbyterian Book Depot, 1959.

Denis, Philippe, ed. *Orality, Memory, and the Past: Listening to the Voices of Black Clergy under Colonialism and Apartheid.* Pietermaritzburg: Cluster, 2000.

Deresiewicz, William. "The Disadvantages of an Elite Education." *American Scholar*, June 1, 2008. https://theamericanscholar.org/the-disadvantages-of-an-elite-education/#.VxmDLz89al4.

———. "The End of Solitude." *Chronicle of Higher Education* 55 (2009) B6, 21.

Desai, Ram, ed. *Christianity in Africa as Seen by Africans.* Denver: Swallow, 1962.

Diamond, Jared M. *Collapse: How Societies Choose to Fail or Succeed.* New York: Penguin, 2005.

Dillistone, Frederick William. *Christianity and Symbolism.* London: Collins, 1955.

———, ed. *Myth and Symbol.* London: SPCK, 1966.

Dionysius of Halicarnassus. *Ars Rhetorica.* Leipzig: Teubner, 1895.

Dodd, C. H. *According to the Scriptures: The Sub-Structure of New Testament Theology.* London: Nisbet, 1952.

———. *The Apostolic Preaching and Its Developments.* London: Hodder & Stoughton, 1936.

———. *The Johannine Epistles.* London: Hodder & Stoughton, 1946.

Du Toit, Cornel W., ed. *The Legacy of Stephen Bantu Biko: Theological Challenges.* Pretoria: Univ. of South Africa, Research Institute for Theology and Religion, 2008.

Dulles, Avery. *Models of the Church.* Garden City: Doubleday, 1974.

Dumas, André. *Die Kirche als Faktor einer kommenden Weltgemeinschaft.* Berlin: Kreuz, 1966.

Dupré, Louis K. *Symbols of the Sacred.* Grand Rapids: Eerdmans, 2001.

Durkheim, Émile. *The Division of Labor in Society.* Glencoe, IL: Free Press, 1947.

———. *The Elementary Forms of Religious Life: A Study in Religious Life.* London: Allen & Unwin, 1926.

Eagleson, John, and Philip J. Scharper, eds. *Puebla and Beyond: Documentation and Commentary.* Maryknoll: Orbis, 1979.

Ebeling, Gerhard. *Luther: An Introduction to His Thought.* London: Collins, 1972.

Edwards, Michael. "The Irrelevance of Development Studies." *Third World Quarterly* 11, no. 1 (1989) 116–35.

El-Bizri, Nader. "Uneasy Meditations Following Lévinas." *Studia Phaenomenologica* 6 (2006) 293–315.

Ela, Jean-Marc. *My Faith as an African*. Maryknoll: Orbis, 1988.

Eliade, Mircea. *The Sacred and the Profane: The Nature of Religion*. New York: Harcourt, 1968.

Elliott, Charles. *Patterns of Poverty in the Third World: A Study of Social and Economic Stratification*. With Françoise de Morsier. New York: Praeger, 1985.

Elliott, Lawrence. *I Will Be Called John*. New York: Dutton, 1973.

Elphick, Richard E., and Rodney Davenport, eds. *Christianity in South Africa: Political, Social, and Cultural History*. Berkeley: Univ. of California Press, 1997.

Elsa Tamez. *When the Horizons Close: Rereading Ecclesiastes*. Maryknoll: Orbis, 2000.

Evans, James H., Jr., comp. *Black Theology: A Critical Assessment and Annotated Bibliography*. New York: Greenwood, 1987.

Fabella, Virginia, and Mercy Amba Oduyoye, eds. *With Passion and Compassion: Third World Women Doing Theology*. Maryknoll: Orbis, 1988.

Fage, J. G. *A History of Africa*. New York: Knopf, 1978.

Fanon, Frantz. *Black Skin, White Masks*. New York: Grove, 1967; orig., 1952.

———. *A Dying Colonialism*. New York: Grove, 1965; orig., 1959.

———. *Toward the African Revolution*. New York: Grove, 1969; orig., 1964.

———. *The Wretched of the Earth*. New York: Grove, 1963; orig., 1961.

Farley, Edward. *Theologia: The Fragmentation and Unity of Theological Education*. Philadelphia: Fortress, 1983.

Fernandez, James W. "Rededication and Prophetism in Ghana." *Cahiers d'études africaines* 10 (1970) 228–305.

Field, Margaret Joyce. *Search for Security: An Ethno-Psychiatric Study of Rural Ghana*. London: Faber and Faber, 1960.

———. "Some New Shrines of the Gold Coast and Their Significance." *Africa* 13 (1940) 138–49.

Fortes, Meyer, and E. E. Evans-Pritchard, eds. *African Political Systems*. London: Oxford University Press, 1940.

Francis, James M. M., and Leslie J. Francis, eds. *Tentmaking: Perspectives on Self-Supporting Ministry*. Leominster, UK: Gracewing, 1998.

Frend, W. H. C. *The Rise of Christianity*. Philadelphia: Fortress, 1984.

Frostin, Per. *Liberation Theology in Tanzania and South Africa: A First World Interpretation*. Lund: Lund University Press, 1988.

Funeral Orations by St. Gregory Nazianzen and St. Ambrose. Vol. 22 of *The Fathers of the Church*. Translated by Leo P. McCauley et al. New York: Catholic Univ. of America Press, 1953.

George, Susan. *The Debt Boomerang: How Third World Debt Harms Us All*. London: Pluto, 1992.

———. *A Fate Worse than Debt: The World Financial Crisis and the Poor*. New York: Grove Weidenfeld, 1990.

Ghana Statistical Service. Population and Housing Census. 2012.

Gibellini, Rosino, ed. *Fanonian Practices in South Africa*. Scotsville, South Africa: Univ. of KwaZulu–Natal Press, 2011.

———. *Frontiers of Theology in Latin America*. London: SCM, 1980.

———, ed. *Paths of African Theology*. London: SCM, 1994.

Gibson, Nigel C. *Fanon: The Postcolonial Imagination*. Oxford: Polity, 2003.

Gifford, Paul. "Africa's Inculturation Theology: Observations of an Outsider." *Hekima Review* 38 (2008) 18–34. https://eprints.soas.ac.uk/7956/1/AfricasInculturationTheology.pdf.

Glazer, Nathan, and Daniel Patrick Moynihan. *Beyond the Melting Pot: The Negroes, Puerto Ricans, Jews, Italians, and Irish of New York City*. Cambridge: MIT Press, 1963.

Gluckman, Max. *Custom and Conflict in Africa*. Oxford: Blackwell, 1955.

———. "Social Aspects of First Fruit Ceremonies among the South-Eastern Bantu." *Africa* 11 (1938) 25–41.

Gold Coast Commission of Enquiry into Mr. Braimah's Resignation and Allegations Arising Therefrom. *Report of the Commission of Enquiry into Mr. Braimah's Resignation and Allegations Arising Therefrom*. Accra: Government Printing Department, 1954.

Goldberg, Michelle. *Kingdom Coming: The Rise of Christian Nationalism*. New York: Norton, 2006.

Grant, Jacqueline. *White Women's Christ and Black Women's Jesus: Feminist Christology and Womanist Response*. Atlanta: Scholars, 1989.

Gray, Richard. *Black Christians and White Missionaries*. New Haven: Yale University Press, 1990.

Greenslade, S. L. "Augustine." *Chambers's Encyclopedia*, 1:774.

———. *Schism in the Early Church*. London: SCM, 1964.

Grenholm, Carl-Henric. *Christian Social Ethics in a Revolutionary Age*. Uppsala: Verbum, 1973.

Griffiths, Paul J., ed. *Christianity through Non-Christian Eyes*. Maryknoll: Orbis, 1990.

Groves, C. P. *The Planting of Christianity in Africa*. London: Lutterworth, 1948–1958.

Gutiérrez, Gustavo. *The Power of the Poor in History*. Maryknoll: Orbis, 1983.

———. *A Theology of Liberation: History, Politics, and Salvation*. Maryknoll: Orbis, 1988.

Hagan, George P. "Human Rights and the Democratic Process." *Symposium on the Concept and Practice of Human Rights in Ghana*. Accra, Ghana Academy of Arts and Sciences, Twenty-First Anniversary Celebration, November 1980.

Hahn, Niels. "US Covert Operations in Liberia: Washington Removes Three Governments." *Africa Watch*, February/March 2016, 57–69.

Haliburton, Gordon Mackay. *The Prophet Harris: A Study of an African Prophet and His Mass-Movement in the Ivory Coast and the Gold Coast, 1913–1915*. London: Longman, 1971.

Hallencreutz, Carl F. *New Approaches to Men of Other Faiths*. Geneva: World Council of Churches, 1970.

Hardy, Barbara Nathan. *Tellers and Listeners: The Narrative Imagination*. London: Athlone, 1975.

Hargreaves, John D. *West Africa Partitioned*. Vol. 2, *The Elephants and the Grass*. Madison: Univ. of Wisconsin Press, 1985.

Hastings, Adrian. *Igreja e Missões Cucujaes*. N.p., 1975.

———. *Wiriyamu*. London: Search, 1974.

Hastings, James, ed. *Encyclopaedia of Religion and Ethics*. Edinburgh: T. & T. Clark, 1910.

Hauerwas, Stanley, and L. G. Jones, eds. *Why Narrative? Studies in Narrative Theology*. New York: Eerdmans, 1989.

Hayford, J. E. Casely. *Ethiopia Unbound: Studies in Race Emancipation*. London: Phillips, 1911.

Hazlitt, William. *Memoirs of Thomas Holcroft*. Vol. 2 of William Hazlitt, *Collected Works*. Edited by A. R. Waller and Arnold Glover. London: Dent, 1902.

Hebblethwaite, Peter. *John XXIII: Pope of the Council*. London: Chapman, 1984.
Hedges, Chris. *Empire of Illusion: The End of Literacy and the Triumph of Spectacle*. New York: Nation, 2009.
Hegel, Georg Wilhelm Friedrich. *Lectures in the Philosophy of World History: Introduction, Reason in History*. New York: Cambridge University Press, 1975.
Herrin, Judith. *The Formation of Christendom*. Princeton: Princeton University Press, 1987.
Herskovits, Melville J. *Man and His Works: The Science of Cultural Anthropology*. New York: Knopf, 1952.
Hetherington, Penelope. *British Paternalism and Africa, 1920-1940*. London: Cass, 1978.
Hinkelammert, Franz. *Crítica a la razón utópica*. San Jose, Costa Rica: Departamento Ecuménico de Investigaciones, 1984.
———. "El cautiverio de la utopía: Las utopías conservadoras del capitalismo actual, el neoliberalismo y la dialéctica de las alternativas." *Passos* 50 (1993) 1–14.
———. "La lógica de la exculsión del mercado capitalista mundial y el proyecto de liberación." In *América Latina: Resistir por la vida*. San Jose, Costa Rica: REDLA-CPID, 1994.
Hodges, Harold M. *Conflict and Consensus: An Introduction to Sociology*. New York: Harper & Row, 1971.
Hofmeyer, J. W., and W. S. Vorster, eds. *New Faces of Africa: Essays in Honour of Ben (Barend Jocobos) Marais*. Pretoria: Univ. of South Africa, 1984.
Howse, Ernest Marshall. *Saints in Politics: The "Clapham Sect" and the Growth of Freedom*. London: Allan & Unwin, 1952.
Hughes, H. Stuart. *Consciousness and Society: The Reorientation of European Social Thought, 1890-1930*. New York: Octagon, 1976.
Humanitas Religiosa: Festschrift für Haralds Biezais. Stockholm: Almqvist & Wiksell, 1979.
Huntington, Samuel P. "The Clash of Civilizations?" *Foreign Affairs* 72, no. 3 (1993) 22–49.
Hussain, Amir. "McGinley Lecture Response: Fall 2010." Fordham University, November 15, 2010.
Irvine, Sandy. "If We Want a Future, It Can Only Be a Green Future." *Independent*, April 1, 1992, 12–15.
Jakobsson, Stiv. *Am I Not a Man and a Brother? British Mission and the Abolition of the Slave Trade and Slavery in West Africa and the West Indies, 1786-1838*. Lund: Gleerup, 1972.
Jevons, W. Stanley. *The Theory of Political Economy*. New York: Macmillan, 1871.
John XXIII. *Ad Petri Cathedram; Encyclical on Truth, Unity, and Peace, in a Spirit of Charity, June 29, 1959*. London: Catholic Tract Society, 1959.
Johnson, James, to Laing, Church Missionary Society, March 9, 1882, G3/A2/1.
Johnstone, Patrick J. *Operation World*. Carlisle, UK: OM, 1993.
Jones, A. H. M. *Constantine and the Conversion of Europe*. London: English Universities Press, 1948.
Jung, Carl G. *Memories, Dreams, and Reflections*. New York: HarperCollins, 1995.
Kanyoro, Musimbi. "Challenges of Feminist Theologies to Ministerial Formation." *Ministerial Formation* 74 (1996) 3–22.
Kanyoro, Musimbi R. A., and Nyambura J. Njoroge, eds. *Groaning in Faith: African Women in the Household of God*. Nairobi: Acton, 1996.
Kaplan, Justin, ed. *Barlett's Familiar Quotations*. 17th ed. Boston: Little, Brown, 2002.
Karis, Thomas, and Gwendolen Margaret Carter, eds. *From Protest to Challenge: A Documentary History of African Politics in South Africa, 1882-1964*. Vol. 3, *Challenge and Violence, 1953-1964*. Stanford: Hoover Institution Press, 1977.

Katjavivi, Peter, et al. *Church and Liberation in Namibia*. London: Pluto, 1989.
Kaunda, Kenneth D. *Letter to My Children*. London: Longman, 1973.
Kaunda, Kenneth D., and Colin Morris. *A Humanist in Africa*. Nashville: Abingdon, 1966.
Keil, Carl Friedrich, and Franz Delitzsch. *Commentary on the Old Testament*. Vol. 1, *The Pentateuch*. Peabody: Hendrickson, 1989.
Kierkegaard, Søren. *Fear and Trembling and the Sickness unto Death*. Translated by Walter Lowrie. Princeton: Princeton University Press, 1941.
Kimble, David. *A Political History of Ghana: The Rise of Gold Coast Nationalism, 1850–1928*. Oxford: Clarendon, 1963.
King, Martin Luther, Jr. *Letter from the Birmingham Jail*. San Francisco: Harper, 1994.
———. *Stride toward Freedom*. New York: Harper & Row, 1958.
———. *Why We Can't Wait*. New York: Signet, 1964.
King, Noel Quinton. *The Emperor Theodosius and the Establishment of Christianity*. London: SCM, 1961.
Kinsler, F. Ross. "Mission and Context: The Current Debate about Contextualization." *Evangelical Missions Quarterly* 14 (1978) 23–29.
Kittler, Glenn D. *The White Fathers*. New York: Harper, 1957.
Klinenberg, Eric. *Going Solo: The Extraordinary Rise and Surprising Appeal of Living Alone*. New York: Penguin, 2013.
Kollbrunner, Fritz. "Die Akkommodation im Geist der Katholizität (1919–1959)." *Neue Zeitschrift für Missionswissenschaft* 28 (1972) 161–84, 264–74.
Kraemer, Hendrik. *Religion and the Christian Faith*. London: Lutterworth, 1956.
Kuma, Afua. *Jesus of the Deep Forest*. Translated by John Kirby. Accra: Asempa, 1981.
Kunambi, B. N. "Women of Africa: Awake!" *African Ecclesiastical Review* (*AFER*) 13, no. 4 (1971) 302–4.
Kwarteng, Kwasi. *Ghosts of Empire: Britain's Legacies in the Modern World*. London: Bloomsbury, 2011.
La Mettrie, Julien Offray de. *L'Histoire naturelle de l'âme* [The natural history of the soul]. 1745.
———. *L'Homme machine* [Man a machine]. 1747.
Langer, Susanne K. *Philosophy in a New Key: A Study in the Symbolism of Reason, Rite, and Art*. Cambridge: Harvard University Press, 1942.
Larbi, Emmanuel Kingsley. *Pentecostalism: The Eddies of Ghanaian Christianity*. Accra: Centre for Pentecostal and Charismatic Studies, 2001.
Laryea, Philip T. *Ephraim Amu: Nationalist, Poet, and Theologian (1899–1995)*. Akropong-Akuapem, Ghana: Regnum Africa, 2012.
Latourette, Kenneth Scott. *A History of Christianity*. New York: Harper, 1953.
———. *A History of the Expansion of Christianity*. New York: Harper, 1937–1945.
Lean, Garth. *God's Politician: William Wilberforce's Struggle*. London: Darton, Longman, and Todd, 1980.
Lederle, Henry I. "The Spirit of Unity: A Discomforting Comforter; Some Reflections on the Holy Spirit, Ecumenism, and Pentecostal-Charismatic Movements." *Ecumenical Review* 42, no. 3–4 (1990) 279–87.
———. *Treasures Old and New: Interpretations of "Spirit-Baptism" in the Charismatic Renewal Movement*. Peabody: Hendrickson, 1988.
Legge, James. *The Chinese Classics: With a Translation, Critical and Exegetical Notes, Prolegomena, and Copious Indexes*. Vol 2, *The Works of Mencius*. 2nd ed. Oxford: Clarendon, 1895.

Lehmann, Paul. *Ethics in a Christian Context*. New York: Harper & Row, 1969.
Lenin, V. I. *Collected Works*. Edited by Robert Daglish. Moscow: Progress, 1946.
———. *The Three Sources and Three Component Parts of Marxism*. Moscow: Foreign Languages Publishing House, 1913; repr., 1961.
Lenski, Gerald. "Religious Pluralism in Theoretical Perspective." *Internationales Jahrbuch für Religionssoziologie* 1 (1965) 25–42.
Lévinas, Emmanuel. *Die Zeit und der Andere*. Hamburg: Meiner, 2003; orig., *Le temps et l'autre* [Time and the other]. Grenoble, France: Arthaud, 1948.
———. *Humanisme de l'autre homme* [Humanism of the other]. Paris: Livre de Poche, 1987.
Lewis, I. M. *Ecstatic Religion: An Anthropological Study of Spirit Possession and Shamanism*. Harmondsworth: Pelican, 1976.
———, ed. *Islam in Tropical Africa*. London: Oxford University Press, 1966.
Lienemann-Perrin, Christine. *Training for a Relevant Ministry: A Study of the Contribution of the Theological Education Fund*. Madras: Christian Literature Society, [1981].
Lietzmann, Hans. *The Beginnings of the Christian Church*. Translated by Bertram Lee Woolf. London: Nicholson & Watson, 1937.
Lightfoot, J. B. *St. Paul's Epistle to the Galatians*. London: MacMillan, 1868.
Lindars, Barnabas. *The Gospel of John*. London: Marshall, Morgan & Scott, 1972.
Livingstone, David. *Missionary Travels and Researches in South Africa; including a Sketch of Sixteen Years' Residence in the Interior of Africa*. . . . London: Murray, 1857.
Long, Charles H. "The Black Reality: Toward a Theology of Freedom." *Criterion* 8, no. 2 (1969) 2–7.
Lossky, Nicolas, ed. *Dictionary of the Ecumenical Movement*. Geneva: WCC Publications, 1991, 2002.
Lugard, Frederick Dealty. *The Dependencies of the British Empire and the Responsibilities They Involve*. London: Birkbeck College, 1928.
———. *The Dual Mandate in British Tropical Africa*. London: Blackwood, 1922.
Lund, John Magne, and Paul Weinberg. *The Church's Secret Agent: Archbishop Walter Makhulu and the Fight against Apartheid*. Oslo: Press Publishing, 2002.
Luther, Martin. *Table Talk*. Translated by William Hazlitt. Rev ed. Gainesville, FL: Bridge-Logos, 2004.
Luthuli, Albert. "Evangelism for Educated Bantu Youth." *South African Outlook* (October 1940; University of KwaZulu-Natal, Killie Campbell Africana Library, Book and Manuscript Collections, KCP 5319, 276, LUT 8832.
Lyimo, Cammilus. "The Quest for a Relevant African Theology." *African Ecclesiastical Review* 18 (1973) 140–43.
Macquarrie, John. *Principles of Christian Theology*. London: SCM, 1966.
Magesa, Laurenti. "Catholic Yet African: Authentic Self-Assertion of the Church and African Culture." *African Ecclesiastical Review* 15 (1973) 110–18.
———. "Return to the World: Towards a 'Theocentric Existentialism' in Africa." *African Ecclesiastical Review* 16, no. 3 (1974) 277–84.
Malinowski, Bronislaw. *A Scientific Theory of Culture*. Chapel Hill: Univ. of North Carolina Press, 1944.
Malinowski, Bronislaw, and Phyllis Mary Kaberry, eds. *The Dynamics of Culture Change: An Inquiry into Race Relations in Africa*. New Haven: Yale University Press, 1946.
Malthus, Thomas Robert. *An Essay on the Principle of Population*. London: Johnson, 1798.

Mandela, Nelson. "Renewal and Renaissance: Towards a New World Order." Lecture, Oxford Centre for Islamic Studies, July 11, 1997. http://www.mandela.gov.za/mandela_speeches/1997/970711_oxford.htm.
Mangcu, Xolela. *Biko: A Biography*. Cape Town: Tafelberg, 2012.
Mannheim, Karl. *Ideology and Utopia: An Introduction to the Sociology of Knowledge*. London: Routledge & Paul, 1960.
Marett, R. R. *Anthropology*. London: Williams & Norgate, 1911.
———. *The Threshold of Religion*. London: Methuen, 1914.
Markus, R. A. *Saeculum: History and Society in the Theology of St. Augustine*. Cambridge: Cambridge University Press, 1970.
Marshall, Alfred. *Principles of Economics*. London: Macmillan, 1890.
Martin, Marie-Louise. *The Biblical Concept of Messianism and Messianism in Southern Africa*. Morija, South Africa: Morija Sesuto Book Depot, 1964.
———. *Kimbangu: An African Prophet and His Church*. Oxford: Blackwell, 1975.
Marx, Karl. *A Contribution to the Critique of the Hegel's Philosophy of Right: Introduction*. [In German.] *Deutsch-Französische Jahrbucher* (1844) 378–91.
Mashele, Prince. *The Death of Our Society*. Pretoria: CPR Press, 2011.
Masson, Joseph. "L'Église ouverte sur le monde." *Nouvelle Revue de Théologie* 84 (1962) 1032–43.
Mawby, Colin. "How Can You Hear Sacred Music without Thinking of God?" *L'Obsservatore Romano* 28, November 2012.
Mayes, Andrew. *Spirituality in Ministerial Formation: The Dynamic of Prayer in Learning*. Cardiff: Univ. of Wales Press, 2009.
Mayson, Cedric. "A Deeply Spiritual Document: The Freedom Charter." *Umrabulo* 11, June–July 2006.
Mazrui, Ali A. "Nkrumah: The Leninist Czar." *Transition* 26 (1966) 9–17.
Mbeki, Thabo. "He Awakened to His Responsibilities." Lecture. University of Fort Hare, South Africa, October 12, 2001.
Mbiti, John S. *African Religions and Philosophy*. New York: Doubleday, 1969.
McCallum, J. Ramsay. *Abelard's Christian Theology*. Oxford: Blackwell, 1948.
Anthropological Society of London. *Memoirs Read before the Anthropological Society of London, 1863–1864*. London: The Society, 1864.
Mesters, Carlos. *Defenseless Flowers: A New Reading of the Bible*. Maryknoll: Orbis, 1991.
Meyendorff, John. *Imperial Unity and Christian Divisions: The Church, AD 450–680*. Crestwood, NY: St. Vladimir's Seminary Press, 1989.
———. *Living Tradition: Orthodox Witness in the Contemporary World*. Crestwood, NY: St. Vladimir's Seminary Press, 1978.
Middleton, John, and David Tait, eds. *Tribes without Rulers*. London: Routledge & Paul, 1970.
Mill, John Stuart. *Principles of Political Economy with Some of Their Applications to Social Philosophy*. London: Routledge, 1847.
Minear, Paul S. *Images of the Church in the New Testament*. Philadelphia: Westminster, 1960.
Mofokeng, Takatso A. *The Crucified among the Crossbearers: Towards a Black Christology*. Kampen: Kok, 1985.
Montesquieu, *De l'esprit des lois*. 1748.
Moreira, Adriano. *Portugal's Stand in Africa*. New York: University Publishers, 1962.
Mosala, Itumeleng J. *Biblical Hermeneutics and Black Theology in South Africa*. Grand Rapids: Eerdmans, 1989.

Moule, C. F. D. *The Birth of the New Testament*. London: Black, 1962.
———. *The Origin of Christology*. Cambridge: Cambridge University Press, 1977.
———. *Worship in the New Testament*. London: SCM, 1961.
Mud Flower Collective. *God's Fierce Whimsy: Christian Feminism and Theological Education*. New York: Pilgrim, 1985.
Mugambi, J. N. Kanyua. *Christian Theology and Social Reconstruction*. Nairobi: Acton, 2003.
———. *From Liberation to Reconstruction: African Theology after the Cold War*. Nairobi: East Africa Educational, 1995.
Mugambi, J. N., and Laurenti Magesa, eds. *Jesus in African Christianity: Experimentation and Diversity in African Christology*. Nairobi: Initiatives, 1989.
Mutiso-Mbinda, John. "Inkulturation: Eine Aufgabe für die afrikanische Kirche." *Zeitschrift für Missionswissenschaft und Religionswissenschaft* 2/3 (1986) 164–71.
Mveng, Engelbert. "Afrikanisches Profil von Theologie und Kirche." *Zeitschrift für Missionswissenschaft und Religionswissenschaft* 2/3 (1986) 154–63.
Nash, Margaret, ed. *Your Kingdom Come*. Braamfontein: South African Council of Churches, 1980.
Neill, Stephen. *Christian Faith and Other Faiths: The Christian Dialogue with Other Religions*. Oxford: Oxford University Press, 1970.
———. *Colonialism and Christian Missions*. London: Lutterworth, 1966.
Nessen, Craig L. *Orthopraxis or Heresy: The North American Theological Response to Latin American Liberation Theology*. Atlanta: Scholars, 1989.
New African 440 (March 2006).
"A New Force of Christian Churches—OAIC Manifesto." *Baragamu: The African Independent Churches' Voice* 1, July 1996.
Newbigin, Lesslie. "The Basis, Purpose, and Manner of Inter-Faith Dialogue." *Scottish Journal of Theology* 30, no. 3 (1977) 253–70.
———. *Theological Education and the Scientific Approach*. Geneva: World Council of Churches, 1980.
Newman, John Henry. *An Essay on the Development of Christian Doctrine*. London: Longmans & Green, 1906; orig., 1845.
———. *The Idea of a University*. Charlotte, NC: Saint Benedict, 2006.
———. *The Idea of a University*. London: Baronius, 2006.
Ngũgĩ wa Thiong'o. *The Black Hermit*. London: Heinemann, 1968.
———. *A Grain of Wheat*. London: Heinemann, 1966.
———. *The River Between*. London: Heinemann, 1965.
———. *Weep Not, Child*. London: Heinemann, 1964.
Nicolson, Ronald. *A Black Future? Jesus and Salvation in South Africa*. London: SCM, 1990.
Niebuhr, H. Richard. *Christ and Culture*. New York: HarperCollins, 2001.
Njoroge, Nyambura Jane. *Kiama Kia Ngo: An African Christian Feminist Ethic of Resistance and Transformation*. Accra: Asempa, 2000.
Nketia, J. H. "The Contribution of African Culture to Christian Worship." *International Review of Mission* 47, no. 187 (1958) 265–78.
———. *Folk Songs of Ghana*. Legon: University of Ghana, 1963.
———. *Music in African Cultures*. Legon: University of Ghana, 1966.
Nkrumah, Kwame. *Axioms of Kwame Nkrumah: Freedom Fighters Edition*. London: PANAF Books, 1967.

———. *Consciencism: Philosophy and Ideology for Decolonization and Development with Particular Reference to the African Revolution.* London: Heinemann Educational Books, 1964.

———. *Ghana: The Autobiography of Kwame Nkrumah.* Edinburgh: Nelson, 1957.

———. *Neo-colonialism: The Last Stage of Imperialism.* London: Nelson, 1965.

———. *Speech at Conference of Independent African States.* Accra: September 15, 1958.

Nolan, Albert. *God in South Africa: The Challenge of the Gospel.* Cape Town: Philip, 1988.

———. *Jesus before Christianity.* Cape Town: Philip, 1976.

Nussbaum, Stan, ed. *Freedom and Independence.* Nairobi: OAIC, 1994.

Nyamiti, Charles. *Christ as Our Ancestor: Christology from an African Perspective.* Gweru, Zimbabwe: Mambo, 1984.

Nzo, Alfred. "The Freedom Charter: A Beacon to the People of South Africa." *African Communist*, second quarter 1980, 23–37.

O'Connor, Daniel, ed. *Three Centuries of Mission: The United Society for the Propagation of the Gospel, 1701–2000.* London: Continuum, 2000.

Ocran, Albert Kwesi. *A Myth Is Broken: An Account of the Ghana Coup d'Etat of 24th February 1966.* New York: Humanities, 1968.

Oduyoye, Mercy Amba. "An African Woman's Christ," *Voices from the Third World* 2, no. 2 (1988) 119–24.

———. *Daughters of Anowa: African Women and Patriarchy.* Maryknoll: Orbis, 1995.

———. *Who Will Roll the Stone Away? The Ecumenical Decade of the Churches in Solidarity with Women.* Geneva: World Council of Churches, 1990.

Oduyoye, Mercy Amba, and Musimbi Kanyoro, eds. *Talitha Qumi! Proceedings of the Convocation of African Women Theologians, 1989.* Ibadan: Daystar, 1990.

Okolo, Chukwudumu B. "Diminished Man and Theology: An African Perspective." *African Ecclesiastical Review (AFER)* 18, no. 2 (1976) 83–86.

Oldham, J. H., ed. *The Churches Survey Their Task: The Report of the Conference at Oxford, July 1937, on Church, Community, and State.* London: Allen & Unwin, 1937.

Olds, Jacqueline, and Richard Schwartz. *The Lonely Americans: Drifting Apart in the Twenty-First Century.* Boston: Beacon, 2009.

Omoyajowo, J. Akin. "Christianity as a Unifying Factor in a Developing Country." *African Ecclesiastical Review* 17, no. 2 (1972) 74–79.

Onyango, Maurice. "Dialogue—The Dialogue: The Holy Spirit on the Move." *Baragamu: The African Independent Churches' Voice* 1 (1996) 2.

Oosthuizen, Gerhardus Cornelis. *Post-Christianity in Africa: A Theological and Anthropological Study.* London: Hurst, 1968.

Orchard, Ronald K., ed. *The Ghana Assembly of the International Missionary Council, 28th December, 1957, to 8th January, 1958.* London: Edinburgh House, 1958.

———, ed. *Witness in Six Continents.* London: Edinburgh House, 1964.

Orczy, Emmuska Orczy. *The Scarlet Pimpernel.* New York: Putnam, 1905.

Ortega, Ofelia, ed. *Women's Visions: Theological Reflection, Celebration, Action.* Geneva: WCC, 1995.

Otto, Rudolf. *The Idea of the Holy: An Inquiry into the Non-Rational Factor in the Idea of the Divine and Its Relation to the Rational.* London: Oxford University Press, 1923.

Ouologuem, Yambo. *Bound to Violence.* New York: Harcourt Brace Jovanovich, 1971.

Oyono, Ferdinand. *Houseboy.* London: Heinemann, 1960.

Pagha, Camille. *Glittering Images: A Journey through Art from Egypt to Star Wars*. New York: Pantheon, 2012.

Pandor, Naledi, et al. "The Challenge of Science in Building Democracy." Nelson Mandela Annual Lecture Dialogue. Nelson Mandela Foundation, July 22, 2011.

Parker, Theodore. *The American Idea; Speech at N.E. Anti-Slavery Convention*. Boston, May 29, 1850.

———. *A Discourse of Matters Pertaining to Religion*. Boston: Little, Brown, 1842.

Parrinder, Edward Geoffrey. *West African Religion*. London: Epworth, 1949.

Parvey, Constance F., ed. *The Community of Women and Men in the Church: A Report of the World Council of Churches' Conference, Sheffield, England, 1981*. Geneva: WCC, 1983.

Patterson, Orlando. *The Sociology of Slavery: An Analysis of the Origins, Development, and Structure of Negro Slave Society in Jamaica*. Rutherford, NJ: Fairleigh Dickinson University Press, 1967.

Paul, Annie Murphy. "Your Head Is in the Cloud." *Time*, March 12, 2012.

Pénoukou, Julien Efoé. *Églises d'Afrique: Propositions pour l'avenir*. Paris: Karthala, 1984.

Perbi, Akosua Adoma. *A History of Indigenous Slavery in Ghana from the Fifteenth to the Nineteenth Century*. Legon, Ghana: Sub-Saharan, 2004.

Perham, Margery Freda. *Lugard: The Years of Adventure, 1858-1898*. London: Collins, 1956.

Pew Research Center. "The Global Religious Landscape." December 18, 2012. http://www.pewforum.org/2012/12/18/global-religious-landscape-exec.

Phiri, Isabel Apawo. "Women, Church, and Theological Education." *Ministerial Formation* no. 71 (1995) 39-43.

Phiri, Isabel Apawo, et al., eds. *Her Stories: Hidden Histories of Women of Faith in Africa*. Pietermaritzburg: Cluster, 2002.

Phiri, Isabel Apawo, and Dietrich Werner, eds. *Handbook of Theological Education in Africa*. Pietermaritzburg: Cluster, 2013.

Pierce, Yolanda. "Restless Spirits: Syncretistic Religion in Edwidge Danticat's *Breath, Eyes, Memory*." *Journal of Panafrican Studies* 3, no. 5 (2010) 68-77. http://www.jpanafrican.org/docs/vol3no5/3.5-6newRestless.pdf.

Pityana, N. Barney, et al., eds. *Bounds of Possibility: The Legacy of Steve Biko and Black Consciousness*. Cape Town: David Philip, 1991.

Platvoet, Jan G. "*Nyame ne Aberewa*: Towards a History of Akan Notions of God." *Ghana Bulletin of Theology*, n.s., 4 (2012) 41-68.

Platvoet, Jan G., and Arie L. Molendijk, eds. *The Pragmatics of Defining Religion: Contexts, Concepts, and Contests*. Leiden: Brill, 1999.

Platvoet, Jan, and Henk van Rinsum. "Is Africa Incurably Religious? Confessing and Contesting an Invention." *Exchange: Journal of Missiological and Ecumenical Research* 32, 2 (2003) 123-53.

———. "Is Africa Incurably Religious? III: A Reply to a Rhetorical Response." *Exchange: Journal of Missiological and Ecumenical Research* 37, 2 (2008) 156-73.

Platvoet, Jan, James Cox, and Jacob Olupona, eds. *The Study of Religions in Africa: Past, Present, and Prospects*. Cambridge, UK: Roots and Branches, 1996.

Pobee, John S. *The Anglican Story in Ghana: From Mission Beginnings to Province of Ghana*. Accra: Amanza, 2009.

———. "Church and State in the Gold Coast in the Vasco da Gama Era, 1492-1947." *Journal of Church and State* 17, 2 (1975) 217-37.

———, ed. *Culture, Women, and Theology*. New Delhi: Indian Society for Promoting Christian Knowledge, 1994.

———, ed. *Exploring Afro-Christology*. Frankfurt: Lang, 1992.

———. *Grundlinien einer afrikanischen Theologie*. Göttingen: Vandenhoeck & Ruprecht, 1981.

———. "I Am First an African and, Second, a Christian." *Indian Missiological Review* 10, no. 3 (1989) 268–77.

———. "Identity, Religion, Nation: The Asante-Opoku-Reindorf Lecture, 2010." *Journal of African Christian Thought* 14, no. 1 (2011) 20–29.

———. "Jesus Christ—The Life of the World: An African Perspective." *Ministerial Formation* 21 (1983) 5–8.

———. *Kwame Nkrumah and the Church in Ghana, 1949–1966*. Accra: Asempa, 1988.

———. "Let Ethiopia Hasten to Stretch Out Its Hands to God." *Ecumenical Review* 49, no. 4 (1997) 416–26.

———. *Politics and Religion in Ghana*. Accra: Asempa, 1991.

———, ed. *Religion in a Pluralistic Society: Essays Presented to Rev. Prof. C. G. Baëta*. Leiden: Brill, 1976.

———, ed. *Religion, Morality, and Population Dynamics*. Legon: Population Dynamics, 1974.

———. *Skenosis: Christian Faith in an African Context*. Gweru, Zimbabwe: Mambo, 1992.

———. *Toward an African Theology*. Nashville: Abingdon, 1979.

———, ed. *Towards Viable Theological Education: Ecumenical Imperative, Catalyst of Renewal*. Geneva: World Council of Churches, 1997.

———. *West Africa: Christ Would Be an African Too*. Geneva: World Council of Churches, 1996.

———. *The Word Became Flesh: The Meeting of Christianity and African Cultures*. London: Catholic Missionary Education Centre, 1984.

———. *The Worship of the Free Market and the Death of the Poor*. Uppsala: Life and Peace Institute, 1994.

Pobee, John S., and Gabriel Ositelu II. *African Initiatives in Christianity: The Growth, Gifts, and Diversities of Indigenous African Churches—A Challenge to the Ecumenical Movement*. Geneva: WCC, 1998.

Pobee, John S., and J. N. Kudadjie, eds. *Theological Education in Africa: Quo Vadimus?* Accra: Asempa; Geneva: World Council of Churches, 1990.

Pobee, Martha. "Gender Issues in the Ghana Foreign Service." *Ghanaian Envoy: Newsletter of the Ministry of Foreign Affairs and Regional Integration*, September 2012, 13–14.

Polish, Daniel F. "McGinley Lecture Response: Fall 2010." Fordham University, November 15, 2010.

Pope Paul VI. *Populorum Progressio*. Encyclical on the Development of Peoples. March 26, 1967.

Preston, Ronald H. *Church and Society in the Late Twentieth Century: The Economic and Political Task*. London: SCM, 1983.

———. *Religion and the Ambiguities of Capitalism*. London: SCM, 1991.

Putnam, Robert D. *Bowling Alone: The Collapse and Revival of American Community*. New York: Simon & Schuster, 2000.

Rahner, Karl, and Herbert Vorgrimler. *Theological Dictionary*. New York: Herder & Herder, 1965.

Rajashaker, J. Paul, et al., eds. *Encounter of Religions in African Cultures*. Geneva: Lutheran World Federation, 1991.

Ramphele, Mamphela. *Conversations with My Sons and Daughters*. Johannesburg: Penguin, 2012.

Ramsey, Ian T. *Models of Mystery*. New York: Oxford University Press, 1964.

Ranson, Charles W. *The Christian Minister in India*. London: Lutterworth, 1946.

———. *A Missionary Pilgrimage*. Grand Rapids: Eerdmans, 1988.

———. *Renewal and Advance*. London: Edinburgh House, 1948.

Rattray, R. S. *Akan-Ashanti Folktales*. Oxford: Clarendon, 1930.

———. *Religion and Art in Ashanti*. Oxford: Clarendon, 1927.

Reston, James, Jr. *Defenders of the Faith: Charles V, Suleyman the Magnificent, and the Battle for Europe, 1520–1536*. New York: Penguin, 2009.

———. *Dogs of God: Columbus, the Inquisition, and the Defeat of the Moors*. New York: Doubleday, 2005.

———. *Warriors of God: Richard the Lionheart and Saladin in the Third Crusade*. New York: Doubleday, 2001.

Ricardo, David. *On the Principles of Political Economy and Taxation*. London: Murray, 1817.

Rich, John M. *Chief Seattle's Unanswered Challenge*. Fairfield, WA: Ye Galleon, 1977.

Richards, Audrey I. *East African Chiefs: A Study of Political Development in Some Uganda and Tanganyika Tribes*. New York: Praeger, 1959.

Roberts, J. Deotis. *A Black Political Theology*. Philadelphia: Westminster, 1974.

———. *Liberation and Reconciliation: A Black Theology*. Philadelphia: Westminster, 1971.

Robins, Wendy S., ed. *Through the Eyes of a Woman: Bible Studies on the Experience of Women*. Rev. ed. Geneva: WCC, 1995.

Robinson, Ronald, and John Gallagher. *Africa and the Victorians: The Official Mind of Imperialism*. With Alice Denny. 2nd ed. London: Macmillan, 1981.

Romero, Óscar. *Voice of the Voiceless*. Maryknoll: Orbis, 1985.

Rooy, Sidney H. *The Theology of Missions in the Puritan Tradition*. Delft, Netherlands: Meinema, 1965.

Rossi, Alice S., ed. *The Feminist Papers: From Adams to de Beauvoir*. Boston: Northeastern University Press, 1988.

Ruether, Rosemary Radford. *Sexism and God-Talk: Towards a Feminist Theology*. London: SCM, 1983.

Rumsfeld, Donald. *Known and Unknown: A Memoir*. New York: Sentinel, 2011.

Runciman, Steven. *The Eastern Schism: A Study of the Papacy and the Eastern Churches during the XIth and XIIth Centuries*. Oxford: Clarendon, 1955.

Russell, Bertrand. *Why I Am Not a Christian*. New York: Simon & Schuster, 1957.

Russell, Letty M. *Church in the Round: Feminist Interpretation of the Church*. Louisville: Westminster John Knox, 1993.

———. "Education as Transformation: Feminist Perspectives on 'The Viability of Ministerial Formation Today.'" *Ministerial Formation* 74 (1996) 23–30.

———. *The Future of Partnership*. Philadelphia: Westminster, 1979.

Russell, William P. *Contextualization: Origins, Meaning, and Implications*. Rome: Pontifica, 1995.

Ryan, Patrick J. *The Atheistic Imagination: A Challenge for Jews, Christians, and Muslims*. With Daniel F. Polish and Amir Hussain. New York: Fordham University Press, 2012.

———. *Boko Haram: Where It Comes From and Where It Is Going*. New York: Fordham University Press, 2014.

———. "The Descending Scroll: A Study of the Notion of Revelation as Apocalypse in the Bible and in the Qur'an." *Ghana Bulletin of Theology* 4, no. 8 (1975) 24–39.

———. *Faith and Culture: Jewish, Christian, and Muslim Perspectives*. New York: Fordham University Press, 2010.

———. *The Faith of Abraham: Bond or Barrier? Jewish, Christian, and Muslim Perspectives*. New York: Fordham University Press, 2011.

———. *Law and Love: Jewish, Christian, and Muslim Attitudes*. With Claudia Setzer and Amir Hussain. New York: Fordham University Press, 2011.

———. "Prophetic Faith and the Critique of Tradition: Jewish, Christian, and Muslim Perspectives." Lawrence J. McGinley Lectures, Fordham University, November 15, 2010. http://www.fordham.edu/downloads/file/3478/fall_2010_lecture.

Sacks, Jonathan. *To Heal a Fractured World: The Ethics of Responsibility*. New York: Schocken, 2005.

Samartha, S. J. *The Hindu Response to the Unbound Christ*. Madras: Christian Literature Society, 1974.

———. *Hindus vor dem universalen Christus: Beiträge zu einer Christologie in Indien*. Stuttgart: Evangelisches Verlagswerk, 1970.

———, ed. *Living Faiths and the Ecumenical Movement*. Geneva: World Council of Churches, 1971.

Samuel, Vinay, and Chris Sugden, eds. *Sharing Jesus in the Two-Thirds World: Evangelical Christologies from the Contexts of Poverty, Powerlessness, and Religious Pluralism*. Grand Rapids: Eerdmans, 1984.

Sanneh, Lamin. *Translating the Message: The Missionary Impact on Culture*. Maryknoll: Orbis, 1989; 2nd ed., 2008.

———. *West African Christianity: The Religious Impact*. Maryknoll: Orbis, 1990.

Santayana, George. *The Life of Reason; or, The Phases of Human Progress*. New York: Scribner, 1905.

Sarbah, John Mensah. *Fanti National Constitution*. London: Clowes, 1906.

Sarpong, Peter K. "African Religion and Catholic Worship." *Standard: National Weekly* 39 (1977) 6.

———. "Christianity Should Be Africanised, Not Africans Christianised." *African Ecclesial Review* 17, no. 6 (1975) 322–28.

———. "Inculturation and the African Church." *Shalom* 6 (1988).

———. *Odd Customs, Stereotypes, and Prejudices*. Accra: Sub-Saharan, 2012.

Sartre, Jean-Paul. *Black Orpheus*. Translated by Samuel W. Allen. Paris: Présence Africaine, 1976.

———. "Orphée noir." Introduction to Léopold Sédar Senghor, *Anthologie de la nouvelle poésie nègre et malgache de langue française*, ix–xliv. Paris: Presses Universitaires de France, 1948.

Sawyerr, Harry. *Creative Evangelism: Towards a New Christian Encounter with Africa*. London: Lutterworth, 1968.

Schaeffer, Francis. *A Christian Manifesto*. Westchester, IL: Crossway, 1981.

Scharper, Philip, and Sally Scharper, eds. *The Gospel in Art by the Peasants of Solentineme*. Maryknoll: Orbis, 1984.

Schillebeeckx, Edward. *The Eucharist*. London: Sheed & Ward, 1968.

———. *The Real Achievement of Vatican II*. New York: Herder & Herder, 1967.
Schineller, Peter. *A Handbook on Inculturation*. New York: Paulist, 1990.
Schreiter, Robert J. *The New Catholicity: Theology between the Global and the Local*. Maryknoll: Orbis, 1997.
Schweizer, Eduard. *The Good News according to Matthew*. London: SPCK, 1976.
Segal, Alan F. *Rebecca's Children: Judaism and Christianity in the Roman World*. Cambridge: Harvard University Press, 1986.
Sembène, Ousmane. *God's Bits of Wood*. London: Heinemann, 1960.
———. *The Money-Order with White Genesis*. London: Heinemann, 1972.
Senghor, Léopold Sédar. *On African Socialism*. Newark: Praeger, 1962.
———. Speech at Howard University, Washington, DC, September 28, 1961. Translated by Mercer Cook. *African Forum* 2, no. 3 (1967).
Setiloane, Gabriel M. "Christus Heute Bekennen aus der afrikanischen Sicht von Mensch und Gemeinschaft." *Zeitschrift für Mission* (1976) 21–32.
Sevenster, Jan Nicolaas. *Paul and Seneca*. Leiden: Brill, 1961.
Shank, David A. "A Prophet for Modern Times: The Thought of William Wade Harris, West African Precursor of the Reign of Christ." PhD thesis, University of Aberdeen, 1980.
Shaull, Richard. *Naming the Idols: Biblical Alternatives for U.S. Foreign Policy*. Ocean City, MD: Skipjack, 1992.
Sheard, Robert B. *Interreligious Dialogue in the Catholic Church since Vatican II: An Historical and Theological Study*. Queenston, Ontario: Mellen, 1987.
Shenk, Wilbert R. *Henry Venn: Missionary Statesman*. Maryknoll: Orbis, 1983.
Shermer, Michael. *Why People Believe Weird Things: Pseudoscience, Superstition, and Other Confusions of Our Time*. New York: Holt, 2002.
Shorter, Aylward. "Secularism in Africa: Introducing the Problem." http://sedosmission.org/old/eng/shorter.htm.
———. *Toward a Theology of Inculturation*. London: Chapman, 1988.
Sigmund, Paul E., ed. *The Ideologies of the Developing Countries*. New York: Praeger, 1971.
Sithole, Ndabaningi. *African Nationalism*. London: Oxford University Press, 1959.
Skinner, Elliott P., ed. *Peoples and Cultures of Africa: An Anthropological Reader*. New York: Doubleday, 1973.
Slovo, Joe. *Slovo: The Unfinished Autobiography*. Randburg, South Africa: Ravan, 1995.
Smith, Adam. *An Enquiry into the Nature and Causes of the Wealth of Nations*. London: Strahan & Cadell, 1776.
Smith, Edwin W. *Aggrey of Africa: A Study of Black and White*. New York: Smith, 1930.
Smith, Janet, and Beauregard Tromp. *Hani: A Life Too Short*. Johannesburg: Ball, 2009.
Smith, M. G. *Government in Zazzau, 1800–1950*. London: Oxford University Press, 1960.
Smith, Wilfred Cantwell. *Faith and Belief*. Princeton: Princeton University Press, 1979.
———. *The Faith of Other Men*. New York: Harper & Row, 1972.
———. *The Meaning and End of Religion*. Minneapolis: Fortress, 1990.
Smith, Wilfred Cantwell, and John W. Burbidge, eds. *Modern Culture from a Comparative Perspective*. Albany: State Univ. of New York Press, 1997.
Smuts, Jan Christian. *Africa and Some World Problems*. Oxford: Oxford University Press, 1930.
Sobrino, Jon. *Christology at the Crossroads: A Latin American Approach*. Maryknoll: Orbis, 1978.
Southern Rhodesia. Land Tenure Act. 1969. Chap. 48, Sec. 69.

Sparrow, Betsy, et al. "Google Effects on Memory: Cognitive Consequences of Having Information at Our Fingertips." *Science* 333 (2011) 776–78.

Speckman, McGlory T., and Larry T. Kaufmann, eds. *Towards an Agenda for Contextual Theology: Essays in Honour of Albert Nolan*. Pietermaritzburg, South Africa: Cluster, 2001.

Stauffer, Ethelbert. *Christ and the Caesars: Historical Sketches*. London: SCM, 1955.

Stinton, Diane B. *Jesus of Africa: Voices of Contemporary African Christology*. Maryknoll: Orbis, 2004.

Sundkler, Bengt. *Bantu Prophets in South Africa*. Nairobi: Oxford University Press, 1948.

———. *Nathan Söderblom: His Life and Work*. Lund: Gleerup, 1968.

———. *Zulu Zion and Some Swazi Zionists*. London: Oxford University Press, 1976.

Swantz, Marja-Liisa. *Ritual and Symbol in Transitional Zaramo Society with Special Reference to Women*. Lund: Gleerup, 1970.

Szamuely, Tibor. "The Prophet of the Utterly Absurd." *Spectator*, March 11, 1966.

Tasie, Godwin. *Christian Missionary Enterprise in the Niger Delta, 1864–1918*. Leiden: Brill, 1978.

Theodorson, George A., and Achilles G. Theodorson. *A Modern Dictionary of Sociology*. New York: Crowell, 1970.

Theological Education Fund. *Learning in Context: The Search for Innovative Patterns in Theological Education*. Bromley, UK: New Life, 1973.

Thirty-Second General Congregation of the Society of Jesus, December 2, 1974, to March 7, 1975. "Decree 4: Service of Faith and the Promotion of Justice," "Decree 5: On Promoting the Work of Inculturation of Faith and of Christian Life," "Decree 6: On Formation."

Thomas, M. M. *The Acknowledged Christ of the Indian Renaissance*. Madras: Christian Literature Society, 1970.

Thomas, Owen C., ed. *Attitudes toward Other Religions: Some Christian Interpretations*. London: SCM Press, 1969.

Thomas, William Isaac. *Social Behavior and Personality: Contributions of W. I. Thomas to Theory and Social Research*. Edited by Edmund H. Volkart. New York: Social Sciences Research Council, 1951.

Thompson, Thomas. *The African Trade for Negro Slaves: Shewn to Be Consistent with Principles of Humanity, and with the Laws of Revealed Religion*. Canterbury, 1772.

Thu, En Yu. "Revising Mission and Vision in ATESEA [Association of Theological Education in South East Asia]." *Ministerial Formation*, July 2007, 14–19.

Tillich, Paul. *Dynamics of Faith*. New York: Harper, 1958.

———. *Theology of Culture*. New York: Oxford University Press, 1959.

Todd, Emmanuel. *L'enfance du monde: Structures familiales et développement*. Paris: Éditions du Seuil, 1984.

Tolstoy, Leo. "What I Believe." In *The Christian Teaching*, vol. 11 of *The Works of Leo Tolstoy*, 447–48. Translated by Aylmer Maude. London: For the Tolstoy Society, Oxford University Press, 1928–37.

Tönnies, Ferdinand. *Community and Association (Genmeinschaft und Gesellschaft)*. Translated by Charles Price Loomis. London: Routledge & Paul, 1955.

Tracy, David. *The Analogical Imagination: Christian Theology and the Culture of Pluralism*. New York: Crossroads, 1981.

Trevor, Meriol. *Pope John*. Leominster, UK: Gracewing, 2000.

Troeltsch, Ernst. *The Social Teaching of the Christian Churches*. London: Allen & Unwin, 1931.

Trompf, Garry W., and Gildas Hamel, eds. *The World of Religions: Essays on Historical and Contemporary Issues in Honour of Professor Noel Quinton King for His Eightieth Birthday.* Delhi: ISPCK, 2002.

Turner, Harold W. *History of an African Independent Church.* 2 vols. London: Oxford University Press, 1967.

———. "A Typology of African Religious Movements." *Journal of Religion in Africa* 1, no. 1 (1967) 1–34.

Tuttle, Lisa. *Encyclopedia of Feminism.* Harlow, UK: Longman, 1986.

Tutu, Desmond. *No Future without Forgiveness.* London: Rider, 1999.

Tylor, Edward Burnett. *The Origins of Culture.* New York: Harper & Row, 1958.

Ukpong, Justin S. *New Testament Essays.* Lagos: Campbell, 1995.

Ullmann, Walter. *The Origins of the Great Schism: A Study in Fourteenth-Century Ecclesiastical History.* London: Burns Oates & Washbourne, 1948.

UNESCO, *Statement on Race and Racial Prejudice.* 1967. http://unesdoc.unesco.org/images/0012/001229/122962eo.pdf.

Van Baal, Jan. "The Political Impact of Prophetic Movements." *Internationales Jahrbuch für Religionssoziologie* 5 (1969) 68–88.

Vandeleur, Seymour. *Campaigning on the Upper Nile and Niger.* London: Methuen, 1898.

Vatcher, William Henry. *White Laager: The Rise of Afrikaner Nationalism.* London: Paul Mall, 1965.

Verkuyl, Johannes. *Contemporary Missiology: An Introduction.* Grand Rapids: Eerdmans, 1978.

Vicedom, George F., ed. *Christ and the Younger Churches.* London: SPCK, 1972.

Villa-Vicencio, Charles. *A Theology of Reconstruction: Nation-Building and Human Rights.* Cambridge: Cambridge University Press, 1992.

Visser 't Hooft, W. A., and J. H. Oldham. *The Church and Its Function in Society.* London: Allen & Unwin, 1937.

Vrijhof, Pieter Hendrik, and Jacques Waardenburg, eds. *Official and Popular Religion: Analysis of a Theme for Religious Studies.* The Hague: Mouton, 1979.

Waardenburg, Jacques. *Classical Approaches to the Study of Religion.* The Hague: Mouton, 1973–74.

Wade, Abdoulaye. "A Plan to Mobilise Capital." *Newsweek*, special issue, December 2002–February 2003, 71–72.

Wainwright, Geoffrey. "The Localization of Worship." *Studia Liturgica* 8 (1971–72) 1–25.

Wakefield, Gordon S., ed. *A Dictionary of Christian Spirituality.* London: SCM, 1983.

Waliggo, John Mary, et al. *Inculturation: Its Meaning and Urgency.* Nairobi: St. Paul Publications–Africa, 1986.

Walls, Andrew F., and Wilbert R. Shenk, eds. *Exploring New Religious Movements.* Elkhart, IN: Mission Focus, 1990.

Ward, W. E. F. *A History of Ghana.* London: Allen & Unwin, 1963.

Warren, Max, ed. *To Apply the Gospel: Selections from the Writings of Henry Venn.* Grand Rapids: Eerdmans, 1971.

Weber, Max. *The Theory of Social and Economic Organization.* Translated by A. M. Henderson and Talcott Parsons. Glencoe, IL: Free Press, 1947.

Weigel, George. *Evangelical Catholicism: Deep Reform in the Twenty-First-Century Church.* New York: Basic Books, 2013.

———. *Witness to Hope: The Biography of Pope John Paul II.* New York: Cliff Street, 1999.

Wengert, Timothy J., ed. *The Pastoral Luther: Essays on Martin Luther's Practical Theology.* Grand Rapids: Eerdmans, 2009.

Werner, Dietrich, et al. *Handbook of Theological Education in World Christianity: Theological Perspectives—Regional Surveys—Ecumenical Trends.* Oxford: Regnum International, 2010.

Westerhoff, John H. *Will Our Children Have Faith?* Harrisburg, PA: Morehouse, 2000.

Whale, John S., ed. *The Pope from Poland: An Assessment.* London: Collins, 1980.

Wilkins, Ivor, and Hans Strydom. *The Super-Afrikaners.* Johannesburg: Bull, 1978.

Williams, Rowan. *Arius: Heresy and Tradition.* London: SCM, 2001.

———. Presidential Address at General Synod of the Church of England. *New African* 440 (March 2006) 36.

Williamson, S. G. "The Lyric in the Fante Methodist Church." *Africa* 28 (1958) 126–34.

Winquist, Charles E. *Epiphanies of Darkness: Deconstruction in Theology.* Philadelphia: Fortress, 1986.

Witte, John, Jr., ed. *Christianity and Democracy in Global Context.* Boulder, CO: Westview, 1993.

Wolff, Otto. *Christus unter den Hindus.* Gütersloh: Mohr, 1965.

Wood, David. *On Paul Ricoeur: Narrative and Interpretation.* London: Routledge, 1991.

World Council of Churches. *Christian Faith and the World Economy Today: A Study Document.* Geneva: WCC, 1992.

———. *Guidelines on Dialogue with People of Living Faiths and Ideologies.* Geneva: World Council of Churches, 1979.

Yankah, Kojo. *Otumfuo Osei Tutu II: The King on the Golden Stool.* Accra-North, Ghana: Unimax Macmillan, 2009.

Yates, Timothy. *Venn and Victorian Bishops Abroad.* London: SPCK, 1978.

Yeebo, Zaya. *Ghana: The Struggle for Popular Power; Rawlings: Saviour or Demagogue?* London: New Beacon, 1991.

Yunus, Muhammad. *Banker to the Poor: Micro-Lending and the Battle against World Poverty.* New York: Public Affairs, 1997.

Yunus, Muhammad. *Creating a World without Poverty: Social Business and the Future of Capitalism.* With Karl Weber. New York: Public Affairs, 2007.

Zaehner, R. C. *Mysticism, Sacred and Profane.* London: Oxford University Press, 1957.

Zahan, Dominique, ed. *Réincarnation et vie mystique en Afrique noire.* Paris: Presses Universitaire de France, 1965.

Zoa, Jean B. "Committed Christian Building a New Africa." *African Ecclesiastical Review* 8, no. 2 (1966) 99–104.

Zorn, Herbert M. *Viability in Context: A Study of the Financial Viability of Theological Education in the Third World, Seedbed or Sheltered Garden?* Bromley: Theological Education Fund, 1975.

Author Index

Abelard, Peter, 55
Abrecht, Paul, 151n41
Achebe, Chinua, 17, 30
Adams, James Tuslow, 5, 8
Adams, William Y., 32n29
Adels, Jill Haak, 95n21
Ahuma, S.R.B. Attoh, 41n2, 44, 113
Ajayi, J. F. Ade, 28n18, 32n28
Albanese, Giulio, 199n14, 200n16, 209
Alexandre, Pierre, 113n20
Allen, Roland, 286n44
Amirtham, Samuel, 2n1, 64n7, 78n37
Amoah, Elizabeth, 165
Amu, Ephraim, 12–13n26
Anderson, Rufus, 286n43
Ansah, Paul, 125n53
Anselm, 4, 68, 70
Aquinas, 32, 83, 140
Aquinas, Thomas, 66, 83, 140
Arendt, Hannah, 56
Ariarajah, S. Wesley, 151n40
Aristotle, 12n25, 66, 93, 189n7, 215–16
Armah, Ayi Kwei, 29n22
Asamoah-Gyadu, J. Kwabena, 278n5, 285n34
Asante, David, 72
Assimeng, J. Max, 138n7
Assmann, Hugo, 164n15
Ataturk, Mustafa Kemal, 107
Augustine of Hippo Regius, 32, 66, 71n24, 79, 86–87, 139n13, 140, 161n7, 170, 187, 198, 216, 267
Austin, Dennis, 219n15
Ayandele, Emmanuel Ayankanmi., 32n28, 41n2, 123n49

Bacon, Francis, 8, 243n31
Baëta, Christian G., 47, 126n61, 135, 281n15, 284n28

Bakare, Sebastian, 100n33, 270
Balandier, Georges, 281n16, 284n31
Balasuriya, Tissa, 164n14
Balcond, Anthony, 17n33
Barberini, Antonio (cardinal), 15
Barr, James, 71n24
Barrett, David B., 276n1
Barry, F. R., 88, 91, 100
Barth, Karl, 150, 194
Bass, Diana Butler, 49n21
Baynes, Norman Hepburn, 139n12, 216n8
Bediako, Kwame, 165, 167n24, 279, 279n10
Bellah, Robert N., 105n1
Ben-Ari, Miri, 14
Benedict XIV (pope), 110
Benedict XVI (pope), 80, 156–57
Bennett, John C., 151n41
Berdyaev, Nikolai A., 232, 233n9
Berger, Peter L., 138n8
Berlin International Conference (1884–85), 27
Bernstein, Basil B., 94n17
Best, Thomas F., 51n24
Beti, Mongo, 29n22, 37
Biko, Stephen Bantu, 122
Bismarck, Wilhelm Von, 27
Blakely, Gloria, 13
Bligh, John, 163n11
Blyden, Edward W., 22
Boff, Leonardo, 111n10, 120n41, 132, 132n9, 164n15, 176, 177n13, 201, 201n17, 242, 281, 282n20
Bonaventure, 70
Bongani, Finca, 55
Bonhoeffer, Dietrich, 19, 69
Bonino, Jose Miguez, 116n30
Bornkamm, Gunther, 160n3
Bosch, David J., 26n12, 69n16, 228n5
Botha, David, 26n11

Author Index

Boulding, Kenneth E., 105n1
Boyd, Robin H. S., 164n14
Brand, Stewart, 74
Bria, Ion, 220n17, 230n7, 239–240
Bridges-Johns, Cheryl, 70n17, 70n19, 71n21
Briggs, John H. Y., 227n2
Brockman, James R., 120n41
Brown, Lalage J., 17n33
Brown, Lester, 245
Brown, Robert McAfee, 119n39
Brown, William Harvey, 104n40
Bruce, F. F., 220n17
Brueggemann, Walter, 103
Buah, F. K., 23–24, 27n15
Bujo, Bénézet, 88, 123, 128, 165, 168n26, 169
Bulhan, Hussein Abdilahi, 30n25
Bunyan, John, 72
Burbidge, John W., 154n44
Burridge, William, 111n12, 111n13
Burtness, James H., 117
Busia, Kofi, 278–79
Busia, Kofi A., 48n15, 52n29, 53, 63n5, 142n21, 278n6, 279n7
Butler, Tom, 252–53
Butty, John, 244n34

Cacioppo, John T., 52n28
Cairns, H. Alan C., 104n40
Calvin, John, 88
Camara, Laye, 29
Camps, Arnulf, 164n14
Cantwell Smith, Wilfred, 7, 8
Carson, Benjamin, 12–13
Carter, Margaret, 262n15, 263n16
Carter, Stephen L., 95
Cary, Joyce, 30n23
Casas, Bartolome de las, 120n42
Cerularius, Michael, 87
Cervantes Saavedra, Miguel de, 32
Césaire, Aimé Fernand, 17, 25n9, 236
Chabal, Patrick, 29n21
Chatterji, Shoma, 198n10
Chittick, William C., 146n31
Christaller, Johann, 166, 167
Chrysostom, John, 236
Clement of Alexandria, 169
Clement XI (pope), 110
Cochrane, Charles Norris, 55n44
Coe, Shoki, 117, 118
Cone, James H., 121n44, 123–24
Confucius, 189n7
Congar, Yves, 114
Conradie, Ernst M., 227n2
Cook, Guillermo, 119n39, 120n41

Couper, Scott, 85, 259n9
Cowper, William, 24
Cox, Harvey, 177
Cox, Idris, 125n53
Crollius, Ary A. Roest, 114n23
Cross, F. L., 110n8
Crowder, Michael, 28n18
Cullmann, Oscar, 160, 160n5
Cyprian, 139n13

d'Alembert, Jean-Baptiste le Rond, 80n40
Daneel, Marthinus L., 281n14, 284, 287
Dangaremgba, Tsiti, 30
Danquah, J. B. (aka Kwame Kyeretwie), 26–27
Davenport, Rodney, 19n37
Day, Laura, 38
de Gruchy, John W., 18, 76n33, 100n34, 118n36
De Maria, Walter, 14–15n31
de Nobili, Roberto, 110
Debrunner, Hans, 282n24
Delitzsch, Franz, 186, 187, 207
Denis, Philippe, 55n46, 56n48, 195n5, 197n7
Deresiewicz, William, 40, 62
Desai, Ram, 12–13n26
Descartes, René, 69–70
Diamond, Jared, 250
Diawara, Fatoumata, 12n26
Dickson, Kwesi A., 123, 165
Diderot, Denis, 80n40
Dionysius of Halicarnassus, 62
Dodd, C. H., 54, 84n3
Du Bois, W.E.B., 31
du Toit, Cornel W., 100n34, 122n47
Dulles, Avery, 105n1
Duncan, Graham, 122n47
Dupre, Louis K., 10
Durkheim, Émile, 174
Dyke, Daniel, 72

Eagleson, John, 119n40
Edwards, Michael, 181n19, 217n10
Ela, Jean-Marc, 48, 76, 76n31, 104, 123, 129
Elliot, T. S., 82
Elliott, Charles, 240
Elliott, Lawrence, 106n3, 107
Elphick, Richard E., 19n37
Evans, James H., Jr., 121n44
Evans-Pritchard, E. E., 141n20

Fabella, Virginia, 165n16
Fanon, Frantz, 17, 30–31, 45n10, 236
Farley, Edward, 66, 74n26
Fernandez, James W., 281n15
Field, Margaret Joyce, 46, 282

Author Index

Foroohar, Rana, 227n3
Fortes, Meyer, 141n20
Francis (pope), 24, 190
Francis, James M. M., 79n38
Francis, Leslie J., 79n38
Frederick the Great, 80n40
Freire, Paolo, 66
Frend, W.H.C., 198n11
Fromm, Eric, 8
Frostin, Per, 121n43

Gallagher, John, 29n21
Gandel, Stephen, 247n40
Gascoyne-Cecil, Robert, 235
Gassmann, Gunther, 51n24
Gaye, Marvin, 13
Geldof, Bob, 236, 237n19
Gensichen, H. W., 149n35
George, Susan, 242
Gibellini, Rosino, 123n50, 164n15
Gibson, Nigel C., 30n25, 125n54
Gifford, Paul, 114
Gilligan, Carol, 198n9
Giri, Jacques, 200
Glazer, Nathan, 25n8
Gluckman, Max, 52–53
Gnanadason, Aruna, 203n21
Grant, Jacqueline, 198n12
Gray, Richard, 23n4, 24n6
Greenslade, S. L., 71n24, 127n63, 140n18
Gregory Nazianzen, Saint, 55
Griffiths, Paul J., 151n40
Groves, C. P., 32n28
Gutierrez, Gustavo, 120n41
Gutto, O. B., 100n33

Hagan, George, 269
Hahn, Niels, 36n36
Haliburton, Gordon Mackay, 281n15, 283n25
Hallencreutz, Carl F., 151n40
Hamel, Gildas, 11n24, 195n5, 198n11
Hardy, Barbara, 17
Hargreaves, John D., 235n16
Hastings, Adrian, 25n9, 267n24
Hauerwas, Stanley, 44n7
Hayes, Graham, 56n48, 195n5, 197
Hayford, J. E. Casely, 41n2, 113, 126, 126n57
Hazlitt, William, 65
Hebblethwaite, Peter, 106n2
Hedges, Chris, 188n4, 188n6, 189, 250, 252
Hegel, Georg Wilhelm Friedrich., 70, 80
Herrin, Judith, 34n32
Herskovits, Melville J., 114n25
Hetherington, Penelope, 29n21

Hillel (sage), 189n7
Hindenburg, Paul von, 244
Hinkelammert, Franz, 5n10
Hobbs, Thomas, 216
Hodges, Harold M., 138n7
Hofmeyer, J. W., 26n12
Hollenweger, Walter J., 111n10, 282, 286
Homer, 66
Howse, Ernest Marshall, 23n4
Hughes, H. Stuart, 57n51
Hume, David, 80n40
Hunt, James, 33
Huntington, Samuel P., 142–43
Huss, John, 88
Hussain, Amir, 83, 146n31, 147n32

Ignatius of Antioch, 95
Innocent II (pope), 140
Irvine, Sandy, 244n34, 245

Jakobsson, Stiv, 23n4
Jansen, Robert, 188
Jefferson, Thomas, 174
Jevons, W. Stanley, 229n6, 234n14
John Paul II (pope), 169, 176, 182, 233–34
John XXIII (pope), 106–9, 182
Johns Hopkins University, 234–35
Johnson, James, 123n49
Johnstone, Patrick J., 276n1
Jones, A.H.M., 139n12
Jones, L. G., 44n7
Jung, Carl Gustav, 258–59
Justin Martyr, 169

Kaberry, Phyllis Mary, 43n5
Kanyoro, Musimbi, 197, 199, 203n23, 204, 207n29
Kaplan, Justin, 266n19, 267n21
Karis, Thomas, 262n15, 263n16
Katjavivi, Peter, 121n43
Kaufmann, Larry T., 118n35
Keil, Carl Friedrich, 186, 187, 207
Kerry, John, 274
Kierkegaard, Sören, 147–48
Kimble, David, 30n26, 125n56
King, Martin Luther Jr., 13, 121n44, 176, 179, 273
King, Noel Quinton, 34n32, 220n17
Kinsler, F. Ross, 117n33
Kittler, Glenn D., 111n12
Klinenberg, Eric, 51n25
Kollbrunner, Fritz, 110n8, 111n11
Kraemer, Hendrik, 153
Kritzinger, Johannes N. J., 100n34

Author Index

Kudadjie, J. N., 24n7, 77n35
Kuma, Afua, 167n24
Kunambi, B. N., 199n14
Kwarteng, Kwasi, 28n16, 28n20, 29n21

Lactantius, 7, 55
Langer, Susanne K., 52n31
Larbi, Emmanuel Kingsley, 46n13, 285n34
Laryea, Philip T., 12–13n26
Latourette, Kenneth Scott, 32n28
Lavigerie, Charles Martial Allemand, 111
Leaver, Robin A., 14n29
Lederle, Henry I., 285n33
Legge, James, 178n14, 215n2
Lemmon, Gayle Tzemach, 201n18
Lenin, V. I., 228, 237, 237n20, 239, 250
Lenski, Gerald, 136
Leo IX (pope), 87
Leo XIII (pope), 181–82
Lepine, Marc, 209n33
Lévinas, Emmanuel, 143–44, 222
Lewis, I. M., 8n18, 9, 113n20
Lienemann-Perrin, Christine, 117n33
Lietzmann, Hans, 54n38
Lindars, Barnabas, 162
Livingstone, David, 237
Livy, 86
Long, Charles H., 121n44
Lossky, Nicolas, 77, 116n30, 119n38, 151n41, 181n20, 203n21, 230n7, 256n1, 260n12
Lubben, Shelley, 188
Lugard, Lord Frederick Dealty, 28–29, 235
Lund, John Magne, 97
Luther, Martin, 14, 61–62, 68, 80, 88, 96, 98, 260
Luthuli, Albert, 85, 259
Lyimo, Camillus, 130n3

MacIntyre, Alasdair, 44, 45n11
Macquarrie, John, 72
Magesa, Laurenti, 165n16
al-Maghīlī, Muhammad, 155
Mahomed, Ismail, 94
Makhulu, Walter Khotso, 96–98
Malinowski, Bronislaw, 43n5
Malthus, Thomas Robert, 234n14
Mana, Kä, 123
Mandela, Nelson Rohihlaha, 50, 179
Mannheim, Karl, 217–18n11
Marett, R. R., 52, 60
Markus, R. A., 216n8
Marshall, Alfred, 229n6
Martin, Marie-Louise, 281n16, 284n30
Marx, Karl, 5

Mashele, Prince, 219
Masson, Joseph, 113n21
Mawby, Colin, 14
Mayfield, Curtis, 13
Mazrui, Ali A., 219n15
Mbeki, Thabo, 260
Mbiti, John S., 10, 48n19, 123, 165, 169n30
McCallum, J. Ramsay, 55n43
McNicoll, Tracy, 12n26
Mencius, 178, 210n38
Menenius Agrippa, 86
Mesters, Carlos, 120n41
Mettrie, Julien Offray de la, 48n17
Meyendorff, Jong, 34n32, 81n41, 87n7, 139n10
Michelangelo, 15
Middleton, John, 141n20
Mijoga, Hilary B. P., 123
Mill, John Stuart, 234n14
Milton, John, 32
Mofokeng, Takatso A., 123n48
Molendijk, Arie L., 7n13
Montaigne, Michel Eyquem de, 93
Montesquieu, Baron de, 267
Moreira, Adriano, 25n9
Mosala, Itumelang J., 123
Moule, C.F.D., 75–76, 160n4, 162–63
Moynihan, Daniel Patrick, 24–25
Mugambi, J. N., 114n27, 165
Mutiso-Mbinda, John, 114
Mveng, Engelbert, 114

Nash, Margaret, 26n11
Naso, Publius Ovidius, 216
Neill, Stephen, 152, 244n33
Nessen, Craig L., 121n43
Newbigin, Lesslie, 118, 119n37, 151n40
Newman, John Henry, 80, 84, 171n2, 264, 265
Ngugi wa Thiong'o, 29, 30
Niblett, W. R., 53n35, 65–66
Nicholas V (pope), 25
Nicolson, Ronald, 121n44
Niebuhr, H. Richard, 32, 42n4, 54
Nietzsche, Friedrich, 28
Njoroge, Nyambura Jane, 204n24, 209, 209n35
Nketia, J. H., 12–13n26, 77n36
Nkrumah, Kwame, 26–27, 29–32, 41–42, 218n12
Nolan, Albert, 118, 118n36
Nussbaum, Stan, 290
Nyamiti, Charles, 123, 168n26, 169

O'Connor, Daniel, 280n12
Ocran, Albert Kwesi, 219n15

Author Index

Oduyoye, Mercy Amba, 123, 165, 203n23, 204–5, 227n2
Okolo, Chukwudumu, 168
Oldham, J. H., 116n30, 151n41
Olds, Jacqueline, 51n26
Omoyajowo, J. Akin, 131n6
Onyango, Maurice, 290n47
Oosthuizen, Gerhardus Cornelis, 281n16
Opoku, Theophilus, 72
Orchard, Ronald K., 32n30, 117n31, 173n6
Orczy, Emmuska, 73
Origen, 79
Ortega, Ofelia, 207n29, 209n33
Oshitelu, Gabriel, II, 111n10, 127n62, 282n22, 286n37, 287n38, 287n39, 291n48
Otto, Rudolf, 10
Ouologuem, Yambo, 28n18, 29n22
Ovid, 216n4
Oyono, Ferdinand, 28n18

Pagha, Camille, 14n31
Pandor, Naledi, 102n36
Paris, Peter, 204
Parker, Theodore, 93, 94, 95n18
Parrinder, Edward Geoffrey, 8n18, 49n20
Parvey, Constance F., 202n19
Patrick, William, 52n28
Patterson, Orlando, 22
Paul, Annie Murphy, 67n13
Paul VI (pope), 108, 109, 217
Pénoukou, Julien Efoé, 168n26
Perbi, Akosua Adoma, 22
Perham, Margery Freda, 28n18
Petrarch, 216n4
Pew Research Center, 2
Phiri, Isabel Apawo, 123n49, 204n24, 204n25, 208n30
Pierce, Yolanda, 136n4
Pityana, N. Barney, 122
Pius X (pope), 107
Pius XI (pope), 106, 182
Pius XII (pope), 108, 182
Plato, 66
Platvoet, Jan G., 2n4, 7n13, 19, 19n37, 19n39, 30, 264
Plotinus, 80n40
Pobee, John S., 2n1, 8n18, 11n24, 24, 27n14, 30n26, 32n28, 35n35, 41n2, 53n34, 57n50, 63n6, 64n7, 70n17, 71n23, 72n25, 76n34, 77n35, 78n37, 111n10, 123, 123n49, 127n62, 138n7, 138n9, 149n35, 158n1, 158n2, 164n13, 166n18, 167n24, 168n26, 169, 176n10, 181n19, 190, 195n5, 198n11, 204, 210n38, 226n1, 246n38, 246n39, 260, 269n25, 276n1, 277n2, 277n3, 279n9, 280n12, 282n22, 283n27, 286n36, 286n37, 287n38, 287n39, 291n48, 292n49
Pobee, Martha, 197n8, 198n10
Polish, Daniel F., 20, 89n9, 90, 147n32
Ponticus, Evagrius, 64, 76
Preston, Ronald H., 233
Putnam, Robert D., 51n25

Rahman-Figueroa, Talyn, 197n8, 198n9
Rahner, Karl, 110
Rajashaker, J. Paul, 138n7
Ramphele, Mamphela, 205n27, 258n6
Rattray, R. S., 13n27, 14–15n31
Reindorf, Carl, 72
Reston, James, Jr., 34n33, 34n34, 139n10, 139n11
Ricardo, David, 234n14
Ricci, Matteo, 110
Rich, John M., 103n39
Richards, Audrey I., 141n20
Ricoeur, Paul, 17n33
Roberts, J. Deotis, 121n44
Robins, Wendy S., 203n22
Robinson, Mary, 269
Robinson, Ronald, 29n21
Romero, Óscar, 120n41
Roncalli, Angelo Cardinal, 106–7
Roosevelt, Franklin D., 234
Rooy, Sidney H., 42n3, 139n14
Rossi, Alice S., 194n3
Ruether, Rosemary Radford, 198n12, 204
Rumsfeld, Donald, 143–44
Runciman, Steven, 87n7
Russell, Bertrand, 90
Russell, Letty, 208
Ryan, Patrick J., 20n40, 83n1, 90n12, 91n13, 146n31, 147, 155
Ryden, Lennart, 14n31

Sacks, Jonathan, 95, 96, 187
Samartha, S. J., 151n40, 164n14
Samuel, Vinay, 165n16, 167n24
Sanneh, Lamin, 72n25, 132, 132n8, 285, 286n35
Santayana, George, 56
Sarbah, John Mensah, 126, 126n60
Sarpong, Peter K., 114n23, 279–280
Sawyerr, Harry, 123, 168
Scharper, Philip J., 119n40, 120n41
Scharper, Sally, 120n41
Schillebeeckx, Edward, 12n25, 109
Schineller, Peter, 114n23
Schreiter, Robert J., 111n10, 282, 288

Schwartz, Richard, 51n26
Schweizer, Eduard, 161n6
Seattle, Chief, 50, 103, 253
Seconder, Charles de, 267
Segal, Alan, 146
Sembene, Ousmane, 29, 30
Seneca, 86
Senghor, Léopold Sédar, 41, 125n53, 218n12
Setiloane, Gabriel, 165
Setzer, Claudia, 146n31
Sevenster, Jan Nicolaas, 86n5
Shakespeare, William, 32
Shank, David A., 281n15, 283n25
Shaull, Richard, 120n42
Sheard, Robert B., 151n40
Shenk, Wilbert R., 283n25, 286n44
Shepperson, George, 126
Shermer, Michael, 38n42
Shorter, Aylward, 19n37, 114n24, 169n29
Sibbes, Richard, 41–42, 139n14
Sigmund, Paul E., 218n12
Sithole, Ndabaningi, 30n26
Skinner, Wilfred Cantwell, 12n26
Slovo, Joe, 261
Smith, Adam, 234n14
Smith, Edwin W., 209n36
Smith, Janet, 254n2
Smith, M. G., 141n20
Smith, N. J., 25n10, 253n1
Smith, Wilfred Cantwell, 8n18, 88, 153
Smith David, 156n46
Smuts, Jan Christian, 173
Sobrino, Jon, 164n15
Sosa, Pablo, 77
Sparrow, Betsy, 67
Speckman, McGlory T., 118n35
Spider, Akan, 13
Stauffer, Ethelbert, 174n9
Stinton, Diane B., 123, 165
Stransky, Tom, 181
Strydom, Hans, 26n12
Sugden, Chris, 165n16, 167n24
Sundkler, Bengt, 151n41, 281, 281n17, 284n29, 284n30
Swantz, Marja-Liisa, 52n31
Szamuely, Tibor, 219n15

Tait, David, 141n20
Tamez, Elsa, 5
Tasie, Godwin, 283n25
Tatian, 79
Tertullian, 32, 54, 79
Theodorson, Achilles G., 114n25, 172n3
Theodorson, George A., 114n25, 172n3

Third Marquis of Salisbury, 27–28
Thomas, M. M., 164n14, 173, 276n1
Thomas, of Aquinas, 66, 83, 140
Thomas, Owen, 150n38
Thomas, W. I., 172
Thomas, William Isaac, 172n5
Thompson, Emma, 243
Thompson, Thomas, 23, 252
Thorogood, Bernard, 119
Thu, En Yu, 18n35
Thucydides, 62
Tillich, Paul, 8, 11n23, 54
Todd, Emmanuel, 200n15
Tolstoy, Leo, 54–55
Toynbee, Arnold, 27
Tracy, David, 75n27
Trevor, Meriol, 106n2
Trimingham, J. Spencer, 113n20
Troeltsch, Ernst, 55n42
Tromp, Beauregard, 254n2
Trompf, Garry W., 11n24, 195n5, 198n11
Turner, Harold W., 278, 281n14
Tuttle, Lisa, 194n2
Tutu, Desmond, 25, 96–97, 134
Tylor, E. B., 43n5

Ukpong, Justin S., 114
Ullmann, Walter, 87n7
Urban VIII (pope), 15

Van Baal, Jan, 194n4
van Rinsum, Henk, 19n37
Vandeleur, Seymour, 28n16
Vatcher, William Henry, 26
Verkuyl, Johannes, 217n11
Vicedom, George F., 165n16
Villa-Vicencio, Charles, 100n34, 114n27, 116
Vincent, David Brown, 41n2, 44n6, 123
Virgil, 66
Visser 't Hooft, W. A., 116n30
Voltaire, 80n40
Vorgrimler, Herbert, 110
Vorster, W. S., 26n12
Vrijhof, Pieter Hendrik, 2n4

Waardenburg, Jacques, 2n4, 10n20, 52n30
Wade, Abdoulaye, 236
Wainwright, Geoffrey, 112, 113n19
Wakefield, Gordon S., 280n12
Waliggo, John Mary, 114
Walls, Andrew F., 164n13, 276n1, 283n25, 286, 292, 292n49
Ward, W.E.F., 123n48125n56
Warren, Max, 131n7

Author Index

Weber, Max, 220
Weigel, George, 66n11, 176n11
Weinberg, Paul, 97
Wengert, Timothy J., 14n29
Werner, Dietrich, 63n6, 123n49
Westerhoff, John H., 3n6
Whale, John S., 234n12
Wilkins, Ivor, 26n12
Williams, Rowan, 23, 79n39
Williamson, S. G., 12–13n26, 77n36, 166n19, 167n23
Wilmore, Gayraud S., 121n44, 123–24
Wilson, Lindy, 122n46
Winquist, Charles E., 4, 36n37, 39, 68n15
Witte, John, Jr., 176n10, 181n19, 269n25
Wole, Soyinka, 28n18
Wolff, Otto, 164n14
Wood, David, 17n33
Wright, Richard, 121
Wycliffe, John, 80, 87, 277

Yankah, Kojo, 166n18
Yates, Timothy, 286n44
Yeats, William Butler, 121
Yeebo, Zaya, 240n25
Yunus, Muhammad, 247–48

Zaehner, R. C., 8n18
Zahan, Dominique, 8n18
Zoa, Jean B., 130
Zorn, Herbert, 62–63, 65
Zwingli, Ulrich, 88

Subject Index

Abacha, Sani, 222
Aborigines Rights Protection Society (ARPS), 41, 102, 112–13, 125–26, 270
Abu Bakr Shekkau, 154
Abu Ghraib prison, 189
accommodation theology, 109–11
Acheampong, Ignatius Kutu, 250
Achebe, Chinua, 17, 30
Acquah, Lieutenant, 99
Ad Petri cathedram (Pope John XXIII), 107–8
adaptation theology, 111–12
Adinkra symbols, 15
Adjepong, Justice, 99
Adult Industry Medical Healthcare Foundation, 189
adultery, 185, 186, 187, 190
affective faith, 3–4
Africa
    church missions, 32–35
    colonialism, 26–32
    communications revolution, 37–40
    denationalization, 44–45
    description of, 21–22
    Europe and, 35–37
    natural resources, 35, 231–33
perceptions of, 199–200
    racism, 24–26
    slavery, 22–24, 238
    sociopolitical organization, 141, 141n20
    stretching wings, 246
Africa Growth and Opportunity Act of 2000 (AGOA), 244
Africa Union (AU), 173
African Christian (author's experience)
    allegiance to Christ, 169–170
    approaches, 168–69
    Christ and, 162–64
    confession of faith and worship, 159
    contextual theological statement, 161–62
    images and symbols, 165–66
    immovable poles, 161
    overview, 158
    personality, 166–68
    Son of man, 165
    third-world Christology, 164, 164n12
    traditions, 159–161
    the Way to imitation of Christ, 158–59
African cultural heritage, 211–13
African cultures, 47–49
African identity, 278–280
African Independent Churches Conference, 291
African Indigenous Religions (AIR), 3
African Indigenous/Instituted Churches (AICs), 47, 276, 280
African Initiatives in Christianity (AIC)
    African identity, 278–280
    African independent churches, 280
    African initiatives, 280
    economic involvement, 228
    Enlightenment style and, 88
    epistemological crisis and, 44–45
    epithet "African," 278
    Ethiopian movements, 284
    genre varieties, 281–82
    historic churches, 289–291
    lessons learned, 286–87
    marks of church, 287–89
    messianic movements, 284
    music and, 14
    overview, 276–77
    Pentecostal churches, 285–86
    prophetic movements, 283–84
    schisms, 277
    sect, movement, church, 280–81
African National Congress (ANC), 254, 259–264

Subject Index

African nationalism, 30
African Peer Review Mechanism (APRM), 224–25
African personality and négritude, 121–23, 166–68
"African Survey" report, 260
African theology
    epistemology and ontology, 129–131, 181, 218
    overview, 128–29
    syncretism, 129–131
African Traditional Religions (ATR), 3, 19, 35, 61, 135, 138
African Union (AU), 22, 51, 224
African wisdom, 268–270
Afrikaner Dutch Reformed Church, 25, 26
Agbebi, Mojola (aka David Brown Vincent), 123, 126
Aggiornamento, 105, 106–9
Aggrey, James Kwegyir, 209
Ahmadiyya tradition, 135
Ahuma, S.R.B. Attoh, 113, 125, 126
Akan society
    belief pertaining to the soul, 48n16
    chieftainship, 141–42, 166
    education and wisdom, 62
    freedom of expression, 274
    freedom of speech, 268–69
    human consciousness, 258
    human dignity, 252
    humaneness of a person, 50
    humanity, 193, 200
    interconnectedness, 258
    on mothers, 211–12
    ritual duties, 48
    self-giving, 178
    seven graces, 175, 234
    symbols and art, 78
    wisdom, 62, 101, 268–270
Akbar (Mogul emperor), 148–49
All African Conference of Churches (AACC), 173
Al-Qaeda in the Islamic Maghreb (AQIM), 155
Al-Shabaab, 156
ancestors, 55, 56–57
Anderson, Rufus, 289
anger, ideologies of, 274–75
Anglican Church of Cyrene (Bulawayo, Zimbabwe), 15–16, 16f
Angola, 4, 25, 31–32, 35, 239
Anti-Balaka (militia), 156
apartheid, 13, 25–26, 97–98, 134, 173, 179–180, 224, 254
Apollonius, 227
apostolicity, 288
Apostolics, 64
Appiah, Joseph William Egyankaba, 47
Arrow of God (Achebe), 17
art, as language of theology, 14–17
Asamoah-Gyadu, Kwabena, 278
Asante society, 146, 166, 167
Asantehene, Nana Otumfuo, 28
Asian Critical Principle, 18
Assaad, Maria, 24
Assembly of Latin American Roman Catholic Bishops (1968), 119
Assmann, Hugo, 119
Ataturk, Mustafa Kemal, 107
Augustine of Hippo Regius, 32, 140
Augustine's theology, 198
authenticity, 18
authority, 220–21
autocephalous churches, 107
Azikiwe, Nnamdi, 30, 31, 219
Azusa Revival (1906–09), 285
Azusa Street Revival, 61

Babalola, Joseph Ayodele (prophet), 283
Baëta, Christian G., 135–36, 205
balkanization, 27
banks, globalization impact and, 241–42, 246–47
Bantu Independent Churches Union of South Africa, 291
Bantu population, 50
Bediako, Kwame, 167
belief, described, 8
bellicosity, 29
Benedict XIV (pope), 110
Benedict XVI (pope), 80, 156–57
Benin, 236
Berlin Conference (1889), 111
Bernstein, Lionel "Rusty," 260
Berquist, James, 117
Beyleveld, Pieter, 261
biblical approach to African Christology, 169
biblical context, 73, 83–84, 89–101
biblical difficulties regarding women's role, 211
biblical input regarding economics, 230–31
biblical sermon tradition, 159–160
Biennial Institute of African Women in Religion and Culture (1989), 203
Biko, Stephen Bantu, 122–23
biography, as story, 195–96
biosocial science, 181
Black Christ, 168
Black Consciousness movement, 60, 112
Black Power, 121

Subject Index

Black theology, 121–23
Blankson, George Kuntu, 125
Blyden, Edward Wilmot, 30
Boff, Clodovus, 119
Boff, Leonardo, 119
Boko Haram, 154–55, 274
Braide, Garrick (prophet), 283
Brazil, Russia, India, China, and South Africa (BRICS), 173, 244
Buddhism
  pluriformity of, 135
  principles, 35
  theology and, 59
  as universal religion, 3
  as world religion, 19
Bujo, Bénézet, 128
Bulgaria, 106
Burundi, 4, 68
Bush, George W., 38, 236–37, 241, 244, 274

Cain, Herman, 183
capitalism, 239
Capuchin church (Rome), 15
Cardenal, Ernesto, 119
carnal knowledge, 184
caste system, 110
Castro, Emilio, 190
Central African Republic, 156
ceremonialism, 52–57
Césaire, Aimé Ferdinand, 125
Chakkarai Chettiar, Vengal, 164
Chalcedonian definition, 160–61
charismatic leadership, 220
charity, 247
Charlemagne, 34
Charles I, 34
Charles II (king of England), 115
Charles V (Holy Roman Emperor), 141
Charles V (king of England), 34
Chatterji's, Shoma, 198
Cherloff, Michael, 38
Chikane, Frank, 99
China, 109–10
Chinese Rites controversy, 110–11
Christ culture and, 54–55
Christaller, Johannes Gottlieb, 33
Christendom, 22, 34, 61, 77, 101, 139–140
Christian Brotherhood Council (Ghana), 291
Christian Institute of South Africa, 292
Christian Reconstructionism, 116
Christian Reformation, 80, 115, 277, 288
Christianity
  in Africa, 19
  human dignity, 265–66

Judaism, Islam, and, 146–48
pluriformity of, 135–37
uniqueness of Christ, 152–53
as universal religion, 3
violence within, 267
as world religion, 19
. *See also* African Initiatives in Christianity
Christo, Carlos Alberto Libanio (Frei Betto), 119
Chrysostom, John, 236
church
  marks of, 287–89
  sect or movement, 280–81
church missions, 32–35
Church of Jesus Christ of Latter-day Saints/Mormons, 64
Church of the Lord (Aladura) in Nigeria, 292
The Church's Secret Agent (Lund & Weinberg), 97
Circle of African Women in Theology (CAWT), 205
Circle of Concerned African Women Theologians, 203–4
civilization clashes, 142–46
classics writings of Western civilization, 66
Clement XI (pope), 110
clientele of AICs, 291–92
Clinton, Bill, 183
Clinton, Hillary, 193–94, 201
Coe, Ivy, 117
Coe, Shoki, 117
coitus, 185, 187–89
colonialism, 26–32, 225, 235–37, 244, 253
Comblin, José, 119
commerce and Christianity, 237–38
Commission on Faith and Order, WCC (1974), 202
common good concept, 181
common religion, 2n4
communication, freedom of, 268–69
communications revolution, 37–40, 66–67
communitarian epistemology and ontology, 51–52, 178, 181, 218
community relationships, 172–73
condescension (*Herablassung*), 109
Congo, 232
conscience, moral, 257–58
conservative theology, 79–81
Constantine the Great, 139, 145
contextual or contextualization theology, 18, 116–19
contextuality principle, 84
Convention People's Party (CPP), 124
corruption, 222, 249–251

Cote d'Ivoire, 4, 39, 283
Council of Jerusalem (50 AD), 277
Council of Nicea (325 AD), 145
Council of Trent (1551 AD), 12
covenant, 83, 90, 102
creativity, 18
creeds, 88
crucifixion, 16
Crusades, 34–35, 140
cultural codes, 11
culture
    African cultures, 47–49
    ceremonialism, 52–57
    character of, 42–47
    Christ and, 54–55
    defined, 43
    human rights, 255
    institutionalized religion, 49–52
    overview, 41–42
    of pluralism, 46–47
    rituals, 52–57
    symbolism, 52–57
cumulative tradition and faith, 153–54
Cyprian of Carthage (saint), 32, 139

da Gama, Vasco, 27
dance, theology and, 60–61
Darfur, 4
Darku, Sir Tsibu, 28
Daughters of Anowa: African Women and Patriarchy (Oduyoye), 204
Day, Laura, 38
de Nobili, Roberto, 110
debtor nations, 242
Democratic Republic of Congo, 15
Deus caritas est (God is love) (Benedict XVI), 80
development, politics and, 217
dialogical style, 101
dialogue, 149–152, 202, 205
Dias, Bartholomew, 27
Dillistone, Frederick William, 15n32, 16, 52
Discourse at the Opening of the Second Vatican Ecumenical Council (Pope John XXIII), 108
diversities of theological constructs models, 67–68
diversity, plurality and, 148
divine religion, 148–49
Divino afflante Spiritu (Pope Pius XII), 108
doctrine or dogma, 73
Donatist controversy and schism, 140, 288
double hermeneutic, 44
double insurance, 129

Douglass, Frederick, 121
Du Bois, W.E.B., 31
"dual mandate," 28, 235
Dutch Pentecostalism, 64
Dutch Reformed Church, 25, 26

Eastern Orthodox Church, 106
Economic Community of West African States (ECO WAS), 22, 51, 173, 240
Economic Cooperation Organization Free Trade Agreement (2003), 142
economics and religion
    biblical input, 230–31
    capitalism, 239
    changes in, 229–230
    Christian thinking on, 181
    commerce and Christianity, 237–38
    corruption, 249–251
    description of economics, 227–28
    diverse ideologies, 235
    economic expansion, 245
    economic groupings, 245–46
    ethical context of the market, 242–43
    ethical imperative, 243
    globalization, hidden side of, 243–44
    globalization, right architecture of, 246–49
    globalization ideology, 240–42
    growth and property rights, 238–39
    human impacts, 233–34
    ideologies critique, 244–45
    ideology and economic construct, 234–35
    interrelationship of, 226–27
    macro and micro economics, 229
    Marxist socialism, 239
    micro credit, 246–49
    natural resources in African, 231–33
    North Atlantic captivity and legacy, 235–37
    overview, 226
    parable of two elephants, 239
    prayer, 243
    religion's place, 228
    self-interest, 235, 245–46
    stretching wings, 246
    sustainability, 245
    telos contribution, 234
ecstatic experience, 9
"Ecumenical Decade of Churches in Solidarity with Women" (1988–98), 203
Ecumenical Theological Education (ETE), 205
ecumenical theology and ecumenism, 14, 51, 173, 202, 208
    . *See also* Second Vatican Ecumenical Council (1962)
education

Subject Index

in age of communications revolution, 66–67
   environment, 65–66
   secular, 33
   theological, 18
   theology and, 62–63
Egyptian Coptic Christianity, 32
Ela, Jean-Marc, 129
Elmina Castle, Ghana, 24
Embassy of God ministry, Ukraine, 278
enemy images, 274–75
Enlightenment
   culture of in African churches, 287
   economics and, 228
   epistemology, 48, 48n17
   ideology and culture, 61, 88, 138
   legacy of, 68–69
   liberal theology and, 80, 80n40
   privatization of religion, 242
   rationality, 57
   styles, 69–71
environment, 53–54, 65–66, 180–82, 232, 245
epiphanies of darkness, 4, 68
epistemology
   African, 129-131, 181, 218
   communitarian, 51–52
   religious traditions and, 44–49
   spiritual, 47–49
eschatological hope, 14
An Essay on the Development of Christian Doctrine (Newman), 80
ethical context of the market, 242–43
Ethiopia and Ethiopianism, 41, 126–27, 232, 239
Ethiopian movements, 284
ethnic and ethnicity, 221n18, 263
etic and emic reading of culture, 45–46, 287
Eucharist, 11–12, 16
Europe, Africa and, 35–37
European Economic Community (EEC), 240
evangelism, 84–85
experienced faith, 3

faith
   belief vs., 8
   cumulative tradition and, 153–54
   described, 2, 2n2
   hope and, 6
   types of, 3
family, 178, 196–97
   . *See also* community relationships
Fanon, Frantz, 45, 125
feminism, 194, 197
feminist God-talk, 207–8
feminist theology, 198–200
fisher-folk community, Ghana, 53

folk religion, 2–4
Food and Agriculture Organization (FAO), 173
forgiveness, 98
fornication, 186
Fourth World Conference on Women, UN (1995), 193, 208
France, 36, 107
Francis (pope), 24, 190
free love, 186–87
free trade and free market concepts, 233, 240–41, 242, 247
freedom, 94–95, 266–69
Frei Betto (Christo, Carlos Alberto Libanio), 119
functional analogy approach, 169
fundamentalism, 154

G7 (industrialized nations), 240
Gagarin, Yuri Alekseyevich, 38
Gamaliel Principle, 214
Gandhi, Mahatma, 164, 256
Garvey, Marcus, 31
Gbedemah, K. A., 124
Geldof, Bob, 236–37
gender, 85, 194, 197, 206–7
   . *See also* mothers and sisters
General Synod of the Church of England (1968), 240
generational inclusion, 85
Gentiles, 277
Ghana
   African Initiatives in Christianity, 228
   Akan (*See* Akan society)
   Asante society, 146, 166, 167
   Basel Mission agents, 72, 72n25
   Bush and Geldof's visit, 236
   Commissions of Enquiry, 222, 222n19
   environmental issues, 180
   fisher-folk community, 53
   IMF negotiations, 241
   independence, 27, 56–57, 117, 219
   indirect rule, 28
   military regime, 99
   Musama Disco Christo Church, 47, 290
   Nanumba versus Konkomba, 263
   Nkrumah (*See* Nkrumah, Kwame)
   Parliamentary Prayer, 250
   polyethnic makeup, 22
   sex scandals, 183
Ghana Council of United Churches, 291
Gilligan, Carol, 197–98
globalization, 222, 240–44, 246–49
God-talk, 195–96, 207–8
Goldie of Nigeria, 29

Subject Index

Good News Institute (Ghana), 292
gospel story, good news, 83–84, 90–101, 127
governments, globalization and, 241
grace, 190
Grameen Bank, 247–48
Great Depression (1929), 5
Great Schism of 1054 (East and West), 87, 288
Greek Orthodox tradition, 87
Grenholm, Carl-Henric, 116–17
griots, 12
"growth ethic," 238–39, 246
Guantanamo Bay Naval Base, Cuba, 224, 254
Gutierrez, Gustavo, 119

Harris, William Wade (prophet), 283
Harrist Movement, 283
Hastings, James, 140n17
hate, ideologies of, 274–75
health care, 33
Henry VIII (king of England), 277
Herablassung (condescension), 109
hermeneutical process and principles, 76–77
heroism, 219
Hill, Anita, 183
Hillary Doctrine, 201n18
Hindenburg, Paul von, 244
Hinduism
    in Africa, 19
    pluriformity of, 135
    principles, 35
    theology and, 59
    as universal religion, 3
historic churches, 276, 289–291
Hitler, Adolf, 250
holism, 49
Holy and Holiness, 10
homo socialis, 172–75
hope
    eschatological hope, 14
    religion and, 4–7
    as vision, 20
human beings and humanity, 50, 233–34
human dignity
    African humanist politician, testimony of, 272–74
    African wisdom, 268–270
    anger, politics of, 274–75
    Christian input, 265–66
    colonialism, 253
    culture of, 255
    enemy images, 274–75
    freedom, 266–69
    Freedom Charter, 259–264
    hate, ideologies, 274–75
    kingdom of God, 266
    land, as measure of, 270
    liberty, 266–69
    moral conscience, 257–58
    overview, 252
    peace, 266–69
    people's consciences, 257
    psychology, 258–59
    racism, 253
    real identity of the other, 254–55
    slavery, 252–53
    UN Charter Preamble, 255–57
    uneven playing field, 253–54
    Universal Declaration of Human Rights, 271–72
    values, 266
human rights, 104
human trafficking, 243
Humanae vitae (Pope Paul VI), 108
humanism, 274–75
humility, 1, 17, 42
Hunt, James, 33
Huntington, Samuel P., 142–43
Hussein, Saddam, 179, 224, 254
Hypatia, 139

"I Have a Dream" speech, King, 179, 273
idolatry, 8, 186
imagery, 11, 165–66, 168
imago Dei, 172
incarnation, 76–77, 84, 169
inculturation theology, 113–14
India, 110, 145, 164
indigenization theology, 112–13
indirect rule doctrine, 28–29
individualism, 258, 287
    . See also self-interest
inflation impacts, 241
injustices, 194–95
Innocent II (pope), 140
Inquisition, 140
insights, 5
Institute of Contextual Theology, 118
institutionalized religion, 49–52
integrity, 18
Inter-American Development Bank, 240
interconnectedness, 50, 218, 253, 258–59, 267
interdisciplinary collaboration, 116
interfaith relationships, 149–152
intergender exchange, 85
intergenerational mission, 85
International Country Risk Guide (ICRG), 238
International Covenant on Civil and Political Rights (ICCPR), 271

Subject Index

International Covenant on Economic, Social and Cultural Rights (ICESCR), 271
International Labour Organization, 243
International Missionary Council (IMC), 119
International Monetary Fund (IMF), 143, 240, 241
interpretation, 85–88
interreligious relations and dialogue, 149
Ireland, 285
Islam
    in Africa, 19, 32, 136–37
    ideology, 143–44
    Judaism, Christianity, and, 146–48
    peace and, 268
    pluriformity of, 135
    politics and, 140–41
    principles, 34–35
    Qur'an, 83
    religious competition, 61
    theology and, 59
    as universal religion, 3
    violence, 145, 154–57
    as world religion, 19
Israel, 274–75

Jeffrey, George, 285
Jehovah's Witnesses, 64
Jehu-Appiah, Jemisemiham, 47
Jesuits, in sixteenth-century China, 109–10
job layoffs, 229
John Paul II (pope), 169, 176, 182, 233–34
John XXIII (pope), 106–9, 182
Johns Hopkins University, 234–35
Judaism, 34, 59, 75, 115, 146–48
Jung, Carl Gustav, 258–59
justice, 94, 96
Justinian I (emperor), 139

Kanyoro, Musimbi, 197
Kaunda, Kenneth, 30, 274–75
kenosis, 76–77
Kenya, 4, 21, 35, 39, 102–3, 156, 219
Kenyatta, Jomo, 29, 219
Kharijis tradition, 135
Kimbanguist university and seminary in Congo (Kinshasa), 292
King, Noel Q., 205
kingdom of God, 92–101, 221, 225, 266
kinship imagery, 168
knowledge, atomization of, 171
Koranteng-Addo, Justice, 99
Korie, Yeboa (prophet), 285
Korle, Nene Mate, 28

L'Abri, Swiss Christian community, 116
Laguma, Jimmy, 261
laity, role of, 182
land, 102–4, 181, 270
Land Tenure Act of 1969 (Zimbabwe), 99
language
    biblical context for African's, 159–161
    cultural index, 72
    interpretation, 85–88
    leadership titles and meanings, 166–67
    multilingualism and, 57, 112
    reduced to writing, 33
    Shona and Portuguese, 31
    Swahili, 113
    theology and, 11–17
    translation, 85–88
    use of temperate language, 97
Larbi, Emmanuel Kingsley, 285
Latin America, 164, 177
Lavigerie, Charles Martial Allemand, 111, 112
leadership, 220–21, 257–58
leadership titles and meanings, 166–67
Lehmann, Paul, 131
Lekganyane, Engenas, 284
Lenski, Gerald, 136
Leo IX (pope), 87
Leo XIII (pope), 181–82
Letele, Arthur, 261
Levinas, 222, 243
Lévinas, Emmanuel, 143–44
Levy, Leon, 261
Liberal study of Scripture, 108
liberal theology, 79–81, 109–11, 116
liberation theology, 119–121, 176, 177, 242
Liberia, 4, 35, 36, 36n36, 39, 236, 283
liberty, 266–69
Life and Work Movement, 150
Litvinenko, Alexander, 275
living alone, 51–52
Lobengula, king of the Matabele, 104
Logos, 86–87
logos approach, 169
Lollards sect, 80, 87, 277
love, 95, 186–87
Lugard, Lord Frederick Dealty, 28–29
Lumumba, Patrice, 30
Luthuli, Albert, 85, 259, 261, 262, 263
Lyimo, Camillus, 130–31

Magesa, Laurenti, 130
Makhulu, Walter Khotso, 96–98
Mali, 155
Mandela, Nelson, 29, 50, 97, 179–180, 261, 261n14

329

Maranke, Johane, 284
Mariam, Mengistu Haile, 239
marriage, 148, 172, 248
martyrdom, 17, 288
Marxist socialism, 239
Mason, Cedric, 261
Matthews, Z. K., 259
Matthews, Zachariah Keodirelang, 260, 263
mediacracy, 39
memory, society's, 56–57
Messianic movements, 284
Methodist Church, 290
microcredit economics, 247–48
middle axioms, 116
Milingo (archbishop), 279
Millennium Partnership for the African Recovery Program (MAP), 224
Milošević, Slobodan, 250
minister's roles, 78–79
mission and worship, 75–76, 84–88
missionaries, 32–35, 264
Mizeki, Bernard, 17
models of theology
    Aborigines Rights Protection Society, 125–26
    accommodation, 109–11
    adaptation, 111–12
    African personality and négritude, 121–23
    African theology, 121–23
    Black theology, 121–23
    contextualization, 18, 116–19
    Ethiopianism, 126–27
    inculturation, 113–14
    indigenization, 112–13
    liberation theology, 119–121
    many designations, one Gospel, 127
    overview, 105
    reconstruction, 114–16
Modernism, 107
Mofokeng, Takatso A., 123
Monica (mother of Augustine), 198
moral character, 191
moral conscience, 257–58
morality, 216
Mormons/Church of Jesus Christ of Latter-day Saints, 64
Morrison, Gresham W. (archdeacon), 283
Mosala, Itumeleng J., 123
motherhood, 212
mothers and sisters
    African context, 201–2
    African cultural heritage, 211–13
    Augustine's theology, 198
    biblical difficulties, 211
    critical and vital resource, 200
    double jeopardy experience, 199–200
    feminism, 194
    feminist God-talk, 207–8
    feminist theology, 198–99, 200–201
    gender, 194, 206–7
    gender issues, 197
    ideology, 197–98
    injustices, 194–95
    ordination of women, 213–14
    overview, 192–93
    personal reflection, 209–10
    preference for, 196–97
    roadblocks, 202–6
    stereotyping, 197–98
    story, biography, God-talk, 195–96
    terminology, 193–94
    transformational constructs, 208–9
    womanist theology, 198–99
movement
    African context, 281–82
    churches as, 280–81
Mozambique, 4, 25, 35
Mugabe, Robert, 29, 222
Muhammad (prophet), 140–41, 148
multilingualism, language and, 57, 112
multitudes before the Lamb
    civilization clashes, 142–46
    Judaism, Christianity, and Islam, 146–48
    names, significance of, 134–38
    overview, 133–34
    political power, 139–142
    rainbow nation, 134
    religious pluralism, 148–49, 152, 153–54
Musama Disco Christo Church (Ghana), 47, 290
music, as language of theology, 12–14, 77–78
myths, 10, 64–65

Naiker, G. M. Monty, 261
nakedness, 184–86
names, significance, 134–38
Namibia, 25
nation building, 218–19
National Council of Pentecostal Churches, 291
National Indian Congress (NIC), 261
nation-state building, 217–18
nativistic churches, 282
natural resources in African, 35, 231–33
natural social distinctions, 178–79
Ndugane, Winston, 105
Négritude, 41, 105, 124–25, 236
New Partnership for Africa's Development (NEPAD), 51, 224

Newbigin, Lesslie, 118–19
Newton, John, 23
Nicene orthodoxy, 79
Nicholas V (pope), 25
Nigeria, 22, 29, 39, 154–55, 219, 222, 263, 274
Nkrumah, Kwame
    African nationalism, 30
    African personality and négritude, 41–42, 124
    as cabinet minister, 97
    chieftainship, 29, 166
    on churches, 32
    Ghana as secular state, 135
    independence, 56, 219
    Pan-Africanism, 31
    political kingdom, 220
    presidency of, 53
No Longer at Ease (Achebe), 17
North Africa, 32
Numinous, 10
Nyerere, Mwalimu Julius, 30, 130, 219

objectivity, 69
Oduyoye, Mercy Amba, 204–5
Ofori Atta I (Kibi), 167
Ofori-Atta, Nana (Akim), 28
Oneness and Jihad in West Africa (MUJAO), 155
ontology
    African theology, 129–131
    communitarian, 51–52, 181, 218
    religious and spiritual, 47–49, 48n16
oral history, 17
ordination of women, 213–14
Organisation of Africa Unity, 224
Organisation of African Instituted Churches (OAIC), 286
Organisation of Petroleum Exporting Countries (OPEC), 240
O'Rorke, Mowbray (bishop), 283
Orthodox Churches, 106–7
owned faith, 4

Padmore, George, 31
Pan-Africanism, 31, 127
Papyri of Zeno, 227
parables, 17
particularity principle, 84
Paschal Mystery approach, 169
patriarchy, 199
Paul VI (pope), 108, 109, 217
peace, 96–99, 156, 217, 266–69
Pentecostal Association of Ghana, 291
Pentecostal churches, 285–86
people's consciences, 257

person, definition of, 256
Pew Foundation survey, 2
philosophy, 59
Pistorius, Oscar, 192
Pius X (pope), 107
Pius XI (pope), 106, 182
Pius XII (pope), 108, 182
Platonism, 85–88
pluralism
    culture of, 46–47
    Enlightenment and, 74
    human dignity and, 254
    religious pluralism, 135–38, 148–49, 152, 153–54, 219
    residuum evangelium and, 101
Pobee, John, 204
political power, 139–142
Political Risk Services (PRS), 238
politics and religion
    charismatic leadership, 220
    international organizing, 223–25
    leadership, power, and authority, 220–21
    nation building, 218–19
    nation-state building, 217–18
    overview, 215–17
    politics for development, 217
    state building, 218–19
    theocracy, 221–23
poor. *See* preferential option for the poor
Poor Christ of Bomba (Beti), 37
population growth, 246
pornography, 67, 188–89, 190
Portugal, 31–32
poverty
    charity and, 247
    liberation theology and, 176
    preferential option for the poor, 177–180
Powell, Adam Clayton, 121
power, 220–21
prayer, 243, 250
preferential option for the poor, 177–180, 201, 242–43
preliterate religions, 19
Prester John, 32
"Problems and Promises for the Mission of the Church in Africa" (1992), 11
Program for Theological Education (PTE), 24, 204–6
proof-texting, 154
property rights, 238–39
prophetic movements, 283–84
prophets, 7, 9
Protestant Christian missions, 139–140
Protestant Reformation, 80, 115, 277, 288

Protestantism, 115, 288
psychic consultants, 38
psychology, 258–59
Pusian High Church tradition, 16
Putin, Vladimir, 275

racism, 24–26, 33–34, 179–180, 189, 253
rainbow nation, 134
Ralebitso, Matumo, 254
Ram Mohan Roy (raja), 164
Ranson, Charles, 117
ratio (reason and rationalism), 68
Rawlings, J. J., 99, 241, 250
Reagan, Ronald, 224
reconciliation, 98–101
reconstruction theology, 114–16
redemption, 120
reform, church reformed by the Spirit, 6
reformation, 115
Reformation, Christian, 80, 115, 277, 288
Reformed Judaism, 115
religion
    cornerstones of, 8–9
    institutionalized, 49–52
    several and diverse, 18–20
    spiritual epistemology and ontology, 47–49
    theology and, 7–8
religious affiliation survey, 2
religious tolerance, 263–64
religious traditions, idolatry and, 8
renewal, 115–16
repentance, 83, 98, 191
residuum evangelium
    covenant, 102
    gospel story, good news, 83–84, 89–101
    incarnation, 84
    land, 102–4
    mission, 84–88
    overview, 82–83
    pluralism, 101
    as story, 101
    threefold cord of theology, 89
reverse mission, 278
revolutions, 114–15
Rhodes, Cecil, 99, 104
Rhodesia (now Zambia), 102–3
Ricci, Matteo, 110
righteousness, 94
rituals, 52–57
Rivonia Trial (1963–64), 261
Robins, Wendy, 203
Roman Catholic tradition
    aggiornamento, 106–9
    Charles I and Charles V, 34

contextual theology, 118
    Enlightenment era, 69
    Great Schism (1054), 87
    inculturation, 113–14, 114n23
    liberation theology, 119–121, 177
    peace effort in Africa, 156
    popes (*See specific popes by name*)
    preferential option for the poor, 177
    racism in Africa, 25
    schisms, 288
    on slavery, 23, 24
    social order, 180–82
    Society of Our Lady of Africa, 111
    transubstantiation, 12
    White Fathers, 111–12
Rome Statute of the International Criminal Court (ICC), 224, 274–75
Roncalli, Angelo Cardinal (later Pope John XXIII), 106–7
Roosevelt, Franklin D., 234, 266, 267
Rudd, Charles D., 104
Rudd Concession, 104
Rumsfeld, Donald, 143–44
Rushdoony, Rousas John, 116
Rwanda, 4, 35, 68, 236, 263

sacred, secular and, 10–11
Sanneh, Lamin, 132
Sarkodie, Justice, 99
Sartre, Jean-Paul, 41n1
Sarvepalli Radhakrishnan, 164
Sawyerr, Harry, 130, 168
The Scarlet Pimpernel (Orczy), 73
Schaeffer, Francis, 116
schisms, 115, 277, 288, 290
science, theology and, 38–40, 53, 61–62
Scillitan Martyrs, 32
scripture. *See* biblical context
searching faith, 4
Seattle, Native American Chief, 50, 103, 253
Second Vatican Ecumenical Council (1962), 108, 109, 119, 169
sect churches, 276, 280–81
secular, sacred and, 10–11
secular ecumenical movement, 173
See-Judge-Act method, 118
segregation of races, 256
Segundo, Juan Luis, 119
Seko, Mobuto Sese, 222
Seleka (rebel coalition), 156
self-interest, 235, 241–42, 245–46
    . *See also* individualism
Sen, Kesbab Chandra, 164
Senegal, 236

Subject Index

Senghor, Léopold Sésor, 41, 124, 125
Sengwayo, 284
sensitivity in theology, 80
Sepede community, South Africa, 56
sepow symbol, 268
Sepsazian, Aharon, 117
September 11, 2001 terrorist attack, 39
Serageldin, Ismail, 102
Serbian Orthodox Church, 68
seven graces, 175, 234
sex
    Africa and, 189–191
    coitus, 187–89
    free love, 186–87
    to know, 184
    to lie with, 184
    nakedness, uncover of, 184–86
    overview, 183
    same sex relationships, 185–86
    sexual prohibitions, 184–86
sexism, 210
Sexism in the 1970s: *Discrimination* Against Women" (1974), 202
Seymour, William J., 61
Shembe, Isaiah, 284
Shepperson, George, 126
Shi'i tradition, 135, 141
Shona independent churches, 291
Sibambo, 284
Sibbes, Richard, 139
Sierra Leone, 4, 35, 39, 130, 168
silence, 12
Simon of Cyrene, 16
simplicity, 1
Sistine Chapel, 15
slavery, 24–26, 238, 252–53
    . *See also* human trafficking
slogans and sloganeering, 245
Smith, Adam, 171, 217
Smuts, Jan Christian, 254, 256–57
Sobrino, Juan, 119
social order, God and
    environment and, 180–82
    homo socialis, 172–75
    overview, 171–72
    preferential option for the poor, 177–180
    theology and, 176–77
    traditional African hints, 175–76
socialis, Marxist, 239
society, as factor in theology, 65
Society of Our Lady of Africa, 111
solidarity, unity and, 182
Somalia, 156
soul music, 13

South Africa
    African National Congress, 254, 259–264
    apartheid (*See* apartheid)
    arms deals with France, 36
    Black Consciousness movement, 60, 112
    colonialism resistance, 26
    contextual theology, 118
    corruption, 222
    member of BRICS, 173, 244
    native lands, 102–3
    Pistorius killing incidence, 134
    precepts of *ubuntu*, 50
    resistance movements, 26, 122
    Sepede community, 56
South Africa Congress Alliance, 261
South Africa Congress of Trade Unions (SACTU), 261
South African Coloured People's Congress (SACPC), 261
South African Congress of Democrats (SACOD), 261
Southern Africa, 4
Southern African Development Community (SADC), 22, 51, 173, 240
Southern Rhodesia (now Zimbabwe), 15–17, 28, 99
Soviet Union, 239
speech freedom of, 268–69
spiritual epistemology, 47–49
Stalin, Josef, 218
state building, 218–19
Steenkamp, Reeva, 192
Stoicism, 85–88
story
    as biography, 195–96
    gospel story, good news, 83–84, 90–101, 127
    as theology, 17
structural sin, 182
subsidiarity principle, 181
suffragette movement, 194
Sulayman the Magnificent, 34
Suleyman I, 141
Sundkler, 284
Sunni tradition, 135, 141
supernatural and natural, 286–87
sustainability, economic, 245
Swahili, 113
Swatson, John, 283
symbols and symbolism, 10, 15, 52–57
syncretism, 129–131, 138
syncretistic movement, 281–82, 286
Synod of Bishops of Africa and Madagascar (1974), 169
synthesis by reduction, 149

333

tabula rasa, 158, 175, 267, 279, 282
Tanzania, 39, 130, 219, 236
Taubman, George (later Goldie of Nigeria), 29
technology, theology and, 38–40, 245
telos, 234
Tertullian, 32
Thatcher, Margaret, 224
theocracy, 221–23
Theodosius I (Roman emperor), 34, 139
theological education, 18, 66
Theological Education by Extension (Zimbabwe), 292
Theological Education Fund (TEF), 116–17
theology
    in Africa, 36–37
    African theology, 128–132
    art and, 14–17
    Augustine's, 198
    biblical context, 73, 83–84, 89–101
    as biography, 71–72
    Black theology, 121–23
    constituencies of, 74–75
    contextual or contextualization, 18, 116–19
    definition, 71
    description of, 1–2, 3, 58–60
    dialogical style, 101
    diversities of models, 67–68
    education and, 62–63, 65–67
    Enlightenment, 68–71
    feminist theology, 198–200
    formative components, 72–73
    hermeneutical process, 76
    language as key to, 11–12
    liberation theology, 119–121, 176, 177
    mission and worship, 75–76, 84–88
    models of (*See* models of theology)
    music and, 12–14
    myths, 64–65
    pluralization of (*See* pluralism)
    reading and, 60–61
    religion and, 7–8
    as scales of music, 77–78
    science and technology, 38–40, 53, 61–62
    social order and, 176–77
    society, as factor in, 65
    story as, 17
    three V's of, 60
    threefold cord of, 89
    ujamaa theology, 130–31
    for whom and for what, 78–81
    womanist theology, 198–200
theory, 68
Things Fall Apart (Achebe), 17
third-world Christology, 164

Thomas, Clarence, 183
Thompson, Thomas, 23
Through the Eyes of a Woman (Robins), 203
Tractarian Oxford Movement, 16
traditional African cultures, 47–49
Traditional African Religions. *See* African Traditional Religions
Trafford, J. L., 283
transactive memory, 67
transformational constructs, 208–9
translation, 85–88
transubstantiation, 12
Treatise Concerning the Christian Priesthood (Chrysostom), 236
tribe and tribal, 221n18
truth and truthfulness, 92–94
Turkey, 106–7
Tutu, Desmond, 25, 96–97, 117, 134
Tutu, Osei, I, 167
two elephants parable, 239
Tylor, E. B., 43

ubuntu precepts, 50, 258
ujamaa theology, 130–31
UN Security Council, 143, 201n18
Una Sancta, 287288
Una Sancta, 135
uneven playing field, 253–54
United Nations Educational, Scientific, and Cultural Organization (UNESCO), 172
United Nations Organization (UNO), 172
United Nations (UN)
    charter, 173–74, 255, 259–260
    charter preamble, 255–57
    Declaration of Human Rights, 255
    Development Programme's Human Development Index, 239
    organization of, 223–24
    Universal Declaration of Human Rights, 255, 271–72
unity
    call to, 291
    solidarity and, 182
Universal Declaration of Human Rights, 255, 271–72
universal religion, 2–4
University of Tübingen, Germany, 73, 87
Urban VIII (pope), 15
utopia, 5

Vacandard, V., 140n17
values, 102, 266
Vatican II, 108, 109, 119, 169
Venn, Henry, 289

Subject Index

Villa-Vicencio, Charles, 116
Vincent, David Brown (aka Mojola Agbebi), 123, 126
violence, 145, 154–57, 223
Vivekananda (swami), 164

Wainwright, Geoffrey, 112
Warren, Max, 131
wars, 253–54, 256, 267, 272, 274
White Fathers, 111–12
Wholly Other, 10
Wilberforce, William, 23
womanist theology, 198–200
women. *See* mothers and sisters; pornography
World Bank, 238, 240
World Council of Churches (WCC), 150, 173, 190, 202, 204–5, 260

World Health Organization (WHO), 172–73
world religions, 19
worship, 75–76
Wovenu (prophet), 284

Yemen, 39
Yusuf, Muhammed, 154

Zaire, 222
Zambia (formerly Rhodesia), 102–3
Zimbabwe, 222
Zimbabwe (formerly Southern Rhodesia), 15–17, 28, 99
Zimmerman, Johannes, 33
Zoa, Jean B., 130

www.ingramcontent.com/pod-product-compliance
Lightning Source LLC
Chambersburg PA
CBHW082027300426
44117CB00015B/2373